Photograph by Studio Edmark.

ESSAYS IN GREEK HISTORY

By H. T. WADE-GERY

OXFORD · BASIL BLACKWELL
MCMLVIII

© Basil Blackwell 1958

PRINTED IN GREAT BRITAIN BY
BILLING AND SONS LIMITED, GUILDFORD AND LONDON

CONTENTS

iii

FOREWORD

Henry Theodore Wade-Gery's seventieth birthday fell on April 2nd of this year. This selection of his essays has been published to mark the occasion and to convey the homage and affection of the many subscribers—individual scholars and institutions of learning—whose names are listed on pp. vii-xi. The quality of his contribution to Greek historical studies, his individual blend of high imagination, clear insight and scholarship, stands out in the essays themselves: by way of preface it remains only to explain a few small editorial points.

The essays are printed without alteration, except for the correction of misprints and the alteration of a few out-of-date references (from the first to the second edition of *I.G.* II-III, from Müller's *F.H.G.* to Jacoby's *F.gr.H.*, etc.); these are not noted in the text. In a few cases, where the author's view has substantially changed and the original text might mislead a reader coming to these questions for the first time, a footnote has been added, in square brackets preceded by an asterisk. Wade-Gery's absence in America during the printing of the book made it impossible to consult him on points of detail, and the responsibility for any editorial error is entirely mine.

My thanks are due to Mr. R. Meiggs for advice on many points; to Mr. W. G. Forrest for help in reading the proofs; to Mr. and Mrs. Forrest and Mr. R. L. Wade-Gery for help with the index; and to Sir Basil Blackwell and the printer throughout for their forbearance and co-operation.

A. Andrewes

LIST OF SUBSCRIBERS

Adcock, F. E.
Anderson, W. J.
Andrewes, A.
Astin, A. E.
Atherley, S. E. P.

Badian, E.
Balsdon, J. P. V. D.
Barnard, D. L.
Barratt, C.
Beattie, A. J.
Beazley, J. D.
Béquignon, Y.
Berlin, I.
Blackwell, B. H.
Bloch, H.
Bob-Manuel, W. K.
Boëthius, A.
Bolton, J. D. P.
Bond, G. W.
Bowra, C. M.
Brunt, P. A.
Burn, A. R.

Calder, W. M.
Carew Hunt, R. N.
Carney, T. F.
Caskey, J. L.
Cawkwell, G. L.
Chamber, M.
Clary, W. W.
Clement, P. A.
Combellack, F. M.
Cooper, P. F.
Cox, C. W. M.
Craig, B. H.
Craig, H. M.

Davison, J. A.
Day, J. H.
Desborough, V. R. d'A.
de Ste. Croix, G. E. M.
Dodd, H. R.

Dodds, E. R.
Dörner, F. K.
Dover, K. J.
Dow, S.
Dundas, R. H.
Dutcher, C.

Edmonson, C. N.
Ehrenberg, V.
Einarson, B.
Eliot, C. W. J.

Felix, D. H. H.
Fine, J. V. A.
Finley, M. I.
Fletcher, G. B. A.
Forrest, W. G.
Fraser, P. M.
Frederiksen, M. W.
Friedli, E.

Gardner, D. B.
Gigante, M.
Goggin, M. G.
Gomme, A. W.
Goodban, G. A.
Gould, J. P.
Granville, W. A.

Haarhoff, T. J.
Hardie, C. G.
Hall, J. G.
Harland, J. P.
Harrison, A. R. W.
Henderson, H. L.
Henderson, M. I.
Hignett, C.
Hill, B. H.
Hjortsö, L.
Hoffleit, H. B.
Holladay, A. J.
Hopper, R. J.
Hudson, R. F.

University and other libraries

Aberystwyth, University College of Wales
Adelaide, University of
Amsterdam, Archaeologisch-Historisch Instituut der Universiteit
Århus, Staatsbiblioteket
Arkansas, University of
Athens:
    American School of Classical Studies
    British School of Archaeology
Auckland University College

Bangor, University College of North Wales
Bishop's University, Lennoxville, Quebec
Bradfield College
Bristol, University of
Bryn Mawr College

California, University of
Cambridge:
    Classical Faculty Library
    Jesus College
    Peterhouse
Canberra University College
Canterbury, University of, Christchurch, N.Z.
Chicago, University of
Cincinnati, University of
Colorado, University of
Columbia University, New York
Concordia Seminary, St. Louis, Missouri
Copenhagen, Royal Library
Cornell University

Dublin, University College

Edinburgh University
Erlangen, University of
Exeter, University of

Flint, Michigan, City of
Frankfurt a. M., Stadt- und Universitätsbibliothek
Freiburg i. B., Seminar für alte Geschichte der Universität

Georgetown University, Washington, D.C.
Glasgow, The Mitchell Library
Glasgow, University of
Gothenburg, Filosofiska Fakultetens Seminariebibliotek

Harvard University
Heidelberg:
    Universitätsbibliothek
    Seminar für alte Geschichte
Hellenic Society
Helsinki, University of
Hull, University of

Johns Hopkins University

Kentucky, University of

Lancing College
Lawrence College, Appleton, Wisconsin
Leeds, University of
Leicester, University of
Liverpool, University of
London Library, The
London, University of:
    Bedford College
    University of London Library
Loyola University, Chicago
Lund, University of

McGill University
McMaster University
Manchester, University of
Michigan, University of
Milan, Università Cattolica del S. Cuore
Missouri, University of
Moravian College, Bethlehem, Pennsylvania
Munich:
    Bayerische Staatsbibliothek
    Kommission für alte Geschichte und Epigraphik e. V.
    Seminar für alte Geschichte

Nancy, Université de
New Brunswick University, Bonar Law Bennett Library
New England, University of, New South Wales
North Carolina, University of, Woman's College
Notre-Dame, University of, Indiana
Nottingham, City of
Novitiate of St. Andrew-on-Hudson, Poughkeepsie, New York
Oberlin College, Ohio
Otago University, Dunedin
Oxford:
    Ashmolean Museum
    Balliol College
    Brasenose College
    Christ Church
    Exeter College
    Merton College
    New College
    Oriel College
    Pembroke College
    St. Anne's College
    St. John's College
    University College
Paris, Bibliothèque Nationale
Pennsylvania, University of
Peterhouse School, S. Rhodesia
Princeton:
    Institute for Advanced Study
    University

Radley College
Reading University
Rome:
    American Academy
    British School

Shadowbrook Library, Chestnut Hill, Mass.
Sheffield, University of
Southampton, University of
Southwestern Baptist Seminary, Fort Worth, Texas

Texas, University of
Toronto, University of
    St. Michael's College
    Trinity College
Tübingen, University of

Uppsala, University of

Victoria University, Wellington N.Z.
Vienna, University of

Wabash College, Crawfordsville, Indiana
Washington University, St. Louis, Missouri
Waterloo College, Waterloo, Ontario
West Baden College, Indiana
Western Ontario, University of
Western Reserve University, Cleveland, Ohio
Worcester, Mass., College of the Holy Cross

Zürich, Zentralbibliothek

BIBLIOGRAPHY

1924

Journal of Hellenic Studies, XLIV. 55–64:
Jason of Pherae and Aleuas the Red.
Cambridge Ancient History, vol. II, ch. xix:
The Dorians.

1925

Cambridge Ancient History, vol. III, ch. xxii:
The Growth of the Dorian States.

1926

Journal of Hellenic Studies, XLVI. 293–7:
Review of U. Kahrstedt, *Griechisches Staatsrecht, Bd. I: Sparta und seine Symmachie.*

1928

PINDAR, Pythian Odes. Translated by H. T. Wade-Gery and C. M. Bowra (London, Nonesuch Press).
Classical Review, XLII. 22:
Review of E. L. Highbarger, *The History and Civilisation of Ancient Megara.*

1930

Classical Quarterly, XXIV. 33–9:
The Year of the Armistice, 423 B.C.
Ibid., 116–18:
A Document of the Restored Democracy of 410 B.C. (*I.G.* I². 114).
Classical Review, XLIV. 14–16:
Review of F. Bölte, V. Ehrenberg, L. Ziehen, G. Lippold: *Sparta* (Pauly-Wissowa, *Real-Enzyklopädie*, III A 1265–1528).
Ibid., 163–5:
A Note on Kleon's Finance.
Numismatic Chronicle, fifth series, X. 16–38:
The Ratio of Silver to Gold during the Peloponnesian War: *I.G.* I². 301.
Ibid., 333–4:

Attic Gold Ratios. A Correction.
Journal of Hellenic Studies, L. 288–93:
An Attic Inscription of the Archidamian War.

1931

Classical Quarterly, XXV. 1–11, 77–89:
Eupatridai, Archons and Areopagus.
Ibid., 129–43:
Studies in the Structure of Attic Society: I. Demotionidai.
Journal of Hellenic Studies, LI. 57–85:
The Financial Decrees of Kallias.
Classical Philology, XXVI. 309–13:
Strategoi in the Samian War.

1932

Mélanges Glotz, tom. II. 877–87:
Horos.
Journal of Hellenic Studies, LII. 205–27:
Thucydides the son of Melesias.
Hermes, LVII. 129–30:
Zu griechischen Epigrammen.

1933

Classical Quarterly, XXVII. 17–29:
Studies in the Structure of Attic Society: II. The Laws of Kleisthenes.
Journal of Hellenic Studies, LIII. 71–104:
Classical Epigrams and Epitaphs.
Ibid., 134–37:
Review of W. S. Ferguson, *The Treasurers of Athena*; B. D. Meritt, *Athenian Financial Documents of the Fifth Century*; M. N. Tod, *A Selection of Greek Historical Inscriptions to the End of the Fifth Century*.

1935

Classical Review, XLIX. 185–6:
Review of B. D. Meritt and A. B. West, *The Athenian Assessment of 425 B.C.*
Journal of Hellenic Studies, LV. 96–7:
Review of G. Lombardo, *Cimone: Ricostruzione della Biografia e Discussioni storiografiche.*
Annual of the British School of Archaeology at Athens, XXXIII (1932–3) 101–6:
Studies in Attic Inscriptions of the Fifth Century B.C.

1936

Greek Poetry and Life, Essays presented to Gilbert Murray on his seventieth Birthday (Oxford University Press) 56–78:
Kynaithos.

Journal of Hellenic Studies, LVI. 101–2:
Review of U. Kahrstedt, *Staatsgebiet und Staatsangehörige in Athen: Studien zum öffentlichen Recht Athens, I.*

American Journal of Philology, LVII. 377–94:
H. T. Wade-Gery and B. D. Meritt, Pylos and the Assessment of Tribute.

1938

American Journal of Philology, LIX. 129–34:
Two Notes on Theopompos, *Philippika*, X.

Ibid., 470–5:
The Islands of Peisistratos.

1939

The Athenian Tribute Lists, by B. D. Meritt, H. T. Wade-Gery and M. F. McGregor, vol. I (Harvard University Press, Cambridge, Mass.).

1940

Perachora, by Humfry Payne and others (Oxford University Press), vol. I, ch. vii:
The Inscriptions on Stone.

Annual of the British School of Archaeology at Athens, XXXVII (1936–7) 263–70:
Themistokles' Archonship.

Athenian Studies presented to William Scott Ferguson (Harvard Studies in Classical Philology, suppl. vol. I) 121–56:
The Peace of Kallias.

1943

Classical Quarterly, XXXVI. 57–78:
The Spartan Rhetra in Plutarch *Lycurgus VI.* A. Plutarch's Text.

1944

Classical Quarterly, XXXVIII. 1–9, 115–26:
The Spartan Rhetra in Plutarch *Lycurgus VI.* B. The Εὐνομία of Tyrtaios. C. What is the Rhetra?

1945

Hesperia, XIV. 212–29:
The Question of Tribute in 449/8 B.C.
Classical Quarterly, XXXIX. 19–33:
Kritias and Herodes.
Proceedings of the Classical Association, XLII. 7–9:
Summary of paper read at General Meeting at Oxford, Tues. April 3rd:
Perikles.
Oxford Magazine, 15 March, 209–10:
Review of C. M. Bowra, *Sophoclean Tragedy*.

1946

Classical Quarterly, XL. 101–4:
The Sixth-Century Athenian Decree about Salamis.

1947

Hesperia, XVI. 279–86:
H. T. Wade-Gery and B. D. Meritt, The Decrees of Kallias.

1948

American Journal of Archaeology, LII. 107–18, J. F. Daniel, O.
Broneer, H. T. Wade-Gery: The Dorian Invasion: 115–18:
What happened in Pylos? By H. T. Wade-Gery.

1949

The Athenian Tribute Lists, by B. D. Meritt, H. T. Wade-Gery and
M. F. McGregor, vol. II (American School of Classical Studies at
Athens, Princeton, New Jersey).
Classical Quarterly, XLIII. 79–81:
A Note on the Origin of the Spartan Gymnopaidiai.
Phoenix, III. 81–93:
Hesiod.
Oxford Classical Dictionary:
Thucydides.
Journal of Hellenic Studies, LXIX. 83–5:
Review of A. W. Gomme, *A Historical Commentary on Thucydides, vol. I:
Introduction and Commentary on Book I*.

1950

The Athenian Tribute Lists, by B. D. Meritt, H. T. Wade-Gery and M. F. McGregor, vol. III (American School of Classical Studies at Athens, Princeton, New Jersey).
Chamber's Encyclopaedia (new edition):
Athens (History).
Greek History (Ancient History).

1951

Journal of Hellenic Studies, LXXI. 212–21:
Miltiades.

1952

THE POET OF THE ILIAD (The J. H. Gray Lectures for 1949, Cambridge University Press).

1953

The Athenian Tribute Lists, by B. D. Meritt, H. T. Wade-Gery and M. F. McGregor, vol. IV (American School of Classical Studies at Athens, Princeton, New Jersey).

1957

Hesperia, XXVI. 183–97:
H. T. Wade-Gery and B. D. Meritt, Athenian Resources in 449 and 431 B.C.

1958

Essays in Greek History, by H. T. Wade-Gery (Oxford, Basil Blackwell) 180–200:
The Judicial Treaty with Phaselis and the History of the Athenian Law Courts.

HESIOD

HESIOD, the poet of whom I am to talk this evening,[1] is not a poet to compare with Homer or Aeschylus, Shakespeare or Dante. But I think in his own range he is a true, even a great, poet. Like the Athenian Solon, with whom one may naturally associate him, he is a good deal besides a poet. He may be called the first Presocratic, that is to say, the first Greek scientist. He was the first Greek poet to break the tradition of anonymousness and to talk about his own concerns, as later Archilochos and Sappho and many others have done. He was also, I believe, of some historical importance. I begin with the first of these aspects: with Hesiod as the first of the 'Presocratic philosophers' or scientists; and with one facet of this aspect, his astronomy.

I

To think in Hesiod's idiom we must forget what we know of the universe, the earth's orbit round the sun and its rotation round its own axis. We must think of the sky as a crystal sphere: or, better still, as a crystal dome—because we know nothing of what is below the horizon. Hesiod indeed probably thought that just below the horizon this dome touched, at its circumference, the stream of *Okeanos*: the earth was a circular island with Ocean all round it. The sun (like most of the stars) climbs out of Ocean into this dome: it climbs from the east, 'culminates' overhead, and sinks in the west. This notion of 'culminating', of reaching the zenith, is important: ἐς μέσον ἔλθῃ οὐρανόν, 'reaches the middle sky' is Hesiod's phrase for it (*Erga* 609–10). The sun culminates at midday. Hesiod knew that in summer it culminates higher over head; in winter it culminates nearer the south horizon. The dazzling level sunlight of midday in winter, when the sun is low in the south and the trees are bare, is a phenomenon which

---

[1] This paper was delivered by Professor Wade-Gery at the annual meeting of the Ontario Classical Association in Trinity College, Toronto, on March 30, 1948.

I   I

even a townsman like myself knows well. There is a day in mid-summer when the sun culminates highest; a day in midwinter when it culminates lowest, nearest the south horizon. Hesiod knew these days. We call them the solstices; he called them the τροπαὶ ἠελίοιο, the days 'when the sun turns'. Till midsummer it climbs higher and higher each day; then, till midwinter, sinks lower and lower: at each solstice, it turns.

Hesiod knew these days and counts his year from them. How was he able to determine them?—And not only he, but his hearers, whose knowledge he can take for granted? It cannot be hard, though I have never actually tried it. You watch some familiar shadow, for example the shadow of your own house: as midsummer approaches, at each midday (each culmination) this shadow is a little shorter—until one day it leaves the whole of some special patch clear of shadow. If on the next day the shadow creeps again *onto* that patch, you know you have seen the summer solstice.

I have spoken of some special patch of ground of which you know that it will, at the actual day of the solstice, be left clear of shadow. You might be more methodical, and lay a marker along the ground and make notches at the two solstices, the longest and shortest shadows. That is how Wilamowitz understood the lines of the *Odyssey* (xv, 403-4) where the swineherd Eumaios describes his home. 'There is an island called Syrie, above Ortygia, where there are markers laid out to show the solstice' (ὅθι τροπαὶ ἠελίοιο). This island called Syrie, above Ortygia, he understood as the island of Syros north of Delos, the modern Syra. This island was the home of the man who was reputed earliest of the Ionian scientists, Pherekydes of Syros. Pherekydes is reported to have possessed a *heliotropion*, a device to show how or when the sun 'turned': Wilamowitz supposed it was not a sundial, but a solstice-recorder. The *Odyssey* poet calls it τροπαὶ ἠελίοιο, the same name as that which Hesiod gives to the solstice.[1]

---

[1] Wilamowitz-Moellendorff, 'Pherekydes' *Sitzungsberichte der preussischen Akademie der Wissenschaften* (1926), 125-46. (*Kleine Schriften* v. 2, 128); *Heimkehr des Odysseus* (Berlin, 1927), 162. Syrie near Ephesos, an island once but later a part of the lower plain of the Kaystros (Pliny, *Natural History* v. 115; ii. 204), lay north of the Ephesian Ortygia: no doubt it too claimed to have been Eumaios' home. Cf. Athenaeus 361E, διαβάντες οἱ Ἐφέσιοι ἐκ τῆς νήσου: this island is no doubt Syrie.

For Hesiod, determining a solstice was elementary: he takes for granted that everyone knows the solstices. He attempted harder things: he attempted to determine the rising of stars. First, what we call the heliacal rising; when the star first appears in the night sky for a minute or two before dawn. At the heliacal rising of the Pleiads (which in Hesiod's time and latitude was some time in May) you should start reaping: this is how he describes this rising (*Erga* 385-7):[1]

> For forty nights in spring they are hidden, they
> Being up by day: then summer comes, and you'll
> See them at sunrise when you whet your sickle.

That is the heliacal rising, when a star, after having been absent from the night sky altogether, appears just for a minute or two at dawn. He knows also what we call the acronychal rising, that is, the first time that the star is up all through the night from the moment of dusk onwards. The acronychal rising of Arcturus was about the end of February: the time to prune vines (*Erga* 564-70):

> When Zeus has counted, from the winter solstice,
> Sixty days more of winter, then Arktouros
> Climbs from the stream of Ocean to the sky
> At point of dusk, and shines all night till dawn.
> And after him Pandion's clamorous girl
> The swallow, comes: and that's the start of spring.
> Prune vines before she's here: that's the best rule.

II

I hope that this has not been too much astronomy. I was leading up to this last passage: if you do not like (in the Greek) that description of spring, you will probably not like Hesiod. It has his special quality, of prosaic poetry. Hesiod, one may say, tries his hardest to write prose (that was an art not yet invented): prose is what he wants to write, but poetry was the only medium he knew; and not only that, but his language and his experience

---

[1] My versions are not literal. I have tried to bring out essential meanings and here I have been more explicit than Hesiod: adding the reason why the stars are hidden ('they being up by day'), and also the time of day when the mower whets his scythe. For Hesiod as for Milton he does it 'at sunrise', before he starts work. No doubt he refreshed the blade at intervals during the day; but the important whetting is at sunrise or dawn, and that is when he gets his first sight of the Pleiades.

were instinct with poetry. That was one reason why I have led up to this passage: the other is that it has been used to give Hesiod a date.

The only enquiry written in English and specifically devoted to the question of Hesiod's date is (so far as I know) T. W. Allen's paper, now about thirty-five years old,[1] reprinted in 1924 as a chapter in his book *Homer, The Origins and Transmission*. This chapter, like the whole book, is written incisively, learnedly, and, when that is appropriate, wittily: Allen's romantic bias towards early dates can be recognized and allowed for. For Hesiod, he reached the conclusion that the *Theogony* was written about 700 B.C.; not by Hesiod but by an admirer of Hesiod. This admirer's admiration is of the type, a legend-making or legend-accepting type, which one could expect him to feel for a man who had lived about a century before himself. Hesiod, therefore, lived about a century before the *Theogony* was written, he lived about 800 B.C. I cannot agree with this reasoning, and in my manner of reporting it I have perhaps betrayed my disagreement. I cannot think it could have persuaded anyone if Allen had not added his astronomical evidence: namely, that these lines point to *c*. 800 as Hesiod's date. It is a difficult argument, and the astronomer Rambaut's letter (which Allen appends) is, I believe, far from supporting Allen's conclusion. Let us look at the lines again.

> When Zeus has counted from the winter solstice
> Sixty days more of winter, then Arktouros
> Climbs from the stream of Ocean to the sky
> At point of dusk, and shines all night till dawn.[2]

In 1948, in Hesiod's latitude, Arcturus's acronychal rising was probably about ninety days after the solstice: it gets rather more than a day later each century. I use these rough figures chiefly because I have not the exact figures at my command: but partly also because the actual and exact date depends on the variable factors of eyesight and horizon. There is a slight uncertainty in translating Hesiod's words: there is a good deal more uncertainty in judging exactly when the phenomenon which Hesiod describes should be deemed to occur. Within the large margin

---

[1] *Journal of Hellenic Studies* 35 (1915), 85–99.
[2] For a discussion of the exact meaning of l. 567, see the 'Note on *Erga* 567' on p. 14.

allowed by these uncertainties, the phenomenon might be held
to occur (on the evening of the sixtieth day after the solstice) more
or less any time in the first millennium B.C. The optimum date
should probably be put somewhere near the middle of that period,
not too far from 500 B.C. I do not press this criterion, but for what
it is worth it indicates that Hesiod wrote the *Erga* after (rather
than before) 700 B.C. So far as I can judge, Hesiod may very well
have watched the sky at about 700 B.C. and have satisfied himself
that it was exactly on the evening of the sixtieth day that the
phenomenon occurred.[1]

This is no doubt the date (in very rough figures) of the *Theogony*
also: did Hesiod write both poems? For myself, I entertain no
shadow of doubt.[2] The enquiry into Hesiod as a person, when he
lived and what he wrote, is easier than such an enquiry into
Homer, because Homer prefers to be anonymous, to keep his
own affairs out of his poem, while Hesiod delights in talking of
himself. If you ask me, whom do I mean by Homer? I will
answer, 'the poet who wrote the *Iliad*', but I am conscious of a
certain margin of doubt. Did any one man write the *Iliad*?
I believe so, indeed, but the margin of doubt is there. With
Hesiod, we are on firmer ground: by Hesiod we mean the man
who had a vision on Mt. Helikon when he was a boy, who won a
prize at Chalkis and dedicated it on Mt. Helikon in the shrine
of the Muses: whose father lived in Kyme in Asia Minor and failed
in his seagoing business and so returned to Boeotia: whose brother
Perses was hard to get on with: who wrote the poem called *Erga*
or *Works* (that is, the *Farmer's Tasks*), who wrote this poem as the
outcome of his quarrel with his brother. All this he tells us of himself in this one poem: and much besides, as that he did not like
the sea, that he had a personal belief in a God who would ensure
that wrong should not prevail. He is an individual confronted with
a historic situation, like the Athenian Solon a century later.

---

[1] See the 'Note on *Erga* 567' on p. 14.
[2] Those who deny to Hesiod the *Theogony* (besides Allen, e.g. Evelyn White, who
edited the Loeb Hesiod) start usually from *Theogony* 22–4, contending that 'Ησίοδον
in 22 and μέ in 24 are different persons. Against this manifestly false contention it
is hardly necessary to quote the practice of, e.g., Catullus, Hipponax. Had he intended
such a distinction, the poet commanded a language which was particularly well qualified to make it clear. Their first thesis compels them to believe that the *Theogony* is a
later poem than the *Erga*: the contrary seems to be proved by the places where the
Erga refers back to the *Theogony*: *Erga* 11, 48, 659 to *Theogony* 225, 537–61, 22–32.

III

Let us begin with his vision. He alludes to it in the *Erga* (650–9): 'I have never been to sea but once,' he says, 'and that was when I crossed from Aulis to Chalkis, to the funeral games, the funeral wake, of Amphidamas. And there (by God!) I got the prize, a fine tripod: I dedicated it to the Muses of Helikon *in the place where they first set me in the path of poetry*'. What had these Muses done to him? He describes the occasion in much more detail in the opening of the *Theogony*. He was keeping watch over his flock by night on Helikon, when he heard them singing: they were hidden in cloud, in one of those patches of low cloud which roll down the mountains' sides in Greece. They had been dancing round Zeus' altar on the mountain top, and had then bathed in one of the high springs ('Permessos or Hippokrene or Olmeios'), and as they came down they were singing of the birth of the gods. And then, they saw him and his fellow shepherds, and spoke to them:

' "You shepherds abiding in the fields, you poor wretches, nothing but stomachs,—we know how to tell the lies that sound like truth: we know besides, when we wish, how to tell the truth itself." So they spoke to me, the daughters of high Zeus, and they put a branch of oleander in my hand, a lovely branch which they plucked: and they breathed poetry into me, that I should tell of the future and the past. And they told me to sing about the birth of the Gods, and to begin and end with themselves.' (*Theogony* 26–34.)

Did he really hear and see them? He most certainly believed that he did. I translated ποιμένες ἄγραυλοι, 'you shepherds abiding in the fields', to recall the words in St. Luke's Gospel, almost the same words: ποιμένες ἦσαν ἀγραυλοῦντες, 'there were shepherds abiding in the fields'. The vision of the Helikon shepherds was the prelude to Archaic Greece, as the vision of St. Luke's shepherds was the prelude to Christian Europe. The immediate result was the *Theogony*, the poem they had told him to write, the poem which he believed he had overheard them singing. The *Theogony* is thus the beginning of Hesiod's career, an earlier poem than the *Erga*: a young man's poem, almost a boy's poem. It has more poetry in it, as we commonly understand poetry, than the *Erga*: more enchantment, far more sense of romantic beauty. There is nothing in his later poetry like the magic of this description of his vision: this is like the dew; the *Erga* is part afire with passion, part humorous and wry and salty.

The *Theogony* itself (as distinct from its Prelude, the *Hymn to the Muses*) is very methodical: it is not exactly matter-of-fact, it is what Kipling calls a 'Just-so Story': it explains how the world, of heaven and earth and Tartaros, came to be. Did he think it all true—that he had had a revelation? Not exactly. The famous words which the Muses used to him ('we can tell lies, and when we wish we can tell truth') have been often interpreted and in many ways: it is often said that what they meant was, to put it crudely, 'Homer told lies, you shall tell the truth.' Nor do I think that that interpretation is entirely wrong: Hesiod did conceive of himself as a scientist rather than an entertainer: there is sense in calling him the first of the Presocratics,—the first of those scientists (or philosophers) who tried on the one hand to fathom the universe, on the other to advance some special technique. In all this his reaction from Homer is not unlike Thucydides' reaction from Herodotos. He did not want to entertain men's fancies; he was speculating about the truth of things, he was attempting to understand the world so that he could control it. But Greek religious thought was singularly free of dogma, it left the field clear for individual experience. Hesiod is not offering a dogma but a hypothesis: as clearly as he could see and formulate it, this was the nature and origin of the gods and the universe. The Muses' power was the power of imagination: imagination may tell you things which are false and only *seem* true; it can also tell you things which *are* true. Their injunction to Hesiod, as I understand it, was to give his imagination rein, and among his hypotheses some would be true.

The imaginative span of the *Theogony* is tremendous. To account for life at all, he posits, in the very beginning, Chaos, and Earth, and Eros (sexual love, 'the most beautiful among the Gods'). From these he derives Heaven and Hell, the known Pantheon of Gods, the Mountains and Rivers, and Good and Evil. It is because of this last preoccupation (Good and Evil) that his genealogy is so full of personifications: Night is mother of Strife, Strife is mother of her brood of evils, including what Professor Beazley has called the terrifying line (228):

Ὑσμίνας τε Μάχας τε Φόνους τ' Ἀνδροκτασίας τε

Battles and Noise-of-Battles, Murders and Massacres.

He tries to account for all, including the figures of fable: so Thetis appears among the Nereids, Kalypso among the daughters of Ocean: the absence of, for example, Proteus and Eidothea is perhaps a sign that he did not yet know the *Odyssey* as we have it.

I imagine he had lain, night after night in his shepherd's camp, teasing his brain with how to grasp the world and God: and then he had his vision. He heard the Muses singing the whole story, and his feet were set by them in the path of song.

IV

The poem which he took to Chalkis, and won his prize with it, was surely the *Theogony*: that is why he gave his prize to the Muses. Hesiod was certainly a professional farmer, poetry was not his main trade: he would no doubt perform at wakes and fairs, but the mature man who writes the *Erga* looks back on his prize at Chalkis as an outstanding event. It was a wake, or funeral: the dead man was Amphidamas, his sons provided the prizes. Plutarch (who thought the whole passage spurious) tells us that Amphidamas fell in the Lelantine War: and to me at least (since I would date the Lelantine War to about 700 B.C.) this seems one of the best clinches for Hesiod's date.[1] That is the time when we are bound to put the man who knew the *Iliad* but not yet the whole *Odyssey*, who is the father of personal poetry in Greece. This visit to Chalkis was all he knew, first-hand, of the sea: this soldier's funeral was all that he knew of war. We shall remember that Boeotia was not concerned in the Lelantine War.

The *Theogony* is followed in our manuscripts by a short 'Hero-

---

[1] It is often repeated (e.g. by F. Geyer, *Topographie und Geschichte der Insel Euboia* (Berlin, 1903), 25 and note 1; 27, note 2) that whereas Aristotle says (fr. 603) that the aristocracy of Hippobotai was ruling Chalkis when her northern colonies were founded, Amphidamas is called 'King'. If then the Lelantine War be made contemporary with these colonies, Amphidamas must be earlier than that war. But in fact Amphidamas is never called King except in the *Certamen* (and the *Vita Hesiodi*: T. W. Allen, *Homer* V (Oxford, 1912), 228, line 64, 222, line 7, both times βασιλέως Εὐβοίας: not a historically convincing title): neither Hesiod nor Plutarch so calls him; and Plutarch in *Moralia* 153 F calls him ἀνὴρ πολεμικός and makes it reasonably certain that he did not think of him as a king. Add Dio, *Orat.* II. 12 (dialogue between Alexander and Philip): καὶ μάλα δικαίως ἡττᾶτο (sc. Homer by Hesiod). οὐ γὰρ ἐν βασιλεῦσιν ἠγωνίζετο ἀλλ' ἐν γεωργοῖς καὶ ἰδιώταις. The *Certamen* is of course childishly irresponsible.

ogony', a poem on the births of the heroes: and that again was followed once by the long poem on the heroines, usually called the *Catalogue of Women*: our manuscripts give the first line of this and then stop. We have many fragments of this *Catalogue of Women* (the first fifty-four lines of the *Shield of Herakles* is one such fragment), and the poem was pretty clearly written some time after Hesiod's death. This means that the *Theogony* was an item in the repertory of rhapsodes and, as such, received additions, chiefly sequels. But the extent of the true *Theogony* is defined in Hesiod's prelude (line 105: cf. lines 21, 33), it is the *births of the immortals*. Only that much of our poem (and not the births of the mortal heroes and heroines) has any claim to be by Hesiod himself.

The *Erga* similarly became a rhapsode's piece, and it too had its sequels: notably the *Hemerai* or *Days*. I do not myself believe Hesiod wrote the *Days*, but I do not feel dogmatic: it contains no autobiography as his certainly genuine poems do.

V

The *Erga* has, we have seen, one brief allusion to the Muses of Helikon and Hesiod's vision. Otherwise they do not appear. In the first line the Pierian Muses, from the foot of Mt. Olympos, are invoked; but the opening Hymn is addressed, not to the Muses as in the *Theogony*, but to Zeus. This short *Hymn to Zeus* is in some ways unique in Greek: it consists of five hexameter couplets, the first four of which are (surprisingly) more or less in rhyme. It states the poem's theme:

> Pierian Muses, you whose song gives fame,
> Come tell of Zeus, your own father proclaim:
>
> Him, who makes men be famous and unfamed,
> Known and forgotten, at his own great will.
>
> Easy for Him to make the strong and break them,
> Easy to abase the great, to raise the obscure;
>
> Crookèd to straighten, proud to quench,—both easy
> For Zeus who dwells 'mid Thunders in the Highest.
>
> Give heed! give eye and ear! make straight Thy justice
> Thou Zeus! whilst I to Perses talk plain truth.

The first theme of the *Erga*, and I think the most important, is
Justice. It is this which gives the poem its historic importance.

Perses has tried to overreach Hesiod, and has got the Judges,
the nobles, on his side: Hesiod has been threatened with a lawsuit
in which the judges have been squared. The poem is about this
quarrel. It is not quite easy to determine exactly the occasion.
In some places, in the early part of the poem, Hesiod speaks with
an agonized suspense and it would seem that the crisis lies ahead.
I quote some of these passages. First, the fable of the *Hawk and
Nightingale* (202–12):

> Now listen, Lords, and well you know
>   The meaning of my tale.
> The Hawk did seize and bear aloft
>   The sweet-throat Nightingale,
> Who wailing in those cruel claws
>   Heard thus the Hawk prevail:
>
> 'Good bird, why all this twittering?
>   A stronger bird than you
> Has got you, singer though you be,
>   And what he will he'll do—
> Will eat you up or set you down
>   As he is minded to.
>
> Match not your strength against the great,
>   It is a foolish thing.
> You lose, friend: and the loser gets
>   (Alas) both shame and sting.'
> Thus spoke the Hawk, the flying Hawk,
>   The bird of widespread wing.

After thus addressing the 'Lords', that is, the Judges, Hesiod turns
to his brother (213–16):

> Perses, heed Justice! and keep clear of Outrage.
> Outrage is not for poor men: even the rich
> Find danger in outrageous acts, and often
> Founder beneath them.

Then come the descriptions of the Two Cities, City of Justice and
City of Outrage (225–47). Then he turns back to the Judges
(248–51, 263–4, 267–73):

You too, my Lords, take note which kind of Justice
Is here. The immortal spirits in our midst
Are taking note of all these crooked Judges
Who grind men down, forgetting that God sees.

*   *   *

Beware then, make your language straight, O you
Gift-hungry Lords: put crookedness clean away.

*   *   *

The eye of Zeus both sees and understands:
At us, if so he please, he is looking now
And sees what sort of Justice Thespia holds.
O who'ld be just, in such a world? not I
Nor son of mine. It's no good being just
Where the unjust will get the better justice.
But Zeus, I think, means it should not end so.

It is the acute tension in these addresses to the Judges, and above
all the momentary wavering of faith in Zeus in those last lines,
which imply that the crisis is still ahead. On the other hand, in
the latter part of the poem Hesiod treats Perses with a sort of
contemptuous affection—as 'a poor thing, but mine own'. The
cry 'O who'ld be just?—not I, nor son of mine!' comes in line 271:
in 286 he is addressing Perses as μέγα νήπιε Πέρση, 'you great
fool, Perses,' and in 299 comes the ironic ἐργάζευ Πέρση, δῖον γένος,
'Perses, my fine gentleman, work!' And the poem thence-forward
is no longer preoccupied with Justice and Outrage, but is advice
to Perses on how to make farming pay.

There can thus be little doubt that when the poem as we have it
was written the crisis was past and Perses had climbed down.
The passages which I have quoted (all of them before line 286)
must have been written earlier. The *Hawk and Nightingale* was,
I imagine, a complete poem: it is like one of Archilochos' poems,
and like them it is designed to work on public opinion. What I
conceive happened is that when the case was pending Hesiod
stumped the country, round Askra and Thespia, making agitation:
and these are his agitation poems, and the agitation was successful.

I would not care to dogmatize about how the poem grew. It
may be that when the crisis was past Hesiod worked up his
occasional poems into the continuous poem which we have. It
may be that the whole of the first part of the poem (1–285), with

its prelude to Zeus and its preoccupation with Justice, was performed while the crisis still pended, and when it was settled
Hesiod added the second part about how to thrive and be honest.
The main thing is that we have both. The first part has the
passion and the fire: the second part has the flavour of earth,
the ripeness and humour.

VI

Historically the poem's importance lies in the fact that the
Nightingale won. The Hawk had said:

> 'Good bird, why all this twittering?
> A stronger bird than you
> Has got you, singer though you be,
> And what he will he'll do.'

But the Nightingale had got its hearing and the Hawk had had to
let it go. We here see Hesiod as the predecessor of Solon, a first
defier of corrupt justice. The differences between them are clear:
Hesiod was fighting for his own hand, Solon for others. Hesiod
had a narrowness which often marks farmer or peasant; he had
little of the magnificent sanguine outlook of the great Athenian
who saw that with a hand's turn Athens could be set on her
incomparable destiny. But Solon quotes Hesiod's language so
constantly that he must have seen in him his forerunner. There
have not been too many ages of the world when public opinion
could really control governments. When we remember what
Homer thought of such an agitator as Thersites, who spoke up
to his betters, we shall recognize the size of Hesiod's achievement.
From Hesiod through Solon to Aeschylus and Euripides, the
Nightingale was a real power in Greek opinion and behaviour,
and the Hawk had to listen. With the Macedonian, and the
Roman, things changed. The Hawk professed benevolence, and
the Nightingale ate out of his hand. Aratos was court poet to
Antigonos, Virgil to Augustus. They both professed to imitate
Hesiod, but it was a strange imitation.

I have spoken of him as astronomer and politician. Neither
of these activities, I imagine, took up much of his life: most of his
time he was a small landowner. We see him at home, coping

with the extremes of cold in winter and of heat in summer (*Erga*
504–60, 582–96, passages of great and vivid beauty); or in another mood, perhaps his most distinctive, giving advice on
neighbours, economy, business (342–56, 368–71):

> Call him who loves you to your feast: your foe
> May wait: and specially invite a neighbour.
> When something happens in a village, neighbours
> Come as they are, your wife's folk wait to dress.
> A bad neighbour's a curse, and that's as sure
> As t'other, that a good neighbour's worth money:
> You'll lose no cattle if your neighbour's honest.
>   Get fair deals from a neighbour: give as good:
> Give better still, if you can manage it;
> So next time you're in need you'll find him ready.
>   Avoid sharp gains, they are ruin. Love the man
> Who loves you, visit him who visits you,
> Give him who gives, refuse him who refuses.
> The giver gets, non-givers are non-getters:
> I like *Give : Help-yourself* I hate, it's death.
>
>   *   *   *
>
> Broaching, and emptying, drink your fill: go slow
> Between: when bottom shows it's no use stinting.
> Have ready a price if you agree it: but even
> If it's your brother, smile—and call a witness.

In one matter Hesiod is almost unique in Greece. The Spartans
said Homer was a poet for warriors, Hesiod for serfs: and it is
true that Hesiod practically never mentions war, and this is as
remarkable in a Greek as, in a modern, never to mention love.
War was, to the Greek imagination, what love has been to the
modern English and American: some praise it, some dispraise it,
but all are intensely interested in it and see in it the experience
which most searches out man's quality. But Hesiod simply ignores
it.[1]

There is no suggestion that Hesiod or Perses or any of their
neighbours is a defence-unit: no suggestion that the Lords are
military leaders, good or bad. The plagues which Pandora lets

---

[1] That is to say, in the *Erga*. I have quoted above the 'terrifying line' in *Theogony*
228: Hesiod was then an imaginative boy. To use Blake's distinction, the *Theogony*
is a Song of Innocence, the *Erga* a Song of Experience.

out of her jar include Pain, Labour, Disease, Death; but not War. In the two ideal pictures, indeed, City of Justice and City of Outrage, we do hear that the former is free of war (228–9), the latter has military disasters (245–7): but compared to these ideal pictures, think of Pandora's plagues 'of which earth and sea are still full' (100–4), and of the Iron Race of men among whom Hesiod actually lives. The Iron Race has every other vice and evil: worry, disease, labour, perjury, no sense of hospitality, none of kinship—all this, but no war (174–200). Hesiod sets no value on military courage or leadership. The Golden Race do not fight, the Silver Race do because they are like spoilt children (134).

In all this, his reaction from the *Iliad* is profound:[1] once more, perhaps, the narrowness of the peasant? Hesiod's is a world whose evils are Poverty and Greed, leading to Perjury and Outrage. The cures for these evils are Justice and Thrift: these are the two themes of the poem of his manhood.

Note on *Erga* 567 (see p. 4 note 2, p. 5 note 1).

1. The slight uncertainty of meaning is due to the word πρῶτον. Editors have observed that a star which rises at the beginning of evening dusk has reached its *last* visible rising: tomorrow it will rise invisibly, in daylight. I do not think that τότε πρῶτον can mean as little as the German *erst dann*, 'tum demum', 'then and not till then'. It could however mean 'as a start', 'as the first thing', and Sinclair aptly compares γενέσθαι πρῶτα in line 784, 'to start [one's life] by being born'. But there must be some process, or a series of happenings, which *starts* with the occasion in question. And it is clear enough, in this case, what the process is: from this night onwards, so soon as it is dark enough to see, Arcturus will be visible. The night in question is the *start* of the period when Arcturus is up all night. The doubt

---

[1] The Heroes fight, of course (*Erga* 161–8). They are like a foreign body in Hesiod's thought and show the direct impact of Homer. Their wars exterminate them: a rather curious anticipation of the Plan of Zeus as conceived in the *Kypria* (fr. I, Διὸς δ'ἐτελείετο βουλή: conceived quite differently from the same words in *Iliad* I. 5, where the scholiast notes the echo). This thought—ὦ Ζεῦ τί μου δρᾶσαι βεβούλευσαι πέρι;—must have crossed many minds in the seventh century when the Cossacks were storming the civilized world: but Hesiod had seen nothing of that. The Heroes' Islands in Hesiod are still at the World's End, beside Ocean (*Erga* 168–71), though Arktinos (if we can trust Proklos) already identified Achilles' Island with Leuke at the Danube's mouth, and Diomed's Island was soon to be found in the Adriatic (schol. Pindar, *Nemeans* x. 12=Ibykos, fr. 38 Bergk: cf. R. L. Beaumont, 'Greek Influence in the Adriatic Sea Before the Fourth Century B.C.' *Journal of Hellenic Studies* 56 (1936), 195). The Hesiodic view survives in the Attic skolion to Harmodius (*scolia anonyma* 11, in Diehl, *Anthologia Lyrica Graeca*).

which remains is whether Hesiod means the *last visible rising*, or rather (one day later) the *first invisible rising*. For the former, we must take the words thus: 'Arcturus starts [sc. its period of all-night visibility] by rising in brightness at the beginning of dusk.' If ἐπιτέλλεται means strictly, 'rises', this is how we are forced to take the words: and this will mean the *last visible rising*. But perhaps ἐπιτέλλεται can mean 'has risen', 'is visible'? In line 383 ἐπιτελλομενάων corresponds to (the future?) δυσομενάων in line 384, and the sense 'when they *have risen*' answers properly to 'when they *are going to set*'. (Similarly 'has risen recently' [νέον] in *Hymn to Hermes* 371.) We could then understand the phrase to mean, 'Arcturus is, for the first time, visible in brightness at the beginning of dusk': and this means the *first invisible rising*. I believe we cannot exclude this second meaning. It should (strictly speaking) alter the count of days by one: but the second uncertainty (that of determining the night when either phenomenon occurs: see para. 2) is so much greater as practically to swamp this one. If we are right in recognizing the phenomenon in the fact (see below) that in 685 B.C. on the night of the sixtieth day after the solstice Arcturus was 2° above the horizon in a 6° twilight, then I am uncertain which translation best represents that occurrence.

2. There is a far greater uncertainty when we try to determine the night on which the phenomenon occurs. When does dusk 'begin'? (sc. when is it dark enough to see the star?): and at what altitude does the star 'rise' (or 'be visible')? Rambaut said, for the former, that effective dusk began one hour after sunset, when the sun was 12° below the horizon: for the latter, the star must not, at the beginning of dusk, be more than 3° above. He gave no figures for any year later than 850 B.C., by which date these conditions are not present, nor anywhere near present. If we extrapolate his figures, we shall find that these conditions are not satisfied till about 400 B.C. If so early a date as 800 B.C., for Hesiod's *floruit*, was 'acceptable to Dr. Rambaut's conscience' (Allen, p. 88), then he must have abandoned his demand for a 12° twilight. In view of his 'Note added later' on p. 97 this is not unlikely, though on p. 94 of his original note he had written 'a 6° twilight is out of the question'. About 685 B.C. on the night in question Arcturus was 2° above the horizon in a 6° twilight: one hundred years earlier, about 785 B.C., Arcturus' altitude (in the same circumstances) was about 3°. Using my own arbitrary judgment, I would suppose that for a star of Arcturus' magnitude, on the eastern horizon (which darkens sooner than the rest of the sky), a 6° twilight (half an hour after sunset) was enough, and that the star's altitude of 2° (as in 685 B.C.) was appropriate: but that 3° (as in 785 B.C.) was excessive, since the star which tonight is 3° above the horizon will have been (in

the same degree of twilight) already visible yesterday or perhaps the day before—that is to say, after fifty-nine (or perhaps fifty-eight) days.

3. The above figures are got by extrapolation from Rambaut's tables (Allen, p. 97). My colleague, H. H. Plaskett, the Savilian Professor of Astronomy, who has most kindly advised me on this whole question, warns me that this is a dangerous process and that a fresh computation is required for any responsible conclusion.

KYNAITHOS

I. The 'Pythian Continuation' of the 'Hymn to Apollo'

THUCYDIDES definitely believed that the *Hymn to Apollo* was the work of Homer himself and contained valuable autobiographic facts. His belief seems to have been shared by Aristophanes. I cannot feel sure that they were wrong. The first 178 lines of the Hymn contain poetry of the first water, full of wilful beauty, unmatched in the Hymns. The rest is now recognized by most readers[1] to be by another hand or hands. Did Thucydides and Aristophanes believe that these last 368 lines were likewise Homer's work? I think they did not. These are tantalizing and debated questions: without presuming to resolve them, I welcome this chance to put to Professor Murray (from whom I learnt to relate Greek poetry to facts) some speculation about the poem's history.

The first 178 lines are about Apollo of Delos (D). The remainder is about Apollo of Delphi or, as the poem calls it, Pytho (P). But this remainder never had independent existence as it stands; our two poems are rather (D) lines 1–178, a Delian poem on Apollo of Delos, and (S) lines 1–546, a Syncretistic poem on Apollo of both Delos and Delphi. So we may conveniently distinguish

D the Delian poem, lines 1–178.
P the Pythian continuation, lines 179–546.
S the Syncretistic poem, lines 1–546.

So far I follow Wilamowitz and Jacoby. I take as established by these scholars that though D can stand alone P cannot; and that P is composed[2] (by the Syncretistic poet) as a sequel to D.

[1] Except Dornseiff, *Die archaische Mythenerzählung*, Berlin, 1933: he returns to the charge in *Nochmals der homerische Apollonhymnos* (*Greifswalder Beiträge* 8, 1935). But I have profited little from his pages, as little as from Bethe's *Der homerische Apollonhymnos und das Prooimion* (SB. Dresden, 1931). On the other hand my deep debt to Jacoby's *Der homerische Apollonhymnos* (SB. Berlin, 1933) will be evident; and of course to Wilamowitz, *Die Ilias und Homer*, pp. 440 sqq., and Allen and Sikes' edition of the Hymns. I have to thank Mr. Bowra for my acquaintance with some of these, and much more for his constant readiness to discuss these problems.

[2] Composed: how far his composition incorporated existing poems it remains to inquire. Since I believe P was composed late and for a Western audience it is likely it incorporated much.

2

Two poets then, the Delian poet and the Syncretistic poet: two poems, D and S. Whether the Delian poet is really Homer is too high an enquiry to pursue yet: to the Syncretistic poet I think we can give a date and a name. In a note on the word Ὁμηρίδαι the scholiast to Pindar, *Nem.* ii. 1, tells us that one of the famous Homeridai was Kynaithos; that he inserted much into Homer's poetry; that he was a Chiot; that (among the works ascribed to Homer) he composed the *Hymn to Apollo*; that he was the first to recite Homer's poetry in Syracuse, about 504 B.C. (the 69th Olympiad).[1] I suggest that this is all true: that Kynaithos composed the Syncretistic poem (enlarging D to S) for performance in Western Greece about the end of the sixth century B.C.

This date has always been rejected, because there are lines in P which were undoubtedly written long before. Especially 299, written before the destruction of the primitive temple in 548 B.C. I would add 269–71, written before the Pythian race-course was made at Krisa (582 B.C. or a little earlier), and 485, written (surely?) before the Sacred War of *c.* 600–590 B.C. On the other hand lines 524–44 are commonly[2] believed to refer to the Sacred War. In considering these passages let us not apply false canons to the rhapsode's art, for S is *ex hypothesi* a rhapsodic poem. There is nothing shocking in his use of lines which he could not possibly have written himself. Perhaps the use of line 299, after the burning of the temple, would be shocking: I therefore start from that passage.

II. *The Foundation of the Temple*

ὣς εἰπὼν διέθηκε θεμείλια Φοῖβος Ἀπόλλων
295   εὐρέα καὶ μάλα καλὰ διηνεκές· αὐτὰρ ἐπ᾽ αὐτοῖς
λάϊνον οὐδὸν ἔθηκε Τροφώνιος ἠδ᾽ Ἀγαμήδης
ο υἱέες Ἐργίνου φίλοι ἀθανάτοισι θεοῖσιν,
ο ἀμφὶ δὲ νηὸν ἔνασσαν ἀθέσφατα φῦλ᾽ ἀνθρώπων·
• κτιστοῖσιν λάεσσιν ἀοίδιμον ἔμμεναι αἰεί.

(297-299 *signa duplicis recensionis addidi.*)

---

[1] The Greek is quoted below, p. 31, n. 3.
[2] Beloch, *Gr. Ges.* I². 2, p. 137; Poulsen, *Delphi* (Eng. tr.), p. 8; Wilamowitz, *Pindaros*, p. 74; Gruppe, *Gr. Myth.*, p. 104; Dornseiff, *Die arch. Myth.*, p. 15. Jacoby and Allen-Sikes are cautious: see p. 24 below.

These lines can be construed: or at least it has been done.[1] But it wants a lot of good will: we must give ἔνασσαν the unique and difficult meaning 'built'; we must believe that the most ancient temple of Apollo comprised a stone structure other than the λάινος οὐδός. Even so, κτιστοῖσιν in 299 cannot be translated. It has been observed[2] that the removal of 298 eases[3] these difficulties. The λάινος οὐδός is now composed (naturally enough) of the 'earth-planted'[4] stones; and ἔνασσαν, being removed, need not trouble us. Alternatively, the removal of 299 (though I do not know that it has been proposed) leaves a good text: ἔνασσαν, relieved of 299, can keep its normal sense, 'they made men dwell round the temple'.

The passage has in fact the symptoms of a double recension: 296–8 make good sense, and 296 followed by 299 makes good sense, but 296–9 make nonsense. Double recensions are not rare in the Hymns: Allen and Sikes, p. xliii, quote several, especially from the *Aphrodite* (add 62, 63): the fragmentary *Dionysos* (Hymn I) seems to be full of them; 13–15, 16; 17–19, 20–1. But the best known and the most certain, and a good parallel to our present case, is in the *Apollo*, 135–9, where the MSS. have noted against 136–8 ἐν ἑτέρῳ κεῖνται καὶ οὗτοι οἱ στίχοι·

ὡς εἰπὼν ἐβίβασκεν ἐπὶ χθονὸς εὐρυοδείης
Φοῖβος ἀκερσεκόμης ἑκατηβόλος· αἱ δ' ἄρα πᾶσαι
135 θάμβεον ἀθάναται· χρυσῷ δ' ἄρα Δῆλος ἅπασα
ϑ βεβρίθει, καθορῶσα Διὸς Λητοῦς τε γενέθλην,
ϑ γηθοσύνῃ, ὅτι μιν θεὸς εἵλετο οἰκία θέσθαι

---

[1] In that case there will be no stop at the end of 298: 'and round the οὐδός the tribes of men built a temple with (something) stones.'

[2] A. von Blumenthal, *Philologus* 83 (1928), pp. 221, 223: he would place 298 after 299. But I think Jacoby (p. 742) is right to say the sequence 296, 297, 299, 298, 300 is stylistically impossible: 297 is intrusive; 298, closing the paragraph after the clausula in 299, is intolerable; nor does, e.g., the exquisite close of *Odyssey* ii provide a parallel.

[3] It does not quite heal them, for 297 still sounds intrusive between 296 and 299. I therefore mark 297 as belonging to the same recension as 298.

[4] 'Aus gegründeten Steinen', von Blumenthal, p. 221. [I think his interpretation of λάινος οὐδός right: he compares *Odyssey* xxii. 127 (and less certainly xx. 258) and the metre-high masonry basis of the cella-wall at the Heraion at Olympia (*Orthostaten-schicht*), whose upper courses were of clay bricks: the physical remains of the Delphic λάινος οὐδός, Courby, *Fouilles* ii. 2, 190 sqq.] κτίζειν seems to mean *to plant*, as one plants a garden or a flower: *to plant* the earth with habitations (χώρην, νῆσον, etc.), or *to plant in the earth* a grove, an altar, a wall or a city (ἄλσος, βωμόν, τεῖχος, ἄστυ): from this, the derived meaning *to establish*.

ο νήσων ήπείρου τε, φίλησε δὲ κηρόθι μᾶλλον·
• ἤνθησ᾽, ὡς ὅτε τε ῥίον οὔρεος ἄνθεσιν ὕλης.

Here, 135–8 make sense, 135 followed by 139 makes sense, 135–9 make nonsense; and here (as Hermann observed) we have no mere indifferent alternative (such as the *Aphrodite* variants appear to be) but evidence of two different shapes of the poem. Hermann believed 139 to be the earlier and to lead on without pause to the account of the Delian festival in 140 sqq.: 136–8 are by a later poet who meant, with them, to end the Delian portion. 'Non dubitandum, puto quin antiqui poetae haec sunt' (135, 139). 'Nam hic quidem poeta recte sic cecinit, quippe statim alia in laudem Apollinis additurus. Interpolator vero qui illa quae sequuntur' (140–78), 'omittere debebat, non potuit non intelligere, si florentem Deli statum uno versu describeret, finem hymni nimis ieiunum futurum esse. Itaque pleniore usus est peroratione' (136–8).[1] This observation of Hermann is the starting-point of what I find the most convincing part of Jacoby's paper.[2] Hermann's first poet is the poet of D, his second poet is the poet of S (the Syncretistic poet had of course no use for so personal a description of the festival). The poet of S made important changes in D; but D survived independently and was used by the compiler of our text for his first 178 lines: the changes which the poet of S had made were recorded as variants.

Jacoby detects further variants in the Delian portion, lines 7–9 (*vice* 6), 14–18 (*vice* 10–13), 72[3] (*vice* 73–9), 96 (*vice* 98), 129 (*vice* 128): all these he considers variants introduced by the poet of S. We are not here concerned with the detail: in general I am convinced.[4] The discovery lets us see the poet of S at work, as he

---

[1] G. Hermann, *Epistula editoris* (in his edition of the Hymns, 1806), p. xxvi.

[2] F. Jacoby, *Der homerische Apollonhymnos* (SB. Berlin, 1933, 682 sqq.), pp. 707–11, 716–25. I cannot here condense his argument. The ground for supposing that (for ll. 1–178) the *main text* of the compiler of our version was the original D and that the changes introduced by the poet of S were recorded as *variants from* that main text, is the fact that 136–8 *are* so recorded in such MSS. as have them, while in the *Mosquensis* (the oldest MS.) they are omitted. The *Mosquensis* likewise omits 96, which later MSS. have in a false position: I take this as valuable confirmation of Jacoby's (and Wilamowitz's) *a priori* opinion that 96 is the version of S (Jacoby, p. 708 sq.). Allen and Sikes's view that '96 fell out from *homoearchon* with 98: the fact has no bearing on its age or genuineness' would have more reason if 97 had fallen with it.

[3] Reading ἀτιμήσῃ.

[4] I note that in line 16 Ortygia is paired with Delos, exactly as Pindar pairs them *Nem.* i. 2–4. Kynaithos wrote, as I believe, for a Syracusan audience; Pindar certainly did. Jacoby's conception of D and S can be conveniently summarized: D contained

prunes his great original, embellishes it with the sacred names, makes it decorous for his purposes: like (if I may be allowed a rather indecent comparison) the editors of *Hymns A. and M.*

Let us return to 296–9. Jacoby finds, and expects to find, no variants in P (the Pythian portion, 179–546).[1] Yet I make bold to say that the variant in 296–9 is as evident as any that he has found in 1–178.[2] The variants in 1–178 are due to the separate survival of D, one of the elements out of which S was composed. Is the variant in 296–9 due to the separate survival of some other element? I am inclined to think so, though I do not insist and am not prepared to define the original extent of such a Χρηστηρίου κτίσις.[3] What I think nearly certain is that the l. 299 which appears to date S before the fire of 548 B.C., only stands in *one of two alternative versions.* It is probably the earlier version, the variation being consequent on that very fire (which would make l. 299 sound foolish). And that the other (sc. 297–8) is in fact the later (the Syncretistic) version, is likely for a further reason: the

---

1–6, 10–13, 19–71, 73–95, 97–128, 130–5, 139–78: S contained 1–5, 7–9, 14–72, 79–95, 97, 96, 99–127, 129–38, 179 sqq.

[1] p. 716: 'der delische Hymnos ist von Varianten durchsetzt, was (das muss mit Nachdruck gesagt werden) im pythischen Teil nicht der Fall ist.'

[2] Jacoby, p. 741, deals with the passage by excision. This gives him a neat resultant text, but it leaves the critical problem (how perfectly good lines came to be 'interpolated' in a nonsensical order) untouched.

[3] It might seem strong evidence for its separate survival (as part of the Hesiodic corpus) that line 241 is in fact quoted by a scholiast on B 523 as from Hesiod (fr. 26 Loeb, on p. 172: the scholiast quotes it with the variant προίει for προχέει: Eustathius, *ad loc.*, quotes it verbatim). Allen and Sikes point out that our Hymns are unknown to the Homeric *Scholia*: i.e. the quotation is not from the Syncretistic poem. I find it hard to weigh this evidence, which is very far from conclusive. Many Hesiodic fragments have details of Central Greek geography (Strabo, ix. 3. 16 says indeed that Hesiod wrote at length about the course of the Kephisos): there would be no lack of suitable contexts for such a line.
The poem might indeed begin with 214 ἢ ὡς τὸ πρῶτον χρηστήριον (compare the opening of the *Aspis* and the other *Ehoiai*: Wilamowitz, *Il. u. Hom.* 443). [Jacoby, p. 702, is rather offended by τὸ πρῶτον, which I take to mean 'at the beginning of (Delphic) history', cf. τὰ πρώτιστα in 237.] Its minimum is the fifty lines 214–43, 278–96, 299, i.e. without Telphusa or the Dragon. But this makes a dull little poem, with no suspension of the action, no act of power. The Telphusa episode improves it and is almost certainly old (see p. 22, n. 1: it could, of course, be old and yet be inserted late, by the poet of S). The trouble about including Telphusa is that she is held by many (cf. Allen and Sikes's note on 375) to presuppose the Dragon: and personally I believe that the Dragon only comes in with the later of the two recensions in 296–9 (l. 298, which belongs to the later recension, leads on to 303 and especially 355). But I think in fact 375 follows on 299 no worse than on 374, and the Dragon is no essential part of Telphusa's deceit. The original poem (seventh century, see p. 22, n. 1) would then be 214–96, 299, 375–87. And it is of course possible that the *Dolphin* 388–522 also belonged to it.

mention of *inhabitants* in 298 leads on to the story of the Dragon (298, 303, 355), and this story, which contains one of the sacred etymologies, must certainly have stood in the Syncretistic poem.

It appears then that the Syncretistic poet did not use l. 299; and ll. 297–8, which he substituted, no longer imply the First Temple's survival. So far as this passage goes, it is in fact likely that he wrote after the fire of 548 B.C. On the other hand it is likely that a poem (on the *Founding of the Temple and Oracle*) whose original form was older than the fire of 548 B.C., and probably older than the Sacred War of *c.* 600–590 B.C.,[1] has been incorporated.

III. *The Dolphin Miracle*

After the Temple has been built and Telphusa punished, Apollo establishes his priests. The rest of the Hymn relates the *Dolphin Miracle*: how Apollo brought a Kretan ship to Krisa by miracle, and the ship's company and their descendants became his priests. Here, as in the Founding of the Temple, there are signs (quite as clear as l. 299) that the story was written long before 504 B.C. It was written probably before the Sacred War of *c.* 600–590 B.C.: before the destruction of Krisa and the 'devotion' of the Krisan Plain.

Delphi stands on the south face of Parnassos; facing, across the Pleistos Gorge, the smaller mass of Kirphis. Below, separating the two masses, runs the Pleistos river: it runs from east to west, and the Kastalia stream (in whose glade Delphi stands) falls steeply into it. About five miles below Delphi the Pleistos issues from its gorge, and flows for a mile or two through the Plain of Krisa to the sea. The ruins of Krisa stand on the south-western spur of Parnassos (near the modern Chryso) overlooking both Gorge and Plain; and the modern road from the coast to Delphi (essentially the same road as is followed in l. 514 sqq. of the Hymn: the same as Karrhotos takes in Pindar, *Pyth.* v. 37 sq.) passes near these ruins, and then slowly climbs east along the south face of the mountain.

---

[1] Since the Kastalian Glade is called Κρίση in 282 sqq. it is likely that the poem dates from the seventh century, whilst Krisa still controlled the Oracle. Nor is it indeed conceivable that 269–71 (from the Telphusa episode) were written after the Pythian Games were established, and the Race-course in the Plain of Krisa. [Dornseiff, *Die arch. Myth.* 13, hardly needs refuting.] It is a thing a poet could not *write*, though a rhapsode might retain it.

From the Sacred War at the beginning of the sixth century, throughout pagan antiquity, Krisa lay in ruins and the Krisan Plain uncultivated. Pausanias saw it in the second century A.D. and records that it was still barren, 'they plant no trees, whether because of the curse or knowing that none will grow';[1] but it is fertile enough in fact, and today it not only has the finest olive woods in Greece, but around the harbour it is green with vines as in l. 438 of the Hymn. The first mention of the curse is in Isocrates, *Plataicus* 31 (written shortly before the battle of Leuktra): in 404 B.C. the Thebans had wished, he says, to enslave the Athenians καὶ τὴν χώραν ἀνεῖναι μηλόβοτον ὥσπερ τὸ Κρισαῖον πεδίον. Aeschines, who had the curse and the oracle and the oaths read out in court, tells us that the land was dedicated to Apollo, Artemis, Leto, and Athena Pronaia ἐπὶ πάσῃ ἀεργίᾳ, and was never to be cultivated:[2] an inscription of 380 B.C. mentions the Hieromnamons' duty of taking fines from any who cultivate it;[3] and from the second century we have a detailed delimitation of the land from sea to sea, and certain individuals who have encroached are named and must evacuate.[4] In this Plain, taken for centuries out of cultivation, the herds and flocks of

---

[1] x. 37. 5. But Strabo ix. 3. 3 calls the plain εὐδαιμον. *Krisa and Kirrha are identical* (for the variation of form compare θρασ-, θαρσ-, θαρρ-). When the harbour town was rebuilt it was called Kirrha, the ruins on the hill were remembered as Krisa. So a distinction grew up in Roman times which need not concern us, any more than Strabo's efforts to locate the two (see, for all this, Pauly-Wissowa, *Krisa*). Their identity in classical times is clear from Pindar: Κίρρᾳ in Pyth. iii. 74 means exactly the same as ἐν Κρίσᾳ in *Isthm.* ii. 18: ὑπὸ Κίρρας in *Pyth.* x. 15 means under the hill-site of Krisa. The distinction for Pindar is metrical: the *iota* in Κρίσα Κρισαῖος is always short. (I do not therefore care for Wilamowitz' idea that Chrysothemis was once Krisothemis, etc.) In the Hymn and the *Iliad* the *iota* is unquestionably long, and (if Pindar's evidence for its natural shortness is valid) must have been long by position. The *Iliad* MSS. have Κρῖσαν apparently without variant: I imagine the true form was Κίρρσα, mentioned by *Et. Mag.* 515. 18 and Herodian i. 266. 11, ii. 385. 26, and extant (as Mr. Lobel points out to me) in Alkaios, fr. 7 [=A 7]. In the Hymn 282, 438, the accusative has the last syllable long, and in 445 the name must begin with Κρ-. The MSS. (here and in practically all classical texts where Krisa is mentioned) vary between Κρίση and Κρίσση: the true reading in the Hymn is perhaps Κρίσση. The form Κρῖσα is, I think, a *monstrum*.

[2] iii. 112: the passage in the text is from 108. On the strength of the Curse Aeschines had raised a Sacred War against Amphissa, which led disastrously to the campaign of Chaironeia the next year. This is from his defence.

[3] Ditt. *Syll³.* 145, l. 18 πρασσοντων τον επιεργαζομενον. This, like Isokrates' reference, is before Philip's Sacred War: all our other evidence is after.

[4] *Syll³.* 826 E: in col. iii, l. 31 one individual is ordered to pull down his house. The encroachers appear to be only on the debatable limit (as Demosthenes implies that Aeschines' Amphissans had been, xviii. 150: see what this has grown to by Strabo, ix. 3. 4).

Apollo grazed[1] and, every four years, the Pythian Games were held.[2]

Of the war's course (to say nothing of its cause) we cannot hope to know much: the story has been pietized. The victors were the Amphiktyons, and they controlled Delphi and the Oracle. The effect of putting the land out of cultivation was to make the priests dependent henceforward on the goodwill of the faithful: Aesop is said to have visited Delphi (early sixth century, Hdt. ii. 134) and commented on this: 'having no land that you can work for your living, you live on Apollo's offerings'.[3] And this no doubt was the real purpose of the war: the religious centre of Greece must not have temporal power.

This state of affairs is described in the last lines of the Hymn (524–44). The Kretans complain that the land will not support them: Apollo answers '*You* don't want land! the offerings of my worshippers will more than support you. Receive them kindly, but if you give offence—' then comes the threat (542–4):

> ἄλλοι ἔπειθ' ὑμῖν σημάντορες ἄνδρες ἔσονται
> τῶν ὑπ' ἀναγκαίῃ δεδμήσεσθ' ἤματα πάντα.
> εἴρηταί τοι πάντα, σὺ δὲ φρεσὶ σῇσι φύλαξαι.

Despite the scruples of Allen-Sikes (note on 542) and Jacoby (p. 749, n. 1), there can be little question that in these twenty or so lines the 'devotion' or desolation of the Sacred Land is explained and accounted for. The desolation is in its first ugliness (οὔτ' εὐλείμων 529: by 498 B.C. Pindar can call it βαθυλείμων). In the rest of the *Dolphin* poem the desolation is unknown: Krisa is green with vines (438), the country is ἐπήρατος (521). This word, standing in the original poem's closing sentence, is very peevishly echoed eight lines later (529): οὔτε τρυγηφόρος ἥδε γ' ἐπήρατος οὔτ'

---

[1] *Syll*³. 636 (178 B.C.), 826 G (117 B.C.). Note that Isokrates xiv. 31 says μηλόβοτον.

[2] The Race-course in the Plain, Paus. x. 37. 4. This is what the *Plain of Krisa* suggested to a fifth-century Greek: e.g. Soph. *El*. 730, Bacchyl. xi. 20, and Pindar, *passim*. The stewards of the Games (corresponding to the Hellanodikai at Olympia) were perhaps called *Pediarchoi*: at least this may be the meaning of an inscription, of the fifth century or earlier, on a miniature bronze chariot-wheel in the Boston Museum, not yet published, which Professor Caskey kindly allows me to quote, Φαλασ πεδιαρχειον ανεθεκε τοπολονι. The wheel is believed to come from near Delphi and the alphabet is Delphic. * [See now *A.J.A.* xl. (1936) p. 310.]

[3] Sch. Ar., *Wasps* 1446; *Peace* 129: ἀποσκῶψαι αὐτοὺς ὅτι μὴ ἔχοιεν γῆν ἀφ' ἧς ἐργαζόμενοι διατρέφοιντο, ἀλλὰ περιμένοιεν ἀπὸ τῶν τοῦ θεοῦ θυμάτων διαζῆν. See some very good remarks in Jacoby, 749, n. 1, on Apollo's priests, the only professional Greek priesthood.

εὐλείμων, 'this is *not* a lovely land; not lovely enough for vines or pasture'.[1]

The epilogue says in effect: 'This is not a rich land, but Apollo's priests do not need rich land, so long as they treat the faithful well. If they do not' (we remember the charges brought against the Krisans, Strabo, ix. 3. 4) 'then of course things will be different.' It is arguable that this is in formal contradiction to the earlier promises: it is certain that no such limiting conditions were in the mind of the poet who wrote 484–5:

> βουλάς τ' ἀθανάτων εἰδήσετε, τῶν ἰότητι
> αἰεὶ τιμήσεσθε διαμπερὲς ἤματα πάντα.

The honours of the Kretan priests are there guaranteed for ever and put beyond the reach of man. Possibly this theme was still more stressed in the poem's original form. Hermann wished to read τετιμένοι in 479, Pierson ἔμελλον in 521 and τετιμένοι in 522. Neither of these corrections should, I believe, be admitted into our texts (which give us S, the poem of 504 B.C.); but both of them, and also τίμιοι for τίμιον in 483, may have stood in the unrevised *Dolphin* poem. I suggest, then, that the *Dolphin* was written before the Sacred War; that it was revised soon after that war (before the Plain had become good pasture); and that it was finally incorporated in S about 504 B.C. Though some of the revision is obvious, and more may be guessed, yet it is vain to hope to recover the *Urform* of a revised poem. But for concreteness I here summarize the *Dolphin* as I conceive it to have stood, using the suggestions of Hermann and Pierson in vv. 479, 521, 522.

Apollo, desiring priests for his new temple, sees a Kretan ship bound for Pylos[2] approaching Peloponnese. In the form of a Dolphin he leaps aboard and miraculously takes control. The ship will not answer her helm, and they are blown by strong

---

[1] I do not know if this odd contradiction between ll. 521 and 529 has been much noticed. Yet is it not proof enough that 529 is part of an afterthought? After all, *whom* is the Kretan contradicting? Not Apollo (521 is not his) but simply the existing poem!

[2] ll. 388–96 can hardly be as they were originally written. Hermann prints a tolerable but hardly likely rearrangement. Mr. W. F. J. Knight suggests to me that 393–6, 'the Kretans who serve Apollo's Oracle at Pytho', may have had their appropriate place in the *propositio* of the original poem. Ἄνακτι without qualification is used of Poseidon in 237 and could be of Apollo here (*pace* Jacoby, 746, n. 1).

winds up the west coast of Peloponnese, till they have opened the
Gulf of Korinth.[1] Then the wind changed:

430　　　　And when Peloponnese was passèd all
　　　　　And now the Gulf of Krisa endless stretched
　　　　　That bounds Peloponnese upon the north,
　　　　　God sent a mighty western wind, high up,
　　　　　That fell in fury from the sky: before it
435　　　　Scudding, the ship made haste upon her voyage.
　　　　　Back then, towards the sunrise and the sun,
　　　　　They sailing (and God's son Apollo led them)
　　　　　Came to far-shining Krisa, green with vines,
　　　　　To harbour: and the ship grounded in sand.
440　　　　　Then leapt ashore Apollo, far-felt king,
　　　　　Shining at noonday like a star; and from him
　　　　　The sparks of fire flew up and lit the sky.
　　　　　He passed through his rich Tripods to the Shrine
　　　　　And kindled fire there, that his arrows shone:
445　　　　Ay, that great light fill'd Krisa, and the wives
　　　　　And fair daughters of Krisa cried aloud
　　　　　Beneath that glare: and fear took every heart.

Apollo has leapt ashore at Itea (or thereabouts) and passed
miraculously up to Delphi, whence his light floods the Plain of
Krisa below. He now, quick as a thought, νόημ' ὥς, comes
down again to Itea and appears to the Kretan sailors in the likeness of a grown but beardless man. They are too terrified to
move; and when he asks why, the master of the ship answers
that they have been taken from their course by a miracle. Then
Apollo declares himself:

475　　　　Strangers who once in wooded Knossos had
　　　　　Your home, but nevermore shall now return
　　　　　Back thither each man to his pleasant house
　　　　　And lov'd wife: rather here shall keep my rich
　　　　　Temple, and many men shall honour [ye]:
480　　　　Lo! I am God's son, I am that Apollo.
　　　　　I brought you here over the yawning waters
　　　　　Nor meant you harm: here you shall keep my rich
　　　　　Temple, and all men shall much honour [ye].

　　[1] Called by our poet, as by Thucydides, the Gulf of Krisa. In view of Thucydides'
practice I do not understand the scruples of Allen-Sikes, ad loc. Jacoby's ἐπεί in 431
seems to me prosaic: cannot ἐπί be an adverb here?

And ye shall know the minds of Gods, and they
485   Shall have you honour'd, ever and for aye.

Here, as I believe, the promise of future honours is made three
times and each time heightened: 479 you shall be honoured by
many men, 483 you shall be much honoured by all men, 485 you
shall be honoured for ever continually throughout the length of
days. The last and most emphatic promise does not rest on an
alteration of text: it is evident that when 485 was written the
descendants of the Kretan priests still had honourable enjoyment
of their office.

Apollo then bids the Kretans dismantle their ship and bring
their goods ashore. They are next to build the altar called
Delphinios close by the shore, in memory of the Dolphin; make an
offering on it and then make their supper beside the ship: after
that he will lead them in procession to the Temple. They do this,
and the poem, as I conceive it first written, ends with the description of this procession:

They went, and first went God's son, Lord Apollo.
515   His harp was in his hand, and sweet he harp'd,
And high and fine he strode. In step behind
The Kretans singing 'Paian' marched to Pytho
(As Kretans aye sing 'Paian', in whose breast
The heavenly Muse hath planted melody).
520   Lightly they climb'd the hill, and lo! before them
Parnassos, and that lovely land, where [they]
522   Must dwell, and many men shall honour [them].
545   And so farewell Thou, God's and Leto's son;
I sing Thee, and another song besides.

Such a poem, relating the miracle of the Dolphin and the establishment of the altar called Delphinios and of the Kretans as
priests in Delphi, and containing four times repeated the God's
promise to those priests, that to compensate for their lost homes
they shall have great honour as priests for ever: such a poem does
not stand in our manuscripts, and I do not present it as more than
a hypothesis. There stands in our manuscripts another and as I
believe a later poem, written when those priests had lost their
honours: the later poet eliminates the promise as far as possible
and concludes with a clear statement that any honours promised
are contingent on good behaviour. Into this later poem the

corrections in ll. 479, 483, 521–2 should not be admitted. They are contrary to the intention of the later poet.

This revision of the *Dolphin* may have happened any time after the Sacred War. I think probably fairly soon after that war.[1]

IV. *The Scenes in Olympos*

What is left to Kynaithos, the poet of 504 B.C.? The Dragon episode, which I fancy he introduced into the *Foundation* poem, is hardly his own writing. It is itself a compilation: ll. 305–55 (Typhaon's birth) can be removed and are intrusive. It is noteworthy perhaps that this story (Typhaon's birth) is Stesichorean:[2] did the poet find it in Syracuse and foist it into the existing Dragon story, and then incorporate the whole in his long Hymn? These are obviously unanswerable questions: I am confident only that Typhaon's birth and the Dragon tale are too ill-knit for either episode to be the rhapsode's own *ad hoc* writing.[3] Who wrote 524–44 (the threat to the priests)? Again the question is hardly answerable: not, I think, Kynaithos in 504.[4] After 590 B.C. the *Dolphin* poem was unusable till those lines were added, and I do not believe it remained nearly a century unused.

From line 214 to the end, then, there is probably little of Kynaithos' own writing. These lines (much more than half the poem) are what Pindar calls ῥαπτὰ ἔπεα, pieces stitched together: he may have stitched elaborately, and lines here and there

---

[1] See n. 4 below.

[2] *Et. Mag.* s.v. Τυφωεύς. In the *Theogony* 927 it is Hephaistos who is conceived without father. [Yet see p. 30, n. 3. Stesichoros travelled in the east and some at least of his poetry was familiar there.]

[3] *Ergo* he (or some predecessor) found the two separate and put them together. [I exclude the hypothesis of any large-scale additions after 504 B.C.] By 'ill-knit' I do not mean simply that Typhaon causes a long digression. That in itself is good rhapsodic art, e.g. the Ἀλκίνου ἀπόλογος and Nestor's tales: cf. later, Catullus' *Peleus and Thetis*, Virgil's *Pastor Aristaeus*. I mean rather that if the *Dragon* tale and *Typhaon's* birth had been written together, or the *Dragon* written to enclose *Typhaon*, or *Typhaon* for insertion in the *Dragon*, we should hardly expect the variation in form, Τυφάονα 306, 352, Τυφωεύς 367 (cf., however, *Theogony*, 306, 821, 869, and Aesch. *Prom.* 356, 372): and, especially, the coupling of Chimaira and Typhoeus in 367–8 would be insensitive, if the poet who wrote had dwelt at length on Typhaon and not mentioned Chimaira. That a rhapsode may *use* lines which he could not *write*, see p. 29, n. 1.

[4] In 529 the priests complain that the land is not εὐλείμων. Yet Pindar calls the Race-course βαθυλείμων (*Pyth.* x. 15) and Strabo says the Plain was εὔδαιμον. I imagine that, fairly soon after it went out of cultivation, it became a good pasture (see p. 24, n. 1). Pindar's βαθυλείμων was written in 498 B.C.: οὔτ᾽ εὐλείμων can scarcely have been written as late as 504 B.C.

may be his own. And of course the shaping, the architectural composition, is his: out of his miscellaneous stock he made of P what it is, a tolerable and not too unharmonious pendant to D. To compose well, in this sense, is work for a great poet, or at least for a great architect of poetry, a great rhapsode. But Kynaithos was hardly a great rhapsode:[1] when we compare S, his Syncretistic poem, with D, the Delian hymn from which he starts, we need not dispute antiquity's judgement, that 'he maltreated Homer's poetry'.[2]

There remain ll. 179–213. Their architectural (rhapsodic) function is manifest, and to my judgement well performed; but their especial interest for this enquiry is that they form what is probably the largest block which we possess of Kynaithos' own writing. Lines 178–81 and 207–13 are mortar: 182–206 (the second scene on Olympos) is a new block. It belongs (if we must still make that dichotomy) to P and not to D, but in style it is utterly different from the rest of P, and strikingly like 7–9, 14–18, which (we have seen)[3] are Kynaithos' own verses in the first Olympos scene.

If I am right, and we have in this second Olympos scene (182–206) a piece of Ionian hexameter verse by a contemporary of Simonides, it is of some considerable interest: we have not too much early hexameter writing which we can really date. It is not the greatest poetry: the theme is conventional, and conven-

---

[1] Kynaithos' rhapsodic art gives to P those three elements which (as often noticed) correspond to elements in D: (1) the second Olympos scene, (2) the choice of the sacred site, (3) its barrenness, perhaps add (4) Hera's jealousy. Of these, only (1) is his own: for (2), (3), and (4) he uses existing material. The instinct to use the given (which dictated choice of subject to the Tragedians: which made Virgil change the context, place, and persons of, but practically never invent, an episode: which determined the Doric entablature) is not laziness but a form of αἰδώς, a respect for the given as such. Because of this validity which the given possesses, a rhapsode can properly use material which he could not have written. And how compatible the use of the given is with the greatest art, and something of the way a great rhapsode might work, can be seen in Shakespeare's use of North's Plutarch in *Coriolanus* and *Antony*. (The passages are noted in R. H. Carr's *Four Lives from North's Plutarch*, Oxford, 1906, and Tucker Brooke's *Shakespeare's Plutarch*, vol. ii, London, 1909: cf. the latter's comments pp. x–xi.) In these later plays he keeps much closer than in the *Julius Caesar*.

[2] See p. 31, n. 3.

[3] Above, pp. 20–21: Jacoby, p. 723 sq. Since these lines are Kynaithos' work, written for Syracusan performance in 504 B.C., I imagine there is now no doubt that Ortygia in 16 is the Syracusan Ortygia: cf. Pindar, *Nem.* i. 2–4, *Pyth.* ii. 6–7. Pindar's phrase 'Ορτυγία Δάλου κασιγνήτα makes this nearly certain. Pindar indeed elsewhere says Delos was once called Ortygia (*Paean* vii b. 12), but that does not help our line 16: he also (alone of early poets) once calls the two gods *twins*, *Paean* xii. 14.

tionally treated (contrast the first triad of *Pythian* i, or even *Nemean* v. 23–5). But it is good: if the most charming *choses vues*

196 ὀρχεῦντ᾽ ἀλλήλων ἐπὶ καρπῷ χεῖρας ἔχουσαι
203 μαρμαρυγαί τε ποδῶν καὶ ἐυκλώστοιο χιτῶνος

have been mentioned before (*Iliad* xviii. 594, 595–6, *Od.* viii. 265), yet they are seen, I think, with new eyes.[1] And in 189–93 the convention is of Homeric quality. Above all, ll. 182–206 are Ionian poetry: nothing else in P is that.

It has been observed that Hymns XXVII and XXVIII have much affinity with the Olympos scenes of the *Apollo*.[2] I hazard the suggestion that they are of the same date and *milieu*—Syracuse about 500 B.C.[3] They are addressed to Artemis and Athena: deities too widely worshipped for this to entitle us to any strong presumptions about the place of writing. But it is worth recalling Cicero's words in the *Verrines* (iv. 118) 'in ea (sc. Ortygia) sunt aedes sacrae complures, sed duae quae longe ceteris antecellant, Dianae una et altera, quae fuit ante istius adventum ornatissima, Minervae'. Of the Ortygian Artemis I need say no more (see p. 29, n. 3): her temple, which must have stood near the Arethusa spring, has not been found. Of the two great archaic temples whose remains are extant, that on the hill-top is commonly taken to be Athena's, built by a certain Agathokles before Gelon expelled the Gamoroi (Diod. viii. 11): the shield upon its roof was a land-

---

[1] *Iliad* xviii. 590 sqq. is the Dance in the Shield of Achilles. Line 594 (where the imperfect ὠρχεῦντ᾽ takes the elision more easily than the present ὀρχεῦντ᾽ in the Hymn) in itself and in its context recalls late geometric drawing: its transplantation from that stylized pattern to the more fluent composition of the Hymn is not unsuccessful: the same words serve different visions. The woven chiton is from the Shield (595–6), the μαρμαρυγαί from the description of the young men dancing to Demodokos (*Od.* viii. 256 sqq.); but the chitons in the Shield do not flicker, they are smooth like oil.—Apollo's 'high fine striding' (202) is taken, I conceive, from 516, where he gives the time not to the Gods in heaven but to the Kretans marching up from Krisa: the earlier poet meant something *andante*, without μαρμαρυγαί, more like (however far in date from) the *Harvester's Vase* from Hagia Triada in Krete.

[2] Gemoll held that xxvii and xxviii were by the same hand, and Allen and Sikes support this by noting that both alike are influenced by the Olympos scenes in the *Apollo*.

[3] The poet of xxviii follows Stesichoros in making Athena be born 'all armed'. But so do the Attic black figure artists from about 550 B.C.: Stesichoros was evidently known in the east. The contracted forms in xxvii and xxviii (xxvii. 4 ὄρη, 15 Μουσῶν, xxviii. 15 τεύχη) do not occur in the *Apollo*; but the uncontracted forms are capable of the same scansion (e.g. *Demeter* 425). The contracted form occurs in the *Hermes* (95 ὄρη): the *Hermes* story is depicted by the Brygos Painter on a cup in the Vatican of about 500 B.C., and I imagine the Hymn was then a *nouveauté*.

mark from the sea (Athen. xi. 6, p. 462 c). The other, at the island's north end, bears on its steps in huge archaic letters Κλεο[?μεν]εσ . εποιεσε τοπελονι. We must therefore add to Cicero's two chief Ortygian temples a third, Apollo's.[1]

V. The Date: Syracuse in the late Sixth Century

The date given, in the Pindaric scholium, for Kynaithos' visit to Syracuse is about 504 B.C. This is commonly rejected because of line 299. I have sought to show that Kynaithos did not use this line but substituted for it 297–8; and that this is perhaps some indication that he composed S after the fire of 548 B.C. So the scholiast's date becomes possible. However, such dates are often wrong; and in this case the assumption that it is wrong is part of the texture of received opinion. Can we find positive reasons for thinking it right?

I note, first, that Kynaithos is known exclusively from the scholiasts on this passage,[2] and the information they give, though it appears miscellaneous, is in fact coherent.[3] Kynaithos was a Homerid from Chios, and wrote the Syncretistic poem, based on a Homeric original, for the first Homeric performances in Syracuse about 504 B.C. Hippostratos is quoted for the visit to

---

[1] See O. Puchstein, 'Die Tempel auf Ortygia' in the Festschrift für H. Kiepert (1898), 199–206. A recent summary of the Athena temple excavations in Pauly-Wissowa, Syrakousai, coll. 1538 sqq.: the latest text which I know of the Apollo inscription is S. E. G. iv. 1. The Athena temple was magnificently rebuilt under Hieron, the Apollo temple retained its archaic form till it fell: this may explain Cicero's selection.

[2] The other passages (from grammarians and lexica) collected by Drachmann, ad loc., are either derivative or strictly parallel. In Athenaeus, i. 40 (p. 22 b), the words Ὅμηρος ἢ τῶν Ὁμηριδῶν τις ἐν τῷ εἰς Ἀπόλλωνα ὕμνῳ are probably an allusion to him, in this same connexion: the lines quoted (514–16) are from S. It is sometimes proposed to identify him with Kinaithon of Lakedaimon: wrongly, I think. But even if he be the same, the argument stands: the information about Kynaithos (sic: the later MSS. of the scholium have κιναιθος but never κιναιθων) is still about Syracuse and the Syncretistic poem and may be presumed to come from Hippostratos: in other aspects he is called Kinaithon.

[3] This is the Greek (Drachmann, Schol. Vet. iii. 29, 31). 1 c. Ὅθεν περ καὶ Ὁμηρίδαι: Ὁμηρίδας ἔλεγον τὸ μὲν ἀρχαῖον τοὺς ἀπὸ τοῦ Ὁμήρου γένους, οἳ καὶ τὴν ποίησιν αὐτοῦ ἐκ διαδοχῆς ᾖδον· μετὰ δὲ ταῦτα καὶ οἱ ῥαψῳδοὶ οὐκέτι τὸ γένος εἰς Ὅμηρον ἀνάγοντες. ἐπιφανεῖς δὲ ἐγένοντο οἱ περὶ Κύναιθον, οὓς φασι πολλὰ τῶν ἐπῶν ποιήσαντας ἐμβαλεῖν εἰς τὴν Ὁμήρου ποίησιν. ἦν δὲ ὁ Κύναιθος τὸ γένος Χῖος, ὃς καὶ τῶν ἐπιγραφομένων Ὁμήρου ποιημάτων τὸν εἰς Ἀπόλλωνα γεγραφὼς ὕμνον ἀνατέθεικεν αὐτῷ. οὗτος οὖν ὁ Κύναιθος πρῶτος ἐν Συρακούσαις ἐραψῴδησε τὰ Ὁμήρου ἔπη κατὰ τὴν ξθ' Ὀλυμπιάδα, ὡς Ἱππόστρατός φησιν.—e. ἄλλως. Ὁμηρίδαι πρότερον μὲν οἱ Ὁμήρου παῖδες, ὕστερον δὲ οἱ περὶ Κύναιθον ῥαβδῳδοί· οὗτοι γὰρ τὴν Ὁμήρου ποίησιν σκεδασθεῖσαν ἐμνημόνευον καὶ ἀπήγγελλον. ἐλυμήναντο δὲ αὐτῇ πάνυ.

Syracuse: he was a recent writer when the *scholia vetera* were taking shape: he was a Sicilian antiquary.[1] We have here no ransacking of libraries, but what Hippostratos had said about the performance of S at Syracuse. At least, this is my impression, that we are not entitled to separate the Hymn from the Syracuse visit; but of course to do so will not make much difference to its date.

If the arrival of the Homeridai was part of the general Ionian impact upon the west, the last decade of the sixth century is a good date. The Persian conquest of Ionia had driven a few Ionians westwards (the Alalia venture, Xenophanes); but the real impact of Ionian taste on Sicily begins in the reign of Dareios. Partly, no doubt, there was some little lag, after the first refugees, before Ionian taste was in demand: partly, the situation in Ionia grew harder. Kambyses' conquest of Egypt, and his resurrection of the Tyrian navy, followed by Dareios' Skythian campaign,[2] very gravely limited Greek exploitation of the east: such things, aggravated by Persian suspicion of Greek enterprise (e.g. Hdt. v. 23), led in due course to the great Revolt. But before the Revolt, many Greeks had preferred to leave the east for the west;[3] and the collapse of Polykrates and then of Hippias had sent many poets and artists on their travels.

But to gauge and date this eastern impact most exactly our evidence will come, eventually, from the material remains, from archaeology. Professor Ashmole, whose *Late Archaic and Early Classical Greek Sculpture in Sicily and South Italy* is still unpublished when I write, lets me quote the following from a letter: 'My impression, from the terracottas and the coins, is that a great impulse comes into art in Sicily and South Italy at the end of the sixth and in the first quarter and probably first half (the dating is difficult, and I fancy there is a big time-lag in some places) of the fifth century. Since it comes at that time, naturally I suspect Ionian immigration as one of the causes, but have not been able

[1] Pauly-Wissowa, *Hippostratos* (7).
[2] Its most concrete result was the conquest of the north Aegean coast. It is hard to say how far it achieved its further aim, which was perhaps the control of the western Black Sea ports: see Momigliano's interesting paper 'Dalla spedizione scitica di Filippo alla spedizione scitica di Dario' in *Athenaeum* xxi (N.S. xi), 1935, pp. 350 sqq.
[3] e.g. Skythes, Hdt. vi. 24. 2: his son Kadmos followed him later, vii. 164. 1 (δεινοῦ ἐπιόντος οὐδενός: does this mean 'before the Revolt' or simply that Kadmos had not involved himself in it?).

to prove it.' Whether this great impulse proves to be specifically (or exclusively) Ionian is not perhaps vital.[1] At the end of the sixth century the West under some influence starts to pull itself more nearly level with the culture of the East—Ionia, the Aegean, peninsular Greece. I suggest Kynaithos may be part of that impulse.

Such is my thesis. Kynaithos performed the Hymn in Syracuse about 504 B.C., consisting of ll. 1–5, 7–9, 14–72, 79–95, 97, 96, 99–127, 129–38, 179–298, 300–546. It was a composite work, ll. 179–213 are the only considerable passage in it which he wrote himself. Let me, for a little, assume this thesis true. Delphi was at her height of glory: the most part of the buildings that dazzled Pindar (*Pyth.* vi. 8–9, vii. 8–9) rose in a time of intensive building which followed the fire and preceded the medism of 480 B.C.: the Temple itself was completed *c.* 505 B.C.[2] A good moment for an Ionian rhapsode, a countryman (a kinsman?) of the blind Chiot who wrote the Delian Hymn, to compose a Syncretistic poem for a western audience. I hardly imagine this Syncretistic poem was much known in the east, where the syncretized elements survived separately: we hear about it and its composer from a Sicilian antiquary of Hellenistic times. Kallimachos probably knew both D and S: our manuscripts appear to give us S revised after comparison with its original elements. Thucydides and Aristophanes, on the other hand, knew D, not S, and knew it as Homer's work. Thucydides quotes (as by Homer) that part of D which is not included in S. Aristophanes refers to l. 114 as by Homer:[3] there is no sign of his knowing S.[4]

---

[1] Mr. T. J. Dunbabin has called my attention to certain pieces: especially to the relief in soft stone of volute and palmette (illustrated in *Mon. Ant.* xxv, pl. 23) which Orsi thinks belongs to the short end of the great altar of the late archaic Athena temple. Its date is towards the end of the sixth century; its Ionian style is conspicuous against the Korinthian of the terra-cotta revetments of the same temple, and appears to be new and intrusive. The statues, Langlotz, *Bildhauerschulen*, No. 67, and Orsi, *Mon. Ant.* xxv, pl. 15, are most likely imported, but are yet some argument for taste: Professor Ashmole thinks the former is Aeginetan. The coinage of Syracuse becomes abundant and magnificent about the end of the sixth century.

[2] Courby, *Fouilles de Delphes* ii. 2. 110: cf. Homolle, *B. C. H.* xxvi. 621.

[3] *Birds* 575 (see the scholium).

[4] It is said sometimes that *Knights*, 1016 ἴαχεν ἐξ ἀδύτοιο διὰ τριπόδων ἐριτίμων is a parody of l. 443. It may be, he may have known the *Dolphin* poem if it had separate existence; but he does not of course suggest it is by Homer. But in fact the phrase διὰ τριπόδων ἐριτίμων must have been frequent in Delphic poetry, oracles, etc., though it happens that only l. 443 and Aristophanes' parody survive. In l. 443 it is (not

A possible parallel for this survival of archaic poetry in the west and not in the Attic sphere is Theognis ll. 255–756. That 1–254 (closed by the famous epilogue to Kyrnos: *exegi monumentum*) stand by themselves and are extremely familiar to pre-Alexandrian writers of the Attic sphere is well known. Fifteen lines[1] from seven different poems are quoted by Plato, Xenophon, Aristotle, Theophrastos, Chrysippos, all by name, from ll. 1–254. From the whole remainder, five lines from one poem are quoted by Plato (434–8). Because of this one quotation Jacoby in his brilliant paper *Theognis* (SB. Berlin, 1931) believes that all of ll. 1–756 circulated in classical Athens. I think this impossible for the following reason. We have for Theognis, unlike most early elegiac and lyric, a first-class book-text, the *Mutinensis*: it is evident that the copy, from which this ultimately derives, contained the *digamma* written at least in ll. 413–574.[2] I take it as certain that no Attic book contained *digamma*: the copy of these lines which reached the Alexandrian library must have come from another place. That it was from Sicily is suggested by the fact that Plato, who alone[3] quotes from this portion, had lived in Sicily and believed Theognis to be a Sicilian.[4] So far, I have spoken only of quotations where Theognis is named. Lines 255–6 are quoted (with variation) by Aristotle as the 'epigram from Delos':[5] he also refers (ap. Plut. *Consol. ad Apoll.* 27. 115 D) to the

---

grossly but rather) out of place, since the new-built and priestless temple will not have gathered offerings yet: understandable, if it were a conventional phrase for the approach to the Adyton.

[1] I do not count the eight lines quoted by 'Xenophon' ap. Stob. 88. 14. Axel Persson has made it likely that this is a scholiast on Xenophon: Xenophon may have quoted the poem (in the passage commented on) but not all eight lines.

[2] The cases are fairly well known (the readings of M are accessible in Hudson-Williams' excellent apparatus): M in 413 has οὐδέ μετ᾽ οἶνος (*sic*, οὐδέ oxytone, μετ᾽ unaccented: O has οὐδέ μεγ᾽ οἶνος), in 440 κἴδιον (*sic*), in 516 κατακεισ, in 548 and 574 εὐγεργεσίης, The copy apparently had οὐδέ με Ϝοινος, Ϝιδίων, κατάϜειφ᾽, εὐϜεργεσίης (*bis*). *Gamma* is elsewhere written for *digamma*, see Hesychius γοῖδα γοίδημι: in Homer (very rare) B 507, μ 44. [Allen, *Origins* 203, no. 3, Cauer, *Grundfragen*³, p. 84.]

[3] Plato's quotation (*Meno* 95 D) was of course familiar; e.g. Aristotle, *Eth. Nic.* x. 10, refers to l. 434. Klearchos (ap. Athen. 256 C) knows the context too; a singular case which needs examination. He does not name Theognis.

[4] *Laws* 630 A. It must be emphasized that l. 247 proves absolutely (as against Beloch and De Sanctis) that Theognis was a native of the Aegean. But he may have gone to Sicily, much as Kynaithos did. The poet of 783 indeed says he has been to Sicily, but one may question whether that poet is Theognis. There can be no question about 247.

[5] *Eth. Nic.* i. 9: in *Eth. Eud.* i. 1 he says it was inscribed on the Propylaion of Leto's temple.

substance of 425–8 (or rather the substance of the hexameters) as being Seilenos' answer to Midas' question on human happiness, and the two hexameters (without the pentameters) are ascribed to Homer in the *Certamen* (already in that early Ptolemaic papyrus[1] which no doubt gives Alkidamas' fourth-century version). Both poems, that is to say, are known to Aristotle as existing in a context other than the *Theognidea*, and in a slightly different form. Both poems are paraphrased by Sophokles; and in each case he keeps closer to the non-Theognidean form.[2] It is a fair inference that though Sophokles knew these poems he did not know them in their Theognidean context. Bacchylides, on the other hand, paraphrases the pentameter, line 426, closely (πάντων μὲν μὴ φῦναι ἐπιχθονίοισιν ἄριστον μηδ᾽ ἐσιδεῖν αὐγὰς ὀξέος ἠελίου ∾ θνατοῖσι μὴ φῦναι φέριστον μηδ᾽ ἀελίου προσιδεῖν φέγγος, Bacch. v. 160), and must have known the Theognidean version. Like Plato he had lived in Sicily.

As is well known, the rest of Theognis (757 sqq.) is not quoted as Theognis until the Christian era, and the Second Book[3] never at all.[4]

VI. *Homeridai*

What did the Homerid bring to Syracuse besides the *Hymn to Apollo*? The *Iliad* and *Odyssey*? The most serious attempt yet made to date the spread of these poems is Johansen's *Iliaden i tidlig græsk Kunst* (Copenhagen, 1934), which is in Danish and I cannot read it; but its pictures are intelligible and its argument is summarized by Beazley, *J. H. S.* liv (1934), p. 84 sq. The author believes the *Iliad* became familiar in Korinth under Periander, in Athens under Hipparchos. We have no comparable mass of

---

[1] The papyrus is given in Allen's Oxford Text of Homer, *Homeri Opera* v. 225.

[2] In the *Kreousa* fragment he paraphrases 255–6, and his third term is ἥδιστον, as in Aristotle's version: Theognis has τερπνότατον. The other passage is *O. C.* 1224 sq., most famous of all Theognidean echoes in literature. He shows no knowledge of the pentameters.

[3] Separate poems are indeed alluded to, but not as *Theognis*. I imagine Bk. II was known in Athens (not, I think, as Theognis, though Isokrates ii. 43 sq. is not decisive). Line 1365 (rather than 1117) is quoted on an Attic vase [so is 939, rather than 695]: Harrison has detected an allusion in Aristoph., *Wasps* 1343 to 1362; and I fancy 1288 sqq. may be the origin of the rather surprising lines on Melanion in Aristoph. *Lys.* 785 sqq. And the beautiful *Prologue* 1231–4, to judge by its instances, was very likely written in Athens in the *Stoa Poikile*.

[4] Into ll. 467, 469, parodied by an Attic comedian, and other gaps in the above statement, I hope to go elsewhere.

material to let us know what poems were best known to Syracusan craftsmen: the little Sicilian sculpture we have from the last half of the sixth century shows more knowledge of Stesichoros than of Homer. What did the arrival of Homeridai mean to a city? What was the Peisistratean (or Peisistratid) recension? I do not desire to beg these large questions. Yet the news that the Homeridai first reached Syracuse[1] about 504 B.C. does not surprise me. If it be established as a fact, it should be of some value to Homeric study.

[1] And the West generally? Theagenes of Rhegion κατὰ Καμβύσην γεγονώς is named by Tatianus *in Graecos* 31 amongst the earliest inquirers into the poetry and family and date of Homer. Born in Kambyses' reign, he may have begun his Homeric studies about 500 B.C.

THE SPARTAN RHETRA IN
PLUTARCH, *LYCURGUS VI*[1]

A. PLUTARCH'S TEXT

(*a*) *Plutarch's commentary: the corrections* τούτως, ἀνταγορίαν

THE Spartan *Rhetra* quoted by Plutarch in *Lyc.* vi. 2 consists of some thirty-seven words in an archaic Dorian or near-Dorian dialect: Plutarch says it was an oracle, and that later an extra clause was added by the kings Polydoros and Theopompos; he quotes this 'added clause' in vi. 8. I believe this *Rhetra* was not an oracle but an act of the Spartan Ekklesia;[2] and I suspect that the 'added clause' was not added, but is an integral part of the original act. But for our first objective this opinion matters less than Plutarch's opinion. Our first objective must be to recover Plutarch's text (for his manuscripts are certainly corrupted to some extent): and to do that, we must understand his interpretation.

In Plutarch's view, then, the *Rhetra* is an oracle. He quotes it to show the importance which Lykourgos attached to the Gerousia: '(vi. 1) he laid such stress on this office that he obtained a Delphic response about it (which they call a *Rhetra*): the response is as follows:

(vi. 2) Διὸς Συλλανίου καὶ Ἀθηνᾶς Συλλανίας ἱερὸν ἱδρυσάμενον (mss.-ος)

---

[1] In citing inscriptions, I have used the abbreviations 'Schwyz.', 'Tod', '*ATL*' respectively for Schwyzer, *Dialectorum graecarum exempla epigraphica potiora*, Tod, *A Selection of Greek Historical Inscriptions*, and Meritt, Wade-Gery, and McGregor, *The Athenian Tribute Lists*, vol. i. I am most grateful to Prof. Ed. Fraenkel for the help he has given me on some points of language and grammar.

[2] Busolt, *Staatskunde* i, p. 43 (esp. note 1) argues rightly (as I believe) that whereas 'Rhetra' means 'formulation', in Sparta a formulation only becomes a Rhetra through legislative act. He therefore concludes that our document is a 'fälschlich als Rhetra bezeichneter pythischer Spruch'. I draw the opposite conclusion: it is an act of the assembly, falsely called an oracle. Busolt, ibid. 44 note 2, quotes Wackernagel's confirmation of Wilamowitz's opinion, that the dialect cannot be recognized as specifically either Laconian or Delphic. I state here my view, to avoid ambiguity, but without prejudice: see the second part of this paper; meanwhile, cf. Latte in Pauly-Wissowa s.v. 'Orakel', pp. 842, 843.

φυλὰς φυλάξαντα καὶ ὠβὰς ὠβάξαντα τριάκοντα γερουσίαν σὺν ἀρχαγέταις καταστήσαντα ὥρας ἐξ ὥρας ἀπελλάζειν μεταξὺ Βαβύκας τε καὶ Κνακίωνος οὕτως εἰσφέρειν τε καὶ ἀφίστασθαι †γαμωδᾶν γορίαν ἤ μὴν† καὶ κράτος.'

As it stands, or with the usual emendations for the obviously corrupted words in the last clause (e.g. δάμῳ δὲ τὰν κυρίαν ἤμεν), this cannot be called 'an oracle about the Gerousia': further, it is not easy to find an appropriate subject which can be common to the three infinitives ἀπελλάζειν εἰσφέρειν ἀφίστασθαι. Both these difficulties are met by the corrections which have been proposed for οὕτως: Hermann's καὶ τώς, Sauppe's αὐτώς. These both use the Doric form of the accusative plural masculine of the second declension (-ως for -ους): they provide a new subject for εἰσφέρειν and ἀφίστασθαι and that new subject will be the Gerousia (the '30 men including the 2 kings' mentioned just above). I would propose to do the same by reading τούτως 'the afore-mentioned'. We shall see that Plutarch appears to assume that the subject both of εἰσφέρειν and of ἀφίστασθαι is the Gerousia, so that some such correction is obligatory.

Plutarch's commentary begins by glossing the hard words:

'(vi. 3) φυλὰς φυλάξαι καὶ ὠβὰς ὠβάξαι means *to divide the population into certain divisions* which he has called φυλαί and ὠβαί. The ἀρχαγέται are the *kings*. Ἀπελλάζειν means ἐκκλησιάζειν: the term is used because he ascribed the beginning and origin of the constitution to the Pythian God.'

I translate προσηγόρευκεν 'he has called' and ἀνῆψε 'he ascribed', though it is not quite clear who or what is the subject. Apollo? or rather Lykourgos, who is innocently conceived as having in fact drafted the form of words? I do not think this greatly matters either way (I shall assume it is Lykourgos, as of ᾤετο in vi. 5 and ἐφεῖτο in vi. 6): it is more important that Plutarch says nothing of ἀπέλλα being Spartan for ἐκκλησία: instead, he derives the word ἀπελλάζειν from Apollo.

Plutarch next (vi. 4) explains Βαβύκα and Κνακίων; citing Aristotle's opinion and thus making it clear that Aristotle had commented on this text.[1] He then proceeds:

---

[1] I am not sure that the lacuna indicated in our texts is essential. 'They now call Babyka-and-Knakion "Oinous", and Aristotle says Knakion is a river and Babyka a bridge.' I leave the localizing of these places to the second part: meanwhile, I suggest that this passage does not compel us to assume that Plutarch drew on a second Rhetra-commentary, besides Aristotle's.

'(vi. 4) They held the Ekklesia's meetings between these two points, without any porticoes or other special buildings: (vi. 5) for he did not think such things helped wise discussion but rather hindered it, etc. (vi. 6) And when the multitude was assembled, he allowed no one else to propose a motion,[1] but *the Gerontes and Kings put the motion forward* and the demos had the decisive vote. (vi. 7) Later, however, the multitude twisted the motions by *taking matter away from them and adding matter to them* (ἀφαιρέσει καὶ προσθέσει) and violently perverted them, and then the kings Polydoros and Theopompos made the following addition to the Rhetra:

(vi. 8) αἱ δὲ σκολιὰν ὁ δᾶμος ἕροιτο τοὺς πρεσβυγενέας καὶ ἀρχαγέτας ἀποστατῆρας εἶμεν.

That is to say, they should not validate [the motion so perverted] but should simply ἀφίστασθαι and dismiss the demos, *which was distorting the motion and changing it for the worse.*'

It is evident (from the first italicized phrase, in vi. 6) that Plutarch assumes the subject of εἰσφέρειν to be the Gerousia. The principle was the same as at Athens: no motion could be proposed from the floor of the house, only the presiding officers could bring a motion forward ('Ἀθ. πολ. xlv. 4: a revolutionary breach of this, ibid. xxix. 4, cf. Thuc. viii. 67. 2).[2] It is further evident (from the second and third italicized phrases, in vi. 7 and vi. 8) that Plutarch conceived the Rhetra as leaving to the Ekklesia wide powers of amendment. It was when these powers were abused (so he believed) that the 'extra clause' was added. This power of amendment does not appear in the Rhetra as the MSS. give it.

The 'extra clause' curtails the power of amendment, or so at least Plutarch thought. How? The Gerousia is to meet a case of excessive[3] amendment by the procedure ἀποστατῆρας εἶμεν: Plutarch takes this to mean much the same as ἀφίστασθαι in the original Rhetra, and he believes that this involves the dismissal of the meeting. The exact meaning of ἀφίστασθαι and ἀποστατήρ must be considered later: meanwhile, note that since

---

[1] Εἰπεῖν γνώμην is here used in its strict sense 'to propose a motion', as Thuc. viii. 68. 1, cf. iii. 49. 1 (where γνῶμαι means 'proposals' not 'opinions', *rogationes* not *sententiae*).

[2] The principle is stated for Sparta in Plut. *Agis* xi. 1.

[3] 'Excessive' is implied in σκολιάν.

Plutarch is evidently assuming that the sense of ἀφίστασθαι in the original Rhetra is the same as of ἀποστατῆρας εἶμεν in the 'extra clause', presumably he is assuming that the subject of the verb is the same in both places, namely the Gerousia.

I have kept the manuscripts' ἔροιτο in the phrase αἱ δὲ σκολιὰν ὁ δᾶμος ἔροιτο. Ehrenberg[1] has rightly protested against the emendations which displace this word (which is evidently cognate with ῥήτρα, so that ῥήτραν can be understood for σκολιάν to agree with)[2] and substitute some form of the quite irrelevant αἱρέομαι. Are we to suppose that the Gerousia act as *agents provocateurs* and offer 'crooked rhetrai' for the demos to *choose*? Of course not: the crookedness is not the result of the demos *choosing* wrong but of its *formulating* wrong. So at least Plutarch understood: ἀφαιρέσει καὶ προσθέσει τὰς γνώμας[3] διαστρεφόντων (vi. 7): ἐκτρέποντα καὶ μεταποιοῦντα τὴν γνώμην[3] παρὰ τὸ βέλτιστον (vi. 8). There can thus be no question but that Plutarch wrote ἔροιτο (or something like it) and not ἔλοιτο or αἱρέοιτο. *If the demos formulates crooked* (that is, amends so as to spoil the original intention), the Gerousia is to take some negativing action. This does not remove the demos' power of amendment altogether, still less does it remove the power of discussion: the contingency αἱ σκολιὰν ἔροιτο is impossible unless both powers remain. Both powers remain: if, on this or that occasion, this results in a case of undue amendment (as we say, an amendment contrary to the preamble), the counter action is prescribed.

How then was the original power formulated? The MSS. give γαμωδᾶν γορίαν ἤ μὴν [or γοριᾶν ἤ μην or γοριανίμην] καὶ κράτος. No doubt ἤ μὴν is for some form of the infinitive ἦμεν (ἤμην, εἶμεν), and γαμω is for δάμῳ (or perhaps the genitive δάμω): if δ' is the

---

[1] Ehrenberg, *Neugründer*, p. 20 and 125.

[2] Prof. Fraenkel advises me that we do not need to supply a cognate noun, nor any specific noun, to account for the feminine σκολιάν. Wilamowitz on Eur. *Herakles* line 681 explains the feminine article in τὰν Ἡρακλέους καλλίνικον ἀείδω by supplying ἀοιδάν from the verb: but after giving some parallels, he adds that many of his instances may be rather instances of the *verwendung des femininums für unbestimmten abstracta* which is common in Greek. See further, to the same effect, Lobeck, *Paralipomena* (1837), p. 363; J. Lohmann, *Genus und Sexus* (1932), p. 17 (I owe these references to Prof. Fraenkel). I feel little competence in this matter: but in our present case, where we have ἔροιτο for the verb, and ῥήτραν is so ready to be supplied, I find it hard to doubt that they are cognate. This means that ἔροιτο (or εἴροιτο?) has nothing to do with the classical ἔρομαι but is the middle voice of the Homeric Ϝείρω or εἴρω: see below, p. 50 and note 3 ibid.

[3] Γνώμας, γνώμην: sc. *rogationes*: see p. 39, n. 1 supra.

connecting particle, we are left with ἄν γορίαν. I would restore ἀν‹τα›γορίαν,[1] and write the whole clause thus:

δάμω δ᾽ ἀνταγορίαν ἦμεν καὶ κράτος.

The forms ἀντήγορος ἀντηγορέω ἀντηγορία do not occur (before late Byzantine times)[2] but the name Αντηγοριων (Αντεγοριον) is found in Euboia in the sixth or fifth century B.C.[3]

The obstacle to such a reading (it is also the obstacle to taking Plutarch's commentary in this chapter as meaning what it says— the obstacle which has been responsible for the emendations of ἔροιτο into ἕλοιτο, etc.) is Aristotle's statement in *Pol*. ii. 11, § 3 (1273ᵃ12) that the demos at Sparta did *not* possess these powers. I return to this later.[4]

(b) The Text

In the following text I do not seek to restore the original spelling of the inscription (if indeed it was inscribed) but rather the form in which Plutarch (and before him Aristotle?) transcribed it in their Ionic alphabet. Probably they normalized to some extent: for example, the infinitive of the verb *to be* is written both ημην and ημεν in a single short (Kretan) inscription of *c*. 600 B.C.,[5] and it appears in the Rhetra in the forms ἦ μὴν and εἶμεν: I have, however, written ἦμεν both times, since it is improbable that Aristotle or Plutarch would have cared to preserve any variation: moreover, in Laconian (or Delphic) as opposed to Kretan script all these forms would appear as εμεν. On the other hand, the corruption of τούτως to οὕτως [and probably of δάμω to γαμω] shows that they kept the Dorian spelling of ω for Attic ου: its disappearance in other words (Συλλανίου, etc.) is presumably due not to Plutarch but his copyists, who have

---

[1] Palaeographically, it would seem that the copyist's eye slipped from Τ to Γ. The corruption of δάμω to γαμω is harder to explain: but the necessity of restoring some form (or some derivative) of δᾶμος is absolute, since Plutarch certainly understood the demos to be spoken of in this clause.

[2] ᾽Αντηγορέω is cited in early editions of Liddell and Scott from Theodorus Studita. See below, p. 51, for a suggestion that ἀνταγόρησεν be restored for ἀνταγόρευσεν in Pind. *Pyth*. iv. 156: cf. the equally unique ἐπηγορέων in Hdt. i. 90. 2, preserved in Hesychios but corrupted in all our MSS. to ἐπηγορεύων. [᾽Ανταγορίαν is, I hear, suggested by Treu in *Hermes* lxxvi (1941).]

[3] *IG* xii, fasc. ix, 56, among the lead tablets (defixiones?) from Styra: Αντεγοριον is no. 19.

[4] See below, pp. 51 f.   [5] Republished by Ehrenberg in *C.Q.* xxxvii (1943) p. 14.

normalized wherever they could understand. I have therefore restored ω throughout: and equally α for η not only in 'Αθανᾶς but also in καταστάσαντα: also ἱαρόν for ἱερόν. The β in ὠβάς is certainly a *digamma*, but no doubt Plutarch wrote it as β and I therefore retain it: by the same principle, in Βαβύκας both or either may be for *digamma*[1], but I write β both times.

I put the 'extra clause' as part (§ III) of the Rhetra: it certainly became part of it eventually. I have divided the earlier part into two clauses (§ I, § II) for convenience of reference.

§ I Διὸς Συλλανίω καὶ 'Αθανᾶς Συλλανίας ἱαρὸν ἱδρυσάμενον (-ος MSS.), φυλὰς φυλάξαντα καὶ ὠβὰς ὠβάξαντα, τριάκοντα γερωσίαν σὺν ἀρχαγέταις καταστάσαντα, ὥρας ἐξ ὥρας ἀπελλάζειν μεταξὺ Βαβύκας τε καὶ Κνακίωνος.

§ II τούτως (οὕτως MSS.) εἰσφέρειν τε καὶ ἀφίστασθαι, δάμω δ' ἀνταγορίαν (γαμωδᾶν γορίαν vel sim. MSS.) ἤμεν καὶ κράτος.

§ III αἱ δὲ σκολιὰν ὁ δᾶμος ἔροιτο, τὼς πρεσβυγενέας καὶ ἀρχαγέτας ἀποστατῆρας ἤμεν.

After a series of aorist participles (which contain instructions for single acts, to be done once for all), the main purport of the Rhetra is *to define the process of legislation*,[2] and in particular to define the respective spheres therein of the probouleutic body (the Gerousia) and of the sovran body (the Ekklesia).

There are certain further questions of interpretation, before we can turn to more historical matters. These are:

(c) Who is the (unnamed) subject of ἀπελλάζειν, and of the aorist participles in the masc. sing. which agree with this subject?

---

[1] I am tempted to connect a form ΒαϜυκά with βαύζω, and to understand it as the Bridge of Shouting. Cf. Thuc. i. 87. 2, κρίνουσι βοῇ, Plut. *Lyc.* xxvi. 3–4: and Aesch. *Pers.* 574–5, δυσβάνκτον βοᾶτιν—αὐδάν. Βαύζω could be expected to give βαϋγή, as οἰμώζω, etc. give (or are given by) οἰμωγή, ὀλολυγή, ἰυγή. I know no such noun in -κή unless ὑλακή be such. For the digamma, cf. αϜυταν in Schwyz. 133 (2) line 3, αϜυτο ib. 760, αϜυταρ ib. app. I. 2, etc.: 'Dittographie zu υ', Meisterhans-Schwyzer, *Grammatik*[3], p. 4, n. 15.

[2] Sc. the *sciscendi ratio*; how the sovran body is to enact its *acta*. Ancient theory did not normally distinguish between *acta* which prescribed regular routine action (like most of Solon's laws) or action in one special situation (like Solon's amnesty or his seisachtheia): both alike were called νόμος or θεσμός (Solon ap. Plut. *Sol.* xix. 4: the locus classicus is Xen. *Mem.* i. 2. 41–3). In Sparta such *acta* were called ῥῆτραι: see the second part of this paper.

(*d*) What does ἀπελλάζειν mean?
(*e*) What do ἀφίστασθαι and ἀποστατήρ mean?
(*f*) How are we to parse ἔροιτο?

(*c*) *The subject of* ἀπελλάζειν

Plutarch glosses ἀπελλάζειν by ἐκκλησιάζειν: the latter word means usually 'to sit in the Ekklesia', as in the title of Aristophanes' play Ἐκκλησιάζουσαι: this is Aristotle's invariable use in the *Politics*, and since the gloss may well go back to Aristotle, this is relevant. But in Ἀθ. πολ. xv. 4 Aristotle says that Peisistratos ἐκκλησιάζειν ἐπεχείρει: the meaning is not quite certain,[1] but certainly Peisistratos is the subject, so that Lykourgos could be the subject of ἀπελλάζειν. If so, it would probably mean *contionem habere*, 'to convoke the Ekklesia'.[2]

There are, I think, only two serious possibilities: either *Lykourgos* is to erect the sanctuary, create or parade the phylai and obai, establish the Gerousia, and then (having done all these things once and for all) at regular intervals and at a set place to *convoke the assembly*: or else *the Spartan demos* is to erect, create, establish, etc., and then at regular intervals, etc., to *sit in assembly*. If, as I believe, the Rhetra is an act of the Spartan assembly, the second must be right: in such an act the unexpressed subject will always be the enacting body itself (as, e.g., invariably in Attic psephismata): any other subject must be expressed. But Plutarch (and Aristotle?) believed that the Rhetra was an oracle delivered to Lykourgos, who was the consultant: and in an oracle, the unexpressed subject is most naturally the consultant. But, e.g., in the prose oracle in Demosthenes xxi. 52 the unexpressed subject is the Athenian demos: and if the consultant is consulting on behalf of his city, he and his city are commonly identified in the answer (e.g. Hdt. vii. 140, 148, *et saepe*).[3]

---

[1] It presumably means the same as in Diod. xxi. 16. 4 (of Agathokles) ἐκκλησιάσας τὸν λαόν, cf. Aen. Tact. ix. 1, sc. *contionem habere*. In the lacuna which follows in Aristotle, Thalheim's supplement [χρόνον μὲν ἠκκλησί]ασεν μικρόν assumes that ἐκκλησιάζειν is used here for δημηγορεῖν: this is improbable, what we want in the supplement is a statement that Peisistratos lowered his voice (e.g. [τῆς φωνῆς ἐχάλ]ασεν μικρόν as Kontos proposed). 'He set about holding an assembly, and rather lowered his voice: when they said they could not hear, he bade them come up closer, to the Akropolis gate.' The passage is not noticed in Liddell and Scott s.v. ἐκκλησιάζω.
[2] See the passages cited in the previous note.
[3] The cases I quote are all a good deal later than the presumable date of the Rhetra

We may doubt, then, whether Plutarch thought of Lykourgos as the subject of ἀπελλάζειν: and the sense of ἐκκλησιάζειν which is required if Lykourgos is to be subject is so much the rarer of its two senses that its use in a gloss would be surprising. Still, it is possible (I do not see that this will much affect his interpretation of the whole)—possible, that is, that Plutarch thought so. I am convinced that if he did he was wrong.

(d) The meaning of ἀπελλάζειν

There is no good evidence for supposing that ἀπέλλα is Spartan for ἐκκλησία. There is indeed no evidence at all for the singular ἀπέλλα. The plural ἀπέλλαι is glossed by Hesychios as σηκοί, ἐκκλησίαι, ἀρχαιρεσίαι:[1] it occurs in two inscriptions of early Roman date from Gytheion in Laconia (εδοξε τωι δαμωι εν ταις μεγαλαις απελλαις, IG. v. 1, 1144[20-1], 1146[40-1]), and several times in the great inscription concerning the phratry[2] of the Labyadai at Delphi (Schwyz. 323). There we learn that απελλαι is one of the phratry's θοιναι [νομιμ]οι, like Boukatia, Heraia, etc. (D 2–3): it is a special day, and on that day and no other the Labyadai have to bring the offerings called απελλαια (A 30–6). It is a yearly festival, since anyone who fails to bring απελλαια is instructed to do so τωι hυστερωι ετει (A 50–1): the Labyadai meet and take decisions on that day. To the Labyadai, in fact (as Nilsson observes, Gr. Feste, pp. 464–5), the Apellai is much the same as the Apatouria to an Attic phratry.[3] It stands first in the list of festivals in D 2–11, just before Boukatia, and comparison with the known list of Delphic months makes it reasonably certain that it

[or of Lykourgos]: at the earlier date the consultant was no doubt more personal and would get a more personal answer. But I am not concerned with the possibility that it is an oracle, so much as with the question how Plutarch's belief that it was will lead him to understand it. Plutarch, who thought it an oracle, may yet have thought the Spartan demos was the subject of ἀπελλάζειν.

[1] Other relevant glosses (the bracketed letters in the lemmata are required by the alphabetic order): ἀπελ(λ)άζειν· ἐκκλησιάζειν· Λάκωνες, and more surprising, ἀππαλλά-ζειν: ἐκκλησιάζειν· Ἴωνες: another pair, ἀπέλλακας: ἱερῶν κοινωνούς and (ἀπ)άλλακες: ἱερῶν κοινωνοί: and ἀπέλλειν: ἀποκλείειν (see Buck, Gr. Dial. § 75).

[2] I use phratry in its Attic sense, for an association comprising more than one Genos. Cf. Pauly-Wissowa s.v. 'Labyadai', xii. 308, lines 8 ff.

[3] Nilsson generalizes this and sees in the Apellai the Dorian counterpart of the Ionian Apatouria, occurring wherever the month Apellaios (see next note) occurs. But are we justified in supposing that the Apellai is usually a phratry festival, just because it is so to the Labyadai? In Tenos the months 'Απελλαιών and 'Απατουρίων coexist (IG xii. v. 872). Cf. also p. 46, n. 1.

fell in the month 'Ἀπελλαῖος, the first month, Βουκάτιος being the second.

It looks as if ἀπελλάζειν means 'to hold Apellai' much as, e.g., θεσμοφοριάζειν means 'to hold Thesmophoria'. At least at Delphi, the word ἀπέλλαι is evidently connected with the offerings called ἀπελλαῖα and the month called 'Ἀπελλαῖος. This month recurs in several calendars, notably at Epidauros, Tenos (in the Ionic form 'Ἀπελλαίων), and probably at Sparta, where (as at Delphi) it seems to be the first month of the year.[1]

What, then, are we to understand by the phrase ὥρας ἐξ ὥρας ἀπελλάζειν 'season after season to hold apellai'? To the Labyadai, the phrase would presumably mean 'to hold Apellai each successive New Year'. Isyllos, in his famous inscription at Epidauros,[2] uses our phrase or something like it: he records a decree, proposed by himself, that Epidauros institute a procession to Apollo and Asklepios, which shall pray for their blessing on the Epidaurians

ωραις εξ ωραν νομον αει τονδε σεβοντας

'so long as they respect this law season after season'. This apparently means 'year by year'.[3] So, too, in Aristophanes' Thesmoph. 950–1, ἐκ τῶν ὡρῶν εἰς τὰς ὥρας means 'at the yearly Thesmophoria'. Possibly we should understand the same in the Rhetra: one yearly assembly is guaranteed. But ὥρα does not mean specifically a year; a recurring date if not annual will most likely be monthly.

---

[1] For Tenos, see the previous note: for Delphi and Epidauros, p. 46 n. 1. It is inferred for Sparta from its occurrence at Herakleia in Italy (Schwyz. 62, lines 2, 95), and further that Panamos (line 101) is there the last and Apellaios the first month of the year: cf. Bischoff in Pauly-Wissowa s.v. 'Kalender': further references, Kubits-chek, ibid. s.v. 'Apellaios'. If μηνος Απολλωνος in a Delphic inscription (Collitz-Bechtel 1931, line 1) is the same as Apellaios, this lends colour to the view that there is a real connexion between Apellai and Apollo: or is it merely a lapsus? We read in the Labyadai inscription (Schwyz. 323, D 44–5) ται δε θυσιαι Λαβυαδαν τωπελλαιου μηνος τωι Διονυσωι.

[2] IG iv,² fasc. 1, 128. Isyllos writes (line 25) ωραις εξ ωραν, and Wilamowitz (Isyllos, p. 11) wished to correct the Rhetra accordingly. The MSS. give two genitives in the singular, ὥρας ἐξ ὥρας [not ὡρᾶν, as Wilamowitz implies], and are surely right. The first ὥρας is the same sort of genitive (partitive?) as e.g. Plato, Phaedo 58 B ἑκάστου ἔτους θεωρίαν ἀπάξειν. [The 'partitive' view of this kind of genitive is given by Meillet-Vendryes, Traité de grammaire comparée (Paris, 1924), p. 509: a different view is taken by, e.g., F. Sommer, Vergleichende Syntax, 1921, p. 22 (who compares λοεσσάμενος ποταμοῖο) and Wackernagel, Vorlesungen über Syntax ii (1924), pp. 210, 212 ('im Genetiv wird der Bereich gegeben'). I owe these references to Prof. Fraenkel.]

[3] Isyllos' law is known only from his verse paraphrase, which gives no date: one naturally assumes the procession is to be annual (rather than monthly or four-yearly). Wilamowitz speaks of 'den alljährlich zu wiederholenden bittgang' (Isyllos, p. 10).

The scholiast on Thucydides i. 67. 3 understands ξύλλογον ... τὸν εἰωθότα as the regular monthly meeting of the Spartan ekklesia, which he says took place every full moon: τὸν εἰωθότα λέγει ξύλλογον ὅτι ἐν πανσελήνῳ ἐγίγνετο ἀεί. If he is right and the custom is ancient, then the phrase in the Rhetra should mean 'to meet *at the full moon of every month*': and so it is commonly understood. But how can this be got out of ἀπελλάζειν? The words ὥρας ἐξ ὥρας cannot, taken by themselves, mean 'every full moon': if that sense is to be understood here, it must be implicit in ἀπελλάζειν. [In Ar. *Thesm.* 950–1, ἐκ τῶν ὡρῶν εἰς τὰς ὥρας (ξυνεπευχόμενος) means in effect 'every 11–13 Pyanopsion', but only because ξυνεπευχόμενος is equivalent to θεσμοφοριάζων.]

With due reserve I would suggest that the 'great apellai' (the μεγαλαι απελλαι of the Gytheion inscriptions) are annual, the apellai of the month Apellaios, at the opening of the year: and that there were 'lesser apellai' in the other months.[1] If the Thucydides scholiast is right, the great and lesser apellai are at the full moon (sc. the 14th or 15th of the month). The meetings were surely monthly,[2] and it enhances the scholiast's credit that he knows this. But these scholia (*neque admodum vetusta nec praestantia insignia*, as Stuart Jones writes in the *Praefatio* of his text, p. iv) show little erudition, so that their testimony has not much weight: in better scholia this might well be derived from Aristotle's commentary on the Rhetra in his *Constitution of Sparta*; with these, we cannot feel much confidence. Plutarch connects ἀπελλάζειν with Apollo,[3] and we know that two monthly dates were marked

---

[1] In Epidauros the τελεια αγορα met on the 4th of Apellaios, for appointing the proxenoi and thearodokoi for the coming year (*IG* iv², fasc. 1, 96): in Delphi, the εννομος εκκλησια met on the 7th or 8th of Apellaios (*Fouilles*, iii. vi. 31, ii. 102, 103): these might correspond to the Great Apellai. Ekklesia on the 6th of every month, at Iasos: *BCH* viii. 219, *JHS* viii. 101, ix. 340 (Busolt, *Staatskunde*, 447, note 3). In Chios *c.* 600 B.C. the *Boule demosie* met every month τηι τριτηι εξ Εβδομαιων: Schwyz. 687=Tod, *SGHI* 1, B 3–4 [the Ebdomaia are thus a monthly event; in the Molpoi inscription from Miletos, Schwyz. 726, line 6, they recur in a very obscure context, but in some connexion with the *eighth* of the month]: we must, I believe, assume that the Demos has met just previously, on or near the Ebdomaia. *[See pp. 198 f. below.]

[2] Ὥρας ἐξ ὥρας must mean either monthly or yearly.

[3] Boisacq, *Dict. Etym.* s.v., while exceedingly doubtful about the etymology of ἀπέλλαι, suggests that 'Απέλλων (which he regards as the original form of 'Απόλλων: it is frequent in Laconian inscriptions) is derived from ἀπέλλαι. [Cf. now *Glotta*, xxvii, p. 32, and *Arch. f. Relig.* xxxii, pp. 142 ff. I owe these references to Dr. Weinstock.] Bechtel, *Hist. Personenname*, p. 61, gives a number of theophoric names in 'Απελλ-, e.g. 'Απελλᾶς, 'Απελλίκων (from 'Απελλικέτης; to this 'Απολλωνικέτης is a good parallel): 'Απελλαῖος (the Elean victor at Olympia in 540 B.C.) he regards as named from ἀπέλλαι not 'Απέλλων (p. 523). Cf. the Spartan Πελλῆς in Xen. *Hell.* iv. 3. 23.

by sacrifices to Apollo: Herodotus says that on the first and seventh *of every month* the Spartan kings offered sacrifice to Apollo at the public cost.[1] Whether the day of apellai was the New Moon or Full Moon or the Seventh, I see little hope of deciding. But in any case, I submit that 'to apellaze season after season' means the same sort of thing as 'to thesmophoriaze season after season', viz. to assemble for the [religious?][2] occasion called *apellai*; and that the exact date was implicit in the name.

(e) ἀφίστασθαι, ἀποστατήρ

I have said that Plutarch glosses ἀποστατῆρας ἦμεν by ἀφίστασθαι, and thus shows that he takes it to mean much the same as ἀφίστασθαι in the phrase εἰσφέρειν τε καὶ ἀφίστασθαι. His actual words are

ἀποστατῆρας ἦμεν· τοῦτ᾽ ἔστι μὴ κυροῦν ἀλλ᾽ ὅλως ἀφίστασθαι καὶ διαλύειν τὸν δῆμον.

---

[1] vi. 57. 2 νεομηνίας δὲ πάσας καὶ ἑβδόμας ἱσταμένου τοῦ μηνὸς δίδοσθαι ἐκ τοῦ δημοσίου ἱρήιον -τέλειον ἑκατέρῳ (sc. τῶν βασιλέων) ἐς ᾽Απόλλωνος. It is perhaps legitimate to infer *e silentio* that there was not a monthly sacrifice to Apollo at the full moon as well.

[2] The Greeks had no hard-and-fast division of days, as at Rome, into *fasti, nefasti, comitiales*, etc. The Boule at Athens is ordered to summon the Ekklesia 'two days after the return of the armed force' and thereafter to have as many consecutive sessions as are needed, and no calendar obstacles are envisaged: IG i². 63=Tod 66=*ATL* A 9, lines 34 ff.: cf. Aeschines ii. 60, iii. 67. In the last instance, Aeschines protests against the disregard of the Dionysia: in the first, it is likely that the meeting was, in fact, adjourned because of a holiday spirit which had nothing to do with the calendar (Plut. *Nic.* vii. 7=Theopompos, *F. gr. Hist.* 115 F 92: cf. pp. 233-4 below). Alkibiades came home on the Plynteria, a *dies nefastus*, ἀποφρὰς ἡμέρα: the narratives are not quite specific, but it looks as if the Boule and Ekklesia met the same day, though many thought it ominous: Xen. *Hell.* i. 4. 20, Diod. xiii. 69. 1, Plut. *Alcib.* 33. 2. Tribute is fixed at the Great Panathenaia, the allies being then conveniently assembled: IG i². 63=Tod 66=*ATL* A 9, lines 27 ff., IG i². 57=Tod 61=*ATL* D 3, lines 8, 31. There was no doubt a prejudice against public business on such occasions: worst on the ἡμέραι μιαραί or ἀποφράδες, Plynteria or Anthesteria (Xen. *Hell.* i. 4. 12, Photius s.v. μιαρὰ ἡμέρα and θύραζε Κᾶρες, Suid. s.v. ἀποφράδες ἡμέραι, Athen. 437 c) when the sublunary order stood in precarious balance: the prejudice on other festivals sprang perhaps from the dislike of work, since a festival was a 'holiday' in our sense, cf. the oracle in Dem. xxi. 53, ἐλινύειν μίαν ἡμέραν, and the sarcasms of ps.-Xenophon, ᾽Αθ. π. iii. 2 and 8. Yet almost all occasions, in an archaic state, are in some sense religious, and religious business was legitimate, e.g. on the Kronia (Dem. xxiv. 29): the Labyadai certainly took decisions at their Apellai. On the whole, I would conclude that the monthly apellai was a 'religious occasion' involving a θυσία (see previous note), but not a holiday. Cf. Nilsson, *Primitive Time-Reckoning*, ch. xiii. For the monthly Ebdomaia at Chios, see p. 46, n. 1. The connexions of Apollo with the *Seventh* are well known: Hesiod, *WD* 770, Proklos *ad loc.*, id. ad Plat. *Tim.* 200 CD, 233, Aesch. *Septem* 800, Kallim. *Hymn. Del.* 251-5, Plut. *Qu. Gr.* 9.

We might understand ἀφίστασθαι καὶ διαλύειν as a pair of synonyms, the former being used to show the connexion with ἀφίστασθαι above, the latter being the unambiguous modern synonym. I think it is possible that this is what Plutarch meant: ἀφίστασθαι is thus nearly (quite?) the same as ἀφίσταναι in the sense of 'to put an end to someone's function' 'to remove from office or function' (e.g. Xen. *Hell.* vii. 1. 45). The Gerousia is instructed, originally, to bring forward the agenda and (after that is finished) to declare the meeting ended: in the added clause, the Gerousia is to close the meeting if it gets out of hand.

Plutarch may have meant that. But Thucydides quotes a Spartan document containing a part of ἀφίστασθαι in a sense which I believe fits our case much more exactly. It is the covering note which the Spartans append to the draft of the Armistice terms in 423 B.C., Thuc. iv. 118. 9.

> 'The Spartans and allies approve the above terms: but if you have any better or fairer terms to suggest, come to Sparta and tell us: οὐδενὸς γὰρ ἀποστήσονται ὅσα ἂν δίκαια λέγητε οὔτε οἱ Λακεδαιμόνιοι οὔτε οἱ ξύμμαχοι.'

Here ἀφίστασθαι means 'to decline to entertain a proposal': the parallel is pretty close; in Plutarch's terms, the Spartans and allies have put forward their γνώμη, and now invite the Athenians to make changes (διαστρέφειν or μεταποιεῖν), and they promise they will not ἀφίστασθαι.

I cannot doubt that ἀποστατῆρας ἦμεν in § III has the same sense as ἀποστήσονται in Thuc. iv. 118. 9. What of § II εἰσφέρειν τε καὶ ἀφίστασθαι? Plutarch, who thinks § III an addition, supposes the practice of excessive amendment was not originally foreseen; he cannot therefore take ἀφίστασθαι in § II as meaning 'to reject *amendments*'. Nor can we, even if we think § III part of the original act; § III would be merely tautologous. Ἀφίστασθαι in § II should refer, not to action in the Ekklesia, but to the preliminary probouleutic process: the probouleutic body is 'to bring motions forward and *to decline to bring motions forward*'. This gives a proper sense to τε καί: the two terms so conjoined must have some specific relation, they may (e.g.) be alternatives: an extreme instance is *Iliad* viii. 167–8

διάνδιχα μερμήριξεν
ἵππους τε στρέψαι καὶ ἐναντίβιον μαχέσασθαι

cf. Aesch. *P.V.* 927 τό τ᾽ ἄρχειν καὶ τὸ δουλεύειν; *Sept.* 427–8 θεοῦ τε—θέλοντος—καὶ μὴ θέλοντος; Pind. *Ol.* ii. 16; Thuc. v. 111. 5 τυχοῦσάν τε καὶ μὴ κατορθώσασαν. The clause τούτως εἰσφέρειν τε καὶ ἀφίστασθαι expresses the same principle which we find in Plut. *Agis*, xi. 1 τοὺς γέροντας οἷς τὸ κράτος ἦν ἐν τῷ προβουλεύειν: Aristotle is (I believe) consciously paraphrasing it when he writes τοῦ μὲν γὰρ τὸ μὲν προσάγειν τὸ δὲ μὴ προσάγειν πρὸς τὸν δῆμον οἱ βασιλεῖς κύριοι μετὰ τῶν γερόντων (*Pol.* ii. 11, § 5, 1273ᵃ6–8: of Karthage—see below, p. 52).

Plutarch's gloss may then (perhaps) be understood thus: 'ἀποστατῆρας ἦμεν: that is, they shall not validate it but simply reject it'. Why, then, does he add καὶ διαλύειν τὸν δῆμον? Does he visualize ἀφίστασθαι as like the act of the judge when he rises from the bench, and the court is adjourned? A cumbrous method of rejection: even if we could believe it was used in the Ekklesia (§ III) it cannot have been in the probouleutic body (§ II). I cannot explain why Plutarch added these words, except by assuming that he understood ἀφίστασθαι as *equivalent* to διαλύειν (above, p. 48). He must be wrong: the word must surely mean the same in the Rhetra as it does in the Spartan[1] phrase in Thuc. iv. 118. 9; and there the genitive οὐδενός makes it plain that we have a specialized form of the more common usage ἀφίστασθαι πόνου, κινδύνου, etc. Kyros, seeing himself out-flanked both right and left οὐδέν τι μᾶλλον ἀφίστατο ἀλλ᾽ ὡσαύτως ἡγεῖτο (Xen. *Cyrop.* vii. 1. 6): all men love virtue ὅτι δὲ διὰ πόνων ἔστι τυχεῖν αὐτῆς οἱ πολλοὶ ἀφίστανται (Xen. *Cyneg.* xii. 18): Kyros *kept to his path*, most men *decline the path* of virtue. The metaphor of the path recurs, I think, in a passage of Pindar where we have something very close to the Spartan usage, *Ol.* i. 52

ἐμοὶ δ᾽ ἄπορα[2] γαστρίμαργον μακάρων τιν᾽ εἰπεῖν· ἀφίσταμαι·

'for me *no road*, to say that a God's belly was ravenous: I *decline that path*'. When a probouleutic council, or the presidents of an assembly, 'decline a path', we should say that they 'rule out of

---

[1] I can make nothing of ℎοπε νομος αποστατο at the end of an early Laconian inscription, *IG* v. 1, 1155 (=Schwyz. 51).

[2] This, and the contemporary *Ol.* x. 40, are the earliest appearances of the word ἄπορος.

order' a proposal or a trend of discussion. Pindar as poet sees himself doing the same.[1]

(f) ἔροιτο

Liddell and Scott quote for εἴρομαι, in the sense 'I say', two Homeric passages, *Iliad* i. 513 and *Od.* xi. 542. In both it seems to me that the sense 'I ask' is admissible: in the former, Thetis 'put her question a second time', in the latter the ghosts 'enquired each about the objects of his care'. I can therefore quote no instance of the *middle* voice of εἴρω (Ϝείρω) 'I say'. The first person singular of the active is certainly attested; always with hiatus preceding, sc. always Ϝείρω: *Od.* ii. 162, xi. 137, xiii. 7: but no other part of the present tense, and no part at all of the middle voice.

Ἔροιτο in our text has been so regularly emended that Liddell and Scott say nothing of it. Yet I believe it certain we have here some form from the root Ϝερ or Ϝρε, from which come (apart from εἴρω cited above) the tenses ἐρῶ, εἴρηκα, εἴρημαι, ἐρρήθην: the adjective ῥητός: the nouns ῥητήρ, ῥήτωρ, ῥῆμα, ῥῆσις, ῥῆτρα: the verb ῥητεύω:[2] the English *word*. The fact that ἔροιτο is unique should not surprise us: unique forms are not infrequent in pre-classical Greek.[3] I think it probable that ἔροιτο is what Plutarch (and Aristotle) wrote, transcribing Ϝεροιτο: whether they should have transcribed it rather as εἴροιτο, I do not know: this will not affect the meaning.

The middle voice perhaps deserves more explanation. I have no suggestion, unless possibly it indicated the fact that, while two parties were in question, the one party 'makes its own formulation' (instead of accepting a formula).

---

[1] For *Pyth.* iv. 145, see p. 51, n. 3. Comparable uses of ἀφίσταμαι in good Attic: Aesch. *Choeph.* 872, Eur. *Med.* 742, Isokr. viii. 81, iv. 83.

[2] In the Argive αϜρετευε, αρητευε (Schwyz. 85 line 14, 91 line 3, 92 line 2, 96 (1) line 4, 99 line 4, cf. 83 B line 25), the α- is usually explained as augment: if so, it presupposes the *nomen agentis* ῥήτας. This 'Speaker' is the eponymous president of the Argive Boule: he is perhaps the 'formulator', the man who formulates the motions before they are voted on. Alternatively the ἀ(Ϝ)ρήτας (contracted from ἀνα(Ϝ)ρήτας) might be the 'announcer' of the votes.

[3] I am most unwilling to correct to ἔροι or εἴροι (-το being a scribe's dittography before τούς) or to assume any corruption graver than ερ- for ειρ-. I hope I have made it plain that I am not claiming that the classical verb ἔρομαι (cognate with ἐρωτάω, ἔρευνα) could bear the sense 'I say': rather, that the totally different archaic verb Ϝείρω could be used in the middle voice.

(*g*) *Translation: and Aristotle* Pol. ii. 11, 1273 a 6–13

§ I. [The Spartan people] shall found a sanctuary of Zeus Syllanios and Athana Syllania, shall create [*or* parade?][1] the phylai and the obai, shall establish thirty men as a Gerousia including the kings: and [these things being done] shall season after season keep Apellai [i.e. assemble on a known day of each month] between Babyka and Knakion.

§ II. The afore-mentioned [Gerontes] shall bring proposals [to the demos] and shall decline to bring proposals: the demos shall have the right to criticize [sc. to make counter proposals?] and the final voice.

§ III. And if the demos formulates crooked, the Gerontes and kings shall decline to accept [that formulation].

I have translated ἀνταγορίαν 'the right to criticize'. In the passage of Aristotle which I believe to be practically a paraphrase of our document, the phrase is τῷ βουλομένῳ τοῖς εἰσφερομένοις ἀντειπεῖν ἔξεστιν. I think ἀντειπεῖν (like ἀνταγορίαν) is not merely 'criticize' but (virtually at least) 'make counter proposals': as Pelias does to Jason in Pindar, *Pyth.* iv. 156. [With due reserve, I suggest that in that passage ἀνταγόρευσεν could be corrected to ἀνταγόρησεν:[2] Jason proposed the motion (138 βάλλετο κρηπῖδα σοφῶν ἐπέων), Pelias makes his amendment:[3] ὡς ἄρ᾽ ἔειπεν· ἀκᾷ δ᾽ ἀνταγόρησεν καὶ Πελίας.]

The grave difficulty about the Aristotle passage is this: though it appears to paraphrase the Rhetra closely, it is written not of Sparta but of Karthage: and the ἀντειπεῖν provision especially

---

[1] Φυλάζω, ὠβάζω, formed (like ἀπελλάζω) from φυλά and ὠβά, do not necessarily imply the *creation* of the bodies in question. This clause, vital for the historical context, is discussed in the second part of this paper.

[2] Pindar would write *ΑΝΤΑΓΟΡΕΣΕΝ*, which might well provoke correction. Cf. Hdt. i. 90. 2, quoted in p. 41, n. 2.

[3] I would emphasize the constitutional idiom in this poem (cf. 110, 153, 265), which has a political aim, as seldom in Pindar: the Sparta-Kyrene connexion through Euphamos is pressed, as well as the further might-have-been connexion (43–51), echoed 254–62, just before the serious politics begin; cf. 22, 175: it recurs in the companion poem *Pyth.* v. 69–81). Here then the words ἔσομαι τοῖος· ἀλλά, etc., suggest a formula of amendment (τὰ μὲν ἄλλα, etc.). Note, finally, lines 145–6: if we accept (as both Wilamowitz, *Pindaros*, 388 note 3, and Schroeder, *Pind. Pyth. erklärt*, ad loc., are inclined to) Chairis' emendation ἀφίσταιντ᾽, we get a good sense from the technical word: Let the Moirai *rule it out of order*, if kinsmen should quarrel.

is stated *not* to hold in Sparta. Aristotle's words are (*Pol.* ii. 11, § 3, 1273ᵃ6):

(A) τοῦ μὲν γὰρ τὰ μὲν προσάγειν τὰ δὲ μὴ προσάγειν πρὸς τὸν δῆμον οἱ βασιλεῖς κύριοι μετὰ τῶν γερόντων
(B) ἂν ὁμογνωμονῶσι πάντες· εἰ δὲ μή, καὶ τούτων ὁ δῆμος·
(C) ἃ δ' ἂν εἰσφέρωσιν οὗτοι οὐ διακοῦσαι μόνον ἀποδιδόασι τῷ δήμῳ τὰ δόξαντα τοῖς ἄρχουσιν, ἀλλὰ κύριοι κρίνειν εἰσὶ καὶ τῷ βουλομένῳ τοῖς εἰσφερομένοις ἀντειπεῖν ἔξεστιν,
(D) ὅπερ ἐν ταῖς ἑτέραις πολιτείαις οὐκ ἔστιν.

D ante C transponendum esse suspicor, vel (*nominibus pronominibusque, necnon* μέν *et* δέ, *leviter immutatis*) C ante A.

The divisions, (A) (B) (C) (D), are added by myself for convenience of reference. In (D) the 'other constitutions' are Krete and Sparta, which have been described immediately before: Aristotle treats the three as a group (1272ᵇ26 αὗται γὰρ αἱ πολιτεῖαι τρεῖς ἀλλήλαις τε σύνεγγύς πώς εἰσι καὶ τῶν ἄλλων πολὺ διαφέρουσιν) and particularly remarks on the resemblance of the Karthaginian to the Spartan (1272ᵇ25 μάλιστα δ' ἔνια παραπλησίως τοῖς Λάκωσιν: 1272ᵇ33 ἔχει δὲ παραπλήσια τῇ Λακωνικῇ πολιτείᾳ τὰ μὲν συσσίτια ... τὴν δὲ τῶν ρδ' ἀρχήν ... τοὺς δὲ βασιλεῖς καὶ τὴν γερουσίαν—[the two latter with certain advantages over the analogous *Ephors* and *Kings and Council* at Sparta]. Such things as are open to criticism, he adds, are mostly common to all the three [sc. Karthage, Krete, Sparta]: of these things open to criticism, some tend rather towards democracy, others towards oligarchy (1273ᵃ5 τὰ μὲν εἰς δῆμον ἐκκλίνει μᾶλλον, τὰ δ' εἰς ὀλιγαρχίαν). Then follows our passage [(A) (B) (C) (D)], an example of a too democratic tendency: next comes a too oligarchic feature, the *pentarchiai*.

If my elucidation of the Rhetra is right, then (A) and (C) give an almost exact paraphrase, in a maturer idiom, of the archaic phrases of clause II

τούτως εἰσφέρειν τε καὶ ἀφίστασθαι, δάμῳ δ' ἀνταγορίαν ἦμεν καὶ κράτος.

Since he is expressly comparing Karthage with Sparta, this is no wonder: he might well choose to express Karthage in Spartan terms. He has indeed phrased the notion of ἀνταγορία καὶ κράτος in such a way (οὐ διακοῦσαι μόνον ἀποδιδόασι τῷ δήμῳ . . . ἀλλά, etc.) as to present it as one of the 'democratic lapses from aristocracy' in Karthage: but this by itself will not prove it to be peculiar to Karthage, since he has just said that most of the criticizable features at Karthage (and these are further defined as lapses towards either democracy or oligarchy) are common to all three states. A more serious difficulty is presented by (D). The Rhetra (if I have rightly restored it to the form which Aristotle knew) shows the features described in (C) as existing in Sparta. Nevertheless, in (D), Aristotle *expressly states that this feature* (more particularly ἀνταγορία) *is peculiar to Karthage.*[1]

Aristotle is not infallible, and I have long resigned myself to the belief that he made a mistake. [That the Spartan Ekklesia had ἀνταγορία, and that Aristotle knew it had it, I have tried to show above.] But there is an alternative solution which some may prefer, namely to change the order of (A) (B) (C) (D). For example, put (D) before (C): Aristotle will then say

(A) The Kings-plus-Council have power to bring some measures to the Ekklesia and to refuse others [sc. εἰσφέρειν τε καὶ ἀφίστασθαι]

(B) *if they are unanimous: (if they are not, this power too passes to the demos,*

(D) *a feature which we do not find in Krete or Sparta):*

(C) the measures which they do bring are not merely heard by the Ekklesia, but the latter has κράτος and ἀνταγορία .

The feature which now becomes peculiar to Karthage is very remarkable indeed, far more remarkable than ἀνταγορία: it is so far as I know unique. It certainly justifies Aristotle in choosing the Karthaginian legislative procedure, with this most distinctive feature, as that which (distinctively) 'lapsed from aristocracy towards democracy'.

There is still a certain awkwardness in καὶ τούτων (sc. κύριός ἐστιν) in (B). It stands for τοῦ τὰ μὲν προσάγειν, τὰ δὲ μὴ προσάγειν; the two infinitives perhaps explain τούτων (rather than τούτου): but why καί? No other power of the demos has been mentioned yet. This may suggest that in an earlier draft of the whole

---

[1] Ὅπερ is presumably ἀνταγορία rather than κράτος, sc. refers to καὶ τῷ βουλομένῳ . . . ἀντειπεῖν ἔξεστιν rather than to [that plus] κύριοι κρίνειν εἰσί.

passage, (B) stood after (C). No mere transposition will restore the earlier draft; I would suppose the order was changed deliberately, and the clauses recast. *Exempli gratia*

(C) ἃ μὲν γὰρ εἰσφέρουσιν[1] οἱ βασιλεῖς μετὰ τῶν γερόντων, οὐ διακοῦσαι μόνον, etc. . . . . ἔξεστιν.

(A) τοῦ δὲ τὰ μὲν προσάγειν, etc. . . . . πρὸς τὸν δῆμον κύριοι οὗτοι [*an retinendum* οἱ β. κ. μ. τ. γερόντων?*]

(B) ἂν ὁμογνωμονῶσι πάντες· εἰ δὲ μή, καὶ τούτων ὁ δῆμος

(D) ὅπερ ἐν ταῖς ἑτέραις πολιτείαις οὐκ ἔστιν.

If so, the clause which has got displaced is not (D) but (C): and the fault lies not with the copyists, but with Aristotle himself (or his amanuensis, however we may conceive the *Politics* written down). And if so, to seek to restore an order both original and final, may be as chimerical as the attempt to rearrange the order of the books. That need not prevent us recognizing that (D) is inapplicable to (C) but appropriate to (B).

B. THE *EYNOMIA* OF TYRTAIOS

(a) Plutarch's (Aristotle's?) Text

Plutarch concludes his chapter on the Rhetra (*Lyc.* 6) with six lines of Tyrtaios:

Φοίβου ἀκούσαντες Πυθωνόθεν οἴκαδ᾽ ἔνεικαν[2]
μαντείας τε θεοῦ καὶ τελέεντ᾽ ἔπεα·
ἄρχειν μὲν βουλῆς θεοτιμήτους βασιλῆας
οἶσι μέλει Σπάρτας ἱμερόεσσα πόλις
5   πρεσβύτας τε γέροντας, ἔπειτα δὲ δημότας ἄνδρας
εὐθείαις ῥήτραις ἀνταπαμειβομένους.

These lines are quoted to confirm Plutarch's statement, that the Kings who added the last clause to the Rhetra (what I have called Clause III, αἱ δὲ σκολιάν, etc.) 'persuaded the city [to accept this addition] on the grounds that it was part of the God's command'.[3] On Plutarch's view, the two Kings added an

---

[1] The indicative has better MS. authority than the subjunctive.
[2] MSS. have οἱ ταδε νικᾶν: see below, p. 57, n. 2.
[3] The Greek is quoted in the following paragraph.

extra clause to an oracle, and justified their action by alleging that Delphi had authorized the clause. It is not immediately obvious how Tyrtaios' lines confirm this view. The Delphic utterance whose substance is given in lines 3–6 approximately paraphrases parts of Clauses I and II (γερωσίαν σὺν ἀρχαγέταις . . . τούτως εἰσφέρειν . . . δάμω δ' ἀνταγορίαν ἦμεν), but where is Clause III? The burden has to be borne by the one word εὐθείαις: 'the Kings and gerontes shall initiate business, the demos shall reply with *undistorted* rhetrai' or 'shall respond to the rhetrai *without distorting them*' (according as we take the dative ῥήτραις as instrumental or as a true dative).[1] If εὐθείαις is given enough weight, the oracle which Tyrtaios quotes may be held to forbid the 'excessive amendment'[2] against which Clause III was (in Plutarch's view) aimed.

Plutarch says that the two Kings who inserted Clause III were Polydoros and Theopompos. Plutarch no doubt believed (as Aristotle certainly did) that Lykourgos lived in the reign of Charilaos, Theopompos' grandfather: and everyone knew that Tyrtaios was two generations (at least) later again.[3] With this sequence in his mind, what did Plutarch understand Tyrtaios to say? Ἔπεισαν δὲ καὶ αὐτοὶ τὴν πόλιν ὡς τοῦ θεοῦ ταῦτα προστάσσοντος, ὥς που Τυρταῖος ἐπιμέμνηται διὰ τούτων. I take these words to mean: 'they persuaded Sparta to accept Clause III [καὶ αὐτοί, sc. as Lykourgos had persuaded her to accept Clauses I and II] on the grounds that it was part of Apollo's command [sc. of his oracle]: and Tyrtaios mentions the oracle as if this were so.'

Apollo's command is the Rhetra itself (which Plutarch regards as an oracle): the two Kings persuaded Sparta to accept Clause III on the grounds that it was really part of the original Rhetra (ὁ θεὸς ταῦτα προστάσσει: 'these are Apollo's words'): the oracle which Tyrtaios quotes, in a metrical paraphrase, *is* the Rhetra, and the word εὐθείαις shows that Tyrtaios accepted Clause III as part of it. This is what I conceive Plutarch's view to have been,

---

[1] See below, p. 62.
[2] Sc. a σκολιὰ ῥήτρα: above, p. 39, n. 3. Εὐθεῖα is the formal opposite of σκολιά: the connexion of this notion with πρόσθεσις and ἀφαίρεσις (Plut. *Lyc.* 6. 7, cf. 13. 3) is illustrated by the lines of Theognis referred to on p. 56, n. 1, τόρνου καὶ στάθμης καὶ γνώμονος . . . εὐθύτερον, etc.: οὔτε τι γὰρ προσθεὶς . . . οὔτ' ἀφελών, etc.
[3] Tyrtaios fr. 4 (Diehl), πατέρων ἡμετέρων πατέρες. At least two generations, since the words might be understood more indefinitely; cf. *Iliad* 20. 308, καὶ παίδων παῖδες τοί κεν μετόπισθε γένωνται.

and Aristotle's. If this is what they thought, we see at once why they thought the Rhetra was an oracle: Tyrtaios (as they understood him) explicitly calls it an oracle.

The morality of the two Kings' action is dubious: but does that matter?[1] Aristotle's reasoning, as I see it, was realistic: 'Clause III is obviously an afterthought, due to experience of how Clause II worked: oracles only contain afterthoughts if they have been tampered with: Tyrtaios regards Clause III as part of the oracle, so the two Kings must have succeeded in passing Clause III off as part of Apollo's words.' This would be logical,[2] if Aristotle understood Lykourgos to have been among the persons who ἀκούσαντες . . . ἔνεικαν (Tyrtaios, line 1). Did he?

Andrewes, in his paper *Eunomia* (*C.Q.* xxxii, 1938, 89 ff.), has argued that the usual ascription of these lines to the poem called *Εὐνομία*[3] is right, since that poem's theme was the authority of the Royal Houses. In fr. 2 (Diehl:=Strabo 8. 4. 10) we hear that 'Zeus has given Sparta to the Herakleidai, who led us from Erineos to Peloponnese', and in the lines before us (=fr. 3[b] Diehl) we hear once more that Sparta is in the care of the Kings, and their authority is strongly emphasized. These considerations lead him (p. 99 f.) to suppose that the subject of ἔνεικαν in line 1 of our

---

[1] How grave a view might be taken of this we may judge from the lines of Theognis, 805–10: 'straighter than a straight-edge the man must be who receives oracles from Delphi: if you add to them, nothing can heal you: if you subtract, your guilt abides'. Cf. Herodotus 7. 6. 3: Onomakritos was evidently forgiven when they were all in trouble together. Theognis no doubt doth protest too much: but oracular business (one may say without cynicism) had to combine pedantic principles with liberal practice. The conjuror will insist that there is no deception. I need not remind my reader that I am not discussing real behaviour (I do not myself believe that the two Kings inserted a clause into an oracle): I am discussing whether Aristotle could allow himself to believe such a story. It seems to me no worse than Cicero's story of the Augur's Wink. The real behaviour which I do posit, and which may not be 'straighter than a straight-edge', is Tyrtaios'. Did he really know that the Pythioi had in their archives an ancient oracle such as he cites? I do not feel censorious about it.

[2] It is true that stories of oracles are often illogical. Plutarch speaks (doesn't he?) as if Lykourgos wrote the Rhetra himself (6. 3, προσηγόρευκεν and esp. ἀνῆψε: see above, p. 38): we could suppose that Aristotle here thinks of the Rhetra as oracle-inspired rather than as Apollo's own words: the inspiring oracle, then, was said by the two Kings to involve Clause III, and Tyrtaios confirms their claim. This saves Aristotle's moral niceness at the cost of his consistency: it still goes some way towards explaining why he thought (still on Tyrtaios' evidence) that the Rhetra was an oracle; only his notion of what he meant by an oracle becomes more hazy. Plutarch's sentence introducing Tyrtaios' lines could no doubt be understood in other ways still, once we allow this haziness.

[3] The poem is so named by Aristotle (*Pol.* 1307[a]) and Strabo (8. 4. 10). Aristotle quotes no lines, Strabo quotes fr. 2 (Diehl). Our lines (fr. 3[b], Diehl) as well as Diodoros' variant (fr. 3[a]) are very frequently ascribed to it by modern scholars.

fragment is the Herakleidai: that in fact this fragment follows fairly closely on fr. 2. I find his argument persuasive, but I do not see that this need prevent Aristotle from thinking that Lykourgos was one of those Heraklids.[1] The Herakleidai fetch the oracle after they have settled in Peloponnese (οἴκαδε shows this[2]), and are not necessarily the same persons, or the same generation, as led the migration from Erineos.[3] And Lykourgos was a Heraklid.

(b) Diodoros' (Ephoros'?) Text

Lines 3–6 are quoted, with small variations, and preceded and followed by lines which Plutarch does not give, in the *Excerpta de Sententiis* from Diodoros (=Diodoros 7. 12 Vogel). A marginal hand adds, ἡ Πυθία ἔχρησε τῷ Λυκούργῳ περὶ τῶν πολιτικῶν οὕτως: if we may trust it (and why not?[4]) Diodoros took the poem to contain the gist of an oracle given to Lykourgos at Delphi. These are rather muddied waters: the excerptor is careless, and Diodoros himself is only too likely to have blunted his original, and that original (whether Ephoros or another) might prove to confuse rather than help the search for Aristotle's meaning. But since we cannot ignore it, I give the text as reported by Boissevain, *Excerpta de Sententiis* (Berlin, 1906), p. 273. The lines are not written as verses: the ten verses (down to πό of πό|λει) take up five lines of the MS., and the heading (ἡ Πυθία, etc.) is written in the margin against these five lines:

ἡ Πυθία ἔχρησε τῷ Λυκούργῳ περὶ τῶν πολιτικῶν οὕτως
δὲ (sic) γὰρ ἀργυρότοξος ἄναξ ἑκάεργος Ἀπόλλων
χρυσοκόμης ἔχρη πίονος ἐξ ἀδύτου
ἄρχειν μὲν βουλῇ (sic) θεοτιμήτους βασιλῆας

---

[1] Andrewes thinks it does, because of the plural (p. 99), and that this is why in Diodoros' version the opening couplet is rewritten. But why must Lykourgos, more than any other inquirer, go without company?

[2] Οἴκαδ' is an emendation, the MSS. have οἱ τάδε νικᾶν: sc. Οἴταδ' ἔνεικαν? 'They brought the oracles from Delphi to Oita.' This might suit very well with Aigimios and his sons, but will not suit at all, I think, with e.g. the tense of μέλει in line 4. We must accept οἴκαδ': the Herakleidai (or whoever) did not bring their oracles with them when they came from central Greece, but fetched them thence after they had settled in Sparta.

[3] Not necessarily: I mean that Aristotle was not bound to infer this, though apparently Hellanikos and Xenophon did. See p. 60.

[4] The *marginale* has been unfairly spat upon. Dindorf writes: *codex inepte ἡ Πυθία, etc.: quasi sequentia, quae sunt Tyrtaei, sint Pythiae.* I question how much of the lines is Tyrtaios': certainly their relevance for Diodoros was that they contained an oracle.

οἷσι μέλει Σπάρτης ἰχερόεσσα (sic) πόλις
5   πρεσβυγενεῖς δὲ γέροντας ἔπειτα δὲ δημότας ἄνδρας
εὐθείην (sic) ῥήτρας ἀνταπαμειβομένους
μυθεῖσθαι δὲ τὰ καλὰ καὶ ἔρδειν πάντα δίκαια
μηδέτι ἐπιβουλεύειν τῇδε πόλει
δήμου τε πλήθει νίκην καὶ κάρτος ἔπεσθαι
10   Φοῖβος γὰρ περὶ τῶν ὧδ' ἀνέφηνε πόλει

I have given all the MS. vagaries (so far as Boissevain reports them), to indicate that we need not shrink from correction.[1] We must clearly write ‹ὧ›δε in line 1, βουλῆς in 3, ἱμερόεσσα in 4, εὐθείαις ῥήτραις in 6 (the last three from Plutarch). I have little doubt we should also write τε for the first δέ in 5, as Plutarch has, and δέ for τε in 9: and if so, it seems misplaced fastidiousness to refuse to write μυθεῖσθαί τε in 7, or in 8 to decline to mend the metre (on the ground that the unmetrical text is meant to be unmetrical).

Should we harmonize the versions of Plutarch and Diodoros? If at all, only with great care. The opening couplet of course cannot be harmonized at all; I agree with Andrewes (p. 99) that Diodoros' opening has the more obvious signs of tampering (due perhaps, as Andrewes suggests, to someone who was embarrassed by the plural ἀκούσαντες in Plutarch's first line—whether or no he wished to make it more Lykourgan). We may therefore fairly suspect the two closing couplets: suspect, I mean, that they have been added by the same poet who wrote the new opening. Andrewes goes farther, and questions whether they even belong to Diodoros' poem.[2] I cannot agree. Diodoros' poem was no doubt poor botched stuff, not very coherent: but I do not doubt that it purported to give the substance of the Rhetra.[3] It gives it

---

[1] Our corrections may be wrong, but I am protesting against e.g. Andrewes, p. 98 'the dubious gain . . . is not worth the cost of a triple corruption in two lines of Diodorus . . .' Andrewes's resolve to think badly of Diodoros' verses makes him unduly tender towards the Excerpta's text.

[2] 'Certainly the last couplet must be separated from lines 3–6. The hexameter . . . amounts to a direct denial of the doctrine' of these lines (p. 98). He then quotes Meyer's view that the couplet is part of a polemic against Tyrtaios, 'but the collocation is more probably a pure accident' (ibid. note 2).

[3] 'The resemblance even of Diodorus' lines to the Rhetra has been greatly exaggerated' (Andrewes, p. 97). Captain Andrewes allows me to say he would withdraw this, and is now prepared to think that even Plutarch's lines refer to the Rhetra. This will (as I see it) involve the abandonment of his view that the Rhetra is later than Tyrtaios (his p. 96 with notes 1, 2, and 3: see my next note). That view is not fundamental to his paper, whose clear thinking has done much to elucidate Sparta's constitutional problems.

with a special emphasis: it stresses the end of Clause II and means to leave no doubt of the sovranty of the Demos. Diodoros got it perhaps from Ephoros. Whether he did or not, we are in a different stream from Aristotle and Plutarch: I must desert for a while the pursuit of Aristotle's opinion, and (for concreteness' sake) state my own.

(c) Tyrtaios and the Rhetra

I believe the Rhetra was an act of the Spartan ekklesia: it was enacted during the crisis which succeeded the Messenian Revolt:[1] its main topic is the *sciscendi ratio*, it defines how the State shall enact its laws: and what most needed definition was the nature and status of the Gerousia (sc. the 'Kings in Council'). Tyrtaios lived to see this crisis, and his poem *Eunomia* was written at that time. The poem was, as Andrewes has shown, a call to loyalty: 'the loyalty which Tyrtaios strove to revive was loyalty to the kings, and with this simple remedy he hoped to cure all Sparta's troubles' (Andrewes, p. 97). The poem, therefore, maintained that the powers reserved by the Rhetra to the 'Kings in Council' were so reserved in conformity with an ancient oracle. 'The Heraklids led us from Erineos to Peloponnese, and Zeus has put Sparta in their care: they also received (long ago?) an oracle from Delphi which gave them, with their Council, certain powers'— powers which are well summarized in a phrase of Plutarch's (*Agis* 11. 1) as τὸ κράτος ἐν τῷ προβουλεύειν, *Probouleutic Control*.

This 'ancient oracle' enjoins of course substantially the same procedure as the ekklesia had just enacted (or was preparing to enact), though no doubt Tyrtaios showed his bias: he was less concerned with the κράτος of the Demos than with the probouleutic κράτος of the Kings and Council, and inside that Council he was less interested in the Gerontes than in the Kings. But for

---

[1] Aristotle Pol. 1306ᵇ speaks of the danger of great wealth and great poverty co-existing, καὶ μάλιστα ἐν τοῖς πολέμοις τοῦτο γίνεται. συνέβη δὲ καὶ τοῦτο ἐν Λακεδαίμονι ὑπὸ τὸν Μεσσηνιακὸν πόλεμον. This was the occasion of Tyrtaios' poem. Andrewes argues from this (p. 96, note 1) that Tyrtaios wrote *during* the war; that ὑπὸ τὸν M. πόλεμον must mean this, since it is an instance of ἐν τοῖς πολέμοις, sc. he takes συνέβη τοῦτο as equivalent to τοῦτο γίνεται. I understand Aristotle to say that these things *come into being* (γίνεται) during wars: this will not prevent the crisis being *precipitated* (συνέβη) after the war is over. I would put the war (and Tyrtaios) a little later than he does (cf. p. 55, n. 3 above), and the Rhetra a little earlier.

all the difference of emphasis, the poem and the Rhetra both enjoin the same procedure: and the likeness did not escape the notice of those (Aristotle, etc.) who were concerned with Sparta's constitution.

If you thought the Rhetra was Lykourgan, it was necessarily much earlier than Tyrtaios. Aristotle (for example) put Lykourgos in the early eighth century[1] and probably put Tyrtaios latish in the seventh: the Kings Polydoros and Theopompos about half-way between them. Consequently, whereas Tyrtaios was really a contemporary of the Rhetra and in his poem seeks to reinforce it with the authority of his ancient oracle, in the eyes of Aristotle and other ancient writers the Rhetra is many generations older than Tyrtaios, and the ancient oracle which he quotes is the Rhetra itself.

The poem was no doubt eagerly consulted. Andrewes has suggested (p. 99 f.) that it was used by Hellanikos, who drew the inference that the constitution was the work of the early Kings; so he left Lykourgos out of it.[2] Xenophon, with his harmonizing mind, clings to Lykourgos, but his date for him, κατὰ τοὺς Ἡρακλείδας, is no doubt from this poem.[3] Aristotle was sure, on other grounds,[4] of Lykourgos' date: and if (as I believe) he understood Lykourgos to be among the persons who ἀκούσαντες . . . ἔνεικαν, he did not let this disturb his date; and indeed it is not likely that the poem was *explicit* about how soon (how many generations) after the arrival in Peloponnese the Herakleidai went to Delphi: though it seems to have *implied*, to Hellanikos and Xenophon, that it was pretty soon. The solid fact was that Tyrtaios ascribed the chief organs of the constitution (Kings, Gerousia, Ekklesia) to an oracle which by this time was ancient. This suited all the theories: I should rather say, all theories were made to suit *this*.

The theorist who evolved Diodoros' version was apparently less

---

[1] Plut. *Lyc.* 1. 2, confirmed by the *Epitome* of the Λακ. πολ. (=Arist. fr. 611, § 10). Lykourgos is contemporary with the First Olympiad. Theopompos will be two generations from Lykourgos, Tyrtaios two from Theopompos.

[2] *F. gr. Hist.* 4 F. 116.

[3] Xen. Λακ. Πολ. 10. 8: quoted by Plutarch, *Lyc.* i. 5–6. The fact that Xenophon uses the phrase κατὰ τοὺς Ἡρακλείδας as an *indication of date* shows that Plutarch is right in understanding him to mean the first Heraklids to settle in Sparta.

[4] The synchronism with *Ol.* I: see n. 1 above. This rested on the *diskos*, which (*pace* Meyer and Jacoby) I am confident he did not discover for himself but owed to Hippias.

scrupulous than most, since he tampered with the poem. He may have been King Pausanias, who seems to have tampered with Herodotos' oracle about Lykourgos:[1] we now know that he attacked Lykourgos[2] and appealed beyond him to Delphi, whose intentions Lykourgos corrupted. The new opening couplet eliminates the consultants and leaves only Apollo: I do not see, however, why King Pausanias should want to stress the sovranty of the Demos, and I am very content to leave Diodoros' poem anonymous. Plutarch's version is better than Diodoros'. When we have to choose, sc. in the opening couplet, I have no doubt that Plutarch is nearer the original poem. I am less certain that Plutarch was right to break his quotation at the participle ἀνταπαμειβομένους. Jacoby has suggested to me possible parallels to such a participle where we should expect an infinitive (or a finite verb), e.g. Archilochos fr. 1

εἰμὶ δ' ἐγὼ θεράπων μὲν Ἐνυαλίοιο ἄνακτος
καὶ Μουσέων ἐρατὸν δῶρον ἐπιστάμενος.[3]

That may be: but Diodoros, once we write μυθεῖσθαί τε, provides the infinitive we look for, and bad as his lines seem, I am unwilling on that ground only to deny that the original poem may have continued in some such way. The last couplet, however, which does not seem specially corrupt, does seem both bad and tendencious: while fairly sure that it is part of Diodoros' poem,[4] I do not wish to give it to Plutarch's, nor to the original Tyrtaios.

[1] King Pausanias' pamphlet containing many oracles is mentioned by Ephoros, *F. gr. Hist.* 70 F. 118: Ed. Meyer suggested that the oracles in Diodoros 7 are from this source, via Ephoros (*Forsch.* i. 215 ff.). Though Meyer misconceived the pamphlet's tendency (see next note), I believe his main thesis still stands. Diodoros 7. 12 (Vogel) gives Herodotos' oracle (1. 65) with two extra lines.

[2] Pausanias' pamphlet was κατὰ τῶν Λυκούργου νόμων, the κατά being guaranteed by the Vatican palimpsest of Strabo: Ehrenberg, *Neugründer*, p. 14.

[3] Or does ἐπιστάμενος depend on εἰμί understood? An unusual construction; cf. *Od.* 4. 231. In Solon fr. 1 (Diehl) line 52, ξυλλέγεται βίοτον can be understood more easily. I know no satisfactory explanation of the participle φυλασσόμενον in Theognis 806 (the passage referred to on p. 56, note 1 above). It is tempting to put the two couplets into *recta* and write ἔπεσθε for ἔπειτα:

ἄρχετε μὲν βουλῆς, θεοτίμητοι βασιλῆες,
οἷσι μέλει Σπάρτης ἱμερόεσσα πόλις,
πρεσβῦταί τε γέροντες· ἔπεσθε δέ, δημόται ἄνδρες,
εὐθείαις ῥήτραις ἀνταπαμειβόμενοι.

[4] As against Andrewes and Meyer: above p. 58, n. 2.

(d) εὐθείαις ῥήτραις

Tyrtaios' poem, in which Delphi enjoins a procedure practically identical with the Rhetra's, persuaded Aristotle that the Rhetra was a Delphic oracle. Yet the word ῥήτρα occurs in the poem, and cannot there possibly mean 'oracle': it must mean either an 'act' of the ekklesia or a 'bill' laid before the ekklesia. After the Kings and councillors have initiated business, the Demos takes its turn

εὐθείαις ῥήτραις ἀνταπαμειβομένους.

This could mean either

(a) 'replying to the straight proposals', or (if we choose to lay on εὐθείαις the weight which Plutarch did) 'replying to the proposals without distorting them':

or else

(b) 'replying with straight enactments', or (with emphasis on εὐθείαις) 'replying with enactments which have not been distorted'.

The latter does more justice to ἀνταγορίαν in Clause II, but I do not know if Tyrtaios wanted to do it justice. The difference is not very substantial: 'responding to proposals' and 'responding with enactments' may come to very much the same thing (once we rid ourselves of an a priori belief in the passiveness of the response), and we shall see that the word ῥήτρα is capable of bearing either sense.

It is curious that with this phrase before him, Plutarch in his *Lycurgus* seems to have believed not only that the Rhetra *was* an oracle, but that the word ῥήτρα meant 'oracle'. In ch. 13 he gives three more Rhetrai, and adds (13. 11) τὰ μὲν οὖν τοιαῦτα νομοθετήματα ῥήτρας ὠνόμασεν ὡς παρὰ τοῦ θεοῦ νομιζόμενα (κομιζόμενα?) καὶ χρησμοὺς ὄντα.[1] In the *Agis* on the other hand he uses the word ῥήτρα frequently, and always (I believe) in the sense of a proposal laid before the Spartan Gerontes or ekklesia. Did he intentionally restrict his usage here to 'proposal' rather than 'enactment'? He may have done, though in fact he elsewhere uses both νόμος and ψήφισμα in the same way as he uses

---

[1] This doctrine is repeated in *de Pyth. or.* 19 (*Mor.* 403 E), αἱ ῥῆτραι δι' ὧν ἐκόσμησε τὴν Λακεδαιμονίων πολιτείαν Λυκοῦργος ἐδόθησαν αὐτῷ καταλογάδην. Elsewhere (e.g. *Mor.* 227 B, C) he treats the three Rhetrai as utterances of Lykourgos himself.

ῥήτρα here, and I think this distinction was not material to him.[1]

If he did make the distinction he was certainly wrong, since long before he wrote Spartan documents use the word to mean 'enactment',[2] and long before the events which he describes the sense 'enactment' is found in contexts which point us to Sparta: the Army of the Ten Thousand;[3] the Spartan colonies of Herakleia and Tarentum;[4] Olympia.

I need not discuss the Olympian Rhetrai (Ϝρατραι) in detail. The most famous,[5] which regulates the rights of private vengeance, is certainly an enactment of the Elean State, and probably some of the others[6] are, though one (see below) is a treaty. These are all headed α Ϝρατρα: in another (whose heading is lost) α Ϝρατρα α δαμοσια is mentioned,[7] probably an 'enactment of the sovran power', but just possibly a judicial pronouncement. Δημο ρητραι are mentioned in the famous Chian law of about 600 B.C.,[8] again most probably 'enactments of the Demos', though the context is too fragmentary to forbid their being judicial pronouncements. These examples, of which the last at least is very early, agree in showing that the word can mean a 'pronouncement of the Demos' quite as well as a 'proposal laid before' the Demos.

One of the Olympian Rhetrai is not an enactment of the Elean State, but a treaty between Elis and Heraia.[9] This comes close to the sense which it bears in its oldest literary use, the 'private treaty' which Odysseus proposes to Eumaios in *Odyssey* 14. 393 ff.

---

[1] See Appendix I (p. 64 below).

[2] *I.G.* v, fasc. 1, no. 20, lines 2–3: no. 1498, line 12.

[3] Xen. *Anab.* 6. 6. 28. The youthful Wilamowitz (*Hom. Unt.*, 1884, p. 280, note 16) said it here means *Vertrag*, and in a Spartiate's mouth. Ed. Meyer corrected him over 50 years ago (*Rh.M.* xliii, 1887, p. 82, note 2) but Liddell and Scott still say it means *covenant*. The man is probably an Arkadian, though he is pleading against a Spartiate defendant and before a Spartiate judge. The ῥήτρα he refers to is an enactment of the Army: it is given in 6. 6. 2, εἴ τις χωρὶς ἀπελθὼν λάβοι τι, δημόσιον ἔδοξεν εἶναι.

[4] The *Tabulae Heracleenses*: *I.G.* xiv, 645, Schwyzer, *Dial. gr. ex. ep. pot.* 62: early Hellenistic. Lines 95–185 are headed συνθῆκα Διονυσω χωρων: if the parties do not fulfil their obligations, they shall be answerable: 145–6 ὑπολογοι εσσονται κατ τας ρητρας και κατ ταν συνθηκαν, in accordance with the laws and with this agreement: 151 ὑπολογος εσσηται κατ τας ρητρας. The usage in this Spartan colony is confirmed for Tarentum by Photius s.v. ῥῆτραι: συνθῆκαι λόγοι ὁμολογίαι (this is the Homeric use). Ταραντῖνοι δὲ νόμους καὶ οἷον ψηφίσματα. παρὰ Λακεδαιμονίοις ῥήτρα Λυκούργου νόμος, ὡς ἐκ χρησμοῦ τιθέμενος (Plutarch's view).

[5] *IvO.* 2: Schwyzer, op. cit. 409.   [6] *IvO.* 10, 11: Schwyzer 414, 415.

[7] *IvO.* 7: Schwyzer 412.

[8] Schwyzer 687 A; Tod, *Selection* 1. * [See pp. 198 f. below.]

[9] *IvO.* 9: Schwyzer 413.

ἀλλ' ἄγε νῦν ῥήτρην ποιησόμεθ'· αὐτὰρ ὄπισθε
μάρτυροι ἀμφοτέροισι θεοί

Eumaios believes Odysseus to be a stranger, and has disbelieved his news: the stranger answers, 'Very well, let us make a *bargain* or *treaty*: if my words prove true treat me well: if false, then put me to death.' 'No, thank you,' says Eumaios. This sense of a sealed covenant or treaty, with the Gods as witnesses hereafter, with contingent forfeits, etc., comes pretty close to the Elis-Heraia treaty. If they had put it in writing in some sacred place which Eumaios controlled as Elis controlled Olympia, it could be appropriately headed α Ϝρατρα Ευμαιοι και τοι ξενοι.

These senses, a treaty between two parties, an enactment of a Demos, possibly a pronouncement of a Demos, cohere very well. A Rhetra is a form of words to which a number of people agree. When it means 'proposal', it is a form of words to which a number of people are asked to agree. I would not deny *a priori* that it might mean a 'divine pronouncement': but this sense would not cohere with the others so well, and (outside the misunderstandings of the 'Lykourgan' Rhetrai) it does not in fact occur.

APPENDIX I: ῥήτρα IN PLUTARCH'S *Agis*

Plutarch uses the word of the Rhetra of Epitadeus in *Agis* 5, and in *Agis* 8–11 of the so-called Rhetra of Agis (really Rhetra of Lysandros? —see below). In both cases it means 'proposal' rather than 'enactment', but I do not know whether the distinction is material for Plutarch. Agis' Rhetra was never enacted. Epitadeus' was enacted, but is called ῥήτρα in the pre-enactment stage: 5. 3, ῥήτραν ἔγραψεν=5. 4, ἴδιον εἰσήνεγκε τὸν νόμον: Plutarch then proceeds οἱ δ' ἄλλοι . . . δεξάμενοι καὶ κυρώσαντες, etc. So he cannot be said to use the word to mean 'enactment' as specifically opposed to 'proposal'. Nevertheless, he uses it as equivalent to νόμος (5. 3–4, quoted above), and his usage here corresponds to his use of ψήφισμα in the Attic lives: ῥήτραν ἔγραψεν[1] corresponds

---

[1] This means 'he drafted a motion': in 9. 1, the motion has been drafted, but not yet accepted by the Gerontes. In the Spartan document of Hellenistic date, *I.G.* v, fasc. 1, No. 1498, the same words are used of the publication on stone of the enacted law: ταν δε ρητραν ταυταν γραψαντες εν σταλαν λιθιναν ανθεντω τοι βιδυιοι. Ehrenberg, *Neugründer* 18, calls the phrase ῥήτραν γράφειν an 'Ungenauigkeit der späteren Autoren,' as if a Rhetra could not be written down. Why ever not? They wrote them on bronze at Olympia, from a very early date. In the archaic inscription from Mykenai, *I.G.* iv. 493, Schwyzer 98, the words κατα (i.e. κατ τα) ϜεϜρεμενα no doubt refer to something which was in writing, as εἰρημένον in Thuc. 5. 39. 3 and εἴρητο in 5. 46. 2 certainly do.

to γράφει ψήφισμα, Pericles 17. 1, cf. 10. 4, 30. 2, 30. 3, 32. 2, 37. 3, *Them.* 10. 4, 11. 1. The constitutional issue in the *Agis* is obscured by emotion, and by the exasperating *lectio incerta* in 8. 1, εἰσέφερε δι' αὐτοῦ or δι' ἑαυτοῦ or εἰσέφερεν ἑαυτοῦ. According to the first reading, Lysandros is the proposer of this Rhetra, according to the other two Agis is. I think the former more likely, because it gives sense to ψηφισαμένοις in 12. 1: ψηφίζεσθαι there cannot mean anything else (so far as I see) than what it certainly does in *Pericles* 13. 11, 20. 2, 24. 1, 25. 1, and perhaps *Alcib.* 35. 1, viz. ψήφισμα γράφειν (a usage which the Lexica do not recognize). If so, the King apparently cannot (in the 3rd century B.C.) introduce a Rhetra himself, but must get an ephor to do it (8. 1). Epitadeus also is probably ephor when he introduces his (5. 3, however we explain the tense of ἐφορεύσας).

The ekklesia apparently meets and discusses the bill before the Gerousia has voted on it: 9. 1, whilst the Gerontes are still disagreeing Lysandros summons the ekklesia; 9. 5, the King speaks in this ekklesia; 10. 1, Leonidas opposes him, etc.; *then*, 11. 1, the Gerontes reject it. This may be a symptom of revolution. Yet we get the same impression in the famous ekklesia of Hetoimaridas (or Etymaridas?)[1] early in the fifth century: Diod. 11. 50. The Gerousia assembles (50. 2), and the ekklesia also assembles (50. 3), and it seems that a great many voices were heard in it. When the issue seemed practically decided, Etymaridas, one of the Gerontes, succeeded in overpersuading *both* Gerousia *and* ekklesia (50. 6).

In both these ekklesiai there seems to be plenty of talk. So there is in the ekklesia of Sthenelaidas in Thuc. 1. 79–87, and though the speakers whom he reports are officials, it is gratuitous to suppose that they had to be. The moral story in Aeschines 1. 180 relates how a notorious evil liver almost carried the Spartan ekklesia with him,[2] till one of the Gerontes intervened. It is not quite clear that the νεώτεροι καὶ τῶν ἄλλων οἱ πολλοί in Diodoros (l.c. 50. 3) actually made speeches, but they evidently made themselves heard; and what of τῶν μὲν πλεόνων in Thuc. 1. 79. 2?

APPENDIX II: V. BLUMENTHAL IN *Hermes*, lxxvii, 212 ff.

I have not yet been able to see Treu's paper in *Hermes*, lxxvi (1941), in which he proposes, as I do, to read ἀνταγορίαν for the αγγορίαν of the

---

[1] Cf. the variants Ἑτοιμοκλῆς (Paus. 3. 13. 9) and Ἐτυμοκλῆς (*Anth. Pal.* 7. 720): the latter form recurs in Xen. *Hell.* 5. 4. 22 and 6. 5. 33.

[2] He made a set speech (δημηγοροῦντος), and unless he is one of the Gerontes, his γνώμη must be an amendment (κατὰ τὴν ἐκείνου γνώμην ψηφίζεσθαι μελλόντων).

5

MSS. So far as I can judge from v. Blumenthal in *Hermes*, lxxvii (1942), 212 ff., which I have seen, he believes, as I do, that the Spartan ekklesia had the power of discussion and amendment, and bases this belief (as I do) on Plutarch's paraphrase, e.g. ἐκτρέποντα καὶ μεταποιοῦντα τὴν γνώμην. 'Dass letztere Deutung nicht richtig sein kann, weil sie dem Wesen der entscheidenden Wehrmännerversammlung widerspricht, scheint mir evident', says v. Blumenthal, and he takes Plutarchs' ἐκτρέποντα, etc. as 'imperfecta de conatu', and in Clause III reads σκολιᾶν (gen. plur.) ἐρέοιτο (from ἔραμαι): 'shows a fondness for crooked rhetrai'. The *a priori* argument seems to me most dangerous, and indeed circular: the question is, was the Spartan ekklesia a Wehrmännerversammlung of the type v. Blumenthal imagines, or not? The Rhetra I believe shows us an ekklesia with a probouleutic council: I do not understand how such an ekklesia, if it may not discuss or amend, ever comes to have a σκολιὰ ῥήτρα before it (above, p. 40).

I have already answered v. Blumenthal's objections to the form of the word ἀνταγορία (above, p. 41 with note 2 and esp. note 3): a gnat to his camel.[1] A small point: he translates ἀνταγορεύειν in Arist. *Frogs* 1072 as 'widersprechen', and he implies that this is how Treu takes it, whereas in Pindar, *Pyth.* 4. 156 it is 'wechselreden'. The context in Aristophanes is quite indecisive: I imagine what he has in mind is episodes like that recorded by Thucydides, 8. 86. 9; perhaps that actual incident. If so, the notion of 'counter-proposal' is apt enough, both here and in Pindar.

C. WHAT IS THE RHETRA?

(a) The Rhetra is an enactment of the late seventh century

In the foregoing parts of this paper[2] I have sought, first (in A. *Plutarch's Text*) to recover Plutarch's text of the Rhetra, which I believe to be also Aristotle's text. It is evident that Aristotle knew and commented on this Rhetra: I take it as my hypothesis

---

[1] He would read δαμώδων γορίαν: the latter word will be part of the Illyrian ('hylleisch') element in Laconian Greek, and correspond to *heriam* in an Illyrian inscription. For δαμώδων see Hesychios δαμώδης: the word is exactly apt, and I think possibly the true original is δαμώδ‹ων› ἀν‹τα›γορίαν. The asyndeton will be an advantage.

[2] This third part has benefited by advice from A. Momigliano and H. W. Parke.

that his account of it in his *Spartan Constitution* was substantially the same as what Plutarch gives us.

Secondly (in B. *The Εὐνομία of Tyrtaios*), I sought to determine why Aristotle had called the Rhetra an 'oracle': I concluded that he had found the evidence for this view in Tyrtaios. Aristotle dated Lykourgos to the First Olympiad: the Rhetra, in his view, was an oracle given by Delphi to Lykourgos in *c.* 776 B.C. (Aristotle's first stage). The Kings Theopompos and Polydoros who in his view added Clause III were about two generations later, contemporary with the conquest of Messenia, about the Fifteenth Olympiad, in the last quarter of the eighth century (Aristotle's second stage). Tyrtaios, some two generations later again (sc. sometime in the seventh century), was understood by Aristotle to show that in the seventh century the whole Rhetra, Clause III and all, was accepted as an oracle which had been delivered to an earlier generation (Aristotle's third stage).

Such, I said, was Aristotle's view, but it was false in so far as it depended on his doctrine that this Rhetra belonged to an historical Lykourgos who could be dated to 776 B.C. I gave as my own belief (pp. 59 f.) that we could eliminate that doctrine and consequently telescope Aristotle's three stages. The Rhetra (Clause III and all) was what the Spartans commonly meant by a 'Rhetra', that is, an enactment of the sovran body. It was contemporary with Tyrtaios: in his *Eunomia* Tyrtaios sought to reinforce its authority by asserting that there was (presumably in the Royal Archives) an ancient[1] oracle enjoining the substance of Clauses II and III.

No one, I suppose, will support Aristotle's date for Lykourgos. My reasons for putting the 'Lykourgan' Rhetra at the time of Tyrtaios, after the close of the Messenian Revolt, sometime towards the end of the seventh century, are substantially the same as those which I adduced in *C.A.H.* iii, p. 562: the most immediately relevant reason is the mention of the Obai (see below).

As for Clause III: if the Rhetra and Tyrtaios be contemporary, and if Tyrtaios' use of the word εὐθείαις does really presuppose

[1] Parke demurs to my phrase '*ancient* oracle', here and above (p. 56 n. 1, p. 59). Did Tyrtaios really offer it as an *ancient* oracle? Aristotle was bound to think so, so that the poem was susceptible of being so understood: but might it not be intended otherwise? Parke thinks that if Delphic authority was sought it would be sought at Delphi and not in the archives: Tyrtaios may have made Ἡρακλεῖδαι the subject of ἔνεικαν and yet have meant his own contemporaries. [Xenophon understood that Lykourgos went *with company* (supra, p. 57, n. 1): Λακ. π. 8. 5.]

Clause III, it follows that Clause III is either an original part of
the Rhetra or was added very early. Why Aristotle made Clause
III into a separate stage (his stage 2) is not an easy question
to answer: but if we are right in telescoping his stages 1 and 3,
his stage 2 will have to be telescoped as well.

(b) Not a construction of fourth-century propaganda

Before I turn to the historical setting, something should perhaps
be said of Meyer's view that the Rhetra is not an authentic
document but a construction of the pamphleteering age which
preceded Aristotle (c. 400–350). In Forschungen, i, pp. 265–9,
Meyer weakens his case by a change of mind: having said (p. 266)
that the Rhetra must have been formulated by a Spartan in
Sparta, since any foreigner would be more explicit about Phylai,
Obai, etc., he then (p. 267) is overpersuaded by Bergk's assertion
that the Rhetra's dialect is Delphic. The latter was a false scent
(see p. 37, n. 2), and his case is more coherent if we eliminate it.
I agree, of course, that the Rhetra was formulated by Spartans
for Spartans; it was formulated (so I think) as a bill to be laid
before the Ekklesia: but Meyer contends that because the Phylai,
Obai, [Gerousia],[1] Demos are mentioned without specific details,
these organs were therefore familiar and long-established, and
he draws the further conclusion that the Rhetra 'formulates the
existing arrangement of the Spartan state: it is not the foundation
on which that arrangement was built' (Meyer, p. 266). These
'basic principles of the constitution' were formulated, so Meyer
suggests, by the theorists of the early fourth century. It was a
tendencious formulation, since the Ephors are left out (p. 267);
the Tyrtaios lines which likewise omit the Ephors are likewise (in
Meyer's view, p. 230) a construction of the early fourth century.

The hexameter oracles given by Diodoros 7. 12 (Vogel) are
indeed fraudulent and tendencious: fraudulent, since they profess
to be the reply which Lykourgos actually received from Delphi.
We owe it to Meyer that this is now an established fact: he was
able to put them in their fourth-century context (see p. 61, n. 1).
He did not make so persuasive a case for the fraudulence of the

---

[1] Meyer includes the Gerousia in his list, but the text I have sought to establish is
quite specific on this.

Tyrtaios lines and the Rhetra.   He was combating the prevalent view, that in this Rhetra we possessed the 'foundation document of the whole Spartan constitution':[1] he made the excusable error of assuming that it professed to be what the prevalent view supposed, and that if it was not such a 'foundation document' it must be fraudulent. 'Is it not clear', he asks (p. 266), 'that this Rhetra rests upon that grossly unhistorical theory which pervaded antiquity, the theory that a constitution arises at the legislator's will, conjured up from chaos or the void?'

But the Rhetra is not, and does not profess to be, the 'foundation document' for the whole constitution of Sparta. It is an enactment which defines certain things about *the composition and powers of the Gerousia*. The Ekklesia to whom it was presented knew what was meant by δᾶμος, by φυλαί, by ὠβαί, by ἀρχαγέται, and no further specification was wanted: it knew too, of course, what γερωσία meant, the Kings must have had some sort of Council of Elders from the beginning of the kingship. What is *specified* is the composition of the γερωσία and its function in the 'process of enactment': these are specified with sufficient precision.

There is, besides, one other specific thing enacted: 'the Spartan people is to *apellaze* regularly,' that is (pp. 44–7) to meet as often as the day of Apellai recurs: that is, once a month. Another factor in the 'process of enactment'.

D. THE AORIST PARTICIPLES IN CLAUSE I

(a) They recapitulate earlier enactments

Let us turn to the text. I give it as determined above on p. 42:

§ I. Διὸς Συλλανίῳ καὶ ᾿Αθανᾶς Συλλανίας ἱαρὸν ἱδρυσάμενον, φυλὰς φυλάξαντα καὶ ὠβὰς ὠβάξαντα, τριάκοντα γερωσίαν σὺν ἀρχαγέταις καταστάσαντα, ὥρας ἐξ ὥρας ἀπελλάζειν μεταξὺ Βαβύκας τε καὶ Κνακίωνος.

§ II. τούτως εἰσφέρειν τε καὶ ἀφίστασθαι, δάμῳ δ᾿ ἀνταγορίαν ἦμεν καὶ κράτος.

---

[1] p. 265 'nach allgemeiner Annahme das Grundgesetz des spartanischen Staates'.

§ III. αἱ δὲ σκολιὰν ὁ δᾶμος ἕροιτο, τὼς πρεσβυγενέας καὶ ἀρχαγέτας ἀποστατῆρας ἦμεν.

This is a real enactment, prescribing for one specific problem, viz. for the process of legislation. It is not the magical formula whereby Lykourgos 'conjured the Spartan state up from the void'. It has survived in isolation, but it is not likely to have been isolated in fact: the things which are left unspecific had no doubt been specified in earlier enactments. One of the decrees of Kallias of 434 B.C. begins with the words [εκποεν τα ενα|ιετια τα λι]θινα και τας Νι[κας τας χ]ρυσας και τα Προ[πυλαια].¹ If we ask 'What pedimental sculptures? How many Golden Nikai?' we know where the answer lay: these things had been prescribed in detail elsewhere, our decree is concerned with something else, the sequel to these things. So here: the sanctuary of Zeus and Athena, the ordering of the Phylai and Obai, have been prescribed in detail already, perhaps too the method of establishing the γερωσία: when these things shall have been implemented, the *process of legislation* in future shall be as follows. To wit: for regular Assemblies, at the Apellai of each month, the agenda shall be prepared by the Council, who shall also preside in the Assembly and make sure that there is no undue departure from the agenda.

That this was more than a routine adjustment, that it was a cardinal moment in the development of the Spartan State, is indicated by the facts that a new sacred area has been designated and the body of citizens is to be reorganized. It is this reorganization of the citizen body which perhaps helps us to date our document.

(b) φυλὰς φυλάξαντα καὶ ὠβὰς ὠβάξαντα

The participle φυλάξαντα is clearly from φυλάζω,² as ὠβάξαντα is from ὠβάζω. 'Having arranged φυλαί as φυλαί and ὠβαί as ὠβαί': this means, I suppose, either that Registers are to be compiled so that every qualified citizen is enrolled in his proper φυλά and his proper ὠβά, or (if that is too elaborate for a society only recently literate) that these units are to be assembled, so that

---

¹ *A.T.L.* I, p. 161. The restorations are not certain, but there is certainly mention of some marble work and the Golden Nikai. *[Cf. *A.T.L.* II D2.]

² Not from φυλάσσω.

every citizen can know to which φυλά and which ὠβά he belongs and who are his fellows. It was long thought that the ὠβά was a subdivision of the φυλά, so that our clause would be tantamount to Nestor's prescription in the *Iliad* (2. 362), κρῖν' ἄνδρας κατὰ φῦλα κατὰ φρήτρας. But it is now fairly clear that there were not more than five Obai in classical Sparta, and that they cannot have subdivided any Tribes. In Roman Sparta it appears that the same unit (e.g. Limnai)[1] can be called both φυλά and ὠβά: yet in our document they can hardly be synonyms. There is, in fact, little serious doubt that in our document the φυλαί are the three 'Dorian Tribes' and the ὠβαί are the five 'Regions' of Sparta. These are two different principles of division, and the Rhetra envisages their coexistence.

(c) Changes in the Spartan Army

The three φυλαί (viz. Hylleis, Pamphyloi, Dymanes) and the five ὠβαί (viz. Pitana, Mesoa, Kynosoura or Konooura, Limnai, Amyklai) formed successively the framework of the Spartan army. By the time of Thucydides and Xenophon both 'Tribal Army' and 'Obal Army' were obsolete and had been superseded by the *Morai*.

The Spartan army which we know in detail, chiefly from Xenophon's *Hellenica* and his *Constitution of Sparta*, is the Army of the *Morai*. Aristotle in his *Constitution of Sparta* appears to have described both the Obal Army and the Army of the Morai (frr. 541, 540), and to have distinguished between them. We know of the Obal Army from him, and from Herodotos (9. 53, 57: see below): of the Tribal Army only from Tyrtaios. Toynbee contends that the Spartan army which Thucydides describes, at Sphakteria in 425 and Mantinea in 418 (*J.H.S.* xxxiii, pp. 265, 267, 269 ff.: possibly also at Tanagra in 457, p. 269), is the Army of the Morai.

The systematic works, Kromayer's *Heerwesen* (1928) and Kahrstedt's *Staatsrecht* (I: *Sparta*, etc., 1922) give no light here. Toynbee

---

[1] *I.G.* v. 1, No. 564, lines 4–5 της Λιμναεων φυ|λης: No. 688 ωβα Λιμναιεω[ν]. So 480, 9–10 φυλης Κονοου|ρεων, and probably της φ[υλης] in 682, 4. They had long performed the function of φυλαί: the Three Tribes were quite as much forgotten as the Four Tribes in Athens.

in his *Growth of Sparta* (*J.H.S.* xxxiii, pp. 246 ff., esp. 262–72) offers a series of bold hypotheses which do (I believe) go far to explain the *Morai* Army and its relation to the Obal Army: but he wrote before the Tyrtaios papyrus was published and so knows nothing of the Tribal Army. For many problems of the Obal Army, Pareti's account (most recently in his *Storia di Sparta arcaica*, 1917, pp. 173–7) is still, I think, the best: though he too is before the papyrus. The Tyrtaios papyrus was published in 1918.

Toynbee has demonstrated (conclusively, I believe) that Thucydides in his account of the Mantineia campaign in 418 (*a*) describes the Army of the Morai, but (*b*) confuses *Lochos* and *Mora* and so calculates the Spartan army at half its strength.[1] Thucydides says that in that battle the Lakedaimonioi, not counting the Skiritai and the corps of promoted Helots (Neodamodeis and Brasideioi), had 6 *Lochoi*[2] of 4 Pentekostyes and 16 Enomotiai apiece: the Enomotia being of about 32 men, that makes rather over 3,000 men in all (Th. 5. 68. 3). If there were in fact 6 *Morai* (and therefore 12 Lochoi), the right figure will be something over 6,000. This is comparable, as it should be, to the 6,000 hoplites at the Nemea River in 394 (Xen. *Hell.* 4. 2. 16).

This establishment of about 6,000 is for the call-out of men up to 55. It includes the perioikoi: this is clear enough in the two cases I have named, as well as in 425 and in 365, and it is stated in principle by Isokrates and Aristotle.[3]

In 479 Laconia put 10,000 hoplites in the field: 5,000 Spartiates and 5,000 perioikoi. They marched out separately, and though

---

[1] In 5. 66. 3 the hierarchy is *King, Polemarchs, Lochagoi, Pentekonteres, Enomotarchoi*: but in 68. 3 he takes count only of *Lochoi, Pentekostyes, Enomotiai*: sc. he leaves out the polemarch's unit, which Xenophon says is the *Mora* (*Λακ. π.* 11. 4). There were polemarchs present, and Thucydides speaks of them as commanding each one Lochos (71. 3): there is no unit left for the Lochagos. It is evident that the polemarch's command was in fact a Mora, and Thucydides' 'Lochoi' are in fact Morai.

[2] 'Seven without the Skiritai' (68. 3): the seventh is the ex-Helots who stood between the Skiritai and the other Lakedaimonioi (67. 1). The Λακεδαιμόνιοι αὐτοί, distinguished from the Skiritai and ex-Helots (67. 1), are the 'regular establishment' of the six Morai.

[3] Isokrates, 12. 180 κατ' ἄνδρα συμπαρατάττεσθαι σφίσιν αὐτοῖς (what he says next, ἀποστέλλειν προκινδυνεύσοντας, will refer to the Skiritai, Xen. Λακ. π. 12. 3, 13. 6). Aristotle, fr. 540, διῄρηνται εἰς τὰς μόρας Λακεδαιμόνιοι πάντες: πάντες includes the perioikoi, cf. Hdt. 7. 234. 2; Xen. *Hell.* 6. 4. 15. Aristotle is no doubt making the contrast with the Obal Lochoi of fr. 541. The order of these two fragments should be inverted: Hesychios, s.v. μόρα: . . . οἱ πάτρι⟨οι⟩ λόχοι μόρα αὖθις ὀνομασθέντες must come ultimately from Aristotle and gives the sequence. [Hesychios takes μόρα as neuter plural.] Prisoners from the Morai include perioikoi: in 425, Th. 4. 8. 9, 38. 5: in 365, Xen. *Hell.* 7. 4. 20, 27.

the two formations were next to each other in the line of battle, they were clearly two formations. The perioikoi are λογάδες. The Spartiates are called ἡ νεότης:[1] it looks as if the call-out was not up to 55 but something less.[2] In Appendix III I suggest it was up to 45, and that the 5,000 Spartiates are 25 year-classes of 200 each.

Xenophon speaks of the six Morai as the creation of Lykourgos (Λακ. π. 11. 4, μόρας μὲν διεῖλεν ἕξ): Thucydides ridiculed Herodotos' reference to the Obal Army at Plataea (Th. 1. 20. 3, τὸν Πιτανάτην λόχον . . . ὃς οὐδ' ἐγένετο πώποτε). We must therefore look a moment longer at this Army of the Morai, which appeared to intelligent contemporaries to be immemorial.

Men in one Mora had close relations in another Mora (sons, fathers, brothers: Xen. Hell. 4. 5. 10), and there were Amyklans in many different Morai (ibid. 11): this can hardly mean other than that the Mora took no count of tribal divisions of any kind but men were just drafted as the army needed them. It was a point of Spartan discipline that any Spartan could fight alongside any other: Spartans, that is to say, depended neither on Nestor's principle that tribesman supports tribesman nor on any of its modern variants.[3] 'When your formation is broken, to be able to remake it with whoever comes to hand (μετὰ τοῦ παρατυχόντος)—this is a hard thing to learn and it needs the training of

---

[1] Hdt. 9. 12 πέμπουσι κήρυκα . . . ἐς τὴν Ἀττικήν, πρότερον . . . ὑποδεξάμενοι σχήσειν τὸν Σπαρτιήτην μὴ ἐξιέναι· ὃς . . . ἔλεγε τάδε· Μαρδόνιε . . . ἐξελήλυθε ἡ νεότης. Should this be pressed? Herodotos is often found to speak the exact truth because he repeats what he hears with all its quiddity and flavour and does not reduce it to commonplace. Here I suspect that his language reveals two facts: (a) that the normal establishment at that time was Spartiates only; (b) that only young men were normally called out. For the relation between this νεότης of 5,000 and the 8,000 ἄνδρες of Hdt. 7. 234. 2, see Appendix III.

[2] The problem of the Eirenes is still unsolved, so that I will not argue from the alleged fact that these youngest soldiers (?) had many casualties and a separate grave: Hdt. 9. 85. 2. Nilsson's interpretation of the Herodotos gloss (Klio, xii. 309 ff.) is no doubt wrong: see the fuller version of this gloss published by Diller, A.J.P. lxii. 500. Yet the fact remains that Xenophon distinguishes εἴρενες from ἄνδρες (Λακ. π. 2. 11) while Herodotos appears to say that the commander of a Lochos was an Eiren. The gloss now appears to say [ἐπ' ἐτῶν should be ἀπ' ἐτῶν?] that you were an ephebos from 14 to 20, and became an Eiren at 20: agreeing with Plut. Lyc. 17. 3–4.

[3] Nestor's rule 'Kin will help kin', Iliad, 2. 362–3. Later, neighbour helped neighbour: the Obal Army, the Kleisthenic army at Athens. Later still, friend (or 'lover') helped friend: the Lochos of Episthenes (Xen. Anab. 7. 4. 8), and the more famous ἱερὸς λόχος (or ἐκ πόλεως λόχος, because their barracks were on the Akropolis) founded by Gorgidas at Thebes, Plut. Pelop. 18. Pammenes is quoted ibid. as saying that this improved on Nestor.

Lykourgos' laws', says Xenophon (*Λακ. π.* 11. 7). Plutarch observes that this failed them at Leuktra: Pelopidas' attack disorganized them 'though the Spartans were disciplined and trained to nothing so much as this, that when their formation was broken they should not be disorganized, but could take anyone without exception as neighbour in line or file and so re-form at the point of danger' (*Pelop.* 23. 3f.).

The change was thus designed partly to let the professional bond override all others: but chiefly, no doubt, to eke out the manpower of the Spartiates. The detailed organization of the Mora need not concern us here: what the proportion was of Spartiates to perioikoi (no doubt it varied), how they were apportioned between the Lochoi, etc. The vital fact (I believe) is that in 479 the 'regular establishment' is of Spartiates: in 418 it is of Spartiates and perioikoi.[1] It was an attempt to meet the crisis of population caused by the great earthquake.

The perioikoi could (in 479 and earlier) be called up, as we see they were for the Persian crisis in 479, but they were called up in separate formations. One such formation seems to have earned its survival: the *Lochos Skirites*. The Skiritai were Arkadian by blood and speech: no doubt their Lochos earned its honours as a scouting formation in those Arkadian wars in which the Obal Army first proved itself (Hdt. 1. 66: *C.A.H.* iii. 365). The 5,000 perioikoi at Plataea were no doubt composed, like the 5,000 Spartiates, of 'regional' Lochoi, and the *Skirites* will have been one of them.

(d) Tribal Army and Obal Army

It is comparatively recently, with Wilamowitz's publication of the Tyrtaios papyrus in 1918,[2] that we learnt for certain that Sparta had once a Tribal Army. In that papyrus, a prospective battle is described, in which the Spartans are to go into action χωρὶς Πάμφυλοί τε καὶ Ὑλλεῖς ἠδ[ὲ Δυμῆνες]. In the Messenian Revolt, then, the units of the Spartan army were those three 'Dorian Tribes', the same as we find in many Dorian cities, racial or 'kinship' groups which purported to be descended from Herakles' three sons, Hyllos, Pamphylos, and Dyman. The

---

[1] I suggest some details in Appendix III.
[2] Wilamowitz, *SB. Berlin*, 1918, 728 ff.: now Tyrtaios, fr. 1, in Diehl's *Anth. Lyrica.*

evidence is conclusive, but there is little other trace of it in our tradition:[1] Aristotle in his *Constitution* appears to know only the two later stages, the Obal Army and the Morai.

The five Obai of the Obal Army were Pitana, Mesoa, Kynosoura (or Konooura), Limnai, Amyklai. The evidence that these are indeed the five 'Regions' of the town of Sparta is assembled by Ehrenberg in Pauly-Wissowa, s.v. 'Obai', pp. 1693–6. The first four are beyond reasonable doubt: Amyklai I think virtually certain, though harder to prove.

The first four are named in conjunction (not as Obai) by Pausanias:[2] three of these (Mesoa is absent) occur in inscriptions of Roman imperial date, as winners in the Obal ball-games (νικασαντες τας ωβας): the *Neopolitai* who also occur here are probably a Hellenistic creation. In these documents Limnaeis occur thrice, Neopolitai twice, Pitanatai once for certain: of three uncertain names, two may be Konooureis, one Pitanatai or (less probably) Mesoatai:[3] and the team of Konooureis are mentioned incidentally in another document.[4] With such figures, we could not be surprised if one name (or even two) were absent: Mesoa's absence, then, means nothing; we may be sure that she competed. I do not myself suppose that Amyklai did: the first four were contiguous and were enclosed in the Hellenistic ring-wall: Amyklai is about three miles to the south, and in the reorganization after 146 B.C. it got the same sort of semi-independence as the towns of the perioikoi. Compare *I.G.* v. 1, No. 26 (and 27) with Nos. 1110, 1114, all of Roman republican date. Amyklai and Geronthrai both issue their own decrees and have their own ephors, though

---

[1] Sch. Pind. *Pyth.* 1. 121a Παμφυλὶς καὶ Δυμανὶς φυλαὶ ἐν Λακεδαίμονι: Hesych. Δύμη· ἐν Σπάρτῃ φυλή· καὶ τόπος (conflated from Δυμήν· ἐν Σπ. φ. and Δύμη· τόπος?). Such passages were enough to suggest that Sparta had once had the Three Tribes, but not that her army had been so composed in historic times. Pareti came very near the truth (see his *St. di Sp. arc.* 173), but thought the Obai much older than the seventh century.

[2] Οἱ Λιμνᾶται Σπαρτιατῶν καὶ Κυνοσουρεῖς καὶ ⟨οἱ⟩ ἐκ Μεσόας τε καὶ Πιτάνης θύοντες τῇ Ἀρτέμιδι ἐς διαφορὰν ἀπὸ δὲ αὐτῆς καὶ ἐς φόνους προήχθησαν (3. 16. 9). The contending parties are Limnai-cum-Kynosoura versus Mesoa-cum-Pitana, eastern versus western Sparta, Eurypontid versus Agiad. It was before Lykourgos (Λυκοῦργος μετέβαλεν, 3. 16. 10), so we do not expect Neopolitai (*aliter* Pareti, op. cit., 175, n. 4): nor Amyklans if (as I think) it recalls a real dichotomy, before the two houses united: the Agiad attempts access to the Eurypontid's altar.

[3] *I.G.* v. 1, nos. 674–87.

[4] *B.S.A.* xxvi, pp. 165, 181. Cf. *I.G.* v. 1, no. 566, line 3 σφαιρεα Κονοουρεα.

these ephors are in each case dated by a Spartan eponymous magistrate. Amyklai's 'independence' is clearly indicated by the phrase in No. 27 (lines 19–20) σειτησιν ε[ν τω | πρυτανειω τω τα]σ ωβα[σ].[1] None of the other four can have disposed of σίτησις ἐμ πρυτανείῳ: I take its appearance in Amyklai to be a mark of the *dioikismos* of 146 B.C.—not to show that it had not been synoikized once.[2]

But though she is independent after 146, we have in these decrees an indication of her former status: she calls herself an ὠβά, while Geronthrai calls herself a πόλις. She had been an ὠβά, and I think that means she had been a 'region' of the Spartiates. That being an ὠβά necessarily means being a Spartiate region is not quite self-evident; nor can I prove, independently, that in Sparta's great days the Amyklans were Spartiates. But I share the general opinion that they were.[3]

Coming now to the 'Obal Army', we are met by the notorious controversy between Herodotos and Thucydides. Herodotos said that one of the Spartan formations at the battle of Plataea in 479 B.C. was the Πιτανήτης λόχος, the Lochos of Pitana. Thucydides discoursing of historical method says that some writers take very little trouble, and he illustrates the mistakes they fall into by this Πιτανάτης λόχος: 'there never was such a thing'. There is little doubt that Thucydides has slipped up badly: he certainly took trouble to find out about the Spartan army, but

---

[1] My supplement is uncertain, but the *sitesis* is certainly part of τα τας ωβ[α]ς τ[ιμια] (line 18).

[2] Synoikisis and πρυτανεῖον, Th. 2. 15. 2.

[3] I do not see that it *follows* from Xen. *Hell.* 4. 5. 11 (Bölte in P-W, 'Sparta', p. 1329, 23). That passage makes it likely, its being an ὠβά makes it likely, its nearness to Sparta and its importance combine perhaps to make it almost certain. [Note, too, perhaps, the statue of *Sparte* at Amyklai and of the *Demos of Spartiatai* at Sparta: Paus. 3. 18. 8 (cf. 2. 16. 4, and Wide, *Lak. Kulte*, 337, n. 1), 3. 11. 10.] My Obal thesis depends on Amyklai being Spartiate and I have no moral doubt of it, but I do not see that it can be proved αὐτὸ καθ᾽ αὐτό.. Every attempted proof begs the question of what exactly the differentia was which distinguished perioikoi from Spartiates.— Nor is it *certain* that the Νεοπολῖται are of Hellenistic date (again I have no moral doubt: cf. Pareti, op. cit. 176–7). I cannot disprove that the classical Five Obai were the known four *plus* the Neopolitai, in fact the ball-game teams. The Neopolitai would then date from the seventh century, and when Aristotle says ('Αθ. π. 21. 4) that Kleisthenes assimilated his νεοπολῖται, he could be understood as contrasting this with the Spartan way.—Against the view that there were only 4 Obai and 4 Obal Lochoi, Aristotle's five names are surely conclusive: nor can Ar. *Lys.* 453 be cited in support of it. The Proboulos orders the assault; Lysistrata says νὴ τὼ θεὼ γνώσεσθ᾽ ἄρα ὅτι καὶ παρ᾽ ἡμῖν εἰσι τέτταρες λόχοι. There can be no reference to the Obal Army: in 411 'four Lochoi' was one-third of the establishment. I suggest there were 4 Lochoi in Dekeleia (soon reinforced, Th. 8. 71. 1).

he found the going hard.[1] In the army of his day there was evidently no Lochos of Pitana, but he extrapolated rashly (we are hardened to his manners). Few historians will now doubt that there was, in 479, a Lochos based on Pitana and composed of Pitanatai: it may not have been called Πιτανάτης λόχος.

Aristotle in his *Spartan Constitution* gave the names of the five πάτριοι λόχοι.[2] One of them is Mesoates, the Lochos of Mesoa: the other four have non-regional names. But if one Lochos is regional, then surely all five must be, though four of them were known by names of honour, or by nicknames: one of the nicknamed four must be the Lochos of Pitana. The 5,000 Spartiates at Plataea are no doubt these five Lochoi (see Appendix III).

Some time between the Messenian Revolt in the seventh century and this battle in the fifth, the three Tribal regiments have been superseded by these five Obal regiments.

(e) The Attic Analogy

The two principles of division, (i) by race or 'tribe', and (ii) by domicile, are familiar in Athens: the pre-Kleisthenic and the Kleisthenic tribes (both alike are called φυλαί). So far as I see, the analogy is good: the ten Kleisthenic tribes, like the five Obai, are regions; the four pre-Kleisthenic tribes, like the three 'Dorian Tribes' are based on race or kinship. The inhabitants of Pitana (or some other Spartan Oba) stand to the descendants of Hyllos (or some other son of Herakles) exactly as the inhabitants of Marathon (or some other Attic Deme) stand to the descendants of Geleon (or some other son of Ion).

The fundamental differences are well known. Laconia had no inhabited centres except Sparta [*plus* Amyklai] on the one hand, and on the other the towns of the perioikoi:[3] nothing, that is, like the Demes of Attica. The perioikoi are unlike the inhabitants of such Demes as Rhamnous or Eleusis[4] in many ways which are

---

[1] Hdt. 9. 53. 2–3, 57: Th. 1. 20. 3. Hard going: Th. 5. 68. 2 (see n. 1 on p. 72), 72. 3, cf. 4. 40. 2 and the apophthegms in Plut. *Mor.* 190 D (Agis 5–6).

[2] Fr. 541: for πάτριοι see n. 3 on p. 72.

[3] Hdt. 7. 234. 2: πόλιες πολλαί . . . Σπάρτη πόλις.

[4] They correspond roughly to e.g. Oropos, Salamis, Eleutherai, but only very roughly. These Attic 'perioikoi' are not called 'Αθηναῖοι but the Spartans' perioikoi are Λακεδαιμόνιοι and moreover πολῖται (n. 1 on p. 84): *cives sine suffragio* perhaps. The fact is that Laconia had no synoikisis in the sense in which Attica did, in the sense that people domiciled in many places had one political centre in which

familiar: for our purpose, they are unlike them in not forming part of the Spartan Ekklesia nor of the Spartan Tribes (whether φυλαί or ὠβαί). It is better to speak of the Spartan Obai not as 'territorial tribes' but as 'tribes based on domicile': the area of the five Obai will not cover the map of Laconia as the Kleisthenic Tribes *do* cover Attica. In Laconia, we must first subtract the whole perioikis: in what is left, the only inhabited centres in which citizens are domiciled were the five villages or small towns which lay within four miles of the foot of the Akropolis. The country estates of the Spartiates[1] were not grouped round villages (as e.g. in Mantineia's territory) but isolated, and anyway the Spartiate's domicile was not on his estate but in Sparta.[2] Sparta was his post of duty and (from the beginning of the Obal period) his barracks. The barracks were not unduly grim: there were married quarters, and children, pleasant open spaces, temples, dancing, and music:

> ἔνθ' αἰχμά τε νέων θάλλει καὶ μῶσα λίγεια
> καὶ δίκα εὐρυάγυια καλῶν ἐπιτάρροθος ἔργων

said Terpander—just before the Obal period, indeed, but Plutarch who quotes him (*Lyc.* 21) quotes Pindar to the same effect. Plato's judgement in the *Laws* is severer: 'In Krete and Sparta', says Kleinias, 'the only singing we know is the community singing of our public dances.' 'More's the pity,' replies the Athenian. 'You live as in a barracks, not a city: like herds of animals: you have no private life and no higher education.' Isokrates had said the same less disparagingly in his *Archidamos*.[3]

---

they shared on equal terms (Th. 2. 15–16): this is the truth behind the moralized account in Isokr. 12. 177–81. Thucydides' denial of synoikisis in Sparta (1. 10. 2) makes quite another point: there *was* a synoikisis of the five Obai in the sense I have just defined, the inhabitants retained their domiciles but pooled their political life. Thucydides' point in 1. 10. 2 is that this process was not accompanied by the usual material signs: he is contrasting it, of course, with Perikles' Athens.

[1] Τὰ χωρία, Xen. *Hell.* 3. 3. 5: you might find one Spartiate in each, surrounded by enemies. The Mantinean χωρία, ibid. 5. 2. 7.

[2] Besides the evidence of barracks life (next note), this domicile in Sparta is implied by Hdt. 7. 234. 2; perhaps too by the narrative of the earthquake (Plut. *Cim.* 16. 4–6; Diod. 11. 63. 6–7).

[3] I have paraphrased Plato's words freely (*Laws* 666 D–667 A): the phrase about the barracks is στρατοπέδου γὰρ πολιτείαν ἔχετε ἀλλ' οὐκ ἐν ἄστεσι κατῳκηκότων: Isokrates' words are (6. 81) τὴν πολιτείαν ὁμοίαν κατεστησάμεθα στρατοπέδῳ καλῶς διοικουμένῳ. When Xenophon speaks of τὰ ἐν τῇ πόλει καλά (*Hell.* 5. 3. 9; cf. πάντα τὰ καλά, ἅπαντα ὅσα καλὰ ἐν τῇ Σπάρτῃ in 5. 4. 32–3) he refers to this barracks discipline: cf. Λακ. π. 5. 2. A well-preserved seventh-century στρατόπεδον is the little town at Vroulia in south Rhodes (Kinch, *Vroulia*, pp. 6–7): walled and tight-packed. The unwalled Sparta is by contrast εὐρυάγυια, εὐρύχορος (Terpander, loc. cit.; *Odyss.* 15. 1).

The Obai were not districts of Laconia but parts of the city of Sparta.[1] The word no doubt means 'village' and could be properly used (like πόλις) both of the region and of its inhabitants. The five Obai, then, are (a) the five regions of Sparta: and since all Spartans are domiciled in Sparta they are (b) the inhabitants of those five regions: that is, the five Regional Tribes into which the Spartan people was divided.

With the above qualification, the Attic analogy is very close. In Athens, the Four Tribes survived: the four φυλοβασιλεῖς were still appointed, the Phratries of which the Four Tribes had been composed still compiled their registers, so that every Athenian was entered in two registers, his Phratry's and his Deme's. Clause I of the Rhetra shows (I think) that in Sparta likewise the Three Tribes survived: in confirmation, we find the 27 Phratries functioning at the Karneia.[2]

It is pretty certain that at Athens the Deme-registers were first compiled in 507: they then introduced a new-model Army. By analogy I would expect the Obal Katalogoi to be first compiled when the Obal Army was formed. The Obal registers, then, are mentioned in Clause I because they are new: the Tribal registers, though not new, could be felt to need this official recognition of the fact that they were to survive. But before the Obal Army, there was no need whatever for two registers.[3]

On this reasoning the terminus post quem for Clause I will be the Messenian Revolt, of the second half of the seventh century. The terminus ante is perhaps the Arkadian wars of the early sixth century, if we may (rather selectively) take from Herodotos (1. 65–6) the fact that the reformed Army shortly preceded these wars. A rather stricter terminus ante is given for Clauses II and III by Tyrtaios' Eunomia: the Revolt and the Rhetra come within one poet's working life.[4]

If the occasion is the creation of the Obal Army, we may adduce,

[1] Strabo is explicit about Mesoa and Limnai (8. 5. 3): Μεσσόαν δ' οὐ τῆς χώρας εἶναι μέρος ἀλλὰ τῆς Σπάρτης καθάπερ καὶ τὸ Λιμναῖον (for the reading see Bölte in P-W, s.v. 'Sparta', p. 1363, 57–9). The passage is polemical but this topographical fact is not: those who equated Messe and Messoa are brushed aside as not having taken account of the topography, not as having held another topographical theory.
[2] Athen. 141 f. The passage about γένη which Kahrstedt quotes from Aelius Aristides refers to Athens (Staatsr. i. 70, n. 1: Aristid. i, p. 314 Dind.).
[3] I don't think that the Spartans were registered for taxation.
[4] An earlier date is excluded, I think, by the operative part of Clause I, which gives the Ekklesia regularity of assembly. This is very advanced: contrast Odyss. 2. 26–8.

for the epithet of Zeus and Athena in Clause I, Hesychios' gloss
Σκυλλανίς· ἡ πολεμική. The feminine adjective looks like the
epithet of a goddess. Von Blumenthal in *Hermes* lxxvii suggests
that we write Σκυλλανίδος in Clause I. Though it is likely that
Plutarch and Hesychios refer to the same goddess, I prefer not to
correct Plutarch's spelling by Hesychios'. Zeus and Athena are
often associated in Sparta: Paus. 3. 11. 11, 3. 13. 6, cf. 3. 17. 6:
most relevant perhaps is the King's offering Διὶ καὶ 'Αθηνᾷ before
he leaves Laconia on a campaign (Xen. *Λακ. π.* 13. 2).[1]

APPENDIX III: πεντηκοστύς, fifty men or a fiftieth part?

The word πεντηκοστύς is used by Thucydides 5. 68. 3 for a division
of the Spartan army, smaller than a Lochos, larger than an Enomotia.
I have discussed the passage above (p. 72, n. 1) and given the arguments for the view, which seems to me practically certain, that
Thucydides has in his calculation overlooked the Mora, so that his
figures must be revised as follows:

> 35 years called out:
> 192 Enomotiai of *c.* 32 men each
> =48 Pentekostyes of *c.* 125 men each
> =12 Lochoi of *c.* 500 men each
> =6 Morai of *c.* 1,000 men each
> =an establishment of *c.* 6,000 men.

This was the field strength of the Spartan establishment in 418 B.C.,
when called out to very nearly its full strength. The 'establishment' is
called (5. 67. 1) Λακεδαιμόνιοι αὐτοί, contrasted as such both to the
Skiritai and to the corps of ex-Helots. It was probably this same
establishment, with 35 years called out, which makes up the 6,000 men
at the Nemea River in 394 B.C. (*Hell.* 4. 2. 16). For Leuktra in 371 B.C.
35 years were called out, but only 4 of the 6 Morai were present (*Hell.*
6. 4. 17): the Enomotia was of something under 36 men (6. 4. 12).
This gives a force of about 4,000; when the King and 1,000 men had
been killed, the polemarchs ceased fighting (6. 4. 15). In 425 B.C. it
looks as if the 420 men who formed the island garrison were one
Enomotia of 35 men from each of the 12 Lochoi: 35 × 12 = 420
(Thuc. 4. 8. 9).

[1] Immediately above, Xenophon records the King's sacrifice Διὶ 'Αγήτορι καὶ τοῖς
σὺν αὐτῷ, which all editors emend (cf. however *Apol.* 24, καὶ τῶν σὺν τούτοις θεῶν). Does
σὺν αὐτῷ perhaps conceal Συλλανίῳ?—'Αγήτορι καὶ [τοῖς] Συλλανίῳ. Earlier in the
seventh century Terpander wrote a poem for Zeus Agetor (fr. 1): at the time of
the Rhetra this Zeus gets this second title?

The Enomotia contained one man from each year-class called out: see Toynbee in *J.H.S.* xxxiii, pp. 262 ff., *Mobilisation-classes and the* ἐνωμοτία (esp. p. 263).[1] For the important occasions I have named, 35 years were called out and the Enomotia was of a nominal 35. In gravest crises 40 years were called out, that is, up to 60 years of age: e.g. after Leuktra in 371 (*Hell*. 6. 4. 17). That was the upper limit (*Hell*. 5. 4. 13): the 42 year-classes which appear to have been called out at first in 418 included the νεώτεροι of 18–20 (Thuc. 5. 64. 2–3, cf. Toynbee l.c.). We do not hear explicitly of the smaller call-outs,[2] but the Mora of 600 men which was destroyed by Iphikrates in 390 was on garrison duty (*Hell*. 4. 5. 11–12) and we may suppose it was composed of 20 year-classes: this would give a paper strength of $32 \times 20 = 640$ men.[3]

These figures are coherent and I believe they confirm the 'corrected' Thucydidean scale. Xenophon's table in Λακ. π. 11. 4 differs considerably from Thucydides, but where it differs is almost certainly wrong. It gives 16 Enomotiai to the Mora, i.e. 96 to the establishment, so that the Enomotia at the Nemea River (*Hell*. 4. 2. 16) would have to be over 60 strong: this is impossible, and there must be twice that number of Enomotiai. It gives 24 Lochoi to the establishment, and this figure must be halved (*Hell*. 7. 4. 20, 7. 5. 10).[4] The 48 Pentekostyes

---

[1] Toynbee's p. 263 contains the clearest account which I know of the Enomotia, and I state at once my few disagreements. I understand the ἐπιτεταγμένοι of Thuc. 5. 72. 3 not as a separate formation but as a rear rank (οὐραγοί): they are included in the Enomotia of '4 × 8', which is not a paper strength but a line of battle. When details and sick were allowed for, about 32 men of the nominal 35 actually paraded. In the last paragraph of the page Toynbee equates the Obal Lochos with the Lochos of the Mora and so gives it 16 Enomotiai. Below, I argue that it has not 16 but 40, and that the five Obal Lochoi at barracks strength came to (not 40 × 16 × 5 =3,200, but) 40 × 40 × 5 = 8,000: see Hdt. 7. 234. 2. I also rather doubt his interpretation of Λακ. π. 2. 4 in n. 70.

[2] The call-out was fixed on each occasion by proclamation of the Ephors: Xen. Λακ. π. 11. 2: τὰ ἔτη εἰς ἃ δεῖ στρατεύεσθαι.

[3] This Mora had sent home all the Amyklans in its ranks (4. 5. 11), and this might reduce even its paper strength to near 600. The order to sally from the ranks is given to the men from 20–30 (4. 5. 14) and later to the men from 20–35 (4. 5. 16): the ranks must therefore have included men at least up to 40. It is not easy, however, to account for all the 600: only 250 were killed (4. 5. 17), and yet practically no one survived except those who were wounded in the early stages (4. 5. 14: the ὀλίγοι τινές of 4. 5. 17 were therefore negligible), Its actual strength must have been well under 600: I think it likely that Ephoros' 'Mora of 500' (Plut. *Pelop*. 17. 2) is from his account of this action.

[4] These two references to an establishment of 12 Lochoi are both after Leuktra, and this prevents the proof being quite formal. But it is unlikely there was any change. The absence of Lochagoi in *Hell*. 3. 5. 22 and 4. 5. 7 is remarkable: in the same way there are no Pentekonteres in *Anab*. 4. 3. 26. The Lochagoi in the army of Asia in *Hell*. 3. 1. 18, 3. 2. 16, are no evidence for the 'establishment'. But the 'half Mora' in 4. 3. 15 must be a Lochos [or 2 Lochoi, if Xenophon's figure in Λακ. π. 11. 4 were right], and must have had its own commander. It is always unwise to infer much from Xenophon's silences.

6

which it gives to the establishment agree with 'corrected' Thucydides and are I believe right. How one figure has come to be doubled, and one halved, could no doubt be accounted for, palaeographically: but I suspect that Xenophon himself gave the wrong figures. The Army of the Ten Thousand adopted Spartan drill, and on one occasion (*Anab.* 3. 4. 21–3) formed a vanguard of 6 Lochoi, each 100 men strong, and subdivided into Pentekostyes and Enomotiai. Xenophon does not say into *how many* of these smaller formations,[1] but the table is pretty clear, viz.:

4 Enomotiai of 25 men each
=2 Pentekostyes of 50 men each
=1 Lochos of 100 men.

Xenophon's own rearguard was probably formed on the same principle, since it too contained Enomotiai (4. 3. 26). I suspect that the memory of this 'para-Spartan' formation has affected the figures in *Λακ. π.* 11. 4. It is quite impossible that the Spartan Lochos was ever as small as this.

The Pentekostys of the Ten Thousand was thus almost certainly *fifty men.* The Spartan Pentekostys was usually much stronger, even in the field: but its battle strength varied, and its barracks strength (which alone was constant) would be higher still: 160 men. On the other hand, there are *forty-eight* Pentekostyes in the establishment, and this is as near to 50 as a multiple of 6 can be. I suggest then that though the Pentekostys may have been often thought of as a 'nominal 50 men' it was in its original meaning a 'fiftieth part'.[2] I find some support for this hypothesis in the fact that it allows a plausible analysis of the Obal Army.

Sparta in 480/479, Herodotos says, was a city 'of 8,000 men': the force of 5,000 hoplites which she sent to Plataea is ἡ νεότης.[3] If we take these figures literally, they give a proportion of 40 to 25: 40 year-classes is 20–60 (the ἄνδρες), 25 year-classes is 20–45 (the νεότης). The νεότης corresponds to the Roman *iuniores*, the field army: the ἄνδρες to *iuniores-plus-seniores*, field army and home guard together.[4] For the field army of 5,000 the 25 year-classes give an Enomotia of 25.

[1] Arrian, *Tact.* 6. 3, is referring to *Anab.* 3. 4. 21 and 4. 3. 26: he ignores *Λακ. π.*

[2] Momigliano calls my attention to the theory of L. Zancan, that *Centuria* originally meant a *hundredth part*: *Atti Ist. Veneto*, xciii (1933–4), p. 869. I am not competent to judge this theory, which Momigliano has criticized in *Studia et Documenta*, ii (1938), p. 510 f., 'Studi sugli ordinamenti centuriati'.

[3] Hdt. 7. 234. 2, 9. 10. 1, 9. 12. 2.

[4] Meyer, *Kl. Schr.* ii, pp. 267–8. I owe this parallel to Momigliano. It seems to me a promising analogy. Were those over 60 excluded from the Obal *Katalogos* and the Ekklesia (*sexagenarii de ponte*, Meyer, 267, n. 3)? If such analogies are valid, I would trace them to the earliest Greek colonists rather than to a common Aryan origin.

Conceivably there were 2 field-enomotiai to a Pentekostys (*fifty men*), and 20 Pentekostyes to a Lochos. This leaves an enormous gap between Pentekostys and Lochos: too large a gap for the system of παραγγέλσεις (Thuc. 5. 66. 3–4). I greatly prefer to suppose that now as later there were 4 Enomotiai to the Pentekostys: this gives the following table:

25 years called out:
200 Enomotiai of 25 men each
=50 Pentekostyes of 100 men each
=5 Lochoi of 1,000 men each
=an establishment of 5,000 men.

Now compare the two armies. The *Obal Army* has 200 Enomotiai of 25 men each: the year-class is 200 strong, 25 years are called out for the occasion of Plataea: the resulting 5,000 are all Spartiates. The *Mora Army* has 192 Enomotiai of 32 men each: the year-class is 192 strong, 35 years are called out for occasions comparable to Plataea: the resulting 6,000 are only Spartiate in part. That is to say: (A) the age has been raised and consequently a rather smaller year-class gives a rather larger establishment; (B) the establishment is no longer pure Spartiate but is laced more or less liberally with 'embodied men';[1] (C) the Obal Army works with exact round figures and is a paper strength, but the Mora Army has non-round figures and calculates with a margin.

The reason of (A) and (B) is fairly clearly the crisis of man-power which followed the earthquake of *c.* 465 B.C. (A) is a *loi de trois ans*:[2] the numerical changes are all consequent upon it. The call-out of 35 years could not give the round figures which the 25 years had done: it produced 6 major formations instead of 5, and 192 and 48 (*vice* 200 and 50) are multiples of 6. Round totals (e.g. 6,000 in *Hell.* 4. 2. 16) are now got by calculating with a margin. Before the earthquake Sparta had reckoned to find 200 Spartiates a year, to make a νεότης

---

[1] The technical term is possibly συντεταγμένοι: Xen. *Hell.* 3. 3. 7, among many other technicalities (but another sense is possible there). Cf. *Vect.* 2. 3, and Plato's ψυχὴ συντεταγμένη σώματι, *Laws* 903 d: in these passages something is *incorporated* in something different. But the word often means simply *enrolled* as one among others (such must be its meaning in 6. 5. 29, since these Helots were not embodied in the establishment): 'under arms' (Dem. 21. 223), 'disciplined' (Th. 3. 108. 3; Xen. *Hell.* 4. 8. 22), 'professionals' (*Hiero*, 10. 6–7).

[2] Sc. it prolongs the time with the colours. Attention was given to the physique of men past youth ἐξ ὧν ἤδη καὶ αἱ μέγισται ἀρχαὶ καθίστανται [I think this means men over 30: cf. Λακ. π. 2. 2] . . . ὅπως δύναιντο . . . στρατιωτικοὺς πόνους ὑποφέρειν: Xen. Λακ. π. 4. 7. It was necessary to raise the age because, though by embodying perioikoi the year-class was kept at almost the old strength (192: 200), yet the perioikoi could not now be asked to provide a substantial second force as in 479. We seldom (e.g. *Hell.* 5. 3. 9) hear of perioikoi outside the establishment, except the Skiritai.

of 5,000 or 8,000 ἄνδρες. After it, she found 192 per year, but only by 'embodying' non-Spartiates. The lacing got more and more liberal. At Leuktra there were only 700 Spartiates, and 300 of these were the Guard, which leaves 400 for the 4 Morai present: 100 per Mora, only one man in ten. Of the 700, 400 were killed (*Hell*. 6. 4. 15): there were 300 survivors from the battle and 200 in the other 2 Morai, 500 survivors in all. Xenophon hardly exaggerates when he says (*Ages*. 2. 24) that the battle cost Sparta half of the whole Spartiate strength: of the fighting age, 20–55, 400 were killed and 500 left. A grim situation.

How were casualties replaced? In the Morai by fresh 'embodiments': here was a large reserve pool which could keep the year-class of 192 always up to strength.[1] In the Obal Army the year-classes of 200 must either have been extremely nominal or we must suppose a reserve of Spartiate population. Probably the latter: the 5,000 was not a *levée en masse*, even of the ages called out: the *Katalogos* was rather larger than the actual formations.[2] This would not meet heavy losses: it could not cope with the earthquake losses. The tradition that the Spartans fought at Dipaia in a single line (Isokr. 6. 99) no doubt preserves the memory of the Obal Army depleted by that catastrophe, before the system of 'embodiment' was adopted. For concreteness, let us suppose that the Enomotia of 25 was normally in 5 lines of 5: the implication will be that each Enomotia had lost four-fifths of its strength, or rather that only one-fifth could take the field in Arkadia.[3]

Could πεντηκοστύς mean a *fiftieth part*? Ἑκατοστύς in the Ionian cities certainly means a 'nominal 100 men' (not a hundredth): χιλιαστύς is a 'nominal 1,000'. Xenophon probably thought πεντηκοστύς meant a 'nominal 50' (*Anab*. 3. 4. 21 ff., cited above) and he uses ἑκατοστύς as his own word for a body of 100 chariots (*Cyrop*. 6. 3. 34). The fractional sense is less likely with high figures: is τριττύς too low a figure to be compared? It sometimes means a *three*, but its standard sense is a *third part*, a 'Riding': and it is near, in place and time, to the Spartan

---

[1] The Morai are regularly called τὸ πολιτικὸν (στράτευμα) or οἱ πολῖται: Xen. *Hell*. 4. 4. 19, 5. 3. 25, 5. 4. 41, 5. 4. 55, 6. 4. 26, 7. 1. 28, 7. 4. 20 (cf. 27): contrast 6. 5. 21. Τῶν πολιτικῶν μορῶν in *Λακ*. *π*. 11. 4 is correct (codd. et Harpocr.) though ὁπλιτικῶν (Stob.) makes sense.

[2] Aristotle says (*Pol*. 1270[a]37) the Spartiates had once 10,000 men (of fighting age? supply ὁπλίτας vel. sim. from 1270[a]30). Aristotle studied the Obal Army, and I would like to take this as a responsible figure: and further to believe that Suidas s.v. ἐνωμοτία goes back to him, 'a formation of 25 men'. But this is no doubt an inference from the view that it is a half-Pentekostys, and goes back rather to Xenophon: and the 10,000 Spartiates are probably only a round figure.

[3] I am positing that Dipaia is between the earthquake and the battle of Ithome (or Isthmos, Hdt. 9. 35. 2): this means immediately after the earthquake, the same time as the 300 are lost in Messenia (9. 64. 2). The 'single line' is legendary, no doubt: so too the faked epiphany in Polyaen. 1. 41. 1. A legendary moment.

πεντηκοστύες, if these be as old as I believe: if, that is, the words ὠβὰς ὠβάξαντα record their creation.

They were created, I believe, like the Attic Demes, to replace the Phratries of the Tribal Army. For that Army we may perhaps compare *Odyss.* 3. 7–8 (a people paraded for a hecatomb, cf. l. 59), with the account of the Karneia which Demetrios of Skepsis gives in Athen. 141 *e, f.* Exact figures are tempting but delusive.

EUPATRIDAI, ARCHONS, AND AREOPAGUS[1]

I. INTRODUCTORY

WILAMOWITZ (*Staat und Gesellschaft*, 74) denies that there was ever any definite status of Nobility ('ein rechtlich irgendwie abgesonderter Stand der Adligen') in Athens: his reason is, that Solon says nothing of such a thing. *E silentio* and very dangerous: and in fact a remnant of Privilege of Nobility survived into the fourth century at least; φυλοβασιλεῖς ἐξ Εὐπατριδῶν (Pollux, VIII. 111). This puts it beyond question that Eupatrid-hood (*a*) was capable of definition, and (*b*) carried privilege.

Except for the Eupatridai, there was no other Nobility of birth in Athens, and the Eupatridai lost the bulk of their privileges by Solon's legislation: the attempt in 580 B.C. to recover some portion came to very little (v. infra).

Toepffer (*Attische Genealogie*, 1889) catalogues the known Athenian Genê (γένη = Clans), and assumes that the aggregate of their members (Gennetai) forms a Nobility. Francotte (*La Polis Grecque*, 1907, pp. 1–91: *L'organisation de la Cité athénienne*) frankly identifies Gennetai and Eupatridai. The identity is assumed by Busolt-Swoboda (*Griech. Staatskunde* II, 1926, p. 772, n. 2). I believe this to be false, and give my reasons in the following pages. For lucidity's sake I append definitions of some of the terms involved.

A GENOS (plural Genê: the members are GENNETAI) [e.g. the Eteoboutadai, ps-Plutarch, *Ten Orators*, 841 B] is technically a group of Athenians connected by fictional common ancestry: fictional, because the alleged ancestor is always mythical. We

---

[1] My references only faintly indicate how much I owe to previous writers, especially those I most attack—Wilamowitz, Toepffer, Francotte, Ledl. I could not indeed remember all my obligations, but I must especially discharge a debt to Professor J. A. Smith, who some years ago pointed out to me the inadequacy of the current views of the fragment of the 'Aθ. πολ., from which my paper starts, and made on that and many other topics suggestions which I hope have not been fruitless.

shall see that Aristotle ascribes their formation to the time of Ion. Membership of a Genos passes in a male line: you belong to the same Genos as your father. Members of a Genos (*Gennetai* technically: Herodotus also uses συγγενέες,[1] 5. 66. 1) shared certain religious cults, and belonged *en masse* to a Phratry.

THIASOS is a non-technical word meaning (in this connexion) a religious group of the size and nature of a Genos: i.e. a Genos is a Thiasos, but not all Thiasoi are based upon fictional kinship. A *Phratry* at Athens was subdivided into Thiasoi (*I.G.* II². 1237, ll. 73 sqq.) of which some may have been Genê. [We do not know if this was true of all Phratries.]

ORGEON ('Ὀργεών=partaker of rites) is a non-technical word for a member of a Thiasos or any similar small religious group. Gennetai could probably be called *Orgeones* in the same way as Peers can be called Gentlemen: but the distinction could also be made (as e.g. in the phrase 'My Lords and Gentlemen').[2]

A PHRATRY [the best known is the Dekeleieis[3] (*I.G.* II². 1237) which I take as typical: but considerable variety of internal organization is likely in the various Phratries] is a religious group composed of several Genê and/or other Thiasoi. Before Kleisthenes had created the Ten (Modern) Tribes (507 B.C.), each of the Four (Ancient) Tribes was, we are told, composed of three Phratries: after Kleisthenes, the Phratries and the Tribes are cross-divisions, neither subdivides the other. Every Athenian citizen[4] must belong both to a Phratry (i.e. be inscribed in a Phraterikon Grammateion) and to a Tribe (i.e. be inscribed in a Lexiarchikon Grammateion[5]).

How did a Gennete differ from a non-Gennete in Aristotle's time? Except for some hereditary priesthoods, the distinction was

---

[1] So Isaeus, *Apollodorus* 26, says γεννῆται, and 27 συγγενεῖς, of the same people.

[2] It appears to be made in Philochorus (*F. gr. H.* 328 F 35), τοὺς δὲ φράτορας ἐπάναγκες δέχεσθαι καὶ τοὺς ὀργεῶνας καὶ τοὺς ὁμογάλακτας οὓς γεννήτας καλοῦμεν.

[3] This, and not Demotionidai, is the name of the Phratry: in which the Demotionidai hold a position like that of the archaic Areopagus in the state. I hope to publish a paper on this later [below, pp. 116 ff.].

[4] So Socrates implies, Plato *Euthydemus* 302 C, D: such exceptional cases as Plangon's children (Demosthenes 39 and 40, bastards of pure Athenian descent) are perhaps exceptions. What became of such bastards' children? Did there arise a large class of half-citizens? I believe not: society contrived (I do not know exactly how) to keep its exceptions exceptional.

[5] The Tribe was subdivided into three Ridings (Trittyes) and each Riding into an indeterminate number of Demes (=civil parishes). The Lexiarchikon Grammateion was kept in each Deme.

unimportant. I think it unlikely that the whole of any one Genos was Eupatrid, since the Eupatridai were conceived as created long after the formation of the Genê.

II. Ion and Theseus

One of the fragments of the lost chapters of the 'Aθηναίων Πολιτεία gives a curious picture of the archaic Athenian nation. 'There were four Tribes (Phylai), in imitation of the four seasons of the year: and each Tribe was divided in three parts, making twelve parts in all, like the twelve months: these parts were called Ridings[1] (Trittyes) and Phratries. And each Phratry had thirty Genê, as each month thirty days: and each Genos had thirty men [called Gennetai].' The passage is quoted, or referred to, by several authors: and in all the quotations we have the further statement that the nation so divided and subdivided was composed of two classes of men, Georgoi and Demiourgoi. It appears quite clear that it was the nation composed of these two classes which was divided into Tribes, Phratries, and Genê: since this point is of importance, I quote the Greek words in question.

γεννήτη: 'Aριστοτέλης φησὶ τοῦ ὅλου πλήθους διηρημένου 'Aθήνησιν εἴς τε τοὺς γεωργοὺς καὶ δημιουργούς, φυλὰς αὐτῶν εἶναι τέτταρας, etc., *Schol. Plat. Axioch.* p. 465 Bk. (cf. Moiris, γεννῆται, who writes διεκεκόσμητο δ ί χ α).

γεννῆται: πάλαι τὸ τῶν 'Aθηναίων πλῆθος, πρὶν ἢ Κλεισθένη διοικήσασθαι τὰ περὶ τὰς φυλάς, διῃρεῖτο εἰς γεωργοὺς καὶ δημιουργούς. Καὶ φυλαὶ τούτων ἦσαν δ', etc., ... ὡς ἱστορεῖ ἐν τῇ 'Aθηναίων Πολιτείᾳ 'Aριστοτέλης λέγων οὕτως· 'φυλὰς δὲ αὐτῶν συννενεμῆσθαι δ', etc.', *Lexic. Demosth. Patm.* p. 152 (*Bull. de corr. hellén.* I. 1877). (A similar quotation in Suidas, s.v.)

It is, I repeat, perfectly clear that the whole nation (divisible into Tribes, Phratries, Genê, Gennetai) consisted of the two Estates, *Georgoi* and *Demiourgoi*. This may seem surprising, and some scholars may still prefer to follow Kaibel-Wilamowitz in their insertion of ⟨Εὐπατρίδας καὶ⟩ before γεωργούς, in spite of the unanimity of the quotations: but the suggestion of Blass, that the words 'τὸ τῶν 'Aθηναίων πλῆθος' and 'τοῦ ὅλου πλήθους' mean 'the whole commonalty (as distinct from the nobility)' is, in this

---

[1] I find the word *Trittys* very unmanageable in English: and *Riding* (=Thirding: cf. farthing=fourthing) translates it exactly.

context, frankly absurd: or will anyone maintain that the Eupatridai were outside the Four Tribes, outside the Genê, and that no Gennete was an Eupatrid?[1]

There is however, as I believe, no difficulty requiring either emendation or special interpretation: the only adjustment needed is to number these passages as 'Fragment 2', and to realize that Aristotle is talking of a time before Theseus. This is indeed so self-evident that I am astounded at the way all editors have followed Rose in placing this fragment (=Rose 385) later than Theseus, and all historians have accepted the implication. Rose had not ch. 41 before him,[2] but his successors have: in ch. 41 § 2 Aristotle says plainly 'the first adjustment was in the time of Ion: *for then first they were divided into the four tribes.*' The Epitome of Herakleides gives two stages before Theseus: (1) Ion; (2) Pandion and his sons: need I argue further that our fragments refer to the 'Ion' stage?

The origin, then, of the *Gennetai*, in the Genê and Phratries and Tribes, was put by Aristotle in the time of Ion, and in Fragment 1 (=Rose 381) we hear of the cult of Apollo Πατρῷος (which was proper to the Gennetai) likewise in the time of Ion. Rose 381 and Rose 385 both belong to the time of Ion, and should be numbered '*Aθ. πoλ.* Fragments 1 and 2. The further implications of this rearrangement are of the first importance, namely:

1. The Gennetai at the time of Ion are conceived as *the whole nation*, numbering over 10,000 ἄνδρες. *They are in no sense a nobility.*

2. At the time of Ion, the Eupatridai are not yet conceived to exist (we shall see their creation belongs to the 'Theseus' stage). The Nobility and Commonalty are not yet distinguished in that

---

[1] Francotte's explanation (*La Polis Grecque*, Paderborn, 1907, p. 10) of these passages deserves attention. He believes it was two different elements of the population which were divided in these two ways: the πλῆθος into Georgoi and Demiourgoi, the others (the Gennetai, whom he conceives as the only full citizens, and exclusive of the πλῆθος: *he identifies them with the Eupatridai*) into Tribes, Phratries, and Genê. This cannot of course be got out of the passages as they stand: Francotte says 'the lexicographers have not grasped Aristotle's thought'. Lexicographers often err, and they follow each other like sheep (though here the remarkable unanimity of the error is not due to copying, for two of the quotations are evidently quite independent of each other). I reject Francotte's view, not because I trust the lexicographers absolutely, but because it contains the fundamental fallacy of his whole essay: *Gennetai cannot be identified with Eupatridai.*

[2] He consequently took Plut. *Thes.* 25 to mean that Aristotle represented Theseus as the creator of the *Three* Estates: a natural enough inference. Next he assumed that the γεννῆται fragments (Rose 385) referred to the creation of the same Three Estates (see his critical note 'omiserunt τοὺς Εὐπατρίδας, Lex. Sch. Moeris').

way: all Athenians are Gennetai, and all are divided into the
Two Estates, Georgoi and Demiourgoi.

3. Many scholars (e.g. Toepffer, Francotte, see above) have,
tacitly or explicitly, equated Gennetai and Eupatridai, and have
regarded both alike as constituting the Nobility of Athens.[1] This
is totally different from Aristotle's conception. For him, the
Eupatridai are a younger institution than the Gennetai, and much
more exclusive.

It is likely that in Aristotle's day a Gennete was far commoner
than a Eupatrid. Neither was a vague term: either you were or
were not inscribed in a Genos: either you were or were not born
in the Caste of Eupatridai. Though Gennetai were commoner
than Eupatridai, not every Athenian was a Gennete: how and
when non-Gennetai entered the citizen body is matter for a separate
enquiry.[2] A Gennete's citizenship was conceived to be very
ancient, more ancient than the nobility of any Eupatrid, though
(since I imagine every Eupatrid family belonged to some Genos)
not more ancient than the Eupatrid's citizenship. But Gennete-
hood implies no nobility:[3] it does not exclude the possibility that
for any given Gennete all the thirty generations (in the 1,000
years between Ion and Aristotle) might be small farmers, or even
labourers or artisans.

Before Theseus, then, and from the time of Ion, the Athenian
nation was, according to Aristotle, divided into the two Estates,
Georgoi and *Demiourgoi*.[4] I postpone to another occasion the consideration of what these Estates meant: and proceed at once to the

---

[1] Typical is Toepffer's note, *Att. Gen.*, p. 170, note 2, on the Hesychidai: who evidently *are* Gennetai and are *not* Eupatridai.

[2] It is the main topic of Francotte's first essay in his *La Polis Grecque*, to which
stimulating and lucid work let me refer, πείθεσθαί γε μὲν οὐ παντάπασιν ὀφείλω.

[3] *Nobility* is not a Greek word: they need be neither εὐπατρίδαι nor γνώριμοι. What
they must be is ἰθαγενεῖς: cf. the constant gloss in Hesychios, γένος τι 'Αθήνησι ἰθαγε-
νῶν (s.v. 'Ησυχίδαι, Λυκομίδαι, etc.).

[4] I note that Strabo agrees with Aristotle in ascribing to Ion the division of the
Athenians both into Tribes and into Estates (βίοι): 8. 7. 1, πρῶτον μὲν εἰς τέτταρας
φυλὰς διεῖλε τὸ πλῆθος, εἶτα εἰς τέτταρας βίους· τοὺς μὲν γὰρ γεωργοὺς ἀπέδειξε, τοὺς
δὲ δημιουργούς, τοὺς δὲ ἱεροποιούς, τετάρτους δὲ τοὺς φύλακας. Here are four Estates,
not two, yet even so no Eupatridai: it was apparently accepted by ancient scholars
that there were no Eupatridai before Theseus.

Whom is Strabo following? Evidently not Aristotle. Are the four Estates due to an
attempt to interpret the Tribe names vocationally? or are the two extra Estates intended to be those whom *later* Theseus called Eupatridai? The notion of an Estate of
φύλακες suggests that Plato's *Republic* has been published for some time; I should think
for some generations.

time of Theseus, and the founding of the Order of Nobility, the Eupatridai.

We have two accounts of this event: one in Plutarch's *Theseus*, ch. 25, which is evidently taken largely from Aristotle and should be printed as a fragment of the 'Aθ. πολ. (as indeed many editors, e.g. Kenyon in *O.C.T.*, print it: only it should be Fragment 3, not Fragment 2): the other in Thucydides 2. 14. That much of the Plutarch passage is taken from Aristotle is clear from a comparison of Plut. *Thes*. 25. 1. with the Epitome of Herakleides, Θησεὺς δὲ ἐκήρυξε καὶ συνεβίβασε τούτους ἐπ' ἴσῃ καὶ ὁμοίᾳ. This is the account:

§ 1. 'Wishing to increase the city still more, he summoned all men on equal terms: and the proclamation "Come hither all ye peoples" is said to be his, when he made a gathering of the whole nation.

§ 2. 'He did not, however, acquiesce in the confusion and mixture produced in the democracy by this influx of an undiscriminated mass: instead, he was the first to separate the Eupatridai and the Geomoroi and Demiourgoi: and, by assigning to the Eupatridai religious authority and a monopoly of the archonship, and by making them teachers of the laws and interpreters (*Exegetai*) of matters sacred and profane, he thus put them on a level, so to speak, with the other citizens: the Eupatridai's strong point was their splendour, the Geomoroi's their usefulness, the Demiourgoi's their number.

§ 3. 'And Aristotle's statement, that he was the first to incline to the crowd and let go the royal power, is confirmed, I think, by Homer, who in the Catalogue used the word *Demos* of no one except the Athenians.'

Plutarch is, of course, notorious for the freedom or laxity with which he paraphrases his sources:[1] there are certain things here which are probably not due to Aristotle. For instance, *Geomoroi* instead of *Georgoi*: and, more important perhaps, Aristotle is likely to have said that he 'separated the Eupatridai *from* the Georgoi and Demiourgoi' rather than that he simply ἀπέκρινε χωρὶς εὐπατρίδας καὶ γεωμόρους καὶ δημιουργούς. That in fact

---

[1] See e.g. Flickinger, *Plutarch as a Source of Information on the Greek Theatre*, pp. 10 sqq.; H. J. Rose, *The Roman Questions of Plutarch*, p. 15.

Plutarch had the former in mind, and not the latter, is fairly clear from the clause following, 'and giving the Eupatridai certain functions, he thus put them on a level (so to speak) with the other citizens: the Eupatridai's strong point was their splendour, the Geomoroi's their usefulness, the Demiourgoi's their number'. The other two Estates had their functions (*ergo* existed) already: Theseus creates certain functions for his new Estate, the Eupatridai, so that honours are now easy.

But indeed the whole chapter, in language and in thought, is so like Plutarch and unlike Aristotle, that those editors (e.g. Thalheim, Mathieu) who print only § 3 as a fragment of Aristotle have some reason: for if we once desert the strait path of explicit quotation, and attempt to include as fragments all passages which seem to have been influenced by Aristotle, we are attempting a problem of literary history harder and more dangerous than the assembling of fragments. Yet § 1 is fairly guaranteed by the Epitome: and in § 3 Aristotle's name is mentioned: it is hardly likely that the information in § 2 is from a different source. The motivation, the moralizing (in a phrase, the Plutarchan style), are Plutarch's: the *information* which remains is—

1. Theseus first separated the Eupatridai from the other citizens.
2. He gave them certain functions, religious, legal, and political (the archonship).

I believe this information is from Aristotle. It exactly fills the gap in his narrative between the 'Ion' stage when there were no Eupatrids, and the 'Solon' stage when the Eupatrid monopoly of the archonship is destroyed.

Before turning to the account in Thucydides (which deals with the συνοίκισις, the unifying and centralizing of Attica), it may be well to consider what part Aristotle ascribed to Theseus in this Synoikisis, and whether he connected it with the creation of the Eupatrid Order.

Plutarch certainly makes this connexion, *Theseus* 32. 1, the complaints of the δυνατοί against Theseus: 'they considered he had taken away their rule and kingship from each of the local Eupatridai (τῶν κατὰ δῆμον εὐπατριδῶν), and enclosing them all in one city used them as subjects and slaves'. Of course, Plutarch or his source may have conflated Aristotle with Thucydides.[1] As for Aristotle himself, the summary in 'Aθ. πολ. 41 does not expressly mention the Synoikisis at all: the Epitome of Herakleides contains one hint of it, namely Θησεὺς δὲ ἐκήρυξε καὶ συνεβίβασε τούτους (sc. the sons of Pandion?) ἐπ' ἴσῃ καὶ ὁμοίᾳ, and the passage here epitomized is probably copied by Plutarch, *Theseus* 25. 1 (quoted above: the proclamation 'Come hither all ye peoples').

This proclamation, and gathering of the peoples, is the only trace I can find in Aristotle of the Synoikisis: it is directly juxtaposed with the creation of the Eupatrid Order. Both he and Thucydides assume that the unity of the Attic nation existed in principle long before: Theseus (according to Thucydides, and I see no reason to doubt that Aristotle agreed) put it into permanent practice by some sort of assembling in the capital, and organizing, of the local chieftains.[2]

I turn to the passage of Thucydides: in which we have, it seems to me, an account of the *origin of the Areopagus* which is less mythical than that of Aeschylus, and far more valuable than the learned speculations quoted by Plutarch in his *Solon*, ch. 19. It has been strangely neglected: Ledl, for instance,[3] reviewing the evidence for the Areopagus before Solon, says there clearly was a Court of Law on the Areopagus, but finds no reason to suppose there was a *Boulé* there: yet he does not even mention this passage.

Thucydides is speaking of the evacuation of the Attic countryside in 431 B.C., and says (2. 14. 2), 'it was difficult, because most

---

[1] This is not very likely. The discontent of which Plutarch speaks (which resulted in the betrayal of Aphidna) appears already in Herodotus 9. 73.

[2] Plutarch gives a full account of the Synoikisis in ch. 24, and this gathering of the peoples in ch. 25: he assumes them to be different, and joins them together with the typical words ἔτι δὲ μᾶλλον αὐξῆσαι τὴν πόλιν βουλόμενος. This sort of phrase is familiar in Plutarch, when, finding one event in two sources, he duplicates it: cf. Kimon's two returns from Ithome (*Kimon* 17), joined by the words οἱ δὲ Λακεδαιμόνιοι τοὺς 'Αθηναίους αὖθις ἐκάλουν ἐπὶ τοὺς ἐν 'Ιθώμῃ.
[Francotte endeavours to detect some difference in principle between Aristotle and Thucydides: Aristotle ascribing the main work to Ion, Thucydides to Theseus; Aristotle conceiving a union of tribes, Thucydides a union of states (*Polis*, pp. 6–8). He admits that his main purpose is to *define* these two procedures, and he begs 'pour plus de facilité à les placer, l'une sous le patronage de Thucydide, ce qui est justifié, l'autre sous le patronage d'Aristote, ce qui l'est peut-être moins.' I do not see (the fundamental point) that Aristotle ascribes the main work to Ion. Francotte does not suggest (as some have done) to alter συνοικήσαντος αὐτοῖς, in the Epitome, to συνοικίσαντος αὐτούς, or to read with Kenyon συνοικισάντων in ch. 41, § 2. See the editors *ad haec loca*, and cf. ch. 3, § 2.]

[3] *Studien zur aelteren athenischen Verfassungsgeschichte*, Heidelberg (1914), pp. 286–336.

of them had been always accustomed to live in the country'. He continues (ch. 15):

§ 1. From very early times the Athenians had observed this custom more than others. For under Kekrops and the first Kings, down to the time of Theseus, the inhabitants of Attica had their separate cities, and the cities had their own Town Halls and magistrates (πρυτανεῖά τε ἐχούσας καὶ ἄρχοντας): and when there was no danger, they did not meet to take part in the King's Council, but the men of each community did their own town business and had their own council: and there were even wars between some of them, as between the Eleusinians (under Eumolpos) and Erechtheus.

§ 2. But when Theseus became king, being a clear-sighted and also a powerful man, he set the land in order, and especially he abolished the Council-Houses and magistrates (τά τε βουλευτήρια καὶ τὰς ἀρχάς) in the separate cities, and establishing one Council-House and Town Hall (ἓν βουλευτήριον ἀποδείξας καὶ πρυτανεῖον), he collected them all in what is now the City: each community was to possess the area it had had before, but he compelled them to make this their single city: which (by this participation of them all) became great, and was bequeathed so by Theseus to his successors. And from his day to the present the Athenians celebrate the *Synoikia* in honour of Athena as a public festival.

§ 3. Previously what is now the 'Akropolis' was the city, with the parts immediately under it, especially to the south.

Thucydides does not mention the Areopagus by name. It is tempting to suppose that he meant, by the ἓν βουλευτήριον which Theseus established, an actual Council-House on Ares' Hill (in the immediate neighbourhood of the Akropolis, as the passage demands). Perhaps he did: at present I would rather not prejudge the questions involved—whether Thucydides had one single building in mind (in the phrase ἓν βουλευτήριον ἀποδείξας καὶ πρυτανεῖον) or two, or none: what and where the *Prytaneion* was: whether in his famous correction of Herodotus (1. 126. 8, Hdt. 5. 71. 2) he means to deny the existence of πρυτάνεις τῶν Ναυκράρων: if not, who they were, and what their relation was to the Phylobasileis who (also) sat in the *Prytaneion*. I hope to examine these questions elsewhere, and meanwhile refer to Eduard Meyer's brilliant speculations.[1] One point: supposing Thucydides meant that Theseus' new Council sat in the *Prytaneion* (as seems to be commonly assumed) they might still be the Areopagus Council. ῾Η ἐξ Ἀρείου πάγου βουλή did not always deliberate on Ares' Hill,[2] nor (so far as I know) is there concrete evidence of a very ancient Bouleuterion there. The function inseparable from the Hill was the trial of certain forms of homicide, and all murder trials at Athens were in the open air. Δικάζουσιν ἐν ἱερῷ καὶ ὑπαίθριοι,[3] in a place consecrated but unroofed. The Areopagites in Aeschylus' *Eumenides* are in the open air.

I leave aside, then, the question whether there was a Bouleuterion on Ares' Hill in these days long before Solon. It does not affect my conclusions:

First: that in this Royal Council[4] established by Theseus, Thucydides is describing the Areopagus. The local nobles are compelled to dissolve their own councils and attend the King's Council.

Secondly: Thucydides associates the formation of this Council with the Union of Attica achieved by Theseus. [N.B.—Thucydides is careful not to imply a creation out of the void. The Royal Council, as a permanent body representative of all Attica, begins with Theseus: but before Theseus such a Council may have met in emergencies, ὁπότε τι δείσειαν.]

Thirdly: Thucydides believed these great events were celebrated at the *Synoikia*.

---

[1] *G. d. Alt.* II., § 233 and § 365. Criticism (not always cogent) of some of his views in De Sanctis, *ATΘIΣ*[2], pp. 187–8. See also Gertrude Smith, *Cl. Phil.* XVI. (1921), 345 sqq., 'The Prytaneum in the Athenian Amnesty Law.'

[2] It often sat in the Stoa Basileia, Demosth. 25. 23. For this Stoa, see Busolt-Swoboda, *Gr. Staatskunde* II. (1926), 792: Judeich, *Topographie* 296 sq.: and for the form, *I.G.* I[2]. 115, line 8.

[3] Aristotle uses these words of the other four homicide courts ('Aθ. πολ. 57. 4), but they apply to the Areopagus also, Pollux 8. 118. Antiphon's evidence is explicit: ἅπαντα τὰ δικαστήρια ἐν ὑπαίθρῳ δικάζει τὰς δίκας τοῦ φόνου (*Herodes* 11).

[4] The President of the Areopagus is, in historic times, the Archon Basileus, 'Aθ. πολ. 57, 4, Pollux 8. 90. For various views on the origin of the Areopagus Council, see J. J. Terwen, *De Areopago Atheniensium quaestiones variae* (Diss. Utrecht, 1894), Cap. I, 'De Areopagi origine vv. doctorum opiniones': and in A. Ledl's valuable book *Studien zur aelteren athenischen Verfassungsgeschichte* (Heidelberg, 1914), the chapter (III. 2, p. 286 sqq.) 'Die Einsetzung des areopagitischen Rates'. Ledl reaches the conclusion that the Areopagus as a Law Court is older than Solon, but as a Council was created by him: this, however, without considering our passage of Thucydides at all. For the natural conjunction of the two functions, see *Hymn to Demeter*, 150 sqq.:

ἀνέρας, οἶσιν ἔπεστι μέγα κράτος ἐνθάδε τιμῆς,
δήμου τε προὔχουσιν, ἰδὲ κρήδεμνα πόληος
εἰρύαται βουλῇσι καὶ ἰθείῃσι δίκῃσιν.

Thucydides, then, says that Theseus first established the Council of the Areopagus as a permanent Royal Council, compelling the local nobles to attend it.

Aristotle appears to say, Theseus was first founder of the Order of Nobility called Eupatridai, and gave them certain religious, legal, and political functions.

Are not these two ways of saying the same thing? The Areopagus and the Eupatrid Order are two aspects of the same Peerage: *Patres* and *Patricii*. Thucydides' Areopagus is composed of the Nobility: Aristotle's Nobility have the functions of the Areopagus. It is remarkable, in a matter of such antiquity, to find two accounts, obviously independent, tallying so well. I will not invoke 'folkmemory'. It cannot be that the truth about Theseus was available to the writers in such solidity that they could (so to speak) draw from the life different aspects of it. How, then, was the tradition of the Synoikisis preserved?

I must here forgo the pleasant enquiry, how Theseus won his place in Hellenic myth.[1] In the lovely archaic group at Eretria, in the metopes of the Athenian Treasure-house at Delphi, in the masterpiece of the Panaitios painter, in the delicious verses of Bacchylides and the graver beauty of the *Oedipus at Kolonos*, he enchants us, τῶν ἐν Ἑλλάδι τερπνῶν λαχὼν οὐκ ὀλίγαν δόσιν. Of the two systematic 'Lives' which have survived, Apollodorus (III. 16 and *Epitome I*) draws, as his custom is, wholly from the earlier[2] poets and mythographers: it is *historia poetica*. Plutarch's *Theseus* covers much of the same ground, but he draws on a second testimony, that of ritual: *Oschophoria, Kybernesia, Synoikia*,[3] *Panathenaia*, and many other feasts and sacrifices. It is this latter element which he gets from Aristotle, or a source similar to Aristotle, the Attic antiquarians.[4] Thucydides' account of the

---

[1] See Gruppe, *Gr. Myth.* (1906), pp. 581 sqq.; Preller-Robert, *Gr. Myth.* (1921) II. 2, pp. 676 sqq.; Roscher, *Lexicon*, s.v. (1919–20). Theseus' greatness is post-Solonian: for our present question, his connexion with the *Synoikia* festival is, I think, a fifth-century speculation: τὸ . . . κήρυγμα Θησέως γενέσθαι φασί, Plut. *Theseus* 25. 1.

[2] I.e. pre-Alexandrian.

[3] MSS. have *Metoikia*: but the date given is 16 Hekatombaion, and this same date is given in Schol. Aristoph. *Peace* 1019 to the *Synoikesia*. It is pretty certain that 'Metoikia=Synoikesia' is the same as Thucydides' Synoikia.

[4] Plutarch appears to have used the Ἀτθίδων Συναγωγή of Istros, the disciple of Callimachus: see M. Wellmann, *De Istro Callimachio* (Diss. Gryphiswald. 1886), Cap. II, 'De Plutarchi Thesei vita'. It is true that much even of pre-Alexandrian poetic myth is partly aetiological, made to explain ritual: as Aeschylus' *Eumenides* and the *Hymn to Demeter*. Yet the antiquarian's aetiology can be distinguished from

Synoikisis, clinched by the reference to the Synoikia, seems to me an early and admirable example of this antiquarianism: that other antiquarians worked at the same vein is evident from Plutarch, *Theseus* 24, where both Synoikia[1] and Panathenaia are referred to Theseus and the Synoikisis.

I suggest, then, that if we had the full ritual of the Synoikia and Panathenaia, we should know how to correlate those accounts of the Synoikisis which have survived. But in fact we know little of them: singularly little, when we consider that the Panathenaia was the greatest of Athenian festivals, that we can establish in some detail the programme of the Panathenaic Games, and that the Panathenaic *Pompe* is depicted on the Parthenon frieze. It would, I believe, be worth while to re-examine the evidence in this light: is not, for example, τὸ κήρυγμα Δεῦρ᾿ ἴτε πάντες λεώι part of the ritual of the Synoikia?[2] Meantime, I assume that the Synoikisis (or some movement towards effective unity) was celebrated at Athens in these two festivals, which stood at the beginning of the Attic year and followed each other in quick succession: the Synoikia on the 16th of Hekatombaion, and the

the poet's: it is quasi-scientific. I note here how strong an influence the Eupatrid *Exegetai* must have had on such aetiologies, since they both prescribed and interpreted ritual, and the *Atthis* tradition is of course dominated by them (Kleidemos, Philochorus, etc., were themselves Exegetai).

[1] See p. 96, note 3.
[2] There is a persistent tradition that Theseus abdicated at the height of his power: persistent, in spite of the great difficulty felt in digesting this into the established story (e.g. by Isocrates, *Helen* 36–7, *Panath.* 129: Aristotle rationalizes, *Ἀθ. πολ.* 41. 2: Pausanias 1. 3. 3 rejects it!).
The *Marmor Parium* appears to synchronize the Synoikisis and 'abdication' at the beginning of the reign (*Ep.* 20: see Jacoby's admirable commentary in his latest edition, *F. Gr. Hist.*, No. 239: Text 1929, Commentary 1930): the constant references in Plut. *Theseus* 24 and 25 (24. 2, 24. 4, 25. 3, cf. *Ἀθ. πολ.* 41. 2) make it certain that this connexion (Synoikisis and abdication) was commonly made. I suggest that the *Synoikia* included a ritual abdication.
The *Synoikia* is a δημοτελὴς ἑορτή, but its ritual was prescribed, interpreted, and aetiologized by Eupatrid Exegetai (see p. 96, note 4): and not even Pericles defied the Exegetai (Lysias VI. 10). Moreover, the main lines of its ritual were probably fixed before Solon, in the full tide of Eupatrid power. The word Synoikia is not, I imagine, derived from, but rather parallel to, Synoikisis: it means the gathering of the (great) houses, and marks the establishment of the Pan-Attic aristocracy. [There is nothing strange in the Democracy celebrating this: Magna Carta still stirs our hearts, though we have removed the Peers' veto.]
This Eupatrid régime began, in its full sense, when the monarchy fell (see the chronographers' tradition in Synkellos 399. 21, μετὰ τούτους ἄρχοντες ἐνιαυσιαῖοι εὑρέθησαν ἐξ Εὐπατριδῶν, ἐννέα τε ἀρχόντων Ἀθήνησιν ἀρχὴ κατεστάθη; and cf. Eur. *Suppl.* 404–7): but the Order was clearly created by a powerful king (so e.g. Thucydides argues, II. 15. 2). Telescope the two (so as to combine the maximum both of antiquity and of legitimate power) and the King must abdicate when he creates the Order.

7

Panathenaia on the 28th of the same month. I assume, further, that these festivals (or their accepted *Aitia*) kept the tradition of the Synoikisis sufficiently constant for a combination of Thucydides and Aristotle to be justified. It gives the following result:

Theseus found Attica a land of separate cities in a loose federation which was not binding except in time of danger. He made a proclamation summoning the whole nation to an assembly (πανδημίαν τινά[1]) and ordered the local rulers to dissolve their local councils and regard Athens as the one seat of government: they were to be members of the Royal Council. To form this Council, he founded an Order of Nobility, called Eupatridai, composed of the local nobles and doubtless certain Athenian nobles also; and he defined their functions. These functions were:

1. They exercised religious authority.
2. The Archons were chosen from their number.
3. They expounded the laws.
4. They were Exegetai in matters sacred and profane.

The subsequent powers of the Areopagus are composed of precisely such functions. Yet it is likely that Aristotle merely recorded, on this occasion, the creation of the Eupatrid Order, with its functions: he does not appear to have constated the other aspect, the origin of the Areopagus Council.

It is well to define as exactly as possible the relation between the Areopagus and the Eupatridai. I conceive it as follows (A and B may, of course, be fictional):

A. The Eupatridai were, first, those local chiefs whom Theseus assembled at Athens and entrusted with certain functions.

B. The Areopagus was, first, the Council composed of those chiefs.

C. The Eupatridai were, later, the descendants in direct male line of those chiefs (or, if A is fictional, members of certain houses supposed to be so descended).

D. The Areopagus was, later, a Council and a Court of Law, composed exclusively of Eupatridai.

How was membership of the Areopagus confined to Eupatridai? It was (for at least some generations before Solon) composed of

---

[1] Which I conceive the *Synoikia* to have represented.

ex-Archons, and only a Eupatrid could be an Archon. If it be true (as Aristotle says, ch. 8, § 2) that the Areopagus appointed the Archons until Solon's time, this amounts to co-option by the Areopagites from amongst the Eupatridai.

Why was membership of the Areopagus confined to Eupatridai? Because its functions were such as in an aristocratic society could only be properly performed by the hereditary *Aristoi*. The words of Plutarch (*Theseus* 25) εὐπατρίδαις δὲ γινώσκειν τὰ θεῖα καὶ παρέχειν ἄρχοντας ἀποδοὺς καὶ νόμων διδασκάλους εἶναι καὶ ὁσίων καὶ ἱερῶν ἐξηγητάς, are a not inapt description of the functions of an aristocracy in an archaic state. They alone inherit knowledge about religion and law, things which have to be done in proper form and in consequence depend upon knowledge:[1] they alone are capable of governing.

A Governing Caste: and the magistrates and the Governing Council chosen from its members.[2]

We shall find that when (owing to the growth of capacity outside the caste) Solon opens the Council to others besides Eupatridai, the Council continues to perform many of its 'noble' functions, though diluted with non-noble blood. It becomes indeed much less important: but such of its old legal and judicial functions as are not usurped by the Demos continue to be performed by the new Areopagus, and are not reserved to the Eupatridai. The same is true of most of its religious functions, but we find some few offices, in this most conservative of all spheres, reserved to Eupatrids right down into the fourth century—the φυλοβασιλεῖς, and the ἐξηγηταὶ ἐξ Εὐπατριδῶν whose authority was required for the cleansing of blood-guilt.[3]

---

[1] Which is incommunicable outside the caste. This obscurantism (if such it be) survives longest in the sphere of *manners*, where it is hardly yet obsolete.

[2] For the notion of *Aristoi* and the causes of their decline, *c.* 600 B.C., see my remarks in the *Cambridge Ancient History*, Vol. III., pp. 533 and 542.

[3] Phylobasileis, Poll. 8. 111, 'Aθ. π. 57. 4, I.G. II.[2] 1357: for Exegetai, and the alleged γένος Εὐπατριδῶν whence they are commonly thought to have been chosen, see Appendix A [pp. 106 ff.]. See meanwhile Toepffer, *Beiträge* 113, *Att. Gen.* 69; Ehrmann, *De iuris sacri interpretibus Atticis* (1908); Boethius, *Die Pythais* (Uppsala, 1918); Persson, *Die Exegeten und Delphi* (Lund, 1918); Busolt-Swoboda, *Gr. Staatskunde* II. (1926) 1105 sq.; *I.G.* I[2]. 77 and 78. Persson and Swoboda take the Eupatridai in question to be the whole Caste; but they still hold to the existence of a 'Genos' called Eupatridai (falsely, as I hope to show). Were the Phylobasileis and Exegetai members of the Areopagus? Not in the fourth century, I imagine, unless they happened to have been archons: but before Solon, perhaps the Exegetai, at least, were. Perhaps *ex officio*: or perhaps only Areopagites could be chosen.

III. Solon and Damasias

I argued in § II. (*Ion and Theseus*) that in the lost chapters of the *Ἀθηναίων Πολιτεία* Aristotle recorded (in connexion with the Synoikisis) the creation by Theseus of the *Eupatrid Order*, from whom the Archons were chosen: that this tallies with Thuc. II. 15: that Thucydides further suggests that the continuous existence of the *Areopagus Council* dates from the same time: that finally *Council* and *Order* stand to each other as *patres* and *patricii* did in Rome.[1] We now approach that part of the *Ἀθηναίων Πολιτεία* where the London Papyrus begins.

Ch. 8 § 2. 'Thus Solon legislated about the 9 Archons. For in the old days, the Areopagus Council called up and adjudged on its own authority the fit man for each magistracy, and gave him the charge for 12 months.'

This is clear enough, and consonant with what we have seen. The Eupatrid Order supplied the Archons: here the Eupatrid Council appoints them. From their own number? The word ἀνακαλεσαμένη 'summoning (from the lower city) up to their presence,' suggests *not*. Aristotle conceives a distinction between the Eupatrid Order and the Eupatrid Council: the Archons are chosen from the Order, and members of the Order pass, through the Archonship, into the Council.

[Ch. 3 § 6. 'The Archons were chosen ἀριστίνδην καὶ πλουτίνδην; and the men so chosen composed the Areopagites.' This may look innocent enough, but I distrust it profoundly. It is the conclusion of the sketch of the 'ancient constitution, before Drakon.' I do not think it seriously misrepresents the facts: the Archons in the seventh and eighth centuries were doubtless 'the best and richest' men in Attica. Nor does it conflict with the view that Archons were then always Eupatrids: for the best and richest men would, in those centuries, be Eupatrids, and, moreover, the words may quite well mean 'the best and richest Eupatrids.'

---

[1] I take the occasion to add two passages in further illustration of § II: (*a*) Bekker's *Anecdota* 257: Εὐπατρίδαι ἐκαλοῦντο οἱ αὐτὸ τὸ ἄστυ οἰκοῦντες καὶ μετέχοντες βασιλικοῦ γένους καὶ τὴν τῶν ἱερῶν ἐπιμέλειαν ποιούμενοι. A careful account: They are of royal blood (not *the* royal blood), i.e. descended from the local rulers (cf. Plut. *Theseus* 32. 1, Herodotus, 9. 73); they have migrated to Athens; they control religion. (*b*) *I.G.* I² 188 (Law of the Deme Skambonidai, early fifth century) lines 60–63, Χσυνοι[κιοι|σ]: εμ πολει: τε[λεον | τ]α [δ]ε κρεα απο[δοσ]|θαι ομα: 'at the Synoikia, on the Akropolis, an entire victim: they shall sell the meat raw.'

But the phrase[1] reeks of the doctrinaire oligarchism of the late fifth and early fourth centuries. That poison is notoriously responsible for ch. 4, and no ingenuity has yet managed to extract the poison from the body of the treatise and leave no wound: ch. 4 is rooted in its context. I plead to include this sentence in the same damnation as ch. 4. I do not doubt that Aristotle wrote both. But neither is evidence for anything except the minds of the oligarchs of *c.* 400 B.C., and neither has been (in spite of careful adjustments) really digested into Aristotle's conception of the development of the Athenian state.]

Before Solon, then, we are to conceive of an Order of Eupatrids from whose number the Eupatrid Council of the Areopagus chose the yearly Archons: the members of the Order who became Archons for a year became thereby Areopagites for life. The Archons and Areopagus between them did the judicial business of the state, interpreted the Laws, and controlled the state religion: they did these things in virtue of the specifically 'aristocratic' functions which Theseus had reserved to the Eupatridai.

Solon's most drastic political change was to ignore the Eupatrid Order. 'He divided the nation, by assessment of property, into four classes.' Some magistracies were open to the top class only, some to the top two, some to the top three: the fourth class had access only to the Ekklesia and Heliaia. Exactly to which class or classes the Archonship was open is uncertain: either the top class only, or else the top two. (Too much must not be made of the order of words in *'Aθ. πολ.* ch. 7 § 3: the only office which we *know* to have been reserved to the top class only was the office of *Tamias*, Treasurer of Athena, ch. 8 § 1. I am inclined to think the Archonship was accessible to *Hippeis*, the second class.[2]) What is important is that the qualification is now property, and

---

[1] For all its archaic sound: cf. αριστινδεν in Drakon's Law, *I.G.* I² 115, line 19. A very different context: the choosing of Phrateres (in default of kin) for the *Aidesis* of an unintentional homicide.

[2] It depends entirely on how large a body the top class, the Pentekosiomedimnoi, were, and this we don't know. The Tamias had clearly to be one of the richest men in the state (cf. Plato, *Laws,* 759e): the need for the Archon to be rich, provided he was a considerable landowner, was not so urgent. Very likely some Eupatrids were only Hippeis. The Archonship was opened to Zeugitai (the third class) in 457 (ch. 26, § 2), whereas the Tamiai continued to be Pentekosiomedimnoi (ch. 8, § 1). Of course, the Archon by then was an unimportant man, but it must have been open to Hippeis for many years at least before then, and thirty years takes us back to the elected Archons, men like Themistokles and Aristeides.

no longer nobility. *Solon has opened the Archonship, and consequently the Areopagus, to the commonalty*, to such *Georgoi* and *Demiourgoi* as can show sufficient property qualification. 'Eupatrid-hood,' the Thesean patent of nobility, henceforth counts for nothing, in the eyes of the state. How this was resented, and resisted, we shall shortly see.

Solon also transferred the election of Archons from the Areopagus to the people.[1] The close ring of Eupatrid government is thus completely broken.

Solon, we are often told, pleased nobody and solved no problems. He did better—he gave functions to classes which had had none, and awoke desires which had been dormant. One of the creators of that unstatic miracle, democratic Athens, he was naturally no millennium-monger. He left behind him a legacy of warring ambitions, and nothing in all his astonishing legislation proved so provocative as his revision of that qualification for Archonship. ᾧ καὶ δῆλον, says Aristotle, of the compromise which was reached about twelve years later, ὅτι μεγίστην εἶχεν δύναμιν ὁ ἄρχων· φαίνονται γὰρ ἀεὶ στασιάζοντες περὶ ταύτης τῆς ἀρχῆς (ch. 13, § 2).

The nature of the conflict in these dozen and more years is best sought in the nature of the compromise which for the moment assuaged it.[2] In the fifth year after Solon, and again in the tenth year, no Archon was appointed: after that, Damasias seized and held the office for two years and two months. After that, ἐξηλάθη βίᾳ: it is not, perhaps, too sensational to suppose he was killed. Then they compromised. Of ten men to be elected for the Archonship, five were to be Eupatrids, five were to be from outside the Nobility. The composition of the non-noble five is further specified: three shall be *Agroikoi* (=Georgoi?) and two *Demiourgoi*. These are, of course, not farmers and artisans (in the first quarter of the sixth century!), but wealthy *Hippeis* (or *Pentekosiomedimnoi*) admitted by Solon in spite of their non-noble estate.

This arrangement is made within the scope of the Solonian law. The property qualification remains. Solon's law, without being contravened, is further defined: the claim of blood, which he had simply disregarded, is here at once recognized and limited.

---

[1] For the question, how the people exercised their vote, see Appendix B.
[2] This is all related in ch. 13.

What proportion of the men eligible under Solon's law had Eupatrid blood? If we could answer that we could say whether this was, on the whole, a Eupatrid victory or defeat. But we can only guess: I should imagine *over* 50 per cent. of the eligibles were Eupatrids, and they are given *only* 50 per cent. representation; it seems like a Eupatrid defeat.

Did Damasias stand for or against the Eupatrid claim? The rare name had occurred in the Archon list in Eupatrid days (Dionysius of Halicarnassus, *Antiqu. Rom.* 3. 36, the Archon of 629-8 B.C.); we may perhaps say it is a Eupatrid name. I imagine Damasias attempted to re-assert the Eupatrid monopoly: he failed, and the Eupatrid claim is reduced.

Neither of the last two questions has admitted of any better answer than a guess. It is the same, when we ask ourselves what exactly did the ten men appointed by this compromise do. They can hardly be ten Archons in place of the usual nine [cf. ch. 13, § 2, ὁ ἄρχων (sc. ὁ ἐπώνυμος) . . . περὶ ταύτης τῆς ἀρχῆς]. Are they the Eponymos in commission, or ten monthly Eponymoi in succession, for the ten remaining months of Damasias' year? I am much attracted by Cavaignac's suggestion (*Rev. de Philol.* 48 [1924] 144 sqq.) that they are the ten πρόκριτοι whom each Tribe elected before the lot was cast between the forty so chosen[1] (ch. 8, § 1). This is not indeed what Aristotle says, nor do I see any way of emending him (should one want to) into such a meaning. But Aristotle is often (in this treatise) wrong, and this seems to me a good correction. If it is right, the compromise may have lasted a good number of years.

I turn with some relief from these dubious enquiries back to the main narrative.

Damasias was quashed about 580: about twenty years later Peisistratos effected his first *coup d'état*. Some time before that, say between 570 and 560, he had created his party of the *Hyperakrioi*, thus adding a third to the two existing parties of *Pedieis* and *Paralioi* (Hdt. 1. 59). These two parties, then, had been in existence *c.* 570, and were led, the Pedieis by Lykourgos, the Paralioi by Megakles.

How do these two parties, Lykourgos' *Pedieis* and Megakles' *Paralioi, c.* 570, stand to the two parties which had compromised

---

[1] For the question whether there *were* actually such πρόκριτοι, see Appendix B.

after the fall of Damasias, *c.* 580? Roughly, I think, the Pedieis have succeeded to those who had upheld the Eupatrid claim (Damasias?), the Paralioi to those who had opposed that claim (the non-nobles admitted by Solon). But I imagine the Pedieis were less exclusive, it is no longer nobles *versus* non-nobles, but landlords *versus* merchants; and the property qualification of the latter is probably no longer landed. For this is the tenour of the sixth century: the party of exclusion is losing, and gets less exclusive, the party of intrusion is winning, and accepts fewer terms. Under Solon, the new rich had been prepared to buy land in order to enter the governing class: they turned themselves into country gentlemen, as Anthemion did, who 'changed from a *Thes* to a *Hippeus*' (ch. 7, § 4), presumably by converting personal into real property. But after a little time, those who had done so ranked and felt as 'landlords,' solid with the old aristocracy; and the new rich maintained the right of the merchant, as merchant, to enter the governing class without becoming a country gentleman first. I do not suppose this change was complete by 570, but it was in process.

The Eupatrid claim to monopolize government is never heard of again. Even the *Pedieis* are soon glad to coalesce with Megakles, and by the Battle of Pallene in 546 have ceased to exist separately, and either submit to Peisistratos or follow Megakles to exile (Hdt. 1. 64). When these 'White Athenians' attempted to fight their way back (under Megakles' leadership, or his son's) and failed, in their song of defeat they called themselves Εὐπατρίδαι (ch. 19, § 3). *Sic transit gloria mundi.* The old Noble Order had sought once to extrude the new rich from partnership in government. One house of tarnished nobility, the accursed Alkmeonid, had turned renegade and led the opposition. Now the proud name is used by the men under his standard.

IV. The Sequel

The Eupatrid monopoly of the archonship was broken by Solon: about 100 years later, in 487, the archonship sank to election by lot ('*Aθ. πολ.* 22. 5), and was never again the goal of the ambitious. In the Strategia, which thenceforward took its place, men of Eupatrid race were long prominent: meanwhile a new aristocracy of blood was growing up, the οἶκοι ἐστρατηγηκότες, just as in Rome *imagines* became the patent of nobility. The Strategoi had one advantage over the archons, they could hold office year after year: one disadvantage, there was no Areopagus of ex-strategoi to secure them against the whim of popular favour. The disadvantage was grave: by the end of the fifth century there is no longer a nobility nor a governing class, only an executive class, despoiled of sovranty, and distrusted by the Sovran. The history of the Areopagus repeats (like a musical canon, always a few beats later) the history of the Archonship. The Tyrants packed the archonship (Thuc. 6. 54. 6), consequently the Areopagus came in time to be a packed body. Perhaps it was so already when Peisistratos answered a charge of homicide before it (*'Aθ. π.* 16, § 8).[1] Certainly it was so when Hippias was finally dethroned. This explains (what indeed needs explaining) why the Areopagus made no trouble about admitting the Laws of Kleisthenes to the Statute book: the Areopagus at that moment was a packed body, whose members were discredited.

From 510 to 487, however, the Archons are once more the leading men in Athens, the Areopagus accordingly recovers its authority. We see it enjoying this authority in 480 (ibid. 23, § 1), when Themistokles, Aristeides, and all the most authoritative men in Athens were Areopagites.

From 487 onwards, the Archons are nobodies: this has not seriously diluted the Areopagus by 480, but the process is cumulative: by 461 there were probably few if any elected archons still sitting in the Council: its hollow prestige is smashed by Ephialtes (ibid. 25).

A change in the personnel of the Archons means a change in the Areopagus, but it takes nearly thirty years for the change to become complete.

In tabular form:

Archons.	*Areopagus.*
546 *onwards* Tyrant's nominees.	507 Powerless against Kleisthenes.

---

[1] Diog. Laert, I. 49, says, when Peisistratos was planning his *coup d'état*, Solon appealed to the Boule: ἡ δὲ βουλή, Πεισιστρατίδαι ὄντες, gave him no help. The story is nonsensical (I think) as it stands: how had Peisistratos packed either Boule, so soon, with his sons? The phrase, however, ἡ βουλὴ Πεισιστρατίδαι ὄντες would not be an inapt description of the Areopagus in the later years of the tyranny: though, if such was the original context of the words, I hardly think it can be recovered now.

510 *onwards* Elected by the
          Demos.   480 Height of authority.
487 *onwards* Chosen by lot.   461 Broken by Ephialtes.

For the rest of the fifth century the Archons are unambitious, solid men, something like our Mayors or Magistrates. There came a time when such men seemed preferable to the hysterical politicians of the war, and during the siege of Athens the Areopagus recovered a measure of political authority (Lysias XII. 69 πρατ- τούσης μὲν τῆς ἐν Ἀρείῳ πάγῳ βουλῆς σωτηρίαν, just before Thera- menes leaves on one of his missions). Of the fourth century I do not speak. The Areopagus of Iso- krates and Aeschines, like that of St. Paul, belongs to another world.

Appendix A.—Alkmeonid and Eupatrid (Isokrates 16. 25)

Πρὸς μὲν ἀνδρῶν ἦν Εὐπατριδῶν, ὧν τὴν εὐγένειαν ἐξ αὐτῆς τῆς ἐπωνυμίας ῥᾴδιον γνῶναι, πρὸς γυναικῶν δ᾽ Ἀλκμεωνιδῶν.

'On his father's side [the great Alkibiades] was of the Eupatridai (a stock whose nobility you may guess from their name), on his mother's side he was of the Alkmaionidai.'

Both *Eupatridai* and *Alkmaionidai* appear in Toepffer's list of the Athenian γένη (*Attische Genealogie*, Berlin, 1889), the former largely on the strength of this passage. Neither, as I believe, are a Genos, in the technical sense of a body of *Gennetai*.

The Alkmaionidai (or Alkmeonidai) lie rather outside my present scope; but I must briefly justify my denial. They are what Herodotus calls an οἰκίη, which is different from, smaller than, a Genos. He says of Isagoras 'he belonged to an οἰκίη of repute, though I know nothing of its early history: his Genos[1] has an altar of Zeus Karios (5. 66. 1).' The Alkmeonid οἰκίη was small and compact enough to share, (*a*) in the first half of the sixth century, in the wealth obtained by Alkmeon at Sardis and Megakles II. at Sikyon, (*b*) in the seventh century, in the curse incurred by the archon Megakles I. It is improbable (indeed impossible) that either such a curse, or such fortunes, were shared by the Gennetai of a whole Genos. And, in fact and practice, Alkmeonid means simply the descendants of these men. No one is called an

---

[1] Συγγενέες here=γεννῆται, as in Isaeus *Apollodoros* 27: and often, though of course not always: συγγενής is not always technical, γεννήτης is. Herodotus is here talking of the *Genos* cults.

Alkmeonid (by our sources) who is not a direct descendant of Megakles II.: no one is called an Alkmeonid even by modern scholars who is not presumed to be a direct descendant of the Alkmeon of *c.* 600 B.C.[1] *Ἀλκμεωνίδαι*, in fact, like *Πεισιστρατίδαι* or *Βουσελίδαι*,[2] are an *οἰκίη*, the descendants of a perfectly historical Alkmeon,[3] the contemporary of Solon.

A *Genos* is wholly different from such an *οἰκίη*. It is a religious corporation, and its antiquity is far greater than the prominence of any historical house. The kinship was, in historic times, fictional: by the sixth century, the Gennetai were frequently scattered over the map of Attica. In cases where we have lists of Gennetai we can test this:

(*a*) *Βρυτίδαι*. Ps.-Demosthenes, *Neaira* 61, names six Gennetai (as witnesses) from six different demes, as wide apart as Kephale, Hekale, Phaleron.

(*b*) *Ἀμυνανδρίδαι*. A large portion of a complete list of the Gennetai arranged in Tribes has survived, from the reign of Augustus, *I.G.* II². 2338. The part preserved covers nine Tribes and includes twenty-five different Demes.

The distribution here found must have existed in Kleisthenes' time, for membership of Deme and Genos both pass strictly in the male line: in case of adoption, the adopted son takes both Deme and Genos of his new father.

Toepffer, calling the Alkmeonidai a Genos, has followed Pausanias 2. 18. 9, who alleges that Alkmeonidai and Paionidai[4] are *γένη* descended from Alkmeon and Paion, immigrant from Pylos after the Trojan War. I do not know if Pausanias is here using 'Genos' technically; nor, if one weighs rather than counts authority, does it matter. On the other hand, Hesychius and Suidas say *Ἀλκμεωνίδαι*: *ἀπὸ Ἀλκμέωνος τοῦ κατὰ Θησέα*. I suggest a possible meaning for this variant (which in itself is worthless). The Alkmeonidai were of Eupatrid stock (since they provide a seventh-century archon): Eupatridai go back by definition to Theseus, Pylian refugees are too recent. [Per-

---

[1] I mean e.g. the Alkmeon and Alkmeonides of *I.G.* I² 472; and the Alkmeon father of Leobotes (Plut. *Them.* 23) who is not, like the Megakles II. line, of the deme Alopeke; and the possibly identical Alkmaion, archon in 508/7.

[2] See the genealogies in Kirchner's *Prosopographia Attica*, to the names Megakles I. (No. 9688), Peisistratos I. (No. 11793), Bouselos (No. 2921).

[3] Megakles I., his father, is never called an Alkmeonid, any more than Hippokrates is called a Peisistratid. The great fortunes of the house dated from the known Alkmeon (Hdt. 6. 125. 1).

[4] Paionidai is the name of a Deme, close to Acharnai: the modern Menidi [= *Μαινίδιο*=*Παιονίδιο*: cf. Mendeli=*Πεντέλη*] lies between the two. It *may* have been the local centre of a *Genos* of Paionidai, though otherwise we know of none such. And Peisistratidai and Alkmeonidai *may* have belonged to that Genos, since the local centre of a Genos says nothing as to the local seat of its members in the sixth century: cf. *Βρυτίδαι* and *Ἀμυνανδρίδαι* above.

haps a good deal of the new 'nobility,' given access to the Areopagus by Solon's law, claimed Pylian blood: for instance, Peisistratos?]

No one, I think, will assert that Eupatridai are an οἰκίη, comparable to Peisistratidai and Alkmeonidai, descended from an historical Eupatros. And if they are not, then Isokrates is already guilty of mixing his categories: and why shouldn't he? Not an οἰκίη: what then are the Eupatridai? I see no reason in this passage for calling them a technical Genos[1]: they are, what we know well enough from countless other passages, a Caste, an Order of Nobility. Careful scholars (such as A. W. Persson in his *Die Exegeten und Delphi*) take pains to write Εὐπατρίδαι when they mean the alleged Genos, and εὐπατρίδαι when they mean the Caste. This is unnecessary, since there is no such Genos: and misleading, since εὐπατρίδαι, as the Caste, is not a mere adjective, =εὐγενεῖς; the Caste of Eupatridai was an exactly bounded caste; their name is a proper name.

Εὐπατρίδης is, of course, an adjective: it is the opposite of κακοπατρίδης, low-born, which Alcaeus[2] uses of Pittakos, and means, simply, 'high-born'. The non-technical adjective is poetical (in the Leipsydrion scolion, and often in Tragic chorus: Sophokles uses it persistently in the *Elektra* with the connotation of being true to your blood[3]): *in Attic (and later) prose it is technical and means always 'of the Eupatrid*

---

[1] I am a little embarrassed by the fact that the Greek word γένος means both 'Caste' (e.g. Hdt. 2. 164) and 'Body of Gennetai.' I use the transliteration 'Genos' in the latter sense only. It has been thought Isokrates' words 'you may guess their nobility from their name' suggest a Genos which happened to have the same name as the Caste of Nobility. He means, in fact, that the name of the Caste is a common (poetical) adjective (see the next two notes). For the alleged Genos see e.g. Busolt-Swoboda, *Gr. Staatskunde* (1926) 772[2], 1102[1], and the scholars there quoted (Wilamowitz, Toepffer, Hirzel, Boethius, even Persson, *Exegeten* 15).

[2] Fr. 67 and 75, Lobel-Page. Not κακόπατρις, which is feminine, Theognis 193, like εὔπατρις (of Elektra, Soph. *El.* 1081: εὐπατρίδης of Orestes, ibid. 162, 859). Do these patronymic forms mean just the same as εὐπάτωρ (Aesch. *Persai* 970) and εὐπατέρεια (Homer)? Or do they rather mean 'son (daughter) of a man who stands well (or ill) in his πάτρα,' εὔπατρος, κακόπατρος? (The most analogous form is Homer's ὄπατρος.) The Eupatridai would thus be the superior members of the πάτρα.
I do not think πάτρα is to be distinguished from φρατρία. It is the 'father house,' in which the members are 'brothers,' φράτερες: the same aggregate of φράτερες can be called φρατρία. The legal fixation of φρατρία at Athens as something probably bigger than πάτρα at Aigina need not mislead us. Dicaearchus (*apud* Steph. Byz. s.v. πάτρα=F.H.G. II., p. 238) speaks as a whimsical philosopher, not an antiquarian: he was not (what Philochorus was) an Exegetes, an 'expert aristocrat,' like the Garter King at Arms.

[3] I.e. Orestes and Elektra are true to Agamemnon: 162, 859, 1081. I do not imagine this connotation was old: Hirzel's theory that Orestes was the ancestor of the (*Genos* of) Eupatridai can be dismissed. Yet I do not know whether Orestes' connexion with the Areopagus might not be partly responsible for the epithet. Of Theseus, Eur. *Hipp.* 152: of Admetos and Alkestis, *Alk.* 920. A very odd late poetical use in Cometas' paraphrase of ch. xi. of St. John's Gospel, *Anth. Pal.* XV. 40, line 20.

Caste'. E.g. in Xen. *Symp.* 8. 40, Arist. *'Αθ. πολ.* 13. 2, Plut. *Theseus* 25 and 32. 1 [Plut.] *Vit. X. Orat.* 834 B, Dorotheus *apud* Athenaeum 9. 78, Vita Aeschyli 1, Polemon *apud* Sch. Soph. *O.C.* 489, Pollux 8. 111, Syncellus 399. 21, Bekk. Anecdota 257, Et. Magn. s.v., Moeris s.v.: and, as we shall see, in Attic inscriptions. To support this, I need only take those passages which have been used as evidence for the 'Genos of Eupatridai'.

The substantial evidence has always been held to be the passage of Isokrates which stands at the head of this Appendix: I will return to it shortly. Corroborative evidence has been sought:

A. In the inscriptions which speak of εξηγηται εξ Ευπατριδων. Toepffer asserted (*Beiträge zur griech. Altertumswissenschaft*, pp. 112 sq.) that such Exegetai belonged to the 'Genos of Eupatridai'. A. W. Persson (*Die Exegeten und Delphi* pp. 15–16) has argued that the Eupatridai here must be the Caste (who are therefore capable of precise definition). I cannot indeed accept all Persson's conclusions (see Appendix B), but this point can, I think, be put beyond dispute.

Of one of these εξηγηται εξ Ευπατριδων, Diotimos, son of Diodoros of Halai (25 B.C. Dittenberger *Syll.*³ 773=*Fouilles de Delphes* III. 2. 59), *we can name the Genos*: it is Bouzygai. In the *Berl. Philol. Woch.* 1902 col. 1095, Prof. Wilhelm states he has completed with a new fragment an inscription of *c.* 30 B.C. in which this same man is given as Βουζυγησ και ιερευσ Διοσ εν Παλλαδιωι.* A man cannot belong to two Genê: if he belongs to the Genos of Bouzygai, εξ Ευπατριδων cannot mean 'of the Genos of Eupatridai'.

B. The actual phrase γένος Ευπατριδων occurs once or twice: it means, *the Eupatrid Caste*.¹ This is certain in e.g. Hellanicus² fr. 170 [Jacoby: =*Vit. X. Or.* 834 B] *'Ανδοκίδης* . . . γένους Ευπατριδων, ώς δ' *'Ελλάνικος* καὶ ἀπὸ *'Ερμοῦ*, καθήκει γὰρ εἰς αὐτὸν τὸ Κηρύκων γένος. Andokides belongs to the Eupatrid Caste, but to the Genos of Kerykes. The scholiast to Soph. *O.C.* 489 quotes Polemon on a sacrifice to the Semnai performed by the Hesychidai: Polemon adds τὸ δὲ τῶν Ευπατριδῶν γένος οὐ μετέχει τῆς θυσίας ταύτης. Again, it is the Eupatrid Caste: and no one who has read Aeschylus' *Eumenides*, and remembers the intimate relation, until Solon, between Eupatridai and Areopagus, will be astonished at this exclusion.

C. Finally, Dorotheus' book³ τὰ τῶν Ευπατριδῶν πάτρια (quoted Athen. 9. 78) cannot, with such a title, refer to anything else than the

* [*Hesp.* IX (1940) 86, no. 17, with new fr.: cf. Jacoby *Atthis* 241 n. 32.]
¹ Γένος is the natural Greek word for 'Caste': see e.g. Herodotus 2. 164 on the seven Castes of Egyptians, ἑπτὰ γένεα. Cf. *I.G.* II² 7447 προγονοισι και γενει Ευπατριδησ.
² Not Hellanicus' own words.
³ Dorotheos is presumably an Exegete, like Kleidemos and Philochoros: and his book an *'Εξηγητικόν*.

privileges and functions of the Eupatrid Caste. It is interesting that our only quotation is concerned with the method of cleansing blood-guilt. When Solon made the Areopagus 'timocratic', it continued to perform the Eupatrid function of judging φονικαὶ δίκαι,[1] but the religious *expertise*, of cleansing the man acquitted, remains with the hereditary Caste.

I come back to Isokrates: who says that Alkibiades, on his father's side, belongs to the Eupatridai. I hope I have made clear that the natural meaning of this is that he belonged to the Caste, not to a special Genos of that name. He does, in fact, belong to a different Genos. In Plato's *First Alkibiades*, 121, Alkibiades says καὶ γὰρ τὸ ἡμέτερον (sc. γένος ἀναφέρεται), ὦ Σώκρατες, εἰς Εὐρυσάκη. The name of this Genos was not Εὐρυσακίδαι but (I think) Σαλαμίνιοι. We possess a decree of this Genos, from the late fourth century, naming its two sanctuaries, which are the temple of Athena Skiras in Salamis and the *Eurysakeion* in Melite close to the Kerameikos.[2]

Isokrates is not pleading before a College of Heralds, but (like the Father of Journalism that he is) is giving an audience of laymen their favourite illusion—'in technical language, XYZ;—but, gentlemen, you can see for yourselves.' If an expert had interrupted and said 'Why, man, Eupatridai and Alkmeonidai are in different categories, one is a Caste, the other a family within that Caste,' Isokrates would have had his audience with him. 'Our learned friend says this and that: yet he cannot show that Alkibiades' ancestry was not of the noblest.' And it makes no serious difference that Isokrates' audience is imaginary.

APPENDIX B.—Κλήρωσις ἐκ προκρίτων AND THE ELECTION OF EXEGETAI IN PLATO *LAWS* 759D

Aristotle *Politics* 1273b 41, ἔοικε δὲ Σόλων . . . οὐ καταλῦσαι . . . τὴν τῶν ἀρχῶν αἵρεσιν, cannot be reconciled with his statements, in *'Aθ. πολ.* 8. 1 and 2, that before Solon the Areopagus chose the Archons, whereas Solon instituted κλήρωσις ἐκ προκρίτων. It is evident he changed his mind, and the *'Aθ. πολ.* is probably his later mind. Were his second thoughts best?

---

[1] I assume, with Gertrude Smith, *Administration of Justice from Hesiod to Solon*, 16 sqq., that the Ephetic courts are, till Ephialtes, manned by Areopagites.

[2] The inscription is *I.G.* II² 1232: given in Toepffer, *Att. Gen.*, p. 287, in rough fac-simile. I have not seen the stone, but suggest for lines 25 sqq. οπωσ αν ειδωσι Σαλα|[μινιοι και ο]ι αλλοι οι αφικνουμενοι ε[ισ | τα ιερα τα Ευρυ]σακ[εια το γενομενο]ν, ο[τι] δ[ι|ατετελεκασ]ι φιλοτι[μουμενοι εισ το γενοσ | και τουσ αλλουσ] πολι[τασ: and possibly for 3 sqq. (cf. τεθυμένος in Xen. *Hell.* 5. 1. 18) [τουσ τεθυμ]ενουσ και τασ τεθυ[μενασ τασ θυσι]ασ υπερ του δη]μου του Αθηναιων και [του γενουσ | του Σαλα-μινιω]ν, Ευφροσυνον Ον[ησιμου, etc.

I believe some light may be thrown on the question by a passage in Plato's *Laws* describing the election of Exegetai.

Plato says:

Τοὺς δὲ ἐξηγητὰς τρὶς¹ φερέτωσαν μὲν αἱ τέτταρες φυλαὶ τέτταρας, ἕκαστον ἐξ αὐτῶν· τρεῖς δέ, οἷς ἂν πλείστη γένηται ψῆφος, δοκιμάσαντας, ἐννέα πέμπειν εἰς Δελφοὺς ἀνελεῖν ἐξ ἑκάστης τριάδος ἕνα.

This is a law for the proposed colony, which is to have twelve Tribes in all.

'Exegetai: three groups of four Tribes each (*lit.* three times over, the four Tribes) shall elect, each group, four; one per Tribe. The state shall put through their Dokimasia the three (in each group) who get most votes, and send (the names of?) these nine to Delphi, who will choose one from each group of three.'

Plato's phrasing cannot be called felicitous or lucid. The change of construction and subject from φερέτωσαν . . . αἱ φυλαί to δοκιμάσαντας . . . πέμπειν, though harsh, has parallels enough in real decrees: the second (unexpressed) subject is, of course, the State whose law this is, τοὺς πολίτας. Ἕκαστον ἐξ αὐτῶν must mean ἐξ ἑκάστης τῆς φυλῆς ἕνα, though I doubt if the words can strictly bear that meaning.²

The method, as I see it, is this: The members of four Tribes choose one man from each of the four Tribes, the whole four Tribes voting in each case. The man of the four who has least votes drops out: three men are left and put through their Dokimasia. This happens three times (since there are twelve Tribes) and you have nine δεδοκιμασμένοι, three groups of three. Delphi chooses one from each group, and this leaves you with three Exegetai.

My interpretation is open to question on two points:

1. (A minor point.) The whole four Tribes vote in each case. I think this must be so, since at the next stage the man [or, on the more usual view, the three men] with fewest votes dropped out. If each Tribe voted for its own man, this directly penalized a Tribe which was numerically smaller. If you are going to compare the numbers of votes, the comparison must be among votes cast by the same constituency, viz. the whole four Tribes.

Nevertheless, I cannot strictly get this from the Greek. Who is αὐτῶν? The only strict construction is to supply ἕκαστον (ἑκάστη ἡ φυλὴ) ἐξ αὐτῶν, and this gives the wrong sense.

2. (The main point.) England, in his commentary on the *Laws*, Ehrmann, *De iuris sacri interpretibus Atticis*, pp. 364 sq., and Persson, *Die Exegeten und Delphi*, p. 10, are unanimous in translating the second clause (the acc. and inf.) quite differently: Persson says Ehrmann has

¹ So the second hand in two MSS.: the uncorrected reading is τρεῖς.
² I.e. the language is slovenly, and will not bear the meaning Plato intends. See below.

proved conclusively that no other translation (than theirs) is possible. They hold that the man of the four who has *most* votes is, straightway, put through his Dokimasia *and becomes an Exegete*. The nine sent to Delphi are *the nine with least votes*: Apollo picks three of them, and you then have *six* Exegetai altogether. They translate 'the state shall put through their Dokimasia (*and thereby appoint*) the three (one from each group) who get most votes, and send the (*remaining*) nine to Delphi, etc.' Plato writes so loosely that I cannot be sure that either rendering of the actual sentence is *per se* impossible: though (like Martial) I prefer my own. In the Greek as Ehrmann, etc., read it, the emphasis seems to me to fall all wrong, and though Plato in the *Laws* writes clumsy and sometimes slovenly Greek, his ear for emphasis remains (I should have said) faultless. Nor do I readily believe that δοκιμάσαντας could include the notion of κυρώσαντας. Further, if τρὶς is right (as I believe), its position in front of φερέτωσαν μὲν seems to me intolerable unless it qualifies both φερέτωσαν μὲν τέτταρας and τρεῖς δὲ δοκιμάσαντας. So far *sprachlich: sachlich* there seems no question at all. Are the nine, who are sent to Delphi, not through their Dokimasia? If not, when do they have it? and what will happen if one of Apollo's choices is rejected? Again, is Apollo to be given the *proxime accessere* to choose from? are the πυθόχρηστοι to be, eventually, inferior to the others? But the sentence which follows in Plato is conclusive. 'They shall be Exegetai for life: and when a vacancy occurs προαιρείσθωσαν αἱ τέτταρες φυλαὶ ὅθεν ἂν ἐκλίπῃ.' Here is nothing of two categories, two modes of election. The orthodox view says, each group of four Tribes has two Exegetai, one πυθόχρηστος, and *one directly elected*: yet in replacing vacancies no distinction is made, and for the alleged latter category προαιρείσθωσαν is meaningless. The matter is perfectly plain if each four-Tribe group has *one* Exegete: when he dies, they once more name three πρόκριτοι (προαιρείσθωσαν) and Delphi chooses one of the three.

The method is, in fact, a form of κλήρωσις ἐκ προκρίτων, Delphi taking the place of the κλῆρος. I do not imagine it was the method actually used at Athens for choosing Exegetai: Plato does not copy directly. [Timaeus in his Platonic Lexikon says of the Exegetai[1] τρεῖς γίνονται πυθόχρηστοι: yet the ten Attic Tribes could not be divided into three such groups as Plato's method requires.] Yet Plato thinks in terms of real procedure, and I believe the passage is not without value to the historian. Two preliminary points: first, Plato is facing the problem of how to man an aristocratic office when he cannot count on the existence of old families [see 759b εἰ δέ, οἷον τὸ πρῶτον κατοικιζομένοις εἰκὸς

---

[1] Presumably the real, not the Platonic, Exegetai. I do not feel quite sure of this, though it is commonly assumed.

γίγνεσθαι περὶ τὰ τοιαῦτα, ‹πάτριαί εἰσιν ἱερωσύναι› ἢ μηδενὶ ἤ τισιν ὀλίγοις] :
secondly, to Plato sortition is no longer the clear voice of God, but
a concession to democracy, giving mechanical equality.[1]
Plato is facing much the same problem, and using much the same
means, as Solon did when he revised the appointment of archons.
When an aristocratic office (such as the archon held in Solon's day,
the Exegete in Plato's) was filled by a hereditary noble, his birth gave
him a clear divine sanction: his fitness was divinely ordered, he was
διοτρεφής. But if you break with heredity, as Solon did, and Plato is
compelled to do, you must replace it with something. By Plato's
method, and by the κλήρωσις ἐκ προκρίτων ascribed to Solon, the
responsibility is shared between man and God, God having the last
word; and, from the point of view of the man chosen, his sanction is
partly at least divine.

I am assuming that sortition was really regarded as the voice of God,
and was really prescribed by Solon for the archonship. Neither fact is
undisputed, and probably the two stand or fall together. I may refer
in general to Ehrenberg's excellent article in Pauly-Wissowa-Kroll on
Losung,[2] and confine myself to a few matters.

Plato's statement about sortition (757b and 757e, quoted in n. 1) is
a religious man's statement, and shows how completely sortition had
lost its religious authority in the fourth century, and become a weapon
of democracy. Contrast *Iliad* 7. 171–180: it is partly perhaps to 'avoid
ill-feeling', but most in order that Zeus may choose his own man, that
sortition is used to determine who shall accept Hektor's challenge.
Solon stands nearer to Homer than to Plato: *his* faith is still innocent.

Further, single combat was an extreme case, demanding especial
personal fitness, and it was frankly recognized that there were men better
at it (φέρτεροι) than Menelaos. Even so, the lot is permitted to choose,
and in their prayers they hope, indifferently, for Aias or Diomedes or
Agamemnon. Things are done in poetry which are not in real life:
if in Solon's lifetime Phrynon really fought a single combat with Pittakos,[3] I don't suppose either was chosen by lot—too great a risk, when
you need your one best man. It is often urged that the same consideration makes it impossible that Solon permitted the lot to choose the nine
archons, one of whom was to be Polemarch, and command in war.[4]

---

[1] 757b and 757e: one has to use it, and hope God will make it a real equality,
τῷ τοῦ κλήρου ἴσῳ ἀνάγκη προσχρήσασθαι δυσκολίας τῶν πολλῶν ἕνεκα, θεὸν καὶ ἀγαθὴν
τύχην καὶ τότε ἐν εὐχαῖς ἐπικαλουμένους ἀπορθοῦν αὐτοὺς τὸν κλῆρον πρὸς τὸ δικαιότατον.
[2] Cf. Klio 19, pp. 106 sqq. and Lehmann-Haupt, ibid. 6, pp. 304 sqq.
[3] Strabo XIII. 1. 38, and the other passages quoted in *Prosopographia Attica* under
Phrynon, 15029.
[4] So *Camb. Anc. Hist.* IV. 51. The generality on p. 155, 'the holder of an office
that is military must be capable of re-election,' is very surprising. Surely the Pole-
marchy could not be iterated?

This is demonstrably wrong. Any good man could command in war, just as any good man could govern, or sacrifice, or give judgment: the notion that the conduct of war is more likely to go wrong, or demands more special skill, is a later notion: the mark of its recognition is when the iterable strategos ousts the yearly-changed Polemarch, about 490 B.C. Till then the yearly change of Polemarch is the proof that, as between a large handful of competent men,[1] it is indifferent who commands. The great professional strategoi of the fourth century have a military prime of about twenty-five years:[2] at this rate, during a great soldier's military prime, sixth-century Athens acquiesced in twenty-five different commanders. This is sufficient to show how little they were concerned to have the one proved man, the Napoleon or Chabrias, in command.

In an aristocratic society, a year of office is a thing which any aristocrat can be trusted to take. This is a fundamental aristocratic conception. Pure aristocracy, by Solon's time, was past its apogee, and Solon abolished the most important of the privileges of birth, the exclusive access to archonship and Areopagus. Time was to show that this was a symptom of aristocracy's mortal sickness: the plain ἀρετή of the Aristoi was being dwarfed by the more specialized ἀρεταί of merchants, revolutionaries, and others. This was not yet evident to Solon's generation: it seemed rather to them that the growth of capacity outside the Caste had moved him to revise the criterion of nobility, to make it property instead of birth. But this new nobility had no such divine sanction as the old,[3] and, for the archonship, the Eupatrid council's chosen Eupatrid[4] had a weight of tradition which the Ekklesia's chosen Rich Man could not possibly claim. Κλήρωσις ἐκ προκρίτων seemed to meet the case (as Plato's method for Exegetai aimed at doing). Each of the four Tribes chose ten men competent to fill the nine archonships: this was ample guarantee against incompetence. Between these forty the lot (a form of oracle) decided: the man it chose was safe from envy, and, in a degree, divinely sanctioned.[5]

Plato, when he wrote the *Laws*, must be presumed to have known Solon's code fairly well, yet I do not think he is necessarily copying him: rather, the cases are analogous. But in one less important point it is

---

[1] A fool or coward would not be among the forty πρόκριτοι.

[2] See their careers in the *Prosopographia Attica*. I compute roughly from their first strategia to their last.

[3] Solon is conscious that wealth, as a criterion, is not good nor even constant: see fr. 4 (Diehl), lines 9–12, especially the last line: χρήματα δ᾽ ἀνθρώπων ἄλλοτε ἄλλος ἔχει.

[4] This is how the archon was chosen before Solon's reform: ʼΑθ. πολ. 8. 2.

[5] Cavaignac's hypothesis, quoted above, that the five Eupatridai and five non-Eupatridai of ʼΑθ. πολ. 13. 2 are really the ten πρόκριτοι of each Tribe would (if right) strongly corroborate the fact of πρόκρισις.

probable he was actually copying the procedure of his day, or at least of his youth: I mean *the dropping of the man with fewest votes*. The aggregate of four Tribes elects four men, one from each Tribe: the one with the fewest votes is then dropped, that Tribe is unrepresented at Delphi. When Perikles, or Alkibiades or another, was Strategos ἐξ ἁπάντων, the other nine Strategoi are from nine Tribes, but the remaining Tribe has no Tribal Strategos.[1] How was it decided which Tribe should be unrepresented? I imagine in the way Plato prescribes. The Tribal Strategoi are elected, from each Tribe, by the whole Demos:[2] the one with fewest votes is dropped, his Tribe has no Strategos.[3]

---

[1] The best known case is the year of the Samian Revolt, when Perikles is ἐξ ἁπάντων, and Glaukon is Tribal Strategos for Akamantis: that year Aiantis has no Strategos. The list is given by Schol. Aristeid. III., p. 485 Dindorf, but is only complete in one MS., published by Wilamowitz, *De Rhesi scholiis*, p. 13: it is conveniently accessible in *I.G.* I², p. 284, lines 60 sqq. *[See now *F. gr. H.* 324 F 38.]

[2] Hdt. 6. 104. 2, Xen. *Mem.* 3. 4. 1: *C.Q.* XXIV., p. 38.

[3] The lists of Strategoi [Krause, *Attische Strategenlisten* (Weimar, 1914); Beloch, *Gr. Ges²*. II. 2, pp. 260 sqq.; Pomello and Zancan, *Riv. d. Fil.* 1927, 361, none of which is complete] make it certain that non-representation was not regularly rotated.

DEMOTIONIDAI

In an earlier paper on this topic, 'Eupatridai, Archons, and Areopagus',[1] I was primarily concerned to recover the views of Aristotle, as expressed in the 'Aθ. πολ., on such elements of Attic Society as Eupatridai, Gennetai, etc. I sought to establish that to him at least these two were not identical: that, more precisely, he recorded two stages of development—

(a) 'Ion': in whose day the whole body of Athenians was composed of Gennetai, while Eupatridai had not yet been created.

(b) 'Theseus': who created the Eupatridai—distinguishing them, as a Third Estate, from those two Estates (Georgoi and Demiourgoi) which had hitherto, since Ion, composed the body of Athenians.

Some few scholars perhaps will regard Ion and Theseus as real people, and these two stages as historic facts. Personally, I cannot: I regard them as fictions, and Aristotle's two stages as a schematic and fictional account of the origins of the Society he knew. But at least one conclusion as to fact may (I believe) be drawn from his fiction—viz. Eupatridai and Gennetai, of whose origin he gives such different accounts, were not identical bodies. This should never have been in doubt, since we are told (by Polemon only:[2] yet it is a fact of a sort which it is scarcely permissible to doubt) that the Gennetai of the Genos Hesychidai performed a certain sacrifice in which no Eupatridai took part. Yet the contrary view, held tacitly or explicitly, has been an axiom in all attempts to diagnose the structure of Attic Society: and a double sense of the word 'Eupatridai' has been posited, which I trust I have proved untrue.[3]

---

[1] Pp. 86–115 above.   [2] Quoted by the scholiast on Soph. O.C. 489.
[3] Pp. 108–110 above.

Proceeding further from Aristotle's fiction to historic fact, I think there is no crucial difficulty about the Eupatridai. It is questionable indeed what, if anything, we may infer from their alleged Thesean origin: I will deal with this later. But I am content to accept Aristotle's view as historic, that the Eupatrid Order was, before Solon, a nobility of birth with a monopoly of access to high office. Indeed I go further, and imagine that the fountain of honour had been the King, and the Eupatrid Order had been created by the Kingship: that for about a century at least (by 594) there had been no King, and consequently the Order had been closed throughout that period of violent social change: that this was one of the reasons why Solon abolished their obsolescent monopoly. However that may be, a 'Eupatrid' after Solon is easy enough to define: he is a descendant in male line of one of those families which had once held a monopoly of all high office, and still retained the monopoly of certain archaic offices (the Phylobasileis and the Eupatrid Exegetai). Nor is their relation obscure to the rest of the body of Athenians as a whole. The Eupatridai had never composed the whole nation: they had been selected out of the nation, and during their monopoly the body of remaining Athenians not eligible for high office had always existed.

The relation of the Eupatridai to the *Genê* and that of the Gennetai to the body of Athenians are not nearly so simple questions. I am not at all prepared to take for granted Aristotle's theory that Gennetai had once composed the whole nation:[1] nor, consequently, that Francotte's question, 'How did the non-Gennetai become part of the nation?' is a *vera quaestio*. Equally incapable of an immediate *a priori* answer is the difficult and important question, 'Does Eupatrid-hood extend to a whole Genos?'—e.g. Kallias is a Eupatrid (Xen. *Symp.* 8. 40) and member of the Genos *Kerykes* (Andoc. *Myst.* 116): does it follow that all members of the Genos *Kerykes* are Eupatrids? It is not even self-evident that the Eupatrid families are all necessarily Gennetai: by Aristotle's fiction (that a Eupatrid is ἰθαγενής as far as Theseus, but a Gennete is ἰθαγενής as far as Ion) Eupatrid-hood does not *eo ipso* carry Gennete-hood.

Now it is evident that progressive statesmen, from Solon on-

[1] As little as I am prepared, *a priori*, to deny it.

wards, were concerned to limit the prerogatives and influence of birth: and that, notwithstanding, certain qualifications of blood were still respected, as late as the fourth century. To understand both the progressive statesmen's task and the power of survival which birth-privilege possessed, it is essential to define these qualifications of blood as exactly as we can. The studies which follow are intended as contributions to this enquiry. That it is not yet time to systematize is evident if I am right in thinking that previous theory has rested on false axioms.

[I treat the terms 'body of Athenians', 'Athenian nation', 'citizen body' as convertible. In the territory of Athens there may be aliens resident (μέτοικοι), whether free (ξένοι) or slaves (δοῦλοι): there may be people on her borders who are under her sovranty (περίοικοι): all these are no part of the nation. All others are, and are Athenian citizens. The extent of their citizen rights may vary to an indefinite extent, and women and children are of course in special categories: but I believe that never in Greece (until the doctrinaire reaction against democracy in the second half of the fifth century) is the theory held that any native adult male in a sovran community has *no concern at all*[1] in the conduct of affairs: I therefore call him a citizen.]

I. THE SO-CALLED 'DEMOTIONID DECREES,' *I.G.* II.² 1237[2]

§ 1. These decrees are resolutions of the Phratry of Dekeleia. This Phratry is, in effect, the 'ecclesiastical parish', the 'Deme of Dekeleia' being the civil parish. The 'congregation' was hereditary and may have included members scattered all over the map of

---

[1] The ὑπομείονες at Sparta are in this position, but we do not hear of them before 400 B.C. The ὅμοιοι were defined c. 600 B.C. (*C.A.H.* III. 562) and it may be said that the notion of ὅμοιοι implies the notion of ὑπομείονες. If that were so, I would have to date as early as 600 those precautions against a power-hungry Demos which I think in fact were first taken about 450 (e.g. in Boeotia, if the arrangements in *Hell. Ox.* XI. date from the Battle of Koroneia). I do not in any case believe that the *Thetes* in Athens were made ὑπομείονες ever, except under the 400, and the 30, and in the Macedonian period.

[2] The most recent text, with full commentary, is Hiller von Gaertringen's in *Sylloge*³ 921. Hiller accepts *in toto* (one slight disagreement in note 35) the position brilliantly established by Wilamowitz *Arist. und Athen* II. 260 sqq. This, though forty years old, is still the fundamental discussion. Add to the references in *Sylloge*³ Busolt-Swoboda, *Griechische Staatskunde*, pp. 879 and 959 sqq., especially 962 and note 2, and further works there quoted: also Toepffer, *Attische Genealogie*, pp. 289–91, and Szanto, *Rh. Mus.* 40 (1885), pp. 506 sqq., the latest writer (I believe) to distinguish the Demotioni-dai from the Phratry.

Attica; yet it had at least this especial connexion with Dekeleia, that the sanctuary and altar of Zeus Phratrios were there. Moreover the Phratry's name was, I believe, Dekeleieis (Δεκελειησ, the Dekeleans): I will come back to this question.

The resolutions of these ecclesiastical parishes are not ordinarily of the first importance. Yet there is a certain interest in seeing how occupied territory will revert to the normal, and Dekeleia in 396 B.C. (the date of the first decree) has this special claim on our notice. Moreover the 126 lines of this inscription are by far the most substantial document which we possess concerning the Attic phratriai; and inexact notions on this topic spoil the clearness of our vision of mature Athens, and for archaic Athens blind us almost completely.

I give, first, a translation of the two decrees: keeping (for convenience of reference) as close as possible to the lines of the Greek. I omit the third decree, that of Menexenos. It is later in date: it is incomplete, and what there is is fragmentary:[1] it may also be fairly called less important.

> [Stele?] of Zeus Phratrios.
> Priest, Theodoros son of Euphantides,
> inscribed and erected the stele.
> They shall give the priest priestly dues
> 5 as follows; from the Meion[2] a thigh, a rib, an ear,
> 3 obols of money; from the Koureion[2] a thigh,
> a rib, an ear, a cake weighing 1 choinix,
> a ½-chous of wine, a drachma of money.
> Resolved as follows by the Phrateres, when
> 10 Phormion was Archon at Athens   396/5
> and the Phratriarch was Pantakles
> of Oion.
> HIEROKLES MOVED: Whoever have not yet been
> scrutinized according to the Nomos of the Demotionidai,
> 15 the Phrateres shall make scrutiny of them
> forthwith, after swearing by
> Zeus Phratrios, carrying their votes from
> the altar. Whosoever seems, not being a Phrater, to have

---

[1] The restorations in the corresponding part of the front face are reasonably certain (50–8).

[2] *Meion* and *Koureion* correspond roughly to Baptism and Confirmation: they are the Sacrifices offered, on behalf of an aspirant member, at infancy and coming of age. This is indeed not more than a hypothesis, since the main text, Pollux VIII. 107 is quite indecisive. See Busolt-Swoboda, *Gr. Staatskunde*, p. 961.

been introduced, his name shall be expunged by the
20 Priest and the Phratriarch from the list
which is in [the archives] of the Demotionidai and from the copy.
He who introduced the man expelled on scrutiny
must pay 100 drachmai, dedicate to Zeus
Phratrios: the money shall be collected
25 by the Priest and the Phratriarch
or they themselves must pay it. The scrutiny
shall in future be in the year following that in which
(the Phratriarch) sacrifices the Koureion, on the Koureotis day
of Apatouria, and they shall carry the votes from the altar.
30 If any one wishes to appeal to the Demotionidai
after an adverse vote, he may:
Synegoroi shall be chosen to sit with them[1]
by the Dekeleia Lodge, 5 men not
less than 30 years old. They shall be
35 sworn, by the Phratriarch and the Priest,
to exercise their function with all justice, and not
to let any man who is not a Phrater be in the Phratry.
Any appellant who gets an adverse vote
from the Demotionidai must pay 1,000 drachmai
40 dedicate to Zeus Phratrios: this
money shall be collected by the Priest
of the Dekeleia Lodge, or he must pay it himself:
and any other of the Phrateres who chooses may
collect it, for the common treasury. The above
45 to hold good from the Archonship of Phormion.   396/5
The Phratriarch shall put the vote concerning those who
are due for scrutiny in the course of each
year: if he fail to put the vote, he must pay
500 drachmai dedicate to Zeus
50 Phratrios, and the Priest shall collect
this money, or any other who chooses,
for the common treasury. In future, they shall bring
Meion and *Koureion* offerings to Dekeleia to the altar,
and if (the Phratriarch) fails to sacrifice them on the altar,
55 he must pay 50 (?) drachmai dedicate to
Zeus Phratrios, and the Priest shall collect
57 this money or himself must pay it.

[At least one line missing, probably to this effect: 'That is to
say, unless there is war or pestilence.']

        [1] επ αυτοισ, lit. 'in addition to them.' Sc. the Demotionidai.

59 In the event of such a hindrance, wherever the
60 Priest shall notify, the *Meion*
and *Koureion* offerings shall be brought there. He shall give
notice
5 days before Dorpia[1] on a white notice board
at least 1 span across, wherever is
the resort of Dekeleieis in Athens. This
65 decree and the priestly dues shall be
inscribed by the Priest on a marble stele
in front of the altar at Dekeleia, at his
own expense. NIKODEMOS MOVED: To concur
in the former decrees laid down concerning the
70 introduction of sons and their
scrutiny: *but* the 3 witnesses mentioned
for the Anakrisis[2] must be found amongst (the father's)
own Thiasotai, to give evidence on the questions asked
and to take the oath by Zeus Phratrios.
75 The witnesses shall give evidence and take the oath
with their hand on the altar. If there are not,
in that Thiasos, so many as 3, they
shall be found amongst the other Phrateres. When
the scrutiny takes place, the Phratriarch shall not
80 put the vote concerning the sons
to the whole body of Phrateres until
the introducer's Thiasotai vote in secret
carrying their votes from the altar.
Their votes shall be counted,
85 in sight of the whole body of Phrateres present
at the meeting, by the Phratriarch,
and he shall declare which way they
have voted. If, when the Thiasotai have voted
that he is a Phrater, the other
90 Phrateres give an adverse vote, the Thiasotai
must pay 100 drachmai dedicate to Zeus
Phratrios, except such of the Thiasotai
as publicly denounce or oppose (the candidate)
during the scrutiny. If the
95 Thiasotai give an adverse vote, and the introducer

[1] The first day of Apatouria (so e g. Hesychius and Suidas, s.v. Ἀπατούρια: other late writers say the second day, but see note 31 to *Sylloge*[3] 921).
[2] A preliminary enquiry, such as the Archon held before cases came into court. The previous decree in which these three witnesses were mentioned is not now extant.

appeals to the whole body, and the whole body
holds that (his candidate) is a Phrater, his name shall be
    entered
in the common lists: but if the whole body
gives an adverse vote, he must pay 100 drachmai
100 dedicate to Zeus Phratrios. If,
after the Thiasotai's adverse vote, he does not appeal
to the whole body, the adverse vote
of the Thiasotai shall stand. The Thiasotai
shall not vote with the whole body
105 on the sons belonging to their own
Thiasos. The Priest shall inscribe
this decree as well on the marble
stele. The oath of the witnesses at the introduction
of sons: *I testify that he whom he is introducing*
110 *is his own son born in wedlock from his lawful*
wife. This is the truth, by Zeus Phratrios:
many blessings on me if my oath is good;
if I forswear myself, the contrary.

These are resolutions of the Phratry. Theodoros the Priest is
priest of the Phratry, and as such receives the fees which the
members pay at the two sacrifices involved in the introduction
of a new member. The Phratriarch Pantakles is, of course,
Phratriarch of the Phratry.

'The priest' and 'the phratriarch' referred to in the remainder
of the document are, presumably, Theodoros and Pantakles or
their successors. For the phratriarch, this is beyond doubt: but
as to the priest, doubts can evidently be entertained, for Toepffer
concludes his account of the Dekeleieis in his *Attische Genealogie*,
p. 291, with the words, 'whether the priest mentioned in line 60
is the priest of the Genos (Dekeleieis) or the Phratry (Demotionidai) cannot be decided.' I will examine the instances.

Theodoros the priest combines with his priestly function that of
a *Grammateus*, or secretary: this stele is erected by him (2/3, 66)
at his own cost (67/8), and consequently his name stands, as that
of a Grammateus in State decrees often stands, at the head of the
stele. It is beyond question, then, that the priest in 2, 66, and 107,
is the same priest—Theodoros or his successor. Further secretarial
duties are—to post the notice in case the sacrifice cannot be held
at Dekeleia (60), and to expunge the name of anyone refused on

scrutiny (19/20): the phratriarch shares this last responsibility. [The inscribing ordered in 97/8 is probably done by the same two, but this is not stated.] In 2, 66, 107, 60, and 19/20, then, we have the priest of the Phratry, Theodoros or his successor. The remaining duties of 'the priest' are—

1. He is, in company with the phratriarch, to administer the oath to the 5 *Synegoroi* appointed to represent the Dekeleieis when appeal is made to the Demotionidai (32 sqq., especially 35):

2. He is to collect certain fines, viz.:

   (*a*) (in company with the phratriarch) 100 drachmas from the introducer of a man refused on scrutiny (25):

   (*b*) 1,000 drachmas from a man who appeals unsuccessfully to the Demotionidai (41/2: he is here called ο ιερευσ το Δεκελειων οικο, 'the Priest of the Dekeleia Lodge):

   (*c*) 500 drachmas from the phratriarch, if he fail to put any name to the scrutiny (50):

   (*d*) 50 drachmas (? the figure is mostly missing) from the phratriarch, if he fail to sacrifice on the altar at Dekeleia (55).

It seems to me most unlikely that 'the priest' in any of these cases is any other than Theodoros (or his successor), the priest of the Phratry; who, as we see, is also secretary and treasurer. In 2 (*b*) he is called 'the priest of the Dekeleia Lodge', and in 1 he administers the oath to men chosen by the Dekeleia Lodge.

I take it, then, that 'the Dekeleia Lodge' (ο των Δεκελειων οικοσ) is the name of the Phratry: or, more simply, Δεκελειησ.[1]

---

[1] Their Eponym is Dekelos, who helped the Tyndaridai to find Helen at Aphidna, Hdt. IX. 73. 2. Herodotus there says of Sophanes that he was ἐκ δήμου Δεκελεῆθεν, Δεκελέων δὲ τῶν κοτε ἐργασαμένων ἔργον χρήσιμον, etc. [the story of Dekelos]: i.e. (I think) Sophanes belonged to *both Deme and Phratry* of Dekeleia. The same distinction appears to be made by Lysias XXIII. 2–3. Pankleon (in Lysias' story) claimed to b? a Plataean, and to have been inscribed in the Deme of Dekeleia, Δεκελειόθεν: the speaker therefore went to the barber's shop by the Hermai, ἵνα οἱ Δεκελειεῖς προσφοιτῶσιν, to enquire: οὕς τε ἐξευρίσκοιμι Δεκελειῶν ἐπυνθανόμην εἴ τινα γιγνώσκοιεν Δεκελειόθεν δημοτευόμενον Παγκλέωνα. It was the Rendezvous of the *Phratry* (Δεκελειεῖς), but they would be more likely than any other group in Athens to know about members of the Deme (Δεκελειόθεν δημοτευόμενοι).—Except in these two passages (where they are being distinguished from the Phrateres) Demesmen of Dekeleia are always, I believe, called Δεκελειεῖς (Δεκελειῆς, Δεκελεῖς, etc.).—See Appendix, ΔΕΚΕΛΕΙΕΙΣ.

This is why the priest has to post his notice at the 'Rendezvous in Athens of the *Δεκελεια*'[1] (64, cf. 122/3).

Some forty years ago[2] Wilamowitz strenuously denied this, asserting that the name of the Phratry is *Demotionidai*: and his view has found, I believe, absolute acceptance. It is universally held that the Phratry is *Demotionidai*, and the *Dekeleieis* are not the Phratry but some portion of it. What, then, can we make of Theodoros, priest of the Dekeleieis and, apparently, priest of the Phratry? Wilamowitz indeed holds that the 'priest of the House of Dekeleieis' is, *ex officio*, priest of the Phratry: but this solution has not satisfied everyone. It is indeed worse to assume that two priests are in question: yet (on Wilamowitz's identification) the priest has a double function—priest of the whole and of a part: why then, when he is for the first time collecting a fine incurred by a vote of the 'whole', is he for the first time called 'Priest of the part' (39-42)? It is certain the fine went to the treasury of the whole (43/4).

The 'so-called Demotionid Decrees' are, I believe, Decrees of the Dekeleieis. I will first develop my own case: next, argue against Wilamowitz:[3] last, face that most difficult question— who, then, are the Demotionidai?

§ 2. The two decrees, of Hierokles and Nikodemos, are written in the same hand. They may well have been passed at the same

[1] This is not a fixed Rendezvous (ὅποι ἂν προσφοιτῶσιν): but the Phrateres would always have *some* favourite resort. At about this moment it was a barber's shop near the Hermai, in the Agora; see preceding note, and Lysias 23. 3, of about this date.— Domaszewski, *Die Hermen der Agora zu Athen* (*Sitzb. Heidelberg*, 1914, *Abh.* 10), thinks (p. 8) the notice can't have been posted at a barber's (why not?), and suggests (p. 11) this is simply where the Riding (τριττύς), in which Dekeleia was (the Inland Riding of Hippothontis), had its parade station. The name of this Riding was, however, inscribed in *I.G.* I². 901, line 3, and was pretty certainly not *Δεκελειεῖς*. I am republishing this inscription in the *Mélanges Glotz*: read (*c.* 12-letter lines) δευρε H[ιπποθο]|ν [τι]σ φυ[λε τελε]|υται Ζε (or Τε, certainly not Πε or Δε) [. . . . . ο]|ν δε τριτ[τυσ—]. The other two Ridings of Hippothontis are *Peiraieis* and *Eleusinioi.*—I also question Domaszewski's translation of προσφοιτᾶν='to parade.' The phylarchoi in Mnesimachos' comedy (quoted by Athen. 402-3—

στεῖχ' εἰς ἀγορὰν πρὸς τοὺς Ἑρμᾶς
οὗ προσφοιτῶσ' οἱ φύλαρχοι)

are off duty.

[2] *Arist. und Athen.* II. 261 sqq.—Szanto (*Rh. M.* XL., pp. 506 sqq.) had distinguished Demotionidai from Phrateres.

[3] I choose Wilamowitz out of homage to a book whose wide and cogent thinking has not been superseded. Subsequent writers, who all accept his main thesis (Demotionidai=Phrateres), have tinkered at details, but only to make inconsequent his subtle and consistent account.

meeting; they certainly are intended to be read together: το δε ψηφισμα τοδε (sc. of Nikodemos) προσαναγραψατω ο ιερευσ εισ την στηλην (106/7).¹—They are not, however, self-explaining: they refer to the Nomos of the Demotionidai and τα προτερα ψηφισματα, and simply supplement these. The two decrees both regulate procedure for admitting a new member.

Hierokles enacts:

A. An immediate emergency scrutiny (13–26). The Phrateres vote: any name refused is deleted from the list, the introducer is fined 100 drachmas.

B. Normal scrutinies for the future, in the year following the candidate's Koureion (26–45). The Phrateres vote:² an introducer whose candidate is refused may appeal to the Demotionidai: if he is refused again, the introducer is fined 1,000 drachmas.

Nikodemos enacts:

A. A modification in the *anakrisis* or preliminary questioning (71–78). The three witnesses required must be from the introducer's Thiasos (unless it has too few members).

B. A modification in the scrutiny itself (78–106). Before the Phrateres vote, the introducer's Thiasos shall first vote by (secret) ballot: the votes shall then be counted in view of the Phrateres. The Phrateres then debate (the Thiasotai taking part) and vote (the Thiasotai abstaining). If the Thiasos has admitted and the Phrateres then refuse, the Thiasos shall be fined 100 drachmas³ (but those Thiasotai who, in the debate, signify their opposition, shall not contribute to the fine). If the Thiasos has refused, the

---

¹ Had Theodorus set his graver to work to inscribe the first decree only, he would probably have got a larger or a smaller stele (or else used smaller or larger writing): either, that is, he would have got the decree on to one face, or spread himself comfortably over both. What he did was to get 58 lines on one face and 9½ on the other.

² The subject of φερεν την ψηφον απο το βωμο is not named: it must be the Phrateres, as in a State decree the unnamed subject is the Athenians. It must also (one would suppose) be the same as in 15 sqq. above, διαδικασαι τοσ φρατερασ, φεροντας την ψηφον απο το βωμο. But, since it is quite evidently the Dekeleieis (since appeal is then allowed from them to the Demotionidai, 30, cf. 32/3), and he refuses to equate the Dekeleieis with the Phrateres, Wilamowitz is forced to hold that the subject of φερεν is *not* the Phrateres.

³ *Centum*, not *centenas*: 100 drachmas in all, not 100 per Thiasote.

introducer may acquiesce (and then there is no fine) or appeal to the Phrateres: if they admit, good: if they refuse, the introducer is fined 100 drachmas.

The principle is constant: an adverse vote of the Phrateres involves a fine of 100 drachmas. Hitherto, the responsibility had lain with the introducer, who had paid the fine. Hierokles expressly enacts it for the emergency scrutiny. For the normal scrutiny, he does not need to enact it (he is concerned with another matter, viz.: appeal *from* the Phrateres, which if unsuccessful involves the tenfold fine of 1,000 drachmas). Nikodemos substitutes, for the conscience of the introducer, the ballot of the Thiasotai. If the introducer heeds their adverse voice, there is no fine: it is as if he had heeded his own conscience. If they encourage him, and he is refused by the Phrateres, the Thiasotai pay the fine: for they, his acting conscience, have failed him. If they refuse him, they decline the responsibility: the introducer is left to his own conscience. If he trusts it and the Phrateres allow his claim, well and good: but if they refuse him, he must pay the fine himself.

The principle is, I repeat, constant: the Thiasotai's ballot was made to replace the introducer's conscience, because (I imagine) it was likely to be more effective.[1] The Phratry was too big to trust its own judgment, so the Thiasoi are made responsible for their members. Nikodemos' two modifications are both in the same direction, more precaution against intruders.

§ 3. 'The Phratry is the Demotionidai: no one else but the *plenum* can give judgment on appeals, and the list of the Phrateres εν Δημοτιωνιδων can only be kept in the Phratry's house. Any other interpretation is wrong.' This is all the argument Wilamowitz devotes to the matter.

It is indeed remarkable that the Demotionidai have such importance: that their νομοσ prescribes the methods of scrutiny, that appeal is allowed to them from the Phrateres, that they keep the chief of the two Phratry-lists on their own premises. Remarkable: though not, I think, more irregular than the position Wilamowitz ascribes to the Dekeleieis. But I leave the Demotionidai till the

---

[1] If the intoducer persists in trusting his own conscience, he may, but the Phratry has been warned. Without doubt the further appeal, to the Demotionidai, is still allowed if anyone chooses to risk the 1,000 drachmas.

next section, and will state now no more than what I consider evident—namely, that the Demotionidai are an aristocratic corporation, with a position of privilege and exegetic functions *vis-à-vis* the Phratry of the Dekeleieis.

Meanwhile, the following considerations seem fatal to Wilamowitz's view:

1. The Scrutiny (Diadikasia) is done by the Phrateres.[1] [*Ergo*, since appeal is allowed from these Phrateres to the Demotionidai (30, cf. 32/3), the equation 'Phrateres=Demotionidai' cannot stand.] This is expressly stated in line 15 (διαδικασαι τοσ φρατερασ), but Wilamowitz claims that the emergency scrutiny there meant should be carefully distinguished from the normal scrutinies.[2] A normal Diadikasia is described in some detail in lines 78 sqq. The phratriarch presides, all the Phrateres are present: the main business is (as in a State Ekklesia) a Debate followed by a Vote. Nikodemos inserts (as a special preliminary to the actual Diadikasia) a secret ballot of the Thiasotai. [That this secret ballot is *not* the Diadikasia is self-evident: it is put beyond question by line 94, the Thiasotai who wish to escape the fine must make their opposition clear εν τηι διαδικασιαι: this cannot be 'in the secret ballot'. It is, of course, 'in the Debate', for the Thiasotai have to abstain in the final Vote (103–6).]

Since then both the emergency and the normal Diadikasiai are done by the Phrateres, it is inconceivable that the unexpressed subject of φερεν την ψηφον in 29 can be other than τοσ φρατεροσ. Nor will anyone who is familiar with the language of Attic Decrees deny the strong presumption that this is so: the subject of such infinitives is the body which votes the decree: εδοξεν τοισ φρατεροιν . . . φερεν την ψηφον: εδοχσεν τει βολει και τοι δεμοι . . .

---

[1] This is indeed allowed by many scholars (see Busolt-Swoboda, *Staatskunde*, p. 962, note 2) who yet cling to the equation *Phrateres=Demotionidai*. The consequences are astounding: I quote Swoboda: 'Es blieb also auch gestattet, gegen einen abweisenden Beschluss der Gesamtheit Berufung an dieselbe Versammlung einzulegen. Das war möglich, weil die Berufung ein neues Verfahren in der Form einer gerichtlichen Verhandlung einleitete.' The appeal is from Demotionidai in Assembly to Demotionidai in Court: as it were, from the Ekklesia to the Heliaia. The thing only needs careful stating (as Swoboda gives it on p. 962) to be seen to be (at least) improbable: and if it were possible, *it is not compatible with the words of the decree.* Appeal from Ekklesia to Heliaia could not be called εσ Αθηναιουσ, nor could appeal *'from Demotionidai in Phratry to Demotionidai in Court'* be called εσ Δημοτιωνιδασ. I therefore disregard this hypothesis.

[2] P. 260. 'Hopeless from the start are all modern explanations which confuse this emergency ruling with the normal institutions which follow.'

ἀποδοναι τα χρεματα . . . ταμιασ αποκναμενεν (*I.G.* I². 91, lines 2, 13, etc.) : *et passim*.

2. The uses of οἱ φρατερεσ, Δεκελειησ, ὁ Δεκελειων οικοσ, correspond respectively to ὁ δημοσ, Ἀθηναιοι, ὁ δημοσ ὁ Ἀθηναιων in State decrees. The instances illustrate this of themselves: I take one instance which is particularly clumsy on Wilamowitz's view (see p. 124 above). The fine of 1,000 drachmas is consequent on a vote of the Demotionidai, but goes to the common treasury: therefore the language is more explicit than usual, 'the priest *of the Dekeleia Lodge* shall be responsible for collecting it, or any Phrater who chooses may collect it for the common treasury'[1] (41–44).

3. *The tariff of fines is constant.* An adverse vote of the Phrateres costs 100 drachmas, an adverse vote of the Demotionidai costs 1,000 drachmas (see p. 126 above). The current view is that when the Thiasoi replaced the Dekeleieis as preliminary investigators, the fine for appeal to the Phratry was reduced by ninetenths: I submit that this is astounding.[2] The appeal to the Demotionidai is appeal *beyond* the Phratry, and is correspondingly expensive.

4. In Attic procedure, *Synegoroi* are sometimes assessors (e.g. *Ἀθ. πολ.* 54. 2³), sometimes advocates (e.g. Hypereides, *pro Euxenippo* 12), sometimes accusers.[4] I have taken them to be assessors, appointed by and from the whole body as assessors to their small

---

[1] The money will not be paid twice, as Wilamowitz suggests (p. 261, note 4). If either the priest hands over 1000 drachmas (no matter whence) or a Phrater chooses to save him the trouble, the transaction is closed.

[2] It is against the whole tenour of the new regulations, which are tightening the strictness of admission.

[3] Λογιστὰς δέκα καὶ συνηγόρους τούτοις δέκα: i.e. they co-operate with the bench. Cf. *Lex. Rhet. Cant.*, p. 672. 20, λογισταὶ . . . καὶ ἄλλοι δέκα συνήγοροι οἵτινες συνανακρίνουσι τούτοις. They help conduct the enquiry and pronounce the decision: they are not briefed for prosecution or defence. A very close parallel in *I.G.* II². 1183, lines 14–15, decree of the Deme Myrrhinous: (ομνυναι) τουσ συνηγορουσ 'συνηγορησειν τωι δημωι τα δικαια και ψηφιεισθαι α αν μοι δοκει (*sic*) δικαιοτατα ειναι.'

[4] Dem. *Meidias* 112, and frequently in Aristophanes, e.g. *Acharn.* 685, 705, *Wasps* 691. The view once held by Hermann, that these are standing public prosecutors (or 'Treasury Advocates'), is, I think, untrue: rather (in Sophocles' words, *Trach.* 814) τῷ κατηγόρῳ συνηγοροῦσι, they support the prosecutor. Public prosecutors (appointed *ad hoc*) are called κατήγοροι in Plut. *Pericles* X. 6. The συνήγοροι in the decree impeaching Antiphon Archeptolemos and Onomakles (ps.-Plut. *X Or.* 833E), appear to be Bouleutai chosen by the Strategoi to support them in the prosecution: παρασχόντων δ' αὐτοὺς (sc. the accused) οἱ στρατηγοί, καὶ ἐκ τῆς βουλῆς οὕστινας ἂν δοκῇ τοῖς στρατηγοῖς προσελομένοις μέχρι δέκα, ὅπως ἂν περὶ παρόντων γένηται ἡ κρίσις: and then κατηγορεῖν τοὺς ᾑρημένους συνηγόρους καὶ τοὺς στρατηγούς.

standing committee. It is impossible *vice versa*: if the Dekeleieis
are only a part, they cannot appoint assessors to the whole.
Wilamowitz recognizes this, and takes Synegoroi as accusers:
they are to lay the Dekeleieis' case before the whole Phratry.
I submit it is improper for *accusers* to take an oath as to what
verdict they will permit (lines 36/7).

§ 4. Who are the Demotionidai?

I have kept this to the end: the most difficult, and the most
interesting, question. Now that I have established (beyond
reasonable doubt, as I hope) that appeal was allowed from the
Phrateres to the Demotionidai, we can enquire who they are,
and possibly enlighten our generalities about the nature of aristocratic privilege. It is disastrous to block enquiry at the start by a
preconceived generality. Our notions about the Attic aristocracy
are exceedingly insecure, and we have to cut *them* to fit the instances, not the instances to fit *them*.

Whose vote could possibly be valid against that of the Phrateres?
The State's:[1] but the Demotionidai are not the State: nor are they
a Tribe (one of the Four or one of the Ten): and there is no corporation known to us (or readily conceivable) which could be
intermediate between the Phratry and the State.[2]

The Phratry appoints 5 Synegoroi to sit *in addition to* the Demotionidai, as assessors[3] representing the Phratry. This suggests to
me (I am not sure with what degree of cogency) that the Demotionidai are themselves a reasonably small body: thus for instance
the State Logistai, 10 in number, are given 10 Synegoroi.[4] I
imagine them as a small committee of experts, keepers of the
Statute Book (line 14, cf. 21: i.e. νομοφύλακες) and *Exegetai* of the
Statutes: these functions are of course hereditary. Their relation
to the Phratry is something like that of the House of Lords to a
Common Jury, in so far as they are the *experts* of the community
and not merely representatives of it. A closer parallel, and closer

---

[1] Solon gave all corporations power to make their own laws unless the State chooses
to interfere. *Lex apud Gaium Dig.* XLVII. 22. 4.
[2] It has been supposed that the Δυαληα, whose inscription (*I.G.* II². 1241) mentions
two Phratriarchoi, are a 'geminated' Phratry. If this is so, the original Phratriai do
not apparently continue their separate existence. We have no evidence of any unit
which subdivides the State and is subdivided into functioning Phratriai: I think we
may safely deny that any existed.
[3] See the end of § 3 above.
[4] *Aθ. πολ.* 54. 2. The 30 Logistai of the fifth century have disappeared.

9

home, is the relation of the Eupatrid Areopagites to the citizen body in seventh-century Athens. It is our fortune that in the small world of the Phratry privilege was not so jealously challenged as in the State, and consequently we see in the Phratry of 396/5 a microcosm of the archaic State, with certain noticeable distortions.

Until Solon, the Areopagus was the seat of pure aristocracy: its members were 'Eupatrids', scions of certain houses of heroic descent, who inherited certain priestly functions and a certain religious competence. In virtue of these functions and this competence they could render great service to the State by dealing with cases of bloodshed, pollution, sacrilege, etc. Whether this was the first nucleus of their more general legal competence, I could not say. Violence is perhaps the most difficult thing a primitive state has to regulate, but it is not the only thing, nor was religion unconcerned in these other cases. The archaic state was regarded, seriously and literally, as a religious entity, whose welfare and health was the concern of certain Gods and Heroes. The distinction between sacred and secular law came very slowly, and so late as 550 B.C. what seems to us a commercial case is partly dealt with by Delphi (Hdt. VI. 86). Common Law in England resides in the breasts of His Majesty's Judges: in seventh-century Athens it resided in the breasts of the Areopagites, and since till Drakon there was no Statute Law, Common Law there comprised the whole field of Criminal, Civil and Constitutional law and custom.

This was the basis of the Areopagites' powers. They claim, like Kallias in the fifth century, νόμον πάτριον λέγομεν.[1] They were a Court of Law and gave judgments: at first, out of their own breasts; and then, when Statute Law began, they became 'Guardians of the Laws,' and kept and controlled the Statute Book. The political decline of Aristocracy began with the arrival of the *nouveaux riches* in the seventh century. Solon was bound to take account of them and admit them to the Areopagus; and so that body, losing its hereditary character, lost the true foundation of its powers. It was more than a century before those powers collapsed: for the Areopagites, although secularized, were men of experience, and their *expertise* (though no longer inherited with their blood)

[1] Andoc. *Myst.* 116.

was still useful to the State. They continued until Ephialtes to give judgment in lawsuits and to have the last word, as legal experts, in admitting Statutes to the Statute Book.[1]

After 461 the State was almost wholly secular: Ephialtes completed the process which Solon had begun and Kleisthenes had drastically continued.[2] We shall find nothing in this secular State to compare with the Demotionidai, unless such pale survivals of Eupatridhood as the *Exegetai*: these may indeed give us our closest analogies, and to them I will return.

Meanwhile, the Areopagites. The powers of the Demotionidai are based on the same hereditary competence with regard to *law*, which is still regarded as sacred law, as those of the Areopagites in their prime. The Law of the Phratry perhaps still resides unwritten in their breasts;[3] if not, it resides written in their keeping. The interpretation of the law, in the last instance, lies with them. I do not suggest that the Demotionidai had as much effective power in the Phratry as the Areopagites in seventh-century Athens. Membership of the Phratry was a matter of consequence in the secular world outside, so the Phrateres have taken their precautions. They freely vote additional psephismata: they appoint assessors to the Demotionidai: and (this is the real anomaly) the Demotionidai have become a court of last instance, i.e. they can override the Phrateres only to admit (not to reject) a candidate.

The anomaly is grave. That experts should form the court of last instance is familiar to us: but in Athens the practice was contrary. Once the non-experts could form an opinion at all, that opinion was final. The Areopagites never were a court of appeal *from* the Heliaia: so soon as the two courts existed, the Heliaia's verdict was final. Wilamowitz's argument ('no one else but the *plenum* can give judgment on appeals') is therefore strong,

---

[1] Νομοφυλακία: I regret that Mr. Walker in *C.A.H.* V., pp. 98–100, is inclined to doubt this meaning. For the sense of the terms 'Statute' (νόμος) and 'Statute Book' (κείμενοι νόμοι): for the practical identity (at least till Eukleides) of νόμος and ψήφισμα: for the distinction between the Statute Book and Solon's Code, etc.: see J. Schreiner, *De corpore iuris Atheniensium* (Dissert. Bonn, 1913): a work remarkable for the candour and cogency of its argument, and for the importance of its subject.

[2] Solon by admitting βέβηλοι to the Areopagus: Kleisthenes by building the State out of Demes instead of Thiasoi.

[3] Cf. Lysias VI. 10, Plato, *Laws* 845E, 916C: all quoted below.

but it will not stand against the weight of evidence. *The anomaly exists*: a consequence of archaic religion surviving into the secular conditions of the fourth century.[1]

The Exegetai were in a similar position. When Solon secularized the Areopagite Court, he converted its judgments from ἐξήγησις (such as 'Theseus' had intended, Plut. *Theseus*, 25. 2) to συμβούλευσις: it is no longer an authoritative verdict, but only an expert opinion. No doubt the opinion was commonly unchallenged: but in principle (since the appeal was allowed) it could be challenged. What power of growth that principle held is well known. In fourth-century Athens, a man jealous for the absoluteness of the pronouncements sanctioned by religion needed to be agile and circumspect: the Exegetai, questioned by [Demosthenes'] client on a matter of behaviour and ritual, are careful to enquire πότερον ἐξηγήσωνται μόνον ἢ καὶ συμβουλεύσωσιν (XLVII. 68). 'Both,' says the client: and they answer ἡμεῖς τοίνυν σοι τὰ μὲν νόμιμα ἐξηγησόμεθα τὰ δὲ σύμφορα παραινέσομεν. Plato, in whose *Laws* the Exegetai are of great consequence, is emphatic that in its own sphere Exegesis is absolute: τὰ μὲν περὶ τὰ θεῖα νόμιμα etc., τοὺς ἐξηγητὰς γίγνεσθαι κυρίους φράζοντας (958D: cf. 775A).[2]

The Democracy though secular was not 'anti-clerical.' Lysias (VI. 10) quotes Perikles' dictum μὴ μόνον χρῆσθαι τοῖς γεγραμμένοις νόμοις περὶ τῶν ἀσεβούντων ἀλλὰ καὶ τοῖς ἀγράφοις καθ᾽ οὓς Εὐμολπίδαι ἐξηγοῦνται. In their sphere (whose delimitation, like that of Delphi's, was a matter of tact and realism) the Exegetai were not advisers to the sovran Demos, but givers of commands to be obeyed: at the least, of authoritative pronouncements to be believed. It was sometimes very hard to delimit the sphere: for most Athenians believed in their religion, and if it *did* affect public life on vital matters, it was not easy to disregard it.[3] The

---

[1] To invest a smaller body than the *plenum* with final powers *ad hoc* is a procedure not unknown in Athens. It is the famous *Autokratia*: cf. Andoc. *Peace* 33, αὐτοκράτορας γὰρ πεμφθῆναι εἰς Λακεδαίμονα διὰ ταῦθ᾽, ἵνα μὴ ἐπαναφέρωμεν: *Myst.* 15, ψηφισαμένης δὲ τῆς βουλῆς, ἦν γὰρ αὐτοκράτωρ (cf. Thuc. VIII. 67. 1, and *I.G.* I². 298, lines 14–15). These are concessions to that notion of the finality of *expertise*, which the pure democratic doctrine denied.

[2] Plato's Exegetai have their own Law: 845E οἱ τῶν ἐξηγητῶν νόμοι: 916C κατὰ τὸν τῶν ἐξηγητῶν νόμον. Cf. line 14 of our inscription, κατα τον νομον τον Δημοτιωνιδων.

[3] In Plato, *Euthyphro* 4B, a (private) matter of life and death is left to the Exegetai.

most famous occasion[1] was the restoration of Alcibiades after his exile. Religion had been mobilized against him, it had now to be demobilized: the Demos asked the Eumolpid Hierophant to take off the curse. 'If he is innocent, I never cursed him' was the dignified (or pedantic) reply with which the Hierophant affirmed his independence.[2] Not all the psephismata in the world could alter the *fact*, that if Alcibiades had committed sacrilege, the curse of the Goddesses was on him.

The Hierophant's authority was the ἄγραφοι νόμοι καθ' οὓς Εὐμολπίδαι ἐξηγοῦνται.[3] The authority of the Demotionidai rests similarly on ὁ νόμος ὁ τῶν Δημοτιωνιδῶν. I imagine they took their function seriously and gave judgment as technical experts: if they had admitted private rancours, they would hardly have survived. Such privilege is indeed threatened as often by the suspicion of the unprivileged as by the real corruption of the privileged. The precaution against any such suspicion or sense of hocus-pocus was the five assessors. Chosen by and from the unprivileged, they sat with the court and saw that the *expertise* was real.

APPENDIX: ΔΕΚΕΛΕΙΕΙΣ (p. 123, note 1).

That Dekeleieis is the name of a Phratry as well as of a Deme, I believe to be certain.

The distinction between Demesmen and Phrateres which I posit in Herodotus IX. 73. 2 and Lysias XXIII. 2–3 is not, however, certain. My hypothesis is, that both are commonly and correctly called Δεκελειεῖς, but Demesmen could be called more distinctively τοῦ δήμου Δεκελῆθεν or Δεκελειόθεν δημοτευόμενοι, and this is done in these two passages: in our Decrees, on the other hand, no such distinction is made or intended, since Δεκελειησ means the Phratry throughout.

It is clear on any hypothesis that Deme and Phratry had much the same personnel, and the chances were, if you belonged to one you belonged to the other. For I take it as certain that the 'Rendezvous of the Dekeleieis' is the same (*a*) in our Decrees and (*b*) in the almost exactly contemporary speech of Lysias: and it is used (*a*) for posting notices of the Phratry and (*b*) for enquiring about Demesmen. More-

---

[1] On an even more famous occasion, the χρησμολόγοι, whose opinion Themistocles combats (Hdt. VII. 143), are clearly not speaking *ex cathedra*.
[2] Plut. *Alcib.* XXXIII. 3. The Hierophant was not actually one of the Exegetai, but his authority was exactly analogous.
[3] Cf. *I.G.* I². 76, lines 36–7, καθοτι αν Εὐμολπιδαι [εχσηε|γο]νται.

over a high proportion of Phrateres, in the Decrees, are Demesmen: and (on my hypothesis) Sophanes is both Demesman and Phrater. The two aspects, however, are distinct.

The matter of my hypothesis is then (I hope) clear: *Herodotus and Lysias, concerned to distinguish the two aspects, Demesman and Phrater, use a distinctive phrase for the former.* I base the hypothesis chiefly on the use of the distinctive phrase, which otherwise is not readily accounted for. And Herodotus' language 'ἐκ δήμου Δεκελεῆθεν, Δεκελέων δὲ τῶν, etc.' is more natural if he is distinguishing two aspects: though this is not conclusive, since the δέ may be the epexegetic δέ of which he is fond. Whether the honours at Sparta of which Herodotus goes on to speak were reserved for Phrateres or Demesmen, I cannot say, and I suspect few Spartans could.

Herodotus is uncertain whether it was *Dekelos* or the *Dekelees* who helped the Tyndaridai, and he does not say explicitly that the 'Dekelees' of whom Sophanes was one were regarded as descendants of Dekelos. Yet I believe it is safe to assume that they were, and this brings me to the last point: was the fiction of an eponymous ancestor ever applied to a Deme? I think not. It is clear at least that the descendants of Philaios were *not* the Demesmen of the Deme Philaidai (where his sanctuary lay) but the Gennetai of the Genos Philaidai (e.g. the older Miltiades, the philosopher Epicurus, etc.).[1] The ἀρχηγέτης τοῦ δήμου from whom Lysis of Aixone was descended (Plato, *Lysis* 205D) may possibly have been called Aixon,[2] but it was hardly as Demesman of Aixone that Lysis traced his ancestry, rather as member of some locally-rooted Genos or Phratry: cf. the Eumolpidai at Eleusis. The Kleisthenic Phratry was no doubt as artificial as the Deme: but the Phratry's fiction was descent, the Deme's fact was domicile.

---

[1] Hdt. VI. 35. 1: Plut. *Solon* X. 3: Diog. Laert. X. 1: Toepffer, *Att. Geneal.*, pp. 269 sqq.

[2] More likely his daughter was Aixone. Cf. the passage in Plato, and Ed. Meyer, *Forsch.* II. 521, note 3: who unwarrantably translates ἀρχηγέτης τοῦ δήμου 'Ahnherr des Demos.' Rather, 'King' or possibly 'founder': to call him 'ancestor' begs the question.

THE LAWS OF KLEISTHENES

As a preliminary to an estimate of the work of Kleisthenes, I have sought in this paper to constate certain facts about the nature of the evidence. Kleisthenes did not dominate popular imagination. The founder of Democracy, in popular thought, was not Kleisthenes but Solon: the destroyer of Tyranny, not Kleisthenes but Harmodios. This circumstance, which historians may regard as fortunate or unfortunate, at least simplifies the tradition: the mythical element (so hard to disentangle in the story of Solon or Harmodios) is confined, I think, to (i) Aelian's moral tale (*Var. Hist.* XIII. 24) that Kleisthenes was the victim of the Ostracism which he invented, and (ii) gossip about his financial relations with Delphi.[1] I do not insist that all else which we are told is therefore true: only that mythopoeic hero-worship or scandal need not be much reckoned with.

I have reached the following tentative conclusions, viz.:

1. The elements of the tradition are—

   (*a*) The narrative of Herodotus, gained I know not whence, possibly in Periklean circles at Athens. This narrative, once in writing, seems to have superseded living memory, and I seek to show that, apart from (*b*), Aristotle and his sources have no information outside it.

   (*b*) Information gained from surviving contemporary documents: *especially the actual Laws of Kleisthenes.* But apart from the Laws we can name two other documents: the decree recording the treason and condemnation of Isagoras and others who accompanied Kleomenes to Eleusis (*c.* 506) and the decree

---

[1] Dem. *Meidias* 144, Isokr. *Antidosis* 232, Philoch. *F. gr. H.* 328 F 115, Ar. *'Aθ. πολ.* 19: cf. Hdt. V. 62. 3, Pind. *Pyth.* VII. 8 sq.: see Wilamowitz, *Ar. und Ath.* I. 33, Pomtow, *Rh. M.* LI. 580 sqq., LII. 105 sqq. It is just conceivable that the fourth-century story represents genuine Delphic tradition, even building accounts.

recording or ordering the *Diapsephismos* (*c*, 510?).
There may well have been others.

2. As to the Laws themselves, I have concluded that they were Psephismata, moved by Kleisthenes as a private citizen and voted by Boule and Demos: that they were extant in the late fifth century (and presumably later too): that the measures recorded in *'Aθ. πολ.* 22. 2 belong to Kleisthenes' legislation, whether or not they stood in his name: that the Law about the Phratriai recorded in Philochoros F 35 is not Kleisthenic.

3. These constatations involve certain further conclusions (which I have accordingly drawn) about the chronology and scope of the Reform.

1. COMPARISON OF THE ACCOUNTS OF HERODOTUS AND ARISTOTLE

The narrative of events in chapter 20 of Aristotle's *'Aθηναίων Πολιτεία* is so remarkably close to Herodotus, not only in substance but in actual phrase, that any definite divergence, on however slight a point, may be important in determining the relation of the two accounts. Aristotle says (*'Aθ. πολ.* 20. 3) that on the surrender of Kleomenes and Isagoras the Athenians πάντας ἀφεῖσαν ὑποσπόνδους. This is definitely contrary to Herodotus, who says (V. 72. 2) ὑπόσπονδοι ἐξέρχονται ἐκ τῆς χώρης ὅσοι ἦσαν αὐτῶν Λακεδαιμόνιοι . . . (4) τοὺς δὲ ἄλλους 'Αθηναῖοι κατέδησαν τὴν ἐπὶ θανάτῳ.

Now it is pretty certain that Herodotus, on this point, is in the wrong. He contradicts himself later, as to Isagoras at least: V. 74. 1 συνεξῆλθε γάρ οἱ (sc. Κλεομένει) οὗτος (sc. 'Ισαγόρης) ἐκ τῆς ἀκροπόλιος: it is evident Isagoras was neither arrested nor killed upon surrender. Nor was he a single exception: for we have what I take to be unimpeachable evidence that Isagoras and his companions were condemned for treason, not upon surrender after this siege, but upon a later occasion, namely the subsequent invasion of Attica in force by Kleomenes. The decree passed by the Athenians on this latter occasion, inscribed on bronze and extant in the centuries following, is preserved for us by the scholiast on Aristophanes' *Lysistrata* 273:

Κλεομένης . . . πολιορκηθεὶς ὑπὸ τῶν Ἀθηναίων καὶ ἀφεθεὶς ὑπόσπονδος, ἀπιὼν οἴκαδε, πάλιν Ἐλευσῖνα κατέσχεν. [Cf. Hdt. V. 74.] *τῶν δὲ μετὰ Κλεομένους Ἐλευσῖνα κατασχόντων Ἀθηναῖοι τὰς οἰκίας κατέσκαψαν καὶ τὰς οὐσίας ἐδήμευσαν, αὐτῶν δὲ θάνατον ἐψηφίσαντο. καὶ ἀναγράψαντες εἰς στήλην χαλκῆν ἔστησαν ἐν πόλει παρὰ τὸν ἀρχαῖον νεών.*

I am not sure that this completely justifies Aristotle's πάντας, though it seems a reasonable *a fortiori* inference that if Isagoras and other Athenians were not excepted from the truce, then no one was.[1] I suggest, in any case, that this *is*, in fact, the ground of Aristotle's divergence: *he has corrected Herodotus' narrative in the light of a contemporary document.* This is a hypothesis: yet we shall find more cases where Aristotle, going beyond Herodotus, seems to derive from such a documentary source.

For in general Aristotle's chapter 20. 1–3 is a mere paraphrase of Herodotus. To illustrate this (it is indeed commonly recognized) I need only write out in Herodotus' words the substance of that chapter, and let Aristotle's text follow. I take for granted a correction of the papyrus in § 3,[2] proposed by Wilamowitz and accepted e.g. by Kenyon in the Oxford Text and Mathieu in the Budé. I put in bold type whatever is not taken, directly and verbally, from Herodotus:

HERODOTUS V. 66. 1. *Ἀθῆναι . . . ἀπαλλαχθεῖσαι τυράννων ἐγίνοντο μέζονες. ἐν δὲ αὐτῆσι δύο ἄνδρες ἐδυνάστευον, Κλεισθένης τε ἀνὴρ Ἀλκμεωνίδης . . . καὶ Ἰσαγόρης Τεισάνδρου . . .* (2) *ἑσσούμενος δὲ ὁ Κλεισθένης τὸν δῆμον προσεταιρίζεται.* [There follows, 66. 2 to 69. 2, an account of the Reform of the Tribes, etc.] 70. 1. *ἐν τῷ μέρει δὲ ἑσσούμενος ὁ Ἰσαγόρης ἀντιτεχνᾶται τάδε· ἐπικαλέεται Κλεομένεα . . . γενόμενον ἑωυτῷ ξεῖνον . . .* (2) *τὰ μὲν δὴ πρῶτα πέμπων ὁ Κλεομένης ἐς τὰς Ἀθήνας κήρυκα ἐξέβαλλε Κλεισθένεα καὶ μετ' αὐτοῦ ἄλλους πολλοὺς Ἀθηναίων, τοὺς ἐναγέας ἐπιλέγων. ταῦτα δὲ πέμπων ἔλεγε ἐκ διδαχῆς τοῦ Ἰσαγόρεω·*[3] *οἱ μὲν γὰρ Ἀλκμεωνίδαι . . . εἶχον αἰτίην τοῦ φόνου τούτου.* 72. 1. *Κλεισθένης μὲν αὐτὸς ὑπεξέσχε· μετὰ δὲ οὐδὲν ἧσσον παρῆν ἐς τὰς Ἀθήνας ὁ Κλεομένης οὐ σὺν μεγάλῃ χειρί, ἀπικόμενος δὲ*

---

[1] Herodotus names, as executed upon surrender, Timasitheos of Delphi. Did he generalize from this single instance? Or is this instance equally erroneous?

[2] *Κλεισθένους ⟨ἀφικόμενος ὁ Κλεομένης⟩.* Many editors have printed the uncorrected text: although thereby Isagoras appears to be the subject of ἠγηλάτει and ἐπειρᾶτο καταλύειν *Ἰσαγόραν δὲ . . . καθιστάναι*: Isagoras is seeking to restore Isagoras. This is of course impossible in Greek prose.

[3] In Aristotle this advice of Isagoras is put in the preceding clause.

ἀγηλατέει ἑπτακόσια ἐπίστια Ἀθηναίων . . . ταῦτα δὲ ποιήσας δεύτερα
τὴν βουλὴν καταλύειν ἐπειρᾶτο, τριηκοσίοισι δὲ τοῖσι Ἰσαγόρεω στασιώτῃσι
τὰς ἀρχὰς ἐνεχείριζε. (2) ἀντισταθείσης δὲ τῆς βουλῆς . . . ὅ τε Κλεομένης καὶ ὁ Ἰσαγόρης καὶ οἱ στασιῶται αὐτοῦ καταλαμβάνουσι τὴν ἀκρόπολιν.
Ἀθηναίων δὲ οἱ λοιποὶ τὰ αὐτὰ φρονήσαντες¹ ἐπολιόρκεον αὐτοὺς ἡμέρας
δύο· τῇ δὲ τρίτῃ ὑπόσπονδοι ἐξέρχονται ἐκ τῆς χώρης ὅσοι ἦσαν αὐτῶν
Λακεδαιμόνιοι . . . 73. 1. Ἀθηναῖοι δὲ μετὰ ταῦτα Κλεισθένεα καὶ τὰ
ἑπτακόσια ἐπίστια τὰ διωχθέντα ὑπὸ Κλεομένεος μεταπεμψάμενοι . . . [the
Embassy to Sardis].

ARISTOTLE 20. 1. καταλυθείσης δὲ τῆς τυραννίδος ἐστασίαζον πρὸς
ἀλλήλους Ἰσαγόρας ὁ Τεισάνδρου **φίλος ὢν τῶν τυράννων** καὶ Κλεισθένης τοῦ γένους ὢν τῶν Ἀλκμεωνιδῶν. ἡττώμενος δὲ **ταῖς ἑταιρείαις**
ὁ Κλεισθένης προσηγάγετο τὸν δῆμον, **ἀποδιδοὺς τῷ πλήθει τὴν
πολιτείαν.** (2) ὁ δὲ Ἰσαγόρας ἐπιλειπόμενος τῇ δυνάμει πάλιν² ἐπικαλεσά-
μενος τὸν Κλεομένην ὄντα ἑαυτῷ ξένον συνέπεισεν ἐλαύνειν τὸ ἄγος, διὰ
τὸ τοὺς Ἀλκμεωνίδας δοκεῖν εἶναι τῶν ἐναγῶν. (3) ὑπεξελθόντος δὲ τοῦ
Κλεισθένους ⟨ἀφικόμενος ὁ Κλεομένης⟩ μετ᾽ ὀλίγων³ ἠγηλάτει τῶν
Ἀθηναίων ἑπτακοσίας οἰκίας. ταῦτα δὲ διαπραξάμενος τὴν μὲν βουλὴν
ἐπειρᾶτο καταλύειν, Ἰσαγόραν δὲ καὶ τριακοσίους τῶν φίλων μετ᾽ αὐτοῦ
κυρίους καθιστάναι τῆς πόλεως. τῆς δὲ βουλῆς ἀντιστάσης καὶ συναθροισθέ-
ντος τοῦ πλήθους οἱ μὲν περὶ τὸν Κλεομένην καὶ Ἰσαγόραν κατέφυγον εἰς
τὴν ἀκρόπολιν, ὁ δὲ δῆμος δύο μὲν ἡμέρας προσκαθεζόμενος ἐπολιόρκει,
τῇ δὲ τρίτῃ Κλεομένην μὲν **καὶ τοὺς μετ᾽ αὐτοῦ πάντας** ἀφεῖσαν
ὑποσπόνδους, Κλεισθένην δὲ καὶ τοὺς ἄλλους φυγάδας μετεπέμψαντο.

Of τοὺς μετ᾽ αὐτοῦ πάντας I have spoken above, of ἀποδιδοὺς τῷ
πλήθει τὴν πολιτείαν I will speak later. Neither of the other
variants entitles us, I think, to assume any narrative source
independent of Herodotus. Ταῖς ἑταιρείαις is a mere inference
from the narrative, little more than an expansion of the idea in
προσεταιρίζεται in Herodotus' next sentence:⁴ we have not here
independent testimony of the existence of *Hetaireiai* as early as
506, probable though that is in fact. Φίλος ὢν τῶν τυράννων is
likewise an inference (a less happy one perhaps) from the narrative: it is to be connected with a sentence in § 4, αἰτιώτατοι γὰρ
σχεδὸν ἐγένοντο τῆς ἐκβολῆς τῶν τυράννων οἱ Ἀλκμεωνίδαι, καὶ
στασιάζοντες τὰ πολλὰ διετέλεσαν. Aristotle interprets the rivalry
between the two men, before Kleisthenes makes his democratic

¹ In Aristotle this unanimity of the people is put in the preceding clause.
² πάλιν=ἀντιτεχνᾶται τάδε.   ³ μετ᾽ ὀλίγων=οὐ σὺν μεγάλῃ χειρί.
⁴ It is indeed hardly more than τῇ δυνάμει in the next sentence (which I have not
thought worthy of bold type in view of ἐδυνάστευον in Hdt. 66. 1 and περὶ δυνάμιος in
66. 2)—a piece of stylistic variation.

gesture, as a rivalry between the Tyrants' enemies (who had turned them out) and the Tyrants' friends (who had acquiesced in tyranny).[1] What of ἀποδιδοὺς τῷ πλήθει τὴν πολιτείαν? This is not in Herodotus: instead is the whole story of the Reformer's legislation, together with that of his grandfather, which (Herodotus suggests) he was imitating. Aristotle reserves the substance of the reform till the next chapter, and provisionally replaces Herodotus' long account with this single phrase. It seems to me a most admirable and succinct statement of Kleisthenes' intention (or achievement), though it has been, as I believe, grossly mistranslated[2] and made the source of grave errors. Let this be as it may: it most certainly is not in Herodotus, and is an inference, not from Herodotus' narrative, but from Aristotle's own far more detailed knowledge of the actual Reform: in fact, from the text of the Laws.

2. How were the Laws voted?

When, after nearly a century, the Democracy was to be discarded, a certain Pythodoros proposed and carried a motion that suggestions for a revised constitution should be laid before the next meeting of the Ekklesia. Anyone who chose might make a suggestion, but thirty men (the συγγραφεῖς) were chosen and especially charged with the duty of presenting at least one such suggestion.

This was the motion of Pythodoros, and a Rider was added by Kleitophon:

'Τὰ μὲν ἄλλα καθάπερ Πυθόδωρος· προσαναζητῆσαι δὲ τοὺς αἱρεθέντας καὶ τοὺς πατρίους νόμους οὓς Κλεισθένης ἔθηκεν ὅτε καθίστη τὴν δημοκρατίαν, ὅπως ἂν ἀκούσαντες καὶ τούτων βουλεύσωνται τὸ ἄριστον·'
(ὡς οὐ δημοτικὴν ἀλλὰ παραπλησίαν οὖσαν τὴν Κλεισθένους πολιτείαν τῇ Σόλωνος.)

I quote from 'Αθ. πολ. 29. 3. We have, evidently, almost the actual words of the Rider; except that the last clause (which I

---

[1] Probably correct enough, if we mean no more than that Kleisthenes led the Exiles, Isagoras the nobles who had stayed and given hostages (Hdt. I. 64). But Isagoras cannot have been an active supporter of Hippias: Kleomenes had made Isagoras' house his Headquarters during the siege (Hdt. V. 70. 1), and Herodotus emphasizes how new a departure it was in Kleomenes' policy when he drops Isagoras and seeks to restore Hippias: Hdt. V. 92. a. 1.

[2] See page 147 below. I translate *universo populo tribuens rempublicam*.

have therefore bracketed) is not part of the Rider, but is a statement of Kleitophon's motive in moving it.

It is a fair inference, indeed an inevitable one, that Kleisthenes' Laws were extant: and any time after 411 B.C. historians and antiquaries knew of them. A knowledge of their contents passed into the 'Ατθίδες: and this is far the most substantial addition which the antiquarians were able to make to what they had learnt from Herodotus about the Great Reform.

I venture now onto less firm ground: Kleitophon's alleged motive. Will anyone accept it as his real motive? There is indeed no reason to doubt that Kleitophon was an oligarch, and that his Rider had an oligarchic tendency: not only the 'Αθ. πολ. (34. 3) speaks of him as being later an ally of Theramenes, but Aristophanes also in the *Frogs* (967) names him with Theramenes as a super-subtle 'Euripidean' sophist. And we may fairly adduce the portrait of him in Plato (and for this purpose it is perhaps indifferent whether the *Clitopho* be Plato's own work,[1] unless we extrude it from the Socratic tradition altogether): in the *Republic* an almost silent listener with some faint Thrasymachean sympathy (340b), he appears in the *Clitopho* as the spokesman of many who are not satisfied that Thrasymachos was fairly heard by Socrates. Plato (if the work be his) is still quicksilver-minded, and lets be stated dramatically a certain scepticism roused by Socrates' doctrine, that political evil could be cured by the knowledge and practice of the Art of Justice. In a vivid passage (407c–e) Kleitophon describes the evils of the time,[2] which only hard work (ἐπιμέλεια) can cure. He denies that the Art of Justice spurs men to this hard work: rather the contrary.

'Your friends tell me, Socrates, that the Art of Justice has its ἔργον, viz.: φιλίαν ἐν ταῖς πόλεσιν ποιεῖν (p. 409D). I cannot find that this is, in fact, true; and am therefore going to Thrasymachos for something better.'

This is the tone of the practising oligarch. The tone, at least,

---

[1] Its genuineness is defended by Grube in *Classical Philology* XXVI. (1931) 302 sqq.: who sees in it a piece of self-criticism not unlike the *Parmenides* or indeed the opening of Book II of the *Republic*. 'It was printed as spurious in the Aldine edition, a mistake for which the editors apologized, but the little work has never recovered from the insult.' It must have been written after *Republic* I., and before the later books.

[2] The passage is curiously like Thuc. III. 82, 83; and strikes me as being equally the work of one who had been a contemporary.

of the man of politics, disillusioned with 'Justice': and for the colour of his politics we may turn to his master Thrasymachos, whose programme was the composing of Stasis, and πάτριος πολιτεία.[1] [Wilamowitz indeed suggests that Aristotle states Kleitophon's motive so confidently because the Academy knew all about him. Hardly. There is comparatively little of Aristotle's own judgment in this part of the book:[2] I strongly share the suspicions of those who see in this mass of documents, tendenciously arranged and commented on, mere extracts from Antiphon's Defence.[3] The motivation is Antiphon's,[4] rather than Academy tradition.]

We have then a Rider proposed by Kleitophon, of whose political reputation we know something: and a motive for it imputed (possibly by Antiphon in his Defence). It is reasonably certain that its purpose was oligarchic. But Antiphon's false candour (if his it be), designed merely to confuse the trail, will not bear examination: even the most moderate oligarchs intended to disfranchise the Thetes, to abolish sortition—*a fortiori*, to destroy the Kleisthenic Boule: they cannot have hoped to find authority for this in the substance of Kleisthenes' Laws. Rather, I suggest, Kleitophon's purpose may be guessed from the immediate sequel ('Aθ. πολ. 29. 4, Thuc. VIII. 67. 2): the suspension of the Oath of the Prytanis, and of the *Graphe Paranomon*. Kleisthenes' Laws were to be studied from the point of view of procedure. What was the sanction of the existing democratic constitution? How

---

[1] Frag. 1 in Diels' *Vorsokratiker*: quoted by Dionys. Hal. *Demosth.* 3.
[2] See e.g. the remarks of Mathieu in the Budé edition, p. xiii sq.
[3] Thuc. VIII. 68. 2: Antiphon fr. III in Gernet's Budé edition [=Pap. Gen., Nicole (1907) fr. I]. See especially Kriegel, *Der Staatsstreich der 400*, Diss. Bonn, 1909, p. 38 *et sqq.* Thucydides had read Antiphon's Defence, and this would explain how he is apparently able to anticipate and correct some of Aristotle's distortions. A notable instance is Thuc. VIII. 67, 2, ἄλλο μὲν οὐδέν, αὐτὸ δὲ τοῦτο, in relation to 'Aθ. πολ. 29. 5. To reconstruct the general argument of Antiphon's Defence (that masterpiece of subtlety, Thuc. VIII. 68. 2, Aristotle *Eudemian Ethics* III. 5, p. 1232b 7) is beyond my ambitions: though the material is abundant, and [Lysias] XX gives a probably instructive parallel.
[4] The Rider (which Thucydides simply disregards, VIII. 67. 1) would naturally be preserved by Antiphon. How he applied his argument, I hardly venture to guess: perhaps he was painting the revolution as reactionary indeed but not contrary to the oath imposed in the archonship of Hermokreon ('Aθ. πολ. 22. 2). The next act of the oligarchs was to dispense the Prytanis from that oath: perhaps Antiphon sought to excuse that decisive step by suggesting it was a legal precaution only, and the oath not actually broken. [By this suggestion I seek only to anticipate the argument that Antiphon could not possibly have imputed such a motive: so I suggest, strictly *exempli gratia*, one possible line for Antiphon's argument.]

had it been established? How could it be superseded by another?

The conclusion reached was, that the two main safeguards of the constitution were the Oath of the Prytanis and the *Graphe Paranomon*:[1] and the thirty Commissioners contented themselves with recommending their abolition. When these two safeguards (which were both subsequent to Kleisthenes' main legislation) were gone, they could create a new constitution by *Psephismata*, as Kleisthenes had done. The comparison with Kleisthenes seems to be relevant only if he had operated with *Psephismata* as they proposed to do.

We may then see perhaps in Kleitophon's Rider an indication that the Laws of Kleisthenes were common *Psephismata*, moved by Kleisthenes as a private citizen, and duly passed by Boule and Demos. The oligarchs proposed indeed to omit the Boule, in virtue of their revised instructions to the Prytanis.[2]

Such is the slender positive proof for what indeed hardly needs proof: that Kleisthenes found in the Ekklesia the authority with which to defeat the reigning Archon. For he defeated the reigning Archon: his laws were passed, in Isagoras' teeth, whilst the latter was still in office.

This is proved by Aristotle's words ἐπὶ Ἰσαγόρου ἄρχοντος πρῶτον μὲν οὖν συνένειμε πάντας εἰς δέκα φυλάς. And this means before the intervention of Kleomenes (so that Aristotle confirms, rather than contradicts, Herodotus): for after Kleomenes began to intervene, Kleisthenes and Isagoras are never again in Athens together. It is mere wantonness to suggest that Isagoras continued to be Archon after his expulsion, or that ἐπὶ Ἰσαγόρου ἄρχοντος can refer to that period. A man cannot be both Head of the State and ὑπόσπονδος: and we may safely assume that the dating

---

[1] Ἀθ. πολ. 29. 4, Thuc. VIII. 67. 2. Thucydides says ἤν τις . . . ἢ γράψηται παρανόμων ἢ ἄλλῳ τῳ τρόπῳ βλάψῃ, and Aristotle defines ἄλλῳ τῳ τρόπῳ more precisely as Eisangelia and Prosklesis: possible alternatives to the *Graphe Paranomon*, which it was safer to abolish at the same time, but which (with the Boule on his side, and the Archon and Aeropagites powerless) are not likely to have troubled Kleisthenes.

[2] Ἀθ. πολ. 29. 4 (ἐπάναγκες ἐπιψηφίζειν): on the strength of this, Peisandros presents his motion straight to the Ekklesia, Thuc. VIII. 67. 3 (68. 1, 69. 1). Aristotle [Antiphon?] obscures this fact, substituting a vague '*Diataxis*', presented by the thirty Commissioners in virtue of their quasi-probouleutic powers. This is that notorious distortion which was apparently already familiar to Thucydides, who tacitly corrects it by his words ἄλλο μὲν οὐδέν, αὐτὸ δὲ τοῦτο (VIII. 67. 2).

ἐπὶ Ἰσαγόρου ἄρχοντος comes from the Laws themselves,[1] and is therefore not a mere annalist's label but gives the real circumstances.

Aristotle depends, for the *story* (that is, the sequence of events), on the narrative of Herodotus, which he can only modify or expand in the light of such documents as survived. He was therefore in no position to correct Herodotus' *sequence*; and the phrase ἀποδιδοὺς τῷ πλήθει τὴν πολιτείαν, rightly understood, makes it reasonably clear that he did not mean to. Kleisthenes (as Kleitophon suspected) had used the procedure of *Psephismata* to revolutionize the State. Two questions: (i) had the Ekklesia really the power (before Kleisthenes reorganized it) to pass such *Psephismata*? (ii) were there no constitutional safeguards to prevent it abusing that power in such revolutionary fashion?

(i) *The Ekklesia's Powers.* The burden of proof lies rather on those who deny this: yet it will be convenient to summarize the evidence for the powers of the 'Ekklesia' (the assembled body of citizens) down to this date. The powers, such as they are, appear to rest on a doctrine that the body of the nation is sovran (and the sovranty of its Kings, etc., merely delegated) which, to go no further afield, we find in Homer. The doctrine in Homer is not absolute, and it has to fight with other doctrines: but both Agamemnon and Telemachos do on occasion convoke the body of the people (the λαός), because theirs is the final voice on such grave questions as whether the Siege of Troy be abandoned or Penelope marry again. It would be unsafe to generalize that *Peace or War* and *Royal Marriages* were questions normally reserved for the people's voice: for there is this common to the two Homeric cases, that Agamemnon and Telemachos are both in difficulties, Agamemnon has quarrelled with Achilles, Telemachos with the Suitors. Popular Sovranty is, in fact, very narrowly limited, since its exercise depends on the ruler's initiative, which he will seldom take except as a last resource: and we may add that the People is still without political consciousness, or any political purpose distinct from its ruler's.

---

[1] So Komeas' name stood in Aristion's decree ('Aθ. πολ. 14. 1) and Hermokreon's in the law mentioned 'Aθ. πολ. 22. 2. Cf. τὸ ἐπὶ Σκαμανδρίου ψήφισμα, of about Kleisthenes' date (Andoc. I. 43: see page 146, note 1 below): and *I.G.* I². 3, lines 16–17, and 4, lines 26–7 (485 B.C.).

In Athens of the seventh[1] century B.C. the situation is similar but slightly more advanced. Of the Massacre of the Kylonians we have two chief accounts. Herodotus, who leaves the People out of his story, seems to be seeking to diminish the Alkmeonid guilt: he says the safe-conduct was given not by the Archon Megakles but by the Presidents of the Naukraroi οἵπερ ἔνεμον τότε τὰς 'Αθήνας (V. 71). Thucydides (I. 126) denies this[2] and in an extremely circumstantial story fastens the responsibility once more upon the Alkmeonids. His account therefore, in which the People plays an important part, deserves the respect due to a deliberate and responsible treatment of a known controversy. This means, in Thucydides, that we need not expect such casual anachronisms as we would find e.g. in Isocrates.

'[When they saw the Kylonians had seized the Akropolis] the Athenians came in from the countryside πανδημεί, and sat down to a siege. Χρόνου δὲ ἐγγιγνομένου οἱ 'Αθηναῖοι τρυχόμενοι τῇ προσεδρίᾳ ἀπῆλθον οἱ πολλοί, ἐπιτρέψαντες τοῖς ἐννέα ἄρχουσι τήν τε φυλακὴν καὶ τὸ πᾶν αὐτοκράτορσι διαθεῖναι. [The starving Kylonians fly to the Great Altar.] ἀναστήσαντες δὲ αὐτοὺς οἱ τῶν 'Αθηναίων ἐπιτετραμμένοι τὴν φυλακήν . . . ἐφ' ᾧ μηδὲν κακὸν ποιήσουσιν, ἀπαγαγόντες ἀπέκτειναν.'

ἐπιτρέψαντες τὴν φυλακήν . . . οἱ ἐπιτετραμμένοι τὴν φυλακήν: this is how, without saying the Archons lifted the suppliants with their own hands, Thucydides fixes the responsibility on them. The part played by the People is thus integral to his story: the People assembles in the emergency, and before dispersing again, delegates to the nine Archons its sovranty (τὸ πᾶν αὐτοκράτορσι διαθεῖναι).[3] This is not unlike the Homeric cases: the rulers (the nine Archons) are in difficulty and therefore welcome the support of the People, their authority is reinforced by the People's voice. The People, moreover, is still feudally-minded: its political purpose is identical with its rulers'. And we may believe that the

[1] I do not discuss the view that puts Kylon's conspiracy in the sixth century. But see page 150, note 1 *sub finem*.
[2] We are bound to take his phrase τότε δὲ τὰ πολλὰ τῶν πολιτικῶν οἱ ἐννέα ἄρχοντες ἔπρασσον as an explicit denial of Herodotus' special pleading.
[3] Αὐτοκράτωρ *'plenipotentiary'* is any person (or body) who has the sovran power delegated to him (or it) for some special business or emergency: so that his acts (within the scope of his *Autokratia*) require no ratification. The notion is well illustrated by Beloch *Attische Politik* 285 sqq.: I quote some leading passages above, p. 132, note 1. [The *Strategos Autokrator* (e.g. Thuc. VI. 26. 1, Xen. *Hell.* I. 4. 20) has this power: there is no authority for using this phrase of the position held by Perikles e.g. in 440; Thucydides' phrase for that is στρατηγὸς δέκατος αὐτός, I. 116. 1. See Beloch loc. cit.]

initiative had lain with Megakles; that he had invited them to bestow this *Autokratia*; had, like Agamemnon or Telemachos, referred to them a delicate situation. Yet when the People grows at all conscious of having interests other than its rulers', it will of course tend to take more seriously the ultimate sovranty implied in such references.

The next Archon (so far as we know) to receive *Autokratia* was Solon. If, in Kylon's case, the threatened aristocrats had been glad to use the voice of the People, it became increasingly hard to neglect that voice, even when, as now, it was formidably hostile and more prepared to create a Tyrant than to destroy one. Solon must have had *Autokratia*: he cannot have consented to legislate until all parties agreed that his legislation should be binding and not need ratifying.[1] Solon was forced upon the Aristocracy which he was going to attack by the pressure of the People behind him. I conceive he was given his *Autokratia* by the People, perhaps (since the ruling class had consented to accept him) on the motion of the outgoing Archon.

Solon, we know, disappointed his supporters, who hoped he would make himself Tyrant. Yet, as he protests, he gave them a lot, things which but for him 'they'd never have set eyes on in their sleep.' Hitherto, they must wait for the Archon's initiative, which they might indeed hasten by threatening revolution: *Solon made them independent of the Archon.* He did this by creating the Lower Boule, independent of Archon or Areopagites, whose function was to summon the People at stated intervals and prepare its business. So Solon left Athens with two Sovranties ranged against each other: on the one side the Archons and Areopagites (like the Kings and Gerontes at Sparta, the Consuls and Senate at Rome), on the other side the Ekklesia and Boule (like the Spartan Apella and Ephors, the Roman Comitia and Tribunes).—Through this every city-state must pass, as it emerges from its archaic phase, aristocratic and religious, into its modern phase, plebeian and secular.

Of the acts of this new Ekklesia we can name very few. The psephisma of Aristion, which gave Peisistratos his bodyguard, was voted by it, and must have been extant long enough for the antiquarians to read in it the name of its proposer (Aristion)

---

[1] In what other way could the Seisachtheia have been executed?

and the reigning Archon (Komeas). The psephisma making torture of citizens illegal should perhaps be put in 510 or 509:[1] the reigning Archon was Skamandrios, the proposer we do not know. But, apart from specific psephismata, the words of the Ephebic oath may perhaps be adduced (Pollux VIII. 105: Stobaeus *Flor.* 43. 48): τοῖς θεσμοῖς τοῖς ἱδρυμένοις πείσομαι καὶ οὕστινας ἄλλους ἱδρύσεται τὸ πλῆθος, ἐμφρόνως: words whose archaic phrasing may well be supposed older than the Laws of Kleisthenes.

(ii) *The Safeguards.* Solon likened the city to a ship, which he had launched indeed, yet claimed to have made it safe by two anchors:[2] the Upper and the Lower Boule. This may reasonably be taken to mean that the Ekklesia was protected against its own inexperience by the προβούλευσις[3] of the Lower Boule and the νομοφυλακία[4] of the Upper. It is a crucial fact, significant of the temper of parties, that the Lower Boule *accepted Kleisthenes' Laws*, in the teeth of the reigning Archon: it was of course within their competence to refuse to present them to the Ekklesia (ἐξενεῖκαι ἐς τὸν δῆμον). It seems that Kleisthenes (like Sulla) sought to guarantee that his *coup* should not be copied by other men: since a few years later he imposed an oath upon the members of the Boule, which (we may be fairly certain, though we do not possess its text) bound the Prytanis not to put to the Ekklesia any motions subversive of the Constitution.[5] [This is one of the sanc-

---

[1] Andoc. *Myst.* 43. For the date see e.g. Cornelius, *Tyrannis*, p. 91, note 1. Skamandrios is a name which suggests the Sigeian War: I am tempted to speculate that he was Archon 510/9, the last nominee of the Tyrants. If he became Archon more or less *ad annum* (as was then usual: Miltiades, the younger Peisistratos, Themistokles, Aristeides) he would be born about 540: his name suggests the Tyrant's circle. His nomination would not necessarily be quashed when Hippias left ('Αθ. πολ. 22. 4).—To abolish torture would be among the early measures of the free city.

[2] Plut. *Solon* 19. 1. As Miss Freeman has pointed out, these words evidently come from Solon's poems, probably the iambic poem of defence quoted 'Αθ. πολ. 12. 4–5. [E.g. ἐγὼ πόλιν τήνδ' ὡς ἐπ' ἀγκύραιν δυοῖν | ὁρμοῦσαν . . . οὐκέτ' ἐν σάλῳ . . .]

[3] Plut. *Solon* 19. 1. προβουλεύειν ἔταξε τοῦ δήμου καὶ μηδὲν ἐᾶν ἀπροβούλευτον εἰς ἐκκλησίαν εἰσφέρεσθαι (Aristotle omits to mention the Lower Boule's functions).

[4] Probably in effect a *veto*.

[5] The Oath imposed, 'Αθ. πολ. 22. 2 (ὃν ἔτι καὶ νῦν ὀμνύουσιν—though it received accretions, e.g. in Glaukippos' archonship, Philochoros F 140). Portions of the Oath quoted [Philoch. loc. cit.]: Andoc. *Myst.* 91: Dem. XXIV. 144, LIX. 4: Lysias XXXI. 1: Xen. *Mem.* I. 1. 18. For the obligation not to put certain motions, see 'Αθ. πολ. 29. 4 (cf. Thuc. VIII. 67. 2), Xen. *Hell.* I.7. 15, Plat. Apol. 32b (the scruples of Socrates), Thuc. VI. 14, and the words [ουκ επιφσ]εφιο εμ [β]ολει ο[υτ εν εκκλεσιαι] in the very fragmentary inscription of Glaukippos' archonship, *I.G.* I². 114, line 28: see also lines 39–41 of that inscription as restored by me in *C.Q.* XXIV, pp. 117 sq.

tions imposed *after* 'Kleisthenes established the democracy (*'Aθ. πολ.* 29. 3)' which the oligarchs therefore abolished in 411, *'Aθ. πολ.* 29. 4.]

As for the *νομοφυλακία* of the Upper Boule (the Areopagite Council), whatever that was, it was scarcely formidable when Kleisthenes was legislating. For almost all the Areopagites were then nominees of the Tyrants (Thuc. VI. 54. 6), and their authority on constitutional correctness would go for little. It was abolished by Ephialtes (*'Aθ. πολ.* 25. 4) and its place was later taken by the *Graphe Paranomon* [the other of the main sanctions abolished by the oligarchs, *'Aθ. πολ.* 29. 4].

The facts which emerge, if not as formally proved, yet as reasonable hypotheses, are:

(i) The Laws of Kleisthenes existed at the end of the fifth century (and, presumably, till the end of antiquity).

(ii) They were voted in due form by the Boule and Demos.

(iii) They contained in due form the name of the reigning Archon, Isagoras.

(iv) The bulk of *'Aθ. πολ.* 21 goes back to them.

Chronology. It follows that they were already voted when Kleomenes intervened in force: for after that (*a*) Kleisthenes was away until Isagoras was expelled; (*b*) when Kleisthenes returned, Isagoras was never again reigning Archon. Aristotle thus confirms (rather than contradicts) Herodotus. It does not, however, follow that the reforms had been *put into practice* before Kleomenes intervened, and this is in fact unlikely: for that would have taken considerable time, and Kleomenes' visits seem to have been fairly frequent (Hdt. V. 70. 1) until this fiasco. The Boule, therefore, which resisted Kleomenes so stubbornly, was the Solonian Boule of 400, which had already voted Kleisthenes' Laws (and thus shown its favour to him), and displayed on this occasion that independence of the Archon for which Solon had designed it.

Aristotle's phrase *ἀποδιδοὺς τῷ πλήθει τὴν πολιτείαν* describes the tenour of Kleisthenes' Laws: it should be rendered *universo populo tribuens rempublicam.*[1] By his Law of the ten Tribes Kleis-

---

[1] Cf. *'Aθ. πολ.* 34. 1. *his igitur mox abstulit populus rempublicam* (not *civitatem*!). But πολιτεία *can* of course mean *civitas*: e.g. 13. 5.

thenes, announcing the break up of the archaic state,[1] vindicated sovranty for Ekklesia and Boule rather than for Archon and Areopagites. The phrase would be applicable to what Cheilon did in Sparta, or the Gracchi in Rome.

3. The Alleged Enfranchisements

'Kleisthenes made those who dwelt in a Deme members of that Deme; so that men should not be called "son of so-and-so", and thereby disclose who were the *New Citizens*' (*'Aθ. πολ.* 21. 4). We need not take too seriously the motives which Aristotle imputes to Kleisthenes, but this sentence reveals (what otherwise we know from a sentence in the *Politics*) that Aristotle considered that Kleisthenes enlarged the body of citizens. In the *Politics* (III. 2. 3: p. 1275 B) he says that after the expulsion of the Tyrants Kleisthenes put into his Tribes many aliens and slaves who were living in Attica.[2]

If the matter were of greater importance, we should have to treat this assertion critically, and enquire what authority Aristotle is likely to have had.—Part of the same or a similar tradition, perhaps, is the statement in *'Aθ. πολ.* 13. 5 'There joined Peisistratos also . . . those whose Attic blood was dubious: these joined him because they were afraid. σημεῖον δέ, ὅτι μετὰ τὴν τῶν τυράννων κατάλυσιν ἐποίησαν διαψηφισμόν, ὡς πολλῶν κοινωνούντων τῆς πολιτείας οὐ προσῆκον.' Though I do not hold (with some critics) that whenever Aristotle says σημεῖον δέ or τεκμήριον δέ we are to assume that he has been merely guessing, yet I take it that in this case his substantial evidence is the fact of a διαψηφισμός, and that for this he had documentary authority. I am therefore sceptical about the statement in the *Politics*, which is perhaps a hasty and careless inference from the same διαψηφισμός: the phrase 'μετὰ τὴν τῶν τυράννων ἐκβολήν', following upon μεταβολῆς γενομένης πολιτείας, is curiously inexact (since he means to imply Kleis-

---

[1] 'Αναμεῖξαι βουλόμενος, ὅπως μετάσχωσι πλείους τῆς πολιτείας: *omnia confundens quo plures in republica versarentur* (*'Aθ. πολ.* 21. 2). By breaking up the aristocratic structure, he invited all men to dare to stand level.

[2] Μετὰ τὴν τῶν τυράννων ἐκβολήν,—πολλοὺς ἐφυλέτευσε ξένους καὶ δούλους μετοίκους. He is seeking a definition for *who is a citizen?* 'Born of citizen parents' will not do when the city is newly founded, and there is a similar difficulty when a city's constitution is changed: thus Kleisthenes, after the expulsion of the Tyrants, put aliens into his Tribes.

thenes' 'change of constitution' of 508/7, yet μετὰ τὴν τῶν τυράννων ἐκβολήν naturally suggests 510 or 509), and it recalls the words used of the διαψηφισμός, 'μετὰ τὴν τῶν τυράννων κατάλυσιν'. The document which recorded or ordered the διαψηφισμός must be presumed (a) to have said that many were in wrongful possession of citizenship ('Aθ. πολ. 13. 5 ὡς πολλῶν κοινωνούντων τῆς πολιτείας οὐ προσῆκον) and (b) to have been dated to 510 or 509: such a document, hastily considered, might possibly produce the statement in the Politics. In that case, when he came to the 'Aθ. πολ. and became more aware of the interval between Hippias' fall and Kleisthenes' Reform, he judged the διαψηφισμός more correctly (as preceding the Reform) and did not specifically impute any large enfranchisements to Kleisthenes: yet his old notion persisted in the mention of the νεοπολῖται.

Such considerations make me sceptical of Kleisthenes' enfranchisements, but they do not of course disprove them. Fortunately, the matter is hardly vital. It is likely enough that certain borderline Athenians were protected by Peisistratos and (they or their children) disfranchised when Hippias fell: and that Kleisthenes, being a liberal-minded man, used his Reform of the Tribes to smuggle them back. Sub rosa and not integral to his main Reform: certainly not the foundation of his popularity. The enormous importance ascribed to these enfranchisements by some modern scholars is due, I conceive, to the belief that the words in 'Aθ. πολ. 20. 1, ἀποδιδοὺς τῷ πλήθει τὴν πολιτείαν, should be understood to mean 'giving back citizenship to those who had lost it.'[1] This sense of τῷ πλήθει is surely impossible per se: to identify the πλῆθος here with the ξένοι καὶ δοῦλοι of the Politics (and the above rendering demands that identification) is quite certainly impossible.[2]

It is even suggested (such a hold have these aliens on the imaginations of some) that the 700 families exiled with Kleisthenes in 508/7 are the νεοπολῖται. The burden of proof is on those who

---

[1] I have stated above (p. 147) what I believe the sentence means: 'universo populo tribuens rempublicam.' It may be suggested that the Plethos here means the Thetes, to whom Kleisthenes gave citizenship. But in Aristotle's view they had citizenship already ('Aθ. πολ. 7. 3): besides, to get his majority in the Ekklesia (not to mention the Boule) Kleisthenes wanted people with votes, not the voteless.

[2] The idea of extensive enfranchisement of aliens by Kleisthenes raises a᾿ urther problem: how did they or their children get into the Phratries? There is certainly no large class of Athenians, in classical Athens, who belong to a Deme but not to a Phratry. Did Kleisthenes force them into both?

say it. From Herodotus,[1] it is clear they are the families under the Curse.

4. THE SECULAR STATE

Τὰ δὲ γένη καὶ τὰς φρατρίας καὶ τὰς ἱερωσύνας εἴασεν ἔχειν ἑκάστους κατὰ τὰ πάτρια ('Aθ. πολ. 21. 6). Kleisthenes did not destroy the religious structure of the state: he merely created alongside of it a secular structure, and transferred the political validity to the latter.

Whether Aristotle is actually quoting from the terms of the Laws (as is possible), or merely inferring *ex silentio*, I dare not determine: in either case it is reasonable to accept his statement, and not to attribute to Kleisthenes any manipulation of the Phratries, unless the evidence is good and positive. Now in the *Politics* he says (VI. 4: p. 1319 B):

'For a certain kind of democracy, measures of a certain kind are useful: the measures used by Kleisthenes at Athens when he was wishing to increase the power of the democracy, and by those who established democracy at Kyrene. For you should change, and increase the number of, your Tribes, and do the same with your Phratries;[2] and should merge the practice of individual cults into a few cults common to all: in fact devise all means for the complete fusion of all elements in the population, and for the breaking up of former associations.'

—How much of this applies to Athens and how much to Kyrene,

[1] V. 70. 2. (πέμπων κήρυκα) ἐξέβαλλε Κλεισθένεα καὶ μετ' αὐτοῦ ἄλλους πολλοὺς 'Aθηναίων, τοὺς ἐναγέας ἐπιλέγων. ταῦτα δὲ πέμπων ἔλεγε ἐκ διδαχῆς τοῦ 'Iσαγόρεω. 72. I. Κλεομένης δὲ ὡς πέμπων ἐξέβαλλε Κλεισθένεα καὶ τοὺς ἐναγέας, Κλεισθένης μὲν αὐτὸς ὑπέξεσχε· μετὰ δὲ οὐδὲν ἧσσον παρῆν ὁ Κλεομένης, ἀπικόμενος δὲ ἀγηλατέει ἑπτακόσια ἐπίστια 'Aθηναίων τά οἱ ὑπέθετο ὁ 'Iσαγόρης. The ἐπίστια are evidently the same as the ἐναγεῖς: Kleisthenes himself withdrew at once, the remainder waited till Kleomenes came and compelled them. The ἐναγεῖς were of Kleisthenes' party (οἱ μὲν γὰρ 'Aλκμεωνίδαι καὶ οἱ συστασιῶται αὐτῶν εἶχον αἰτίην τοῦ φόνου τούτου) and Isagoras believed their exile would cut the heart out of it. 700 families is not too many (Herodotus says the Curse was on ἄλλους πολλοὺς 'Aθηναίων), for the Curse had passed for three or four generations in both lines, male and female [Megakles' daughter, Hdt. I. 61; Perikles, Thuc. I. 127. I], and was shared in the original generation by all who had accepted the surrender of the Kylonians: see Thucydides' narrative, I. 126. II, οἱ τῶν 'Aθηναίων ἐπιτετραμμένοι τὴν φυλακήν (he does not mean the Archons lifted the suppliants with their own hands).—We cannot tell how large a detachment of 'watchers' the Archons employed: but that they had multiplied by 508 B.C. to 700 families is one more proof of how wrong is the theory of Beloch and his followers, that Kylon's conspiracy lay only one generation back from that date.

[2] φυλαί τε . . . καὶ φρατρίαι. Since the *Tribes* were changed at Athens, we may suppose the *Phratries* were at Kyrene; the τε . . . καὶ seems to mean, not that *both* things must be done on each occasion, but that *both* are recommendable courses.

the passage itself does not say, but in view of 'Aθ. πολ. 21. 6, I assume that the changing of Phratries and the curtailing of individual cults belong to Kyrene. Kleisthenes, then, according to our evidence, never touched the Phratries. Why should he? He was not concerned to reform the Church, only to disestablish it. Organized religion, he thought, favoured the Aristocracy: his remedy was not to change the organization, but to take away its political, its military, and a great part of its social, significance: for his new Secular State, built up of Demes, was what mattered for the political,[1] the military, and a great part of the social, life of Attica.

A 'great part of' social life: this limitation should perhaps give us pause. It could not be indifferent to an Athenian, if he was refused admission to a Phratry: and if Kleisthenes really created a large number of new citizens, somehow he had to gain for them admission to Phratries.[2] I have given above my reasons for being sceptical about these 'new citizens.' I do not think they existed in any large number: but if they did, Kleisthenes must have found Phratries for them.

Evidence that he did so may possibly be sought in Philochoros F 35: Τοὺς δὲ φράτορας ἐπάναγκες δέχεσθαι καὶ τοὺς ὀργεῶνας καὶ τοὺς ὁμογάλακτας [οὓς γεννήτας καλοῦμεν]. The word ἐπάναγκες shows that this is a decree not of any individual Phratry, but of the State: Francotte and others ascribe it to Kleisthenes (who thus compels the Phratries, composed hitherto only of Homogalaktes, to admit Orgeones also). If so, the ὀργεῶνες appear to be the same as the νεοπολῖται, since, until the Reform of Kleisthenes, the citizen body was simply the aggregate of the Phratries, and persons in need of compulsory admission to Phratries are therefore new citizens.

I cannot accept this, and will try to give reasons. Since the Law compels the Phratries to accept two types of members, it

---

[1] The Archon, however, in his Dokimasia, had to prove his membership of a Phratry or subdivision thereof: 'Aθ. πολ. 55. 3.

[2] Sokrates says, in Plato's Euthydemos 302C: ἔστι γὰρ ἔμοιγε καὶ βωμοὶ καὶ ἱερὰ οἰκεῖα καὶ πατρῷα καὶ τὰ ἄλλα ὅσαπερ τοῖς ἄλλοις Ἀθηναίοις τῶν τοιούτων. I do not suppose this includes absolutely all Athenians: the decrees of the Dekeleieis (see above, pp. 116 sqq.) are fatuous if no one was ever in fact refused, and refusal cannot have eo ipso entailed loss of citizenship. But we may infer from Sokrates' language that not to have a Phratry was an abnormal and uncomfortable position, for which Kleisthenes' νεοπολῖται would hardly have said Thank you.

would appear that till then some Phratries had discriminated against one of these types: in fact against the Orgeones, who are the non-Gennetai (since I accept Philochoros' equation, Homogalaktes=Gennetai). The Law compels the admission of the non-Gennetai, *viá* the Phratries, into the Religious State.

Who are the non-Gennetai? According to the thesis under consideration, they must be aliens (recent immigrants).—This gives indeed a quite consistent story. The citizen body, till Kleisthenes, is divisible into Phratriai and Genê: all citizens are Gennetai. Kleisthenes extends the citizen body by introducing certain aliens, who had immigrated during the preceding century. He does not force them upon the Genê: instead, he combines them into certain artificial cult-groups, and compels the Phratries to admit the members of these artificial cult-groups (the Orgeones) alongside the members of the Genê (the Homogalaktes).—The story is consistent, but I do not believe it. It involves three assumptions which can neither be proved nor disproved, but I doubt all three of them:

1. That Kleisthenes *did* introduce aliens (Ar. *Pol.* III. 2: p. 1275B: but see pp. 148–9 above).

2. That all Athenians, till Kleisthenes, were Gennetai (no evidence).

3. That the Law quoted by Philochoros belongs to Kleisthenes (no evidence).

I believe Philochoros' Law is earlier than Kleisthenes, perhaps Solonian. The situation it implies seems to me this:—Among the members of a Phratry, some (by some real or fictitious family-consciousness) have formed themselves into groups called Genê: the members of less powerful families have formed similar groups, but with no bond of kinship. The Phratry shows a tendency to discriminate in favour of the former, and the State hereby forbids such discrimination.

The situation fits Solon's time, and the remedy is appropriate. For then

(*a*) the citizen body was the aggregate of the Phratries

(*b*) the extrusion of weaker elements was rife and needed correction (*c*) membership of the citizen body was becoming more important, from the new status given by Solon to the Ekklesia. I imagine it is part of the same Law from which Gaius has preserved a portion under Solon's name (*Dig.* XLVII. 22. 4[1]):

ἐὰν δὲ δῆμος ἢ φράτορες ἢ ἱερῶν ὀργίων θύται ἢ σύσσιτοι ἢ ὁμόταφοι ἢ θιασῶται ἢ ἐπὶ λείαν οἰχόμενοι ἢ εἰς ἐμπορίαν, ὅτι ἂν τούτων διαθῶνται πρὸς ἀλλήλους κύριον εἶναι, ἐὰν μὴ ἀπαγορεύῃ δημόσια γράμματα.

Kleisthenes left the system of the Phratries untouched, but juxtaposed the system of the Demes. In the same way, he[2] left the lunar year, of twelve or sometimes thirteen lunations (about 355 or 385 days) untouched, but juxtaposed the solar year of 365 or 366 days, made up of ten Prytanies of thirty-six or thirty-seven days. The lunar year is the year of months, the year of the religious Calendar of Feasts: it belongs to the archaic Religious State,[3] and accordingly the Archons and the Tamiai (Treasurers of Athena) hold office by the lunar year. The solar year belongs to the modern Secular State: the Lower Boule holds office and the Ekklesia assembles by the solar year (i.e. by Prytanies). Both years begin about Midsummer. The Archons hold office from the first day of Hekatombaion (the lunar New Year), the Tamiai from Hekatombaion 28 (the Panathenaia): the Boule holds office from the first day of the first Prytany (the solar New Year). It has been established beyond question that the Strategoi also (strange as it seems) enter office about Midsummer: it can hardly be doubted that they keep the solar year, and hold office (like the Boule) from Prytany I. 1.

I argue in my next paper (on the *Strategoi*)* that Kleisthenes

[1] Cf. Poland, *Gesch. d. gr. Vereinswesens*, p. 14. This law is preserved not by an antiquarian but by a lawyer; so that neither its phrasing nor the list of possible associations can be ascribed to Solon himself. It remained always valid, and presumably passed from code to code and underwent changes analogous to those suffered by the Amnesty Law in its successive re-enactments: compare the Decree of Patrokleides (Andoc. *Myst.* 77–9) with Solon's own Amnesty Law, quoted from the Axones αὐτοῖς ὀνόμασι by an antiquarian (Plut. *Solon* 19).

[2] Meritt, *Athenian Calendar*, pp. 72, 124: *Athenian Financial Documents*, p. 153.

[3] The solar year is, astronomically, the year of the four seasons, marked by solstice and equinox. This is a thing far harder to determine than a lunation: consequently archaic religious calendars are commonly fixed by lunations, not by solstice and equinox. We have a similar juxtaposition today: our months divide the solar year, our feasts (Easter, etc.) are tied to a year of lunations.

*[Not published.]

created the Strategoi *c.* 500 B.C., as a Secular[1] Executive destined to displace the Archons: the Archons' degradation was a corollary of the creation of Strategoi, yet this corollary was postponed for fourteen years, since Kleisthenes lost power *c.* 499 B.C. The three juxtapositions—Demes beside Phratries, Solar Year beside Lunar, Strategoi beside Archons—reveal his method: to make the religious structure politically insignificant, by creating alongside it a secular structure.

The Kylonian Curse had no doubt embittered the Alkmeonids against 'priest-craft': but Kleisthenes' sense that the State should be secular does not of course argue him an enemy of religion. Of his personal convictions we must be content to know nothing: but his relations with Delphi argue as much the opposite, and it has struck me that the conventional date, 1506 B.C., given by the *Marmor Parium* for the first founding of the Panathenaic Games by Erichthonios, reflects perhaps some especial solemnity in the celebration of 506;—the first democratic Panathenaia ranked as the millenary. A programme of irreligion, like that of the French or Russian revolutionaries, would have been wholly unacceptable to Kleisthenes' followers.

Kleisthenes in fact was as well aware as anyone how religion can be mobilized for political ends: played his part in the game: and took his measures to restrict the game thenceforth. This was his share in that valiant fight against obscurantism and for spiritual integrity, which gives Greek history its eternal significance.

---

[1] It is, I think, typical that the Strategoi can summon the Ekklesia (e.g. Thuc. IV. 118. 14: Perikles' power of *suspending* the Ekklesia is, I imagine, an emergency power, Thuc. II. 22. 1):—a thing no Archon could do, after Solon.

MILTIADES

THE red-figure plate in the Ashmolean Museum bearing the inscription Μιλτιαδες καλος has been ascribed, by the scholar* to whom these pages are dedicated, to the Cerberus Painter; and dated to 520–510 B.C.[1]

We ask ourselves inevitably: is this the great Miltiades? and he who tries to answer is unusually incurious if he does not ask the second question: is the beardless mounted archer, here depicted, Miltiades himself? He looks to be under twenty, Marathon was fought twenty to thirty years later. What age was Miltiades at Marathon in 490? what age was he between 520 and 510 B.C.?

The earlier dates in Miltiades' life are all controvertible.[2] I offer the following *fasti*:[3]

A. *His father Kimon.*

1. Circa 585: born.
2. 536 (or shortly before); exiled by Peisistratos.
3. 536: while in exile wins the chariot race at Olympia.
4. 532: wins a second time, has his victory announced in Peisistratos' name, is reconciled and recalled to Athens.
5. 528: wins a third time.
6. 528/7: within a few months Peisistratos dies, and during the crisis of Hippias' succession Kimon is murdered; possibly on Hippias' orders.

*[Sir John Beazley.]

[1] *A.R.V.*, p. 55, Cerberus Painter 8. *C.V. Oxford* 1 (1927), pl. I, 5, text p. 2. Cf. Schoppa, *Die Darstellung der Perser* (diss. Heidelberg 1933), p. 23. The inscription is not visible in the photograph: it describes a semicircle round the top half of the field. I am greatly indebted to my wife for advice and help throughout this paper.

[2] Berve devoted *Hermes*, Einzelschrift 2 (1937), to Miltiades (henceforward cited by author's name only). Inevitably my references are mainly to disagreements.

[3] The passages of ancient authors (chiefly Herodotos) can be found in Kirchner, *P(rosopographia) A(ttica)*, nos. 8426 and 10212. Add, for the Skythian invasion of Chersonese, Strabo XIII. 1. 22; and for the capture of Lemnos, Diodoros X. 19. 5, Hesychios Ἑρμώνειος χάρις, Zenobios III. 85, and Charax in Stephanos Ἡφαιστία (*F. gr. H.* 103 F 18: the parallel passages are quoted in the commentary).

B. *Miltiades himself.*

1. Circa 550 (554?): born.
2. From 528 to circa 516: Hippias 'treats him well in Athens'.
3. 524: appointed archon for 524/3.
4. Between 528 and 516: first marriage.
5. Circa 516: death of his brother Stesagoras: Hippias sends Miltiades to take over the principality in Chersonese. Accession troubles. [Second marriage (Thracian wife)— or later ? see p. 167, note 5.]
6. 514: Danube episode.
7. Circa 514: Skyths invade Chersonese: Miltiades retires (to Thrace? to Athens?) for a few months, then returns. At the same time Hippias breaks with him and makes alliance with his enemies in Lampsakos.
8. Circa 507: Kimon (son of his Thracian wife) born.
9. From 499 to 493: Ionian Revolt.
10. 499 or 498: occupies Lemnos and Imbros.
11. 493: leaves Chersonese and comes to Athens: acquitted of 'tyranny' at his first trial.
12. 492–489: elected strategos in successive years.
13. 490: Marathon.
14. 489: Paros fiasco: found guilty of 'false public statement' at his second trial. Dies in prison.

The matters which most need justification are:

    (i) A 3–5: the dates of Kimon's victories.
    (ii) B 6: date of Danube episode.
    (iii) B 5, 7: interpretation of Herodotos, VI. 40.
    (iv) B 10: Lemnos and Imbros.
    (v) *passim*, esp. A 6, B 2–5, 7: Miltiades' relation to Hippias.
    (vi) B 1: Miltiades' age.

(i) The story of Kimon the 'Simpleton'[1] is told in Herodotos, VI. 39. 1 and 103. 1–3. He was exiled by Peisistratos: in exile he won the Olympic chariot race twice running. He caused the second victory to be announced in Peisistratos' name, and having

---

[1] Plutarch *Cim.* 4: ὅν δι' εὐήθειάν φασι Κοάλεμον προσαγορευθῆναι. He three times achieved the height of earthly ambition, and never had the wit once to enjoy it in his own name and his own home.

made this gesture he was recalled. After this he won a third time with the same horses: 'having won this third victory, it befell him to die at the hands of Peisistratos' sons, Peisistratos himself being by then dead'. The same team of horses won all three times. No doubt, then, all three wins were consecutive: this means an interval of 8 years between the first win and the last (otherwise, the interval is of twelve years or more). Peisistratos is dead at the time of, or at least very soon after,[1] the third win: since he died in the year 528/7, this third win was either in 528 or else in 524. The latter, it has been often assumed:[2] but the former is surely more likely.

If we accept the *later* dates, we must assume (what is likely enough) that Peisistratos' death in the Attic year 528/7 came after the Olympia of 528. The reconciliation has to be more or less a deathbed reconciliation, the old tyrant hears the news of the race, recalls his generous adversary, and dies. The murder will come (on this view) four years later, in 524/3, and will surely have had a quite funest effect on that union of hearts which the archon-list suggests was being aimed at.[3]

If we accept the *earlier* dates, it becomes indifferent whether Peisistratos dies before or after the race: his death comes anyway within a few months, and produces the crisis of the succession. During that crisis, Kimon's enhanced prestige would be formidable: it is not impossible that he *was* disposed to dispute Hippias' claim, and (whether or not) he must at least have seemed dangerous. I do not know whether Hippias was really privy to the murder: but the motive (real or alleged) is surely better during this succession crisis than four years later. The crisis once over, the dangerous man removed and Hippias safe on his throne, it was then time to establish goodwill. Herodotos reports this sequence of moods, rather sourly: 'as if they had not, forsooth, been privy to his father's death', Hippias and his brother now 'treat Miltiades well': they see to his advancement in Athens, and eventually send him to rule in Chersonese. In these circum-

---

[1] 'Der dritte Olympiasieg ereignete sich nach Peisistratos' Tod' (Berve, p. 40, note 1). No: it is the murder which is after Peisistratos' death: the Olympic victory is not necessarily so. It cannot of course have been much earlier.

[2] E.g. Kirchner, *P.A.* no. 8426: Berve l.c. But Cadoux in *J.H.S.* LXVIII (1948), p. 110, note 217, gives what I believe the correct dates.

[3] The fragment of archon-list covering the early years of Hippias' reign was published in *Hesperia* VIII (1939), pp. 59–65: *S.E.G.* X. 352. See below, p. 164.

stances, the archon Miltiades of 524/3[1] is likely to be this young man: the archonship is part of his advancement. Hippias' use of the archonship is noticed by Thucydides, VI. 54. 6, and illustrated by the extant fragment of archon-list (see below, p. 164).

For these reasons I prefer the earlier dates. Let us look once more at the implications of the later dates. Kimon's third victory is now in 524, during the archonship of a Miltiades who may be his son and (if not that) is probably of his family. This third victory makes Kimon look dangerous enough to kill: and he is killed when leaving the archon's table.[2] In the fifth year of Hippias' reign we have a suspected conspiracy in the family of the chief archon. This is dramatic, sensational, not perhaps impossible: but not, to my mind, probable. It makes the relations between the two houses persistently ambiguous: the favour shown *after this* to Kimon's son in Athens, the establishment some 8 or 9 years later of this son on the throne of Chersonese, become things melodramatic and (if I may so put it) *opaque*: I conceive Hippias' reign in more transparent terms.[3] I can understand how Kimon's violent death during the crisis of succession could be followed, *more Polycrateo*, by the advancement of his son: the more tangled story is to my mind unlikely.

Why was he exiled in the first place? I think, if we may judge by the sequel, that Peisistratos fancied himself threatened by the prestige of Kimon's racehorses. The quarrel, if so, may be imagined as flaring up when Kimon started for Olympia in 536.[4]

(ii) Herodotos records (IV. 83–142) that Dareios crossed the Bosporos into Europe, and then crossed the Danube and invaded Skythia. Mandrokles of Samos bridged the Bosporos for him, a Greek fleet accompanied him and bridged the Danube. Of the Greek princes who followed him many were Asiatics (e.g. from Lampsakos, Lesbos, Miletos) and a few Europeans (Ariston of

---

[1] Dionysios, *Ant R* VII. 3. 1: the name is also in the inscribed list (p. 157, note 3). See Cadoux, *J.H.S.* LXVIII (1948), p. 110, note 216.

[2] Herodotos, VI. 103. 3: κατὰ τὸ πρυτανήιον νυκτός. Olympic victors dined in the Prytaneion: Preuner, *Hermes* LXI (1926), pp. 472 ff.

[3] 'Transparency' characterizes the Attic skolia, the Hipparchos herms. For the kind of quarrel (as I suppose it) see the following note.

[4] This date is of course quite arbitrary: it does not affect the argument. The *type* of quarrel matters more. I am supposing something like the stage quarrels, between Oedipus and Kreon, Theseus and Hippolytos: sc. that Kimon, like Kreon or Hippolytos, stood close to the throne, was its natural prop. The sequel is less bizarre if this is so.

Byzantion, and Miltiades). These were left to guard the Danube crossing: when Dareios by misadventure overstayed his time, the Skythians invited the Greeks to break the bridge, and Miltiades advised that they do so: but most of the Greek princes opposed him, so that Dareios found the bridge still guarded and intact. This is the *Danube episode.*

Most modern scholars think this episode, or at least Miltiades' proposal, fictitious:[1] the event which we will therefore try to date is Dareios' European campaign. There is a growing consensus to put it in about 513 B.C.: so Berve, p. 42, note 3, and Cameron in a careful note in *J.N.E.S.* II (1943), p. 313, note 32. Dareios' eastern preoccupations forbid any date substantially earlier, Hippias' medising alliance with Lampsakos forbids any substantially later. Dareios' 'list of peoples', on the foundation block of the Persepolis terrace, which mentions the 'Lands oversea', was probably inscribed very soon after the European campaign, and it was inscribed in some year not very much before 511:[2] it could well be of 514 or 513. The approximate date is thus hardly in question.[3] Chance has preserved only one ancient statement of

[1] See Berve, pp. 41–2.

[2] Kent, *J.N.E.S.* II (1943), pp. 302 ff. *Old Persian Texts IV: The Lists of Provinces*; Cameron, ibid., pp. 307 ff. *Darius, Egypt, and the 'Lands beyond the Sea'.* The Persepolis list (Darius Persepolis e) is no. II on p. 302. Line 14, hitherto misread and mistranslated as 'Lands in the east', is here given as *dahyāva: tyā: para: draya:* (terrae quae trans mare). This is the first time European subjects are mentioned: later they are specified, as *Skudra* (Thraces), *Yaunā: tyaiy: paradraya:* (Graeci qui trans mare), etc.: see Kent's Table 2 on p. 305 [I venture to disagree with his separation of *Yaunā* in cols. 3 and 5 from the relatives which follow]. This unspecific mention of 'Lands oversea', and the absence of *Putāyā* (sc. Libyans: see Cameron, p. 309, note 12), indicate that Dareios' campaign is still recent and that Aruandes' simultaneous campaign in Libya (Herodotos, IV. 145. 1) is not yet digested. Cameron observes that the Canal Stelai from Egypt (evidently of the same date) complete the picture: they list Libya but have no oversea people.—For the sense in which the stone which bears the Persepolis list is a 'foundation stone', see Cameron, p. 312, and for a further description of it, p. 307. The earliest extant 'Fortification Tablets' are of 511 and by then the terrace was in use.

[3] An earlier date (517) is suggested in *C.A.H.* IV, mainly in the belief that the Danube campaign was mentioned and dated on the Behistun Rock, OP col. V. The best available text of this column (pending Cameron's publication of the whole) is Kent's in *J.N.E.S.* IV (1945), pp. 40–1. The campaign was certainly in Turkestan and probably in Dareios' third year: it is mentioned in Polyainos, VII. 11. 6 and VII. 12. Polyainos also (VII. 11. 7) mentions a visit of Dareios to Egypt, when the sacred Bull was being mourned. The sacred Bull no doubt died more than once or twice in the reign, but we know of one such mourning in autumn 518 (*J.N.E.S.* II, p. 311); this may be when Dareios came, since the Canal Stelai say that he visited Egypt early in his reign. That visit has of course no connexion with Aruandes' quarrel with Dareios much later (Herodotos, IV. 166), and gives no date (unless perhaps *post quem*) for the Danube campaign.

Polyainos' knowledge of Dareios' early years is perhaps derived from Deinon, a fourth century writer.

the date, in the *Chronikon Romanum* (*F. gr. H.* 252 B 8). Here it is
synchronized with the murder of Hipparchos and both are dated to
513/2. This absolute date is one year too low for Hipparchos'
murder. I believe it is also one year too late for Dareios' campaign:
that is to say, the synchronism is correct though the absolute date
is wrong by one year.[1]

This synchronism is, I think, implied in Thucydides' statement
(VI. 59) that Hippias' reaction to Hipparchos' murder was to
make a marriage alliance with Lampsakos: for this alliance was
in fact Hippias' reaction (and a prompt reaction) to both events
alike. After the murder, Thucydides says, Hippias' rule became
harsher: he killed many citizens and also took stock of the external
situation. '*At any rate* [γοῦν: *for this reason or another*] *he now proceeded
to marry his daughter Archedike to Aiantides, son of Hippoklos the ruler of
Lampsakos: though he was Athenian and these were Lampsakenes, he saw
how well they stood with King Dareios*'. Hippoklos was one of the
Asiatic Greeks who followed Dareios to the Danube, and when
Miltiades suggested deserting Dareios, Hippoklos was one of those
who opposed him and saved the King and his army. Thucydides
(as I understand him) presupposes this: Hippoklos enjoyed
Dareios' favour because he had proved loyal on the Danube.

Thucydides here confirms the substantial truth of Herodotos'
story. The alliance was paradoxical,[2] since Lampsakos had a
long-standing feud with the Athenians in Chersonese: this is
Hippias' decisive break with Miltiades. In concrete terms, he
now detaches Sigeion from Chersonese and attaches it to Lampsakos: his communications now run from Sigeion via Lampsakos
to Sousa.[3] This *volte face* is called for only if Miltiades has to some

---

[1] The interval (528 years) is computed from A.D. 15/6. The compiler speaks of the
Kimmerian Bosporos, a venial error.—I do not think there is any reason *a priori* to
respect his synchronism more than his absolute date: the synchronism happens to be
right.—Note that B 6–9 have four Persian items in succession: Kyros captures Sardis
(date lost), Kambyses conquers Egypt (525/4), Dareios crosses into Skythia (513/2),
Xerxes crosses the Hellespont (date incomplete).

[2] Berve, p. 35, speaks of this alliance as the culmination of constant hostility between
Sigeion and Chersonese. He starts from his belief in the 'fortdauernde Feindschaft
zwischen den beiden Familien', and finds any other relation between the two places
'denkbar unwahrscheinlich'. I do not know how he understands Thucydides' words
Ἀθηναῖος ὢν Λαμψακηνῷ (VI. 59. 3). I understand them to mark the singularity of the
act. See p. 166 note 1.

[3] Thucydides, VI. 59. 4: ἔς τε Σίγειον καὶ παρ' Αἰαντίδην ἐς Λάμψακον ἐκεῖθεν δὲ ὡς
βασιλέα Δαρεῖον.. Unless Herodotos is wrong (V. 91–6) it took him some years to reach
Sousa.

degree compromised himself, or (as I would prefer to say) if the policy of keeping Thrace for Athenians (rather than Asiatic Greeks) has proved futile. I do not know how far Miltiades had shown his hand on the Danube: but Dareios' advance into Europe had certainly been against Athenian interests. The Asiatic Greeks who supported Dareios (and had saved his life) were now getting their rewards at Athens' expense. Athens' three main interests in the north (Strymon, Troad, Chersonese) were all coveted by Dareios' benefactors. The two chief benefactors (Histiaios and Koês, in Miletos and Lesbos) coveted the Strymon and the Troad:[1] Hippias struck his bargain with Lampsakos, which coveted the Chersonese. Miltiades whom (a very short while before) Hippias had established as ruler in Chersonese, must now be sacrificed to the changed circumstances.

This was most satisfactory for Dareios, who knew something of the quality of Greek civilisation and the value to him of a medising Athens: and correspondingly disquieting for Sparta. The Spartan attacks on Hippias are the consequence; and the first of these (Anchimolios) can hardly be later than 512.[2] The marriage belongs then probably to 513: it followed fairly promptly on Hipparchos' murder. I would expect that it followed equally promptly on the Danube campaign, since Hippias could not afford to wait long before adjusting himself to his dangers in Thrace and the Troad. The marriage in 513 is Hippias' prompt reaction to both events, so that the *Chronikon's* synchronism is good. Both events were in 514.

(iii) Herodotos, in VI. 40, is closing a longish digression. His main theme is the collapse of the Ionian Revolt and the punitive cruise of the Phoenician fleet along the Aegean coast of Asia Minor: this is in 493. This fleet reaches Chersonese at VI. 33: at VI. 34 Herodotos digresses to explain how Miltiades came to be there. He tells of the arrival of Miltiades *senior*, the founder;

---

[1] Koês suggested guarding the bridge (IV. 97), Histiaios preserved it (IV. 137). Their rewards: Koês is made ruler of Mytilene, Histiaios is given Myrkinos on the Strymon (V. 11). A ruler of Mytilene favoured by Persia was a danger to Sigeion: see, for a generation earlier, V. 94–5; and the possessions of Mytilene in the Troad a generation later can be measured, roughly, from the 'Aktaian cities' ceded by Mytilene in 427: *A.T.L.* I [or II], A9 III. 124–141, A 10 IV. 14–27, *A.T.L.* II, D 22, lines 13–15.

[2] Between Hipparchos' murder in August 514 and Hippias' expulsion probably in spring 510, we should probably put the Alkmeonid attempt at Leipsydrion in 513, the Spartan seaborne attack (Anchimolios) in 512, the preparation of a land approach (sc. Megaris) in 511.

of his death and the death of Stesagoras his successor (34–38);
next, the accession of the younger Miltiades (39. 1), his accession
trouble (39. 2), and the worse which followed (40). The closing
sentence of 40 is, as it stands, nonsense: the necessary correction
(as I see it) was made by Dobree, who deleted the words [τρίτῳ
ἔτει] and [τῶν τότε μιν κατεχόντων] and left the simple statement:
'this then happened earlier: but now, in 493, etc.'
This correction leaves the narrative fairly clear.[1] In 39 we
read how Miltiades' predecessor has been assassinated, leaving
everything uneasy: how Miltiades takes the drastic steps which
are required (mass arrests, foreign bodyguard, etc.). The story
proceeds (40)

> 'So this Miltiades, Kimon's son, had just arrived. And after
> his arrival there befall him troubles even worse than these:[2] for
> after two years he must run before the Skyths. These Skyths were
> nomads, who having been provoked by King Dareios, rallied and
> pursued as far as this Chersonese. Miltiades did not wait their
> attack but withdrew, until the Skyths went away and the Dolonkoi
> fetched him back.
> All this happened earlier: but now, in 493 . . .'

The Skythian attack comes two years after Miltiades' arrival.
It was a consequence of Dareios' campaign, evidently an immediate consequence:[3] Dareios' campaign therefore was just under

---

[1] Dobree's correction is supported with very strong arguments by Enoch Powell,
C.Q. XXIX (1935), p. 160. Note, also, how like the restored sentence is to V. 2. 1:
τὰ μὲν δὴ − − πρότερον γενόμενα ὧδε ἐγένετο. τότε δέ, etc. For further corrections
introduced by Powell in his *Translation*, see the next note.

[2] The two *comparanda* are evidently (a) the trouble he had encountered at his first
arrival (described in ch. 39) and (b) the worse trouble which came two years later,
namely the Skythian raid on Chersonese. For (a) neither of the two variants τῶν
καταλαβόντων πρηγμάτων and τ. κατεχόντων πρ. sounds quite right: perhaps Herodotos'
felicity deserted him. There is, to my ear, a rather uneasy play on the verb καταλαμβάνω:
38. 2, κατέλαβε: 39, 1, καταλαμφόμενον τὰ πρήγματα: 40. 1, κατέλαμβανε − − ἄλλα τῶν
καταλαβόντων πρηγμάτων χαλεπώτερα. He was sent to take charge of the situation, but
it took charge of him? In his *Translation* Powell proposes to change τῶν καταλαβόντων
to τῶν κατέλιπε οἴκοι: this rather violent change destroys the sense, since so far as
Herodotos has told us Miltiades left no troubles at Athens (39. 1).

[3] Unless we alter the text this Skythian raid is only two years after Miltiades' arrival,
and is therefore less than two years after Dareios' campaign. It was surely a pursuit
(though by translating ἤλασαν 'pursued' I beg this question). Strabo, XIII. 1. 22,
confirms that the Skyths reached Chersonese, but gives no further precision about the
date. The Skythian embassy to Sparta (Herodotos, VI. 84), if it belongs to this occasion will imply that they stayed more than a few weeks.
It is clear that Dareios was in some trouble: the Bosporos bridge was broken,
Byzantion, Chalkedon and Perinthos all required punishment (V. 1. 1, V. 26): this
is evidently why Dareios crossed, in this tumultuary fashion, at Abydos. Did Miltiades

two years after Miltiades' arrival. If we put that campaign in 514, the Skythian attack will come in 514 or 513, and Miltiades' arrival in 516 or 515.

(iv) The date of Miltiades' action in Lemnos and Imbros makes little difference to the present enquiry. I am accepting D. Mustilli's recent statement, that the contents of the earliest Greek burials at Hephaistia in Lemnos can all be later than 500 B.C., though the deposits of the pre-Greek temple stop perceptibly earlier. The temple, Mustilli supposes, was destroyed by Otanes when he captured the two islands in 513 (Herodotos, V. 26–27). Both islands had then still their pre-Greek (Pelasgian) inhabitants. Otanes put in Lykaretos (a Samian) as governor at Lemnos: Lykaretos died (was perhaps killed?) and Lemnos apparently regained its independence under Hermon, presumably a Pelasgian. Hermon handed Hephaistia (one of the island's two cities) over to Miltiades; who captured the other after a siege and then presented the whole of Lemnos to Athens. The Pelasgians were now evacuated and Athenian colonists took possession.[1] Imbros (which Miltiades kept for himself) was perhaps captured in the same operation.[2]

The action was hostile to Persia. Miltiades might possibly venture on hostile action at various times, but Athens' complicity (she accepts possession of Lemnos) probably fixes this to the very beginning of the Ionian Revolt, 499 or 498.[3] We have from Hephaistia in Lemnos part of a list of names, arranged by Attic tribes, in the Attic script of this date.[4] It was no doubt a catalogue of some of the Athenian colonists.

help at this point, and so escape his punishment? or was he, when Otanes came, still in flight from the Skyths? Perhaps Chersonese was for Hippoklos to deal with: whether he did so, how he did so, why he did no more, are questions we cannot answer.

[1] D. Mustilli, *L'occupazione ateniese di Lemnos e gli scavi di Hephaistia*, in *Studi – – offerti a E. Ciaceri* (1940), pp. 149–58. Cf. also A. Passerini, *Miltiade e l'occupazione di Lemno* (1935). Herodotos says nothing of Hermon, for whom see the authors named p. 155 note 3.

[2] He called at Imbros on his way home in 493, Herodotos, VI. 41. 2, 104. 1. In the Attic tribute lists, Imbros was probably, down to 447, one of the items covered by *Cherronesitai*: see e.g. *A.T.L.* III, p. 46.

[3] The alternative date is 510–508: after Hippias' fall, and before the new alliance with Sardis made in 508/7 (Herodotos, V. 73) and voided after the second embassy in *c.* 500 (96. 2, 97. 1). To judge by its position in Diodoros, X. 19. 6, Ephoros told the story of Hermon [note 1 above] as part of, or a pendant to, the Danube campaign. But so far as we can judge Ephoros' principles of arrangement, this is no reason for preferring the earlier date. It is to be hoped that eventually the material from Hephaistia will be decisive.

[4] *B.C.H.* XXXVI (1912), pp. 329–38 (photographs): *A.T.L.* III, pp. 290–1.

(v) Thucydides says (VI. 54. 6) that Peisistratos and Hippias left the constitution untouched except that they contrived to have 'always one of themselves' in the archonships.[1] The archon-list from the Agora[2] reveals how this worked in Hippias' reign: so soon as he is safely established, the three archons first appointed, in 526, 525, 524, are himself, Kleisthenes, Miltiades. The concept 'one of ourselves' is stretched to include the leading houses of Athens. For this I have (above p. 157) borrowed Dr. Tarn's phrase, a 'union of hearts'. The reign was to be founded upon a cordiality between the three families, Peisistratids, Alkmeonids, Kimonids.[3]

It seems that Herodotos did not know these facts. This is intelligible, if the text was not publicly displayed before about 425 B.C.[4] The memory of cordial relations with Hippias was not

[1] VI. 54. 6: αἰεί τινα σφῶν αὐτῶν ἐν ταῖς ἀρχαῖς. I accept Schwartz' argument for changing the text in 54. 5: we must read οὐδὲ γὰρ τἆλλ' ἡ ἀρχὴ [misread as τ αλλη αρχη?] ἐπαχθὴς ἦν. The subject of this sentence will thus be 'the tyranny', not 'Hipparchos'; τύραννοι οὗτοι in the next clause will mean 'Peisistratos and Hippias' (not 'Hippias and Hipparchos'), and these will be the subject of ἐπεμέλοντο in 54. 6.
[2] See p. 157 note 3 above.
[3] I use the term 'Kimonid' for Kimon Koalemos and his descendants. Modern scholars usually call them 'Philaids', but no ancient writer does and the term as applied to them is meaningless. Miltiades *senior* was descended in male line from Philaios (Herodotos, VI. 35. 1; Pherekydes, *F. gr. H* 3 F 2) and may be thought therefore to belong to the genos Philaidai (for which see *Diog. Laert.* X. 1), but the only known tie of blood between Kimon Koalemos and Miltiades *senior* is the woman who married first Miltiades' father and then Kimon's. That tie of blood, though it did not make Kimon a Philaid, did nevertheless bind the half-brothers very closely: Miltiades *senior* being childless looked for heirs not among his father's relations but in his mother's second family. I expect this means that her family was important, perhaps more important than the Philaids. The Philaids were not (I think: see p. 167, note 1) Eupatrids; but the pre-Solonian archon Miltiades (*P.A.* no. 10205: cf. Cadoux, *J.H.S.* LXVIII, 1948, p. 90, note 86) shows that Miltiades was an Eupatrid name, which perhaps descended through this woman. E.g. thus:

Miltiades
(*archon c.* 660)
|
Son
|
Kypselos = daughter = Stesagoras
| |
Miltiades   Kimon
(*Senior*) (Koalemos)
|
Stesagoras   Miltiades

This whole group (which includes all the Kimonids and also Miltiades *senior*) may be termed 'the Miltiades house'. This is the house whose dealings with the Athenian tyrants we have to clarify.
[4] Jacoby, *Atthis*, p. 171 and note 20 on p. 346.

a thing which either Alkmeonids or Kimonids would treasure. Herodotos asserts that the former stayed in exile till Hippias fell,[1] and this makes it certain he did not know of Kleisthenes' archonship. Of the latter he gives a more ambiguous account: this is no doubt because it reflects two things, a charge of undue complicity with the tyrants, and a defence against that charge.

In his last phase, when he was a plain citizen of Athens, Miltiades was twice put on trial; the first time (in 493) on the charge of 'tyranny'.[2] He was acquitted. I believe that Themistokles was his judge, resolved (if necessary, for the public weal) to override the evidence.[3] It was certain in 493, whatever his past record had been, that Miltiades was now the enemy of Hippias and of Hippias' Persian friends: and for Themistokles that was enough. But the prosecutors no doubt made play with the fact[4] that Miltiades had been Hippias' viceroy in Chersonese. Herodotos has more than one echo of this case: the controversy attending Miltiades' return to Athens has caused us to know more about some episodes of his career than about most things in Hippias' reign. This information is 'forensic'. In the Danube episode the motives assigned to Miltiades' opponents (IV 137. 1–2) are assigned forensically: they give the story its value for a defence against the charge of 'tyranny'. It is equally clear, I think, that all of VI. 39 was meant (not by Herodotos, but by the parties whom he echoes) to be damaging: the treacherous arrests, the foreign wife, the bodyguards, not least the help from Hippias, all have the smell of tyranny.[5]

In my judgment, the principality of Chersonese was associated closely with the tyranny at Athens. During most of the principality's duration the Peisistratids possessed Sigeion in the Troad. The relation between these two places (just astride the Hellespont mouth) cannot have been indifferent: they must have been either

---

[1] VI. 123. 1. For the sense of τὸν πάντα χρόνον see p. 166 note 3.
[2] He was indicted under the current version of the law whose earlier and later formulations we have in 'Aθ. π. 16. 10 and Andokides, I. 97. But the trial was surely argued by both parties, and decided, on political grounds.
[3] Plutarch, Arist. 2. 5: below, pp. 177–8.
[4] Herodotos, VI. 39. 1: καταλαμψόμενον τὰ πρήγματα ἐπὶ Χερσονήσου ἀποστέλλουσι τριήρει οἱ Πεισιστρατίδαι. As I say in the text, this was no doubt a prosecutor's allegation; but no doubt also true.
[5] Cf. Herodotos, I. 64. 1. No doubt VI. 40 is also prosecutor's matter, especially the closing words 'such is his past record: and now here he is again on the run' (see p. 162, note 1 above). It is like Herodotos, to echo both parties with this impartial gusto.

enemies or close friends. When we ask ourselves, *which*? the answer can hardly be in doubt: it was (until 514) a relation of close friendship.[1] It had been the same in Phrynon's time, *c.* 600 B.C.: Phrynon's twin foundations were Sigeion and (in Chersonese, immediately opposite) Elaious.[2] The Danube episode in 514 changed this: it made Hippias cut his losses, give up his projects in Thrace, and attach Sigeion to Lampsakos and Persia.

The principality was established (so I believe) in 546, soon after the battle of Pallene. Miltiades *senior* was (Herodotos says) a man of consequence who found Peisistratos' rule irksome.[3] Motives in Herodotos are not above question, but this motive may be true. He had already won the Olympia chariot race (perhaps in 548?): this no doubt was what irked both parties alike. Yet the trouble was hardly more than irksome. I believe that the two men, Peisistratos and Miltiades *senior*, both belonged to the wealthy

---

[1] Berve's contention, in his Kapitel I, is that these Athenian colonies were something quite distinct from the Athenian state and must not be presumed to have common interests. I think this is totally false: the quarrel between Sigeion and Mytilene is, for Alkaios and Herodotos and no doubt for Periander also (Herodotos, V. 95), a quarrel between Athens and Mytilene: that between Chersonese and Lampsakos is, for Thucydides (VI. 59. 3: see p. 160, note 2 above), between Athens and Lampsakos. This is not of course true of all colonies (the word ἀποικία does not define any strict international status: see Herodotos, IX. 106. 3; Thucydides, I. 38. 3), but of these particular colonies it clearly is.

[2] Elaious, at the southern point of Chersonese, is the modern Cape Helles (which appears on early maps as *Eles Burun*). In *A.T.L.* III, p. 289, note 75, we quote ps. Skymnos 707–8:

ἐξῆς Ἐλαιοῦς, Ἀττικὴν ἀποικίαν
ἔχουσα, Φρύνων ἦν συνοικίσαι δοκεῖ.

where the MS. gives φορβοων. The corruption was probably caused by a confusion (very common in Byzantine hands) between *upsilon* and *beta*. This produced φρβνων: or (νν misread as βο) φρβοων.

[3] Herodotos, VI. 34–6. When Miltiades left Athens, Peisistratos was supreme (35. 1); after arrival, Miltiades had time to enjoy Croesus' friendship before Sardis fell (37). Herodotos (I think) considers Peisistratos' first two attempts relatively unimportant: in VI. 123. 3 τὸν πάντα χρόνον certainly does not include them, nor (almost certainly) the '36 years' rule' in V. 65. 1: I do not think he refers to them here (in VI. 35. 1). The 36 years began in 546 with the victory at Pallene, which Herodotos puts perceptibly earlier than the fall of Sardis: Croesus had heard about Pallene before he sought Sparta's alliance, *a fortiori* before he attacked Kyros (I. 59, 65). See *C.A.H.* IV. According to Herodotos, then, Pallene was in 546 and Sardis fell perceptibly later. Either he is wrong, or else the conjecture is false in the Babylonian *Chronicle* which makes Kyros march against Lydia in 547 and kill its King: see Sidney Smith, *Isaiah ch.* XL–LV (Schweich Lectures for 1940), p. 36 and notes on p. 135. Although I cannot judge the conjecture, I prefer Herodotos. I think the battle between Argives and Spartans at Thyrea was in 544, separated from that at Sepeia (in 494) by a 50-year truce: and Herodotos synchronizes Thyrea with the fall of Sardis (I. 82). If Pallene was in 546 and Sardis fell in 544, there is time enough between for Miltiades to be taken prisoner at Lampsakos, and for Croesus to demand his release (VI. 37).

non-Eupatrid families which Solon has recently admitted to public life:[1] both were from Brauron in east Attica and both no doubt belonged to the *Hyperakrioi* faction.[2] If neither the faction nor Attica was big enough for both men, this was put right when Miltiades went abroad. Trouble started again when Kimon looked likely to rival his half-brother's exploits. Kimon may have been a simpleton, but the Olympic victor sat in the Prytaneion with the high annual officers of state; he stayed there year after year while archons came and went. I do not suppose the Tyrant had this privilege—until Kimon ceded to Peisistratos his second victory in 532. (He had not the wit to cede his third, in 528, to Hippias.)

Jealousy of the family's four victories, in 548 (?), 536, 532, 528, accounts, I believe, for what discord there was. Basically, the two houses[3] were allied. After Kimon's death the Peisistratids saw to Miltiades' civic advancement.[4] So long as he was young and tractable, his place would be next to the reigning house. Of his first wife we know only that her son Metiochos was honourably received by Dareios in 493: this may suggest she had been related to Hippias.[5] If Miltiades stood as close as I suppose to the

---

[1] Both Miltiades *senior* and Peisistratos claimed descent from Homeric heroes (Aias and Nestor): I do not suppose any Eupatrid house claimed to have entered Attica later than the Trojan War. Before Solon only Eupatrids became archons (Plutarch, *Thes.* 25, no doubt from Aristotle): Solon admitted all families which had sufficient landed wealth. (I hope some time to improve what I wrote on this subject in *C.Q.* XXV, 1931, pp. 1 ff., 77 ff. [above, pp. 86 ff.].)

[2] The name *Hyperakrioi* (Herodotos, I. 59) no doubt indicates the *periphery* of Attica, outside the ring of Hymettos, Pentelikon, Parnes, Aigaleos: opposed to the *Plain* and *Coast* inside that ring and visible from Athens. Brauron on the east coast is *peripheral*. Peisistratos probably retired there between his two first (relatively futile) attempts at tyranny: it was only after the second failure that he 'left Attica altogether' (I. 61. 2). Early collaboration between the two Brauronian families may perhaps be seen in the fact that the great Panathenaia were begun in Hippokleides' archonship (Pherekydes, *F. gr. H.* 3 F 2). I suggest above (p. 166, note 3) that Miltiades *senior* left Attica in 546; his race at Olympia could then be 548. The hypothesis is too uncertain to pursue much further, but I should like to know whether he shared Peisistratos' exile. He may have done; it would have given him Thracian interests, and exiles could train horses and win races (Herodotos VII. 103. 2: cf. Pindar, *Pyth.* VII): but I rather suppose he has stayed in Attica. The whole Hyperakrian faction did not emigrate.

[3] That is, the Peisistratids and the 'Miltiades house': see p. 164, note 3.

[4] Herodotos, VI. 39. 1: ἐν Ἀθήνῃσι ἐποίευν εὖ. No doubt a prosecutor's allegation (cf. p. 165, notes 4, 5), but the substantial fact was the archonship, notorious to all in 493. Herodotos on the other hand was very likely ignorant of this archonship, as he certainly was of Kleisthenes'.

[5] Kirchner, *P.A.* no. 10212, suggests that the second marriage came after the Danube episode: and though this is not what Herodotos says (VI. 39. 2) it is surely possible: the second marriage will then mark his breach with Hippias.

throne, it is possible that he was made archon exceptionally young, before he was thirty: but I do not think this very likely.[1]

(vi) I have argued above, especially under (i) and (v), that the archon of 524/3 was the great Miltiades. An archon is probably not under thirty, so he was born not *later* than 554. This makes him 64 at Marathon, so that he is hardly likely to have been born much *earlier* than 554. This will give the following ages:

> 532: returns with Kimon from exile: aged 22
> 524: appointed archon: aged 30
> 516: goes to Chersonese: aged 38

If he was made archon exceptionally young [see (v) above], and/or if his father's exile ended in 528 instead of 532 [see (i) above], we have further possibilities. He could return in 532 aged 22 (as above) or in 528 aged 26, or (if he was archon at 23)[2] he could return in 532 aged 15 or in 528 aged 19. I do not think these alternatives very probable.

The Ashmolean plate was painted (if the above dates are anywhere near right) at about the time when Miltiades went to Chersonese (*c.* 516): I suspect the painter celebrates that event. The young archer perhaps is saying that Miltiades is a fine chap: he may be an aide-de-camp[3] who will accompany the prince to his principality. The archer cannot be Miltiades himself unless the painter (for some reason) represents him as almost twenty years younger than he was. Yet may I with the utmost reserve suggest one possible reason why he might have done just that? I have in mind the Akropolis marble statue of a mounted archer, to whom the Ashmolean plate has been so often compared. Akropolis inventory no. 606; Dickins, *Acrop. Cat.* I, pp. 138–41; Payne and Young, *Arch. Marb. Sculpt.*, p. 52, pl. 134. 2–3, 135. 3;

---

[1] If the archon of 522/1 be Hippias' son Peisistratos (as I believe: Cadoux, *J.H.S.* LXVIII, 1948, pp. 111–2), it is possible that he too was under thirty when archon. But I am very doubtful of this: Hippias may have married in the middle 'fifties (Kleidemos, *F gr H* 323 F 15).

[2] This would put his birth in 548/7, within a few months, perhaps, of Miltiades *senior's* Olympic victory (see p. 167, note 2). If so, we may see why he took his uncle's name (Herodotos, VI. 103. 4) although not he but his elder brother was to be that uncle's heir (VI. 38. 1). But there are many ifs here, and some of them not easy: I think in fact that he was born much earlier; and that his name was a family name (p. 164, note 3), requiring no such occasion.

[3] Beardless youths in archer's dress are frequent in late bf. painting, and frequently accompany hoplites (as ὑπηρέται, aides-de-camp?): a catalogue of both bf. and rf. examples, Schoppa (as p. 155, note 1), pp. 9–24.

Schuchhardt, in Schrader *Die archaischen Marmorbildwerke der Akropolis* no. 313, Textband pp. 225–9 (Abb. 249–53), Tafelband 138–9. Payne and Schuchhardt differ widely in their dating. There are three pieces which come into question. First, the 'courtyard horse' (or horseman): this has no number in the Akropolis inventory but stands in the museum courtyard [Schuchhardt adds several numbered fragments, esp. 568 and 4169, probably parts of the rider]: Payne p. 52 note 1, pl. 134. 1: Schuchhardt no. 316, pp. 233–7, Abb. 258–64. Next, the mounted archer (as above): Akropolis 606 [+ 569, 331, 556, 558, 357a]: Payne, as above: Schuchhardt no. 313, as above. Last, the 'Epiktetos horseman:'[1] Akropolis 700 [+ 485]: Payne p. 52, pl. 137–8: Schuchhardt no. 314, pp. 229–31, Abb. 254, Taf. 140–1. I will call these three, respectively, Sch. 316, Sch. 313, Sch. 314.

Both scholars agree that Sch. 313 comes between the other two. But whereas Payne, very tentatively, suggested 'perhaps about 550–540' for Sch. 316, and 'near 520' for Sch. 314, Schuchhardt puts the former 'rather after than before 520' and the latter between 510 and 500 'or rather, about 500' (eher noch am Ende des Jhs.). His date for 316 depends largely on the treatment of the chiton in the fragments of the rider (Abb. 261).[2] The question is whether the rider belongs to the horse (see Schuchhardt's careful statement on p. 236: there is no actual join): if he does belong, I imagine Payne's early date is quite impossible. Schuchhardt says 316 is 'only a little earlier than 313' (p. 228): 313 thus comes apparently between 520 and 510,[3] which is more or less

---

[1] I use this name because (as Payne points out, *A.M.S.*, p. 52) Epiktetos has made a careful drawing of the horse. The drawing (*A.R.V.*, p. 50, Epiktetos no. 78) completely changes the action: the cavalryman is dismounted and leads his horse.

[2] The references on p. 235 to Abb. 261 and 262 seem to have been transposed in error.

[3] There are I think some small inconsistencies in his datings especially on p. 228. He there says (*a*) 316 is 'only a little' earlier than 313: (*b*) 316 cannot be before 520 B.C. (see p. 237): (*c*) 313 is 10 years later than 316: (*d*) 313 is about 520 B.C. Conceivably *ein Jahrzehnt* in (*c*) is a misprint? But even so: if 316 is after 520 B.C., and 313 is (even a little) later again, this should bring 313 somewhere near 515 B.C., yet he says (p. 228) that since Miltiades did not go to Chersonese till 516 or 515 there are *chronological* difficulties in connecting 313 with that event. Finally, (p. 231) 314 is 'at least 10 years' later than 313 and this brings 314 'into the last decade, or rather to the end, of the century'.

The treatment of the chiton in Akropolis 568 (which Schuchhardt ascribes to 316) cannot possibly, I believe, be much earlier than 520 and Schuchhardt thinks it later. If we hang his chronology on that, we get the following: 316, *c.* 520– B.C.: 313, *c.* 515 B.C.: 314, *c.* 500 B.C. The snag is that 500 B.C. is very late for 314 if Epiktetos drew his horse from it.

contemporary with the Cerberus Painter's drawing. An objection to this, perhaps, is that Sch. 314 has now to be put some 10 years later again, close to 500 B.C.: and this will make Epiktetos' drawing of it (see p. 169, note 1) almost impossible. Schuchhardt believes there is no such particular likeness (p. 231).—There is, further, some divergence between the two scholars on how good our mounted archer (Sch. 313) is. 'Kein Werk ersten Ranges' (Schuch- hardt p. 227). Payne on the contrary says that it, 'as is generally recognized, must have been the finest of the whole series': and he includes in this comparison, if I understand him, both the Rampin rider and the Epiktetos horseman.

Payne did not, I think, wish to put the mounted archer as early as 530. The hypothesis which I shall venture to suggest requires (I believe) a date even earlier, namely 532; for that is when I believe Miltiades returned with his father to Athens. This hypo- thesis is, briefly, that the statue was dedicated by (or in honour of) Kimon when he returned from exile in 532: that it represented his son Miltiades:[1] that in c. 516 the Cerberus Painter made a rough likeness of it.[2]

I have not, I hope, disguised from the non-archaeologist that responsible opinion puts the statue much later. The rider fragments assigned to the courtyard horse (Sch. 316) cannot possibly (I believe) be so early as this: if they are rightly assigned, my hypothesis demands that the courtyard horse is later than the archer. The hypothesis must be defended in some such way as this: the Epiktetos horseman, whose horse Epiktetos drew, is not later than about 520: the archer is some ten years earlier, and (if it be work of the quality which Payne says) may be earlier than it looks. I doubt if this is a good defence: if it will not hold, then either my dates for Miltiades are wrong, or else the mounted archer does not (either in statue or drawing) portray him.

---

[1] The Megakles pinax, I think, represents the son of a returned exile (Pfuhl, pl. 175).

[2] A rough likeness, but I think a real one, in spite of considerable differences, e.g. in what the rider wears: Payne p. 52, Schuchhardt p. 228. The marble, relatively unfinished on the left side (e.g. horse's left ear, rider's left foot), was meant to be seen from the right; sc. he appeared to be moving to the spectator's right: the drawing quite systematically inverts this. (The Amphiaraos crater seems likewise to have in- verted what stood on the kypselos chest. What, incidentally, was the time-interval here between original and copy?) Schoppa, p. 24, thinks that the marble is part of a group which included an adult horseman, presumably on the archer's left. Even so, since the archer's body is turned to the right, the right is no doubt the 'Hauptansicht,' at least for him (and indeed, so far as I can envisage Schoppa's group, for the whole composition).

THEMISTOKLES' ARCHONSHIP

I. THE ARCHON'S POWERS

WHILST archon, in 493/2 B.C.,[1] Themistokles began his constructions at Peiraeus, which he got finished in 479/8 (Thuc. I. 93. 3). On the latter occasion he persuaded (ἔπεισε) the demos: on the former he evidently acted in virtue of the archon's powers. What powers?[2]

The classical archon's functions were mainly two: to conduct certain public festivals, and to see to such lawsuits as pertained to the family. Not unimportant functions, at least not unimportant in the archaic state: when his discretion in his own court was still considerable,[3] the man who could, e.g., dispose of heiresses had much power and enjoyed much confidence. But not by any means enough to account for his known importance. Aristotle, noting how eagerly the archonship was sought in the sixth century, comments ᾧ καὶ δῆλον ὅτι μεγίστην εἶχεν δύναμιν ὁ ἄρχων · φαίνονται γὰρ ἀεὶ στασιάζοντες περὶ ταύτης τῆς ἀρχῆς (᾿Αθ. π. 13. 2). This is 'the archon', the eponymos: of the college of nine archons, Thucydides tells us that in the seventh century τὰ πολλὰ τῶν πολιτικῶν οἱ ἐννέα ἄρχοντες ἔπρασσον (I. 126. 8). He is speaking of the Kylonian curse, which we know rested most heavily on the descendants of Megakles, who was the eponymos.[4] That the classical archon has lost not only the use of his discretion in his own court,

---

[1] Dionys. A.R. 6, 34: there is little to add to Busolt's decisive note, G.G. II², p. 642, note 1. As Busolt insists, Themistokles cannot have been chosen by lot: the story I quote in my last section is an episode of his election campaign, see note 3, p. 178. He evidently became archon at about thirty, as did others, e.g. Aristeides (490/89): a relic of Tyrant policy, so we may add Miltiades in 524/3 (cf. Hdt. 6, 39, 1, ἐν ᾿Αθήνῃσι ἐποίευν εὖ) and I would say Peisistratos in 522/1 (Hesperia VIII, p. 60, no. 21, line 8: Thuc. 6. 54. 6 gives him as an instance of those whom the Tyrants contrived to have as archon during the tyranny, so that Meritt's date for him, ibid. p. 63, seems to me impossible: apart from the twelve Gods' altar, Thuc. ibid. and Hdt. 6. 108. 4): both these must have been very young.

[2] Kahrstedt, Magistratur, p. 88, believes (on the strength of Philochoros F 30), that at this time the nine archons presided in Boule and Ekklesia. This, even if true, would hardly account for the Peiraeus undertaking.

[3] ᾿Αθ. π. 3. 5.   [4] Plut. Solon 13.

but considerable other powers of which no trace at all survived, is clear. It has been noted how this fact misled Aristotle: seeking to reconstruct the archaic archon from the functions of the archon of his own day, he was forced to the conclusion that 'the archon' was a later creation than the polemarch: a conclusion surely false.[1] Besides his construction in Peiraeus, Themistokles had charge, some time before 480, of a water supply. In that capacity he levied fines on people who diverted the water for their own uses, and used the money for a bronze *hydrophoros* (female, two cubits high) which he dedicated, presumably to Athena: years later, when himself an exile, he saw his hydrophoros in the temple of the Mother at Sardis, and 'whether he pitied her for being a prisoner of war,[2] or simply wished to let Athens know his influence with the King,' he asked the satrap to restore her to Athens. The story is in Plutarch, *Them.* 31. 1: the satrap indignantly refused, and the bronze no doubt remained in the Metroon at Sardis. Plutarch (or his source) speaks of it as a known piece: the fact that Themistokles had once dedicated it in Athens, and in what circumstances, was no doubt temple tradition, quite likely justified by its dedicatory inscription.[3]

The constructions at Peiraeus were suspended for some years, and resumed in 478 (Thuc. l.c.): the provision of Peiraeus with a water supply comparable with what Peisistratos had provided for Athens was not completed till after the great Plague (Thuc. II. 48. 2), perhaps by Meton (Ar. *Birds* 997 *cum sch.*): for the remains of the work, see Judeich, *Topographie*,[2] 203. Plutarch calls Themistokles ὑδάτων ἐπιστάτης: was this also a function of his archonship? Whether as archon, or as epistates *ad hoc*, it was no doubt in his own court that the fines were imposed:[4] where perhaps, like the archaic Areopagus, he was κύριος καὶ ζημιοῦν καὶ κολάζειν, καὶ τὰς ἐκτίσεις ἀνέφερεν εἰς πόλιν (in the form of a bronze figure), though, unlike them, ἐπιγράφων τὴν πρόφασιν τοῦ ἐκτίνεσθαι.[5]

---

[1] 'Aθ. π. 3. 3: Ledl *Studien z. älteren athen. Verfassungsgesch.* 1914, pp. 252 ff.

[2] *I.e.* the bronze was taken at the sack of Athens in 480.

[3] For the inscription, compare perhaps *I.G.* I². 393: there the Tamiai appear to 'dedicate' ([ανεθεσαν]?) bronze objects which were never their own property; they had 'collected' them in their official capacity (συνλεχσαντεσ: cf. *I.G.* I². 301, lines 3, 58, *et saepe*, [το επετειο h]ο αυτοι χσυνελεχσαμεν).

[4] Aeschines 3. 14, οἱ τῶν ἔργων ἐπιστάται πάντες ἡγεμονίᾳ χρῶται δικαστηρίου.

[5] Cf. 'Aθ. π. 8. 4. If he used the verb ἐπιστατεῖν, it would not determine whether he was a special epistates, or the epistasia was a function of archonship.

Whatever the exact procedure, Themistokles appears to have handled fines imposed in his own court with surprising freedom. The archaic archon's greater power perhaps lay in two things chiefly: the wider scope of his jurisdiction,[1] and his more absolute control of it.

2. EPHESIS

The decline of the archon's powers is thus described and explained in the 'Aθ. π.:

3.5. (the archons in the ἀρχαία πολιτεία) κύριοι ἦσαν καὶ τὰς δίκας αὐτοτελεῖς κρίνειν καὶ οὐχ ὥσπερ νῦν προανακρίνειν.

9.1. (Solon's τρία δημοτικώτατα) τρίτον δὲ <ᾧ καὶ> μάλιστά φασιν ἰσχυκέναι τὸ πλῆθος, ἡ εἰς τὸ δικαστήριον ἔφεσις· κύριος γὰρ ὢν ὁ δῆμος τῆς ψήφου κύριος γίγνεται τῆς πολιτείας.

Ephesis, the right of appeal, is what enabled the populus to usurp the magistrate's powers: the magistrate who once gave a final verdict, by Aristotle's time gave no verdict at all, but conducted a mere preliminary interrogation. There are two very similar passages in the Politics: IV. 14 (1298a),[2] and II. 12 (1274a);[3] but ephesis is not mentioned in them and the dikasterion's part in upsetting the balance is consequently conceived in questionable terms: κύριον ποιήσαντα (sc. Solon) τὸ δικαστήριον πάντων, κληρωτὸν ὄν. This is not the only respect in which the 'Aθ. π. has an exacter conception of Solon's reforms than the Politics. Among Aristotle's works Hesychios records περὶ τῶν Σόλωνος ἀξόνων ε̄: it seems a reasonable hypothesis that the axones existed, and were studied by Aristotle or under his direction, and that to this study the exactness of the 'Aθ. π. is due.

The word Heliaia, which Solon appears to have used for the court to which he allowed appeal (Lys. 10. 16, Dem. 24. 114) is, I imagine, the same as, e.g., ἁλίη in Herodotos (1. 125; 5. 29, 79; 7. 134) and αλιαια common in Peloponnesian inscriptions,[4] and

---

[1] If, that is, he imposed these fines as archon.

[2] Τὰς ἀρχὰς περὶ μηθενὸς κρίνειν ἀλλὰ μόνον προανακρίνειν· ὅνπερ ἡ τελευταία δημοκρατία νῦν διοικεῖται τρόπον.

[3] The unfavourable view of Solon: he did not keep a good balance, but found the aristocratic-oligarchic element in existence (viz. archons and Areopagus) and upset it by his democratic invention, the dikasterion. Ephialtes, Perikles, etc., developed this evil element, and so τὴν πολιτείαν εἰς τὴν νῦν δημοκρατίαν κατέστησαν.

[4] Cf. Schwyzer, dial. gr. exempla epigr. pot. 83 B.24, 90. 2, 91. 2, 92. 2 (Argos); 99. 2 (Mycenae); 666. 6 (Orchomenos); 656. 24 (Tegea, αλιασται). I write Heliaia, since it

means what was later called the Ekklesia. Ἔφεσις εἰς τὴν ἡλιαίαν is *provocatio ad populum*.

3. DEFINITIONS OF TERMS

What was the effect of *ephesis*? It converted the magistrate's interrogation (*anakrisis*) from a final adjudication into a mere preliminary: it converted the magistrate from a judge into a mere *eisagogeus*, a 'conveyer'. It did not do these things at once: before seeking to trace the stages, I would like to offer definitions of the terms.

Ephesis, not exactly 'appeal', since it could be automatic,[1] means the referring of a case from one tribunal to another. In classical Attic law it is automatic so far as the archon and thesmothetai are concerned: any case which comes before an archon, if admitted at all, must be judged by a heliastic court. Consequently, the archon's interrogation (anakrisis) is no longer a real trial, and he gives no verdict: he merely acts as 'conveyer' (eisagogeus) and conveys the case to the heliaia. But ephesis is not always automatic even in classical procedure. The public arbitrators (diaitetai), who in conjunction with the deme-dikasts (or 'the 40') handled a high proportion of Attic lawsuits, could offer a verdict which the parties might accept: only if one party appeals (ἄν ὁ ἕτερος ἐφῇ τῶν ἀντιδίκων, Ἀθ. π. 53. 2) does the case come before heliasts: if there is no appeal, the case is finished (ἔχει τέλος ἡ δίκη, ibid.). And some non-heliastic verdicts were not appealable: the deme-dikasts (who are normally mere eisagogeis, like the archons) could pronounce verdicts involving not more than 10 drachmas, and no appeal lay (μέχρι δέκα δραχμῶν αὐτοτελεῖς εἰσι δικάζειν, Ἀθ. π. 53. 2). More important were the equally unappealable verdicts pronounced in certain cases by the Areopagus.

It is not known when ephesis became automatic—indeed, that is the crux of the enquiry: but I take it as certain that Solon did not make it so, that Solon's ephesis was real 'appeal'.

---

seems pedantic to change so familiar a word, but I imagine Eliaia is the true form. It has no aspirate in Attic inscriptions: *I.G.* I². 39. 75, Meritt and West, *Ath. Ass.* p. 44, line 14, cf. *B.S.A.* XXXIII, p. 121, line 40: nor does αλιαια in the aspirated Argive inscription, Schwyzer 83 B.24, nor αλια in the Delphic, Schwyzer 323 A.21.

[1] Bonner and Smith *Administration* II. 1938, p. 232: 'If the *ephesis* depends upon the volition and action of the losing party in the original proceedings, it is to all intents and purposes an "appeal" as it is known in Anglo-American law and practice. But if the *ephesis* is required by law, it is in no sense an appeal.'

Anakrisis, the magistrate's 'interrogation', is a form of judicial enquiry which (so soon as ephesis became automatic) became a mere preliminary to the real trial in the Heliaia: this is προανα-κρίνειν. The magistrate then does not even offer a verdict: his only discretion is to decide whether to refuse the case or not.[1] But ἀνακρίνειν does not, without προ-, have any necessary notion of preliminariness. If ephesis is not automatic, the magistrate will offer a verdict which the parties may or may not accept: the diaitetai do this (see above, under *Ephesis*), and their interrogation is no doubt an anakrisis (cf. Isaios, 5. 32, ἀνακρίναντες ἡμᾶς πολ-λάκις οἱ διαιτηταί). The dokimasia of magistrates by the Boule was an anakrisis (Lipsius, Att. Recht II, p. 272), and originally was not appealable, νῦν δ᾽ ἔφεσίς ἐστιν εἰς τὸ δικαστήριον (᾽Αθ. π. 55. 2). I think it possible that an Areopagite trial is, in fact, an anakrisis: in their special sphere, the classical Areopagites, like the archaic archons, still αὐτοτελεῖς κρίνουσι καὶ οὐ προανα-κρίνουσι.

But in all cases which came before the archon or the thesmo-thetai, ephesis was automatic in classical Athens, and the anakrisis consequently a mere pro-anakrisis, carrying no verdict appealable or otherwise.

By an *Eisagogeus* I mean[2] any magistrate who conducts an anakrisis, and then, as a result of ephesis, 'conveys' the case to the heliasts. The eisagogeus will preside in the heliastic court to which the case comes: he is thus the same as a ἡγεμὼν δικαστηρίου (Aeschines, 3. 14, 29).[3] The classical archon is a 'mere' eisagogeus, he offers no verdict at his anakrisis, and reveals no opinion or bias whilst presiding in his heliastic court: for how he should behave, see Lysias, 15. 3–4.

I will use the terms ephesis, anakrisis, eisagogeus, as defined above. I will also speak of the heliastic trial which follows an anakrisis, as an '*eisagoge*'. The use of the word is perhaps justified by Isaios, 4. 12 (see Appendix); it is at least convenient.

We have, then, in the normal lawsuit, two judicial enquiries, the anakrisis and the eisagoge. both conducted by the eisagogeus. They are separated by the ephesis, which is automatic, and results

---

[1] Εἰ ὅλως εἰσάγειν χρή (Harpok. ἀνάκρισις). This represents the classical practice.
[2] For justification of this usage, see the last paragraph of the Appendix.
[3] The reading in *I.G.* I². 41. 1, [h]ο ηεγ[εμον], is extremely doubtful.

in there being no verdict in the former, and the verdict of the latter being final.

4. THEMISTOKLES

Wilamowitz truly says that Athena in the *Eumenides* appears as the foundress of the Heliaia rather than of the Areopagus (*Ar. und Ath.* II. 334). After the anakrisis in 397–489, she declines of her own volition to give a verdict: in a case involving such passion, one person's judgment cannot satisfy, she needs the comfort of numbers (470–9). In the succeeding eisagoge (482 ff.) she behaves as Lysias demands an eisagogeus shall (15. 3–4), not pleading for Orestes until the voting is over (734–41).

Had the system of eisagoge received some expansion in the reforms which shortly preceded the *Eumenides*? Was it Ephialtes who made ephesis automatic, and converted the archon from a judge into an eisagogeus? The presentation of Athena as an eisagogeus is, of course, no proof of this; but is there in fact any more likely date? It cannot, surely, have been later: that it was not very much earlier (not, e.g., as early as Kleisthenes) is perhaps indicated by a small piece of evidence with which I will cope my edifice of conjecture.

Plutarch tells a story of Themistokles; *Aristeides* 2. 5: πρὸς τὸν εἰπόντα καλῶς ἄρξειν αὐτὸν Ἀθηναίων ἄνπερ ἴσος ᾖ καὶ κοινὸς ἅπασι ʿ μηδέποτε ʾ εἰπεῖν ʿ εἰς τοῦτον ἐγὼ καθίσαιμι τὸν θρόνον ἐν ᾧ πλέον οὐδὲν ἕξουσιν οἱ φίλοι παρ' ἐμοὶ τῶν ἀλλοτρίων.ʾ[1]

There can be little doubt that καλῶς ἄρξειν Ἀθηναίων means 'be a good archon of Athens.' In stricter idiom this should be 'Αθηναίοις: Herod. 8. 51 Καλλιάδεω ἄρχοντος Ἀθηναίοισι (480/79): Thuc. 1. 93. 3 (of Themistokles) ἐπὶ τῆς ἐκείνου ἀρχῆς ἧς κατ' ἐνιαυτὸν Ἀθηναίοις ἦρξε: 2. 2, 1, Πυθοδώρου ἔτι δύο μῆνας ἄρχοντος Ἀθηναίοις (432/1): 6. 54. 6, ἦρξαν τὴν ἐνιαύσιον Ἀθηναίοις ἀρχήν: Simonides 77 (Diehl),

ἦρχεν Ἀδείμαντος μὲν Ἀθηναίοις ὅτ' ἐνίκα
Ἀντιοχὶς φυλὴ δαιδάλεον τρίποδα (477/6):

I.G. I². 220.2, ερχε δε Αθηναιοισ Αριστιον (421/0): *I.G.* II.² 7404,[2] Καλλιασ Σκαμβωνιδησ

---

[1] Also in *Praecepta ger. reip.* 13 (807*b*). The variants are hardly material: πρὸς τὸν ἀποφηνάμενον ὡς ἄρξει καλῶς ἴσον ἅπασι παρέχων ἑαυτόν—εἰς τοιοῦτον. . θρόνον—τῶν μὴ φίλων.

[2] I owe this reference to Mr. Tod.

ἤρξας Ἀθηναίοισι Δικαιοσύνην δε πάρεδρον
Καλλία εκτήσω δαίμονα σεμνοτάτην (412/1).

But I think we must impute the genitive to Plutarch's own style: the parallel version (p. 176, note 1) has ἄρξει alone, as in Dem. 21. 178, τοῦ βελτίστου Χαρικλείδου, τοῦ ἄρξαντος (363/2). 'Sitting on the throne' is going to be an important part of his function; that can hardly mean other than sitting in court,[1] and though, e.g. a strategos sometimes sat in court, it was not his typical function: it was the archon's.

Themistokles is encouraged, then, to shew himself impartial when he occupies the archon's chair: he replies that he would be ashamed not to have helped his friends. Now, in classical Athens an archon's opportunities for graft were few: that no doubt explains the great reputation of the body of ex-archons, the Areopagus. But before ephesis was made automatic, the opportunities were more: Ephialtes was able to get many Areopagites condemned περὶ τῶν διῳκημένων, which may well include their behaviour as archons. The story, then, is out of colour for classical Athens, but may well be in colour for the time before Ephialtes: I would take this as a token of authenticity: not that Themistokles ever used those witty and shocking words (though I would not deny this obstinately); rather, that it is a contemporary comment on his behaviour.

In 493 there were two famous trials. Early in the year, Phrynichos the poet was condemned for a breach of the peace, after the performance of his 'Fall of Miletos'. Later the same year (but under the new archon?) Miltiades was acquitted on a charge of 'tyranny'. It was a moment when public policy was in the balance. Phrynichos had stressed the disgrace of the attempted appeasement of Persia, Miltiades (an escaped rebel) was sure to press for war: both were dangerous to those who still hoped for peace. Herodotos tells us that the acquittal of Miltiades was seen to

---

[1] For θρόνος, see G. M. A. Richter *Ancient Furniture* 3 ff. It means simply a fine chair, but especially a chair of honour. As a judge's chair, Hdt. 5. 25, τὸν θρόνον ἐς τὸν ἵζων ἐδίκαζε, and μεμνῆσθαι ἐν τῷ κατίζων θρόνῳ δικάζει (Persia); Aesch. *Eum.* 511–2, ὦ Δίκα ὦ θρόνοι τ' Ἐρινύων. King's chair (and so, 'office'), Soph. *Ant.* 166; cf. Aesch. *Prom.* 909–12, ἐκ τυραννίδος θρόνων τ', and ἦν ἐκπίτνων ἠρᾶτο δηναιῶν θρόνων (Zeus and Kronos). In the Parthenon frieze, I conceive that Zeus alone sits on a thronos, the other gods on diphroi: and thus I imagine Παλλάς, οἵ τ' ἐφήμενοι, in *Eum.* 629. The tamias Alkimachos sits on a diphros: Acropolis no. 629 (Payne and Young *A.M.S.* Pl. 118, 3–5) with *I.G.* I². 548+663, cf. *J.H.S.* 58, p. 217. Κάθημαι=δικάζω, Theognis 1281.

agree with the popular vote, when Miltiades was made strategos.[1] He might have added that the condemnation of Phrynichos[2] was seen as clearly to disagree with it, when Themistokles was made archon.

The courts could still give judgments which might, or might not, agree with popular sentiment: the trials were still anakriseis, ephesis was not automatic, cases did not necessarily come to the Heliaia. One may wonder why Phrynichos did not appeal: perhaps, since it concerned the discipline of the Dionysia, it lay peculiarly in the archon's competence (cf. Dem. 21. 179, more than a century later). But we may believe it was a *cause célèbre*, and a matter of scandal and indignation. That I conceive is the setting of Plutarch's story. Themistokles is talking with his backers[3] and one of them says 'No more scandals when you are archon: you will be fair.' 'Fair? I'll be better than fair, I'll make certain the right side wins.'

I have said I doubt if Themistokles used those words. No man was better qualified, by that creative quickness which Thucydides admired (which makes me glad to dedicate a study of him to the scholar we are honouring*), to have done so: but I fancy it is *post eventum*, though close to the event. For surely the trial of Miltiades is glanced at: he was the friend whom Themistokles would be ashamed to go home without having acquitted.[4] The gay words reveal the clear sight and firm purpose of the man whose nerve and wit saved Athens and Greece and Europe: *non vero ma ben trovato.*

APPENDIX: εἰσάγειν δίκην.

The function of an eisagogeus is εἰσάγειν δίκην, but there has been some confusion about this phrase. Liddell & Scott distinguish εἰσ.

---

[1] 6. 104. 2, αἱρεθεὶς ὑπὸ τοῦ δήμου, evidently for 492/1. There is no reason to think this refers to the election of 490; Miltiades is evidently strategos continuously, from his return to his death.

[2] 6. 21.

[3] Plut. *Arist.* 2. 5, εἰς ἑταιρείαν ἐμβαλὼν ἑαυτὸν εἶχε πρόβλημα καὶ δύναμιν οὐκ εὐκατα-φρόνητον, ὥστε καὶ πρὸς τὸν εἰπόντα καλῶς ἄρξειν αὐτόν etc. For clubs in elections, Thuc. 8. 54. 4, Calhoun, *Athenian Clubs*, 127 ff. In 'Aθ. π. 20. 1. ἡττώμενος ταῖς ἑταιρείαις ὁ Κλεισθένης meant in fact that Isagoras was elected archon.

*[Sir John Myres.]

[4] Miltiades was accused of 'tyranny': this was presumably a charge analogous to δήμου κατάλυσις and would, later, have come before the Thesmothetai. But while the magistrate still had discretion, and such cases were consequently worth hearing, I imagine the archon took his pick.

δίκην from εἰσ. τινά, but say the former is used of the *prosecutor*: the examples cited are, however, either of the eisagogeus (*Eum.* 580, 582; *P. Hal.* I, 125 etc.) or else not of δίκην (Dem. 24. 10, where the object is νόμον; here, as often in παρανόμων cases, the νόμος is spoken of as if it were the defendant). Conversely, Plat. *Laws* 910*e*, cited under εἰσ. τινά, is of the eisagogeus and the object is δίκην. The distinction between εἰσ. δίκην and εἰσ. τινά is overlooked by Lipsius, *Att. Recht*, 978, Add. to p. 55 note 6, and Busolt-Swoboda, *Gr. Staatsk.* 966[4], 1031[3], 1152[1]: even Kahrstedt, whose treatment of the εἰσάγουσα ἀρχή (= eisagogeus) is generally satisfactory, says, *Magistratur*, p. 203 note 3, 'gelegentlich sagt man εἰσάγειν auch von der Partei': this is false of εἰσ. δίκην, while of εἰσ. τινά it is true not gelegentlich, but habitually.

We may formulate: εἰσ. δίκην (γραφήν, εὔθυναν, etc.) is invariably of the eisagogeus, and in this usage δίκην is frequently omitted (e.g., *Eum.* 580, *I.G.* I² 65 lines 46–7=Meritt, etc. *Ath. Trib. Lists* D8, 47–8): this is too common to need many instances: e.g. Antiph. 6. 42, Lys. 15. 3, *Ἀθ. π.* 45. 1, 48. 5, etc. Εἰσ. τινά is normal of the prosecuting party: Antiph. 6. 38, Andok. 1. 135, Lys. 13. 36, Isaios 3. 3, 5. 12, Dem. 24. 10 (νόμον), *Ἀθ. π.* 29. 4, Plat. *Gorgias* 521*c*, *Laws* 958*c*, *Apol.* 24*d*, 25*d*, 26*a*, 29*a*, Ar. *Pol.* 6. 5 (1320*a*), *I.G.* I² 84 line 30: but is said of an eisagogeus in certain circumstances, e.g. regularly of the Eleven (e.g. *Ἀθ. π.* 52. 1, Dem. 24. 105), who were eisagogeis (Ar. *Wasps* 1108, Lys. 15. 3, Harpokr. Παράβυστον), but who also had charge of the defendant's person; so perhaps the Hipparch in Xen. *Hipparch.* I, 9–10 (cf. Dem. 39. 17); the Logistai, Dem. 18. 117.

I base my use of the term *eisagogeus* (for any magistrate who εἰσάγει δίκην) on Dem. 37. 33: οἱ δὲ νόμοι καὶ τούτων διδόασι τὰς παραγραφὰς ἀντιλαγχάνειν περὶ ὧν οὐκ εἰσὶν εἰσαγωγεῖς. Cf. Bekker *An.* I, p. 246, εἰσαγωγεῖς ἦσαν ἑκάστου δικαστηρίου οἱ ἄρχοντες οἳ εἰσῆγον αὐτοῖς τὰς δίκας. I use *eisagoge* for a case so brought (a δίκη εἰσαγομένη, Lys. 15. 3): I can only cite Isaios 4. 12, ἐν μόναις δὲ ταῖς τῶν κλήρων εἰσαγωγαῖς 'only in probate cases'.

THE JUDICIAL TREATY WITH PHASELIS AND THE HISTORY OF THE ATHENIAN COURTS

1. Text and Translation

The judicial treaty (or rather, the modification of a judicial treaty) between Athens and Phaselis survives inscribed on marble, *I.G.* II¹. 11; *I.G.* I². 16; Tod, *S.G.H.I.* 32 (cf. *S.E.G.* X. 16). The marble slab is virtually unbroken, but the surface is badly damaged, so that the beginning of each line is lost and what survives is difficult to read. Yet it is only in a few places that the text is seriously doubtful, and my object is not to offer a new text: I am concerned here with the light which the inscription throws on the history of the Attic lawcourts. It is (as I believe) a cardinal document, and its importance has not been fully realised.

The following text is not materially different from Tod's or Wilhelm's. I have left two names in lines 3 and 4 uncompleted: such supplements must be guesses; to go on repeating such guesses becomes misleading prosopographically. Two letters which Wilhelm reads in 7 and 21 I have put outside the brackets. In 12 I keep the text of *I.G.* II¹, in 16 I follow (with some misgiving, since I cannot myself read the doubtful letter at the beginning) the reading and text of Photiadis, whose supplement I accept for 18.[1]

---

[1] Besides Tod (to whose *Selection* I refer henceforth by author's name alone) and the two editions of *I.G.*, the valuable paper of Photiadis in the Greek *Ephêmeris Archaiologikê*, 1922, 62–5, 79, with a photograph, needs special mention here. The approximate date was determined by Wilhelm, *Goettingsche gelehrte Anzeigen* (1898), 204. I quote Wilhelm's text from his *Attische Urkunden* IV. (1939), 60: I follow it almost exactly except in lines 12 and 18. I have to thank Miss Jeffery and Mr. Woodhead for examining the stone in Athens for me: it is on their advice that I read the first visible letter in line 12 as *nu* and not *iota*, and in line 16 as *nu* and not *upsilon*. The letter *nu* varies greatly on this stone: some examples are almost or quite vertical; e.g. in lines 2 and 8: others slope forward; e.g. in ξυμβολων in 12. The first visible stroke in 12 is the third stroke of a fairly vertical *nu* (not vertical enough for *iota*, and also too much to the right). At the beginning of 16 only one stroke is quite clear. It has been usually taken for the right-hand tip of *upsilon*, and I must admit that in the squeeze the letter looks to me like *upsilon*: Miss Jeffery thinks the stroke is not curved enough for this. The letter, if *nu*, will have been much sloped forward. No good restoration with *upsilon*

The vitally important reading in 18 I have verified in two squeezes in the Institute for Advanced Study at Princeton.¹

    [εδο]ξεν τηι βοληι και τωι δ[η]   *stoichedon* 22.
    [μωι Α]καμαντισ [ε]πρυτανευε
    . ΝΑΣΙΠΠΟΣ εγραμματευε ΝΕ
    . . . . ΔΗΣ επεστατει Λεω[ν ε]ι
5   [πε· τοι]σ Φασηλιταισ το ψ[ηφ]ι
  I [σμα αν]αγραψαι· οτι αμ με[ν] Αθ
    [ηνησι ξ]υ[μβ]ολαιον γενηται
    [προσ Φ]ασηλιτ[ω]ν τινα Αθη[ν]η
    [σι τασ δ]ικασ γιγνεσθαι παρ
10 [α τωι πο]λεμαρχωι καθαπερ Χ
  II [ιοισ και] αλλοθι μηδε αμο· τω
    [ν δε αλλω]ν απο ξυμβολων κατ
    [α τασ οσασ] ξυμβολασ προσ Φα
  III [σηλιτασ] τασ δικασ εν[α]ι· τασ
15 IV [δε εκκλη]το[σ] αφελεν· εαν δε τ
    [ισ αλλη τω]ν αρχων δεξηται δ
    [ικην κατα] Φασηλιτων τινοσ
    [παρα τοδε ε]ι μεν καταδικασ
  V [ει η καταδικ]η ακυροσ εστω· ε
20 [αν δε τισ παραβ]α[ι]νηι τα εψη
    [φισμενα οφ]ε[λετ]ω μυριασ δ[ρ]
  VI [αχμασ ιερ]ασ τηι Αθηναιαι· τ
    [ο δε ψηφισ]μα το[δε] αναγραψα
    [τω ο γραμμ]ατευσ ο τησ βολησ
25 [εστηληι λιθι]νηι και καταθ
    [ετω εμ πολει τ]ελεσι τοισ τω
    [ν Φασηλιτων] *vacat*

'Resolved by Boulê and Assembly: prytany of Akamantis:

has been suggested. Photiadis made clause V part of clause IV, ε[αν δε] in 19/20 responding to [ε]ι μεν in 18, with the same subject for both verbs. The responsion would be better if both verbs could be restored in the indicative (with e.g. ε[πειδη δε] in 20), but the subjunctive termination in 20 is certain. We must no doubt assume that the μεν in clause IV had no responsion: close parallels in Aristotle, 'Αθ. π. 42. 1, 48. 5; cf. also *I.G.* I². 44 *sub fin.* Clause V perhaps helps to explain the talk of certain fines, τὰ ἐπιτίμια, in Dem. 35. 46 (the *paragraphê* of Lakritos, see App. B below). For the proper names see p. 182, note 1.

¹ The *mu* was earlier read as *nu* or *lambda*, but is surely *mu*. The restoration [ε]ι μεν (in which *I.G.* I², Photiadis, Tod and Wilhelm agree) is virtually certain. The Ionic script forbids us to restore [τ]μεν (for τιμην). If we swallowed this large obstacle and restored [η δ ηλιαια τ]μεν καταδικασ[ηι], that might perhaps circumvent the vital evidence. This is exceedingly unlikely and I note it only *ex abundanti cautela*. There will remain the evidence of clause I.

[Mnasippos?] was Secretary: [Neilonides?] presided:[1] Leon proposed:

To inscribe for the Phaselites' benefit this Decree, viz.:

I. In the case of a contract made at Athens involving a Phaselite the actions at law arising from it shall (as in the case of Chians) be heard at Athens *at the Polemarch's tribunal* and nowhere else.

II. In the case of other contracts the actions at law which involve Phaselites shall be heard on treaty terms according to the existing treaty.

III. Except that the provisions for appeal shall be deleted.

IV. If any other magistrate shall contrary to this decree accept an action at law against any Phaselite *if he gives judgment against the Phaselite* the judgment shall be void.

V. If anyone transgresses against what has been decreed he shall be debited with a payment of 10,000 drachmas to Athena's treasure.

VI. The Secretary of the Boulê shall inscribe this decree on marble and shall place it on the Akropolis and the Phaselites shall pay.'

I have underlined the two vital phrases. The seond is the most vital. The first I have perhaps over-translated.

2. Clause IV

The approximate date, somewhere not very far from the middle of the fifth century B.C., is not open to question: Wilhelm has sufficiently shown that the writing is of that time. The date between 469 and 462 for which I argue will perhaps make it the earliest public document which we have from the time after the Persian

---

[1] The Secretary, [*M*]ναοιππος. If the να is certain, then (as Wilhelm says) [M]nasippos is as good as [O]nasippos: better indeed since we have now three Attic examples (*I.G.* II². 5567, 1st cent. B.C.; Sundwall, *Nachträge*, s.v., 2nd cent. B.C.; *I.G.* II². 678, line 22, 3rd cent. B.C.). The Presiding Officer is restored as E(pi)medes in *I.G.* I² and Tod, but I can see no trace of the letters μη in the squeeze and I wonder who in fact ever read them. (The restoration is credited to Leonardos: yet I doubt if he *read* the letters μη, since Photiadis, reporting Leonardos, has the letters bracketed.) My suggestion, Νε[λωνι]δησ, is based on Raubitschek's reading of the Endoios basis, *I.G.* I². 983, in *Jahreshefte* 31 *Beiblatt*, p. 62; Friedländer, *Epigrammata* 69, *S.E.G.* X. 435; cf. *J.H.S.* 24. 337. Since the first syllable is scanned long but is written with *epsilon*, we should transcribe it as 'Neilonides'.

invasion.[1] The vital phrase in clause IV ('if he gives judgment against the Phaselite') envisages a judicial power which no magistrate possessed in 'classical' Athens, the Athens of the Orators. In classical Athens it is the Jurors, the *Dikastai*, who give judgment: the magistrate who presides in the court (most often one or more of the Nine Archons) has conducted a preliminary interrogation of the parties (the *Anakrisis*); but at that interrogation he has offered no verdict, and once in court he is strictly confined to matters of procedure and may make no observations *ad rem*. 'How angry you would be', says Lysias, 'if the Thesmothetai were to get up and ask for such and such a verdict: you would hold it outrageous if those who preside at the contest and put the question to the vote should advise the Jury about what verdict they should give. What more shameful or outrageous thing could you imagine in Athens, than that the Archon (for example) in cases involving heiresses should beg and pray the jurors for whatever he wanted done, or that the Polemarch, or the Eleven, should make such entreaties in the cases which they put before you?' The duties of such a magistrate are clear: he brings the case before the court, he supervises procedure, he puts the question to the vote: but he says nothing *ad rem*, he does not sum up or instruct the jury. He is quite unlike an English Judge.[2]

It had not been so always. Aristotle says in the *Politics* (1298a30) that it is a mark of developed democracy that the magistrates

[1] The arguments which have led scholars recently to place it near 450 (the type of *prescript*, and the identity of *Leon* the proposer: see Oliver, *Hesperia* 2. 495–7) were never more than tentative. The *prescript* is normal: the hypothesis was that before Ephialtes' Reform it should have been 'abnormal', but this was a mere hypothesis. *Leon* may perhaps as Oliver suggests be a supporter of Kimon: if he is, a date in the sixties suits him as well as can be. But even if these indications pointed more clearly, they would not, in my judgment, outweigh (a) the fact that the magistrate is credited with a power which is totally unknown in classical Athens, (b) the improbability that he lost this power later than 462. I do not suggest that the 'classical' lawcourts sprang into existence full-grown in 462. They did not: for instance, the great part played later by the Circuit Judges ('The Forty') cannot have begun before 453 ('Aθ. π. 26. 3, 53). Much positive construction was left to do after 462: but (in my judgment) the negative act, the destruction of the magistrates' power, was the vital preliminary and must be Ephialtes' own work.—Such is my judgment: if I am wrong, if Ephialtes did not strip the magistrates of these powers, then 462 will no longer be the *terminus ad quem* for our document.

[2] Lysias, 15. 2–3. In *T.A.* (see next note), p. 176, I note that in the trial of Orestes in Aeschylus' *Eumenides* (performed 458) Athena behaves as Lysias demands: she conducts the interrogation (397–489), declining to give a verdict (470–9): in the main trial (582 ff.) she directs procedure: only when the voting is over (734) does she speak *ad rem*. (Cf. Wilamowitz, *Aristoteles und Athen* II. 334.) Bdelykleon in Aristophanes' *Wasps* is naturally much less scrupulous (especially line 949).

'give verdicts in no cases but only make the preliminary interrogation', and more positively in '*Aθ. π.* 3. 5 that in the older constitution (before Solon) the Nine Archons had the power 'to render verdicts with no appeal against them, not (as now) just to make the interrogation'. In a paper on *Themistokles' Archonship*[1] I argued that the Archons had not lost the whole of these powers in 493 when Themistokles was Archon, and stated my belief that they did not lose the whole until Ephialtes' 'Reform Laws' in 462, but since I overlooked this decree I was not able to do much more than state a belief. This decree provides the positive evidence which was wanted. No one will question that it is later than Kleisthenes (507 B.C.), later than the formation of the Delian League (477 B.C.): no one will seriously question that it is later than the Eurymedon campaign (469 B.C. or possibly a little later) since Phaselis joined the League immediately before that battle (Plutarch, *Cimon* 12. 3–4). And here is a magistrate who still renders a verdict. It is not earlier than 469, and Ephialtes' Reform is in 462. I believe that two conclusions follow: (1) the magistrate's power to render a verdict was removed by Ephialtes' Reform (or at least not materially earlier); (2) the Phaselis decree was voted between 469 and 462.

The Phaselite's case must be heard before the Polemarch. Supposing it is heard elsewhere and judgment goes against him, the judgment is to be quashed. I doubt if after Ephialtes the Assembly would presume to quash a judgment of the courts: it was rather the courts which quashed the Assembly's decrees. After Ephialtes the Phaselite's remedy, if he were brought before the wrong court, would have to be a plea *in bar of action (paragraphê)*, and unless the court upheld his plea a judgment given against him later, in a court other than the Polemarch's, would have to stand. (The Phaselite Lakritos uses this method of *paragraphê* in the speech ascribed to Demosthenes, no. 35). This offer to quash a court's judgment is no doubt another mark of pre-Ephialtes date. It is not, taken by itself, so decisive a mark as the magistrate's power of judgment, since the unassailable authority of a court's verdict was perhaps not immediately recognized in 462, and the *paragraphê* procedure no doubt was not immediately defined. But it is good corroboration, and it throws

[1] Above, pp. 171–9: henceforth referred to as *T.A.*

its light on the climate in which justice was administered before 462.

It is a climate in which a magistrate gives a judgment, but the dissatisfied party can appeal against that judgment to the sovran people (§ 6 below). In this climate an act of the sovran people may, reasonably, quash the judgment of a court.

3. CLAUSE I

Further corroboration is given by the phrase παρα τωι πολεμαρχωι in clause I. In a later decree this phrase would be replaced by προσ τον πολεμαρχον (*I.G.* I². 28, 152, 153),[1] 'suits shall be filed at the Polemarch's office'. Our phrase probably means 'suits shall be heard at the Polemarch's tribunal'.

To translate thus is indeed to substitute a quite explicit phrase for one which (in other contexts certainly and perhaps even in this context) might have other meanings. Examples of παρά used with the dative of such a magistrate as the Polemarch are not wanting in classical Attic, at a time when these magistrates had little[2] or no judicial discretion: Lysias, 23. 3; Aristophanes, *Eccles.* 655; Dem. 30. 6 (twice), 26; 35. 47–8 (four times); 37. 46. These cases are exceptional and one may account for them in various ways,[3] but in most of them we must assume that the force of παρά is mainly locative and the possibility remains that it is the same in our clause I.

Yet instead of ranging it among these few exceptions, it is no doubt better to let παρα in our clause I have its full force, the force which it normally has in judicial contexts and metaphors. Παρ' ἐμοί means *meo iudicio* (e.g. Herod. 1. 32. 9), παρὰ δικασταῖς ὑμῖν in Thuc. 1. 73. 1 means 'at your tribunal', παρ' ἡμῖν αὐτοῖς ibid. 77. 1 means 'before our own juries'. In the Attic lawcourt speeches

---

[1] It should therefore probably not be restored in *I.G.* I². 49a, line 6 (Wilhelm, *Att. Urk.* IV. 50–1, = *S.E.G.* X. 49).

[2] The Archon Eponymos had some limited discretion: see the law quoted by Demosthenes, 43. 75. This perhaps affects the instances from Dem. 30 and 37. For the last passage (37. 46) compare Isaios 3. 46–7. Many of my citations from the Demosthenic corpus are from speeches which Demosthenes did not write, but since this fact can hardly affect the present discussion, I have for simplicity cut out the usual distinction between 'Dem.' and '[Dem.]'.

[3] See previous note. The four examples in Dem. 35. 47–8 (the *paragraphê* of Lakritos) are possibly an echo of our clause (see App. B). The hardest to account for is, no doubt, the Aristophanes. My list is probably not exhaustive.

παρ᾽ ὑμῖν occurs probably more than 100 times (over 50 in Demosthenes alone) in the sense of 'at your tribunal'.[1]

The dative after παρά, in judicial contexts, means normally the person (or persons) who gives judgment.[2] Because of the exceptions, I would not have argued from clause I alone that the Polemarchs still gave judgments. But since clause IV makes it virtually certain that magistrates comparable to the Polemarchs did still give judgments, I think there can be no doubt that the Polemarchs did also, and clause I should be understood in this sense.

4. WHAT WAS PROVIDED FOR PHASELIS?

A. CLAUSES I, II, IV

The main concern of this paper is the light which this document throws on the Athenian courts. What it provides for Phaselis raises quite other questions: which I must now broach because the date of our treaty needs to be controlled from this side as well. Various opinions are held on these treaties called ξυμβολαί, and specially on those between Athens and her allies.[3] Our document is always one of the important witnesses.

Most of the supplements (5–10, 14, 17, 21–7) may count as reasonably certain, the sense being fairly clear without them. But

---

[1] E.g. Andok. 1. 7; Lysias, 1. 2, 7. 14; Isaios, 7. 5; Isokr. 18. 10, 63; Aischines, 3. 1, 230; Hypereides, 2. 5, 4. 1 (Kenyon's numbering); Lykourgos, 110, 150; Deinarchos, 1. 3, 49; Dem. 19. 137, 21. 182, 54. 39, 29. 2, 20. 147. The phrase occasionally has other meanings: quite other, as Aisch. 3. 240; sometimes metaphorical (in your opinion, as men not judges); and in those lawcourt speeches which deal with public affairs (notably Dem. 18, 20, 23) the judicial context is often overridden and it means, not 'at your tribunal', but 'in Athens'. These examples are not of course included in the figures given above: those form the great majority of cases and in them it means precisely 'at your tribunal'. The basic sense is no doubt locative. The five examples I have chosen from Demosthenes all refer to the courts as a whole, not the particular jurors present: the first three cannot be taken as locatives but mean specifically *vestro iudicio*.

[2] See Kühner-Gerth, *Grammatik* II. 1. 511 (II. 2. c), *L.S.J. Lexicon* s.v. παρά B II. 3. In Powell's *Lexicon to Herodotus*, s.v. παρά C 2 b and C 3, it can be seen how the metaphorical use ('in my judgment' etc.: e.g. 1. 32. 9, 86. 5) arises out of one special form of the common usage 'at the court of', 'in the presence or in the eyes of', a King, etc. (e.g. 1. 115. 2). The metaphor was early established and is common in poetry, e.g. Soph. *Trach.* 589, Pindar, *Ol.* 6. 10, *Py.* 2. 72. In Homer, see Cunliffe's *Lexicon* s.v. (II) (1) (b).

[3] E.g. Lipsius, *A.R.* 63 ff., 965 ff.; and more recently Hopper, *J.H.S.* 63, 1943, 35 ff., *Interstate Juridical Agreements in the Athenian Empire*, esp. pp. 39–45.—I have profited from discussing this difficult topic with my colleague A. R. W. Harrison.

in three lines particularly (11, 13, 15) the supplements vitally affect the sense. No likely alternatives have been offered for 11 and 15, but in 13 instead of Bannier's [οσασ] the older editors followed Sauppe and supplied [Χιων].

The word X[ιοισ] in 10–11 presumes that the Chian status served as model for the Phaselite in clause I. In 13 the word [Χιων] presumes the same Chian model for clause II, whereas [οσασ] introduces a new notion, namely that there existed already a treaty with Phaselis which is abrogated for clause I but retained for clause II. Clause II on either view (whether the Chian model or an existing Phaselite treaty is to be substantially followed) is modified by clause III: how it is modified depends again on the supplement, but if we accept [εκκλη]το[σ] in 15, then there are to be no *ekkletoi dikai*.

These supplements (sc. X[ιοισ] in 10–11, [Χιων] in 13, [εκκλη]το[σ] in 15) were made in the belief that the decree was of the early fourth century. The use of the Chian model was explained by the fact that Chios led the way in the new confederacy.[1] When the decree was recognized to belong to some time not far from 450 B.C., Eduard Meyer (*Forschungen* II. 5-6) called attention to Plutarch's words in *Cimon* 12. 3–4 (p. 189, note 2 below), which make the Chian model particularly apt for a Phaselite treaty of the second quarter of the fifth century. Bannier (*B.P.W.* 1917, pp. 91 and 1342) brought the date down to *c.* 430 and therefore denied the relevance of Chios: he proposed χ[ρεωσ] instead of X[ιοισ] in 10–11, and [οσασ] instead of [Χιων] in 13. Recent editors have compromised, retaining X[ιοισ] in 10–11 and adopting [οσασ] in 13. They assume (rightly, I believe[2]) that whereas the Chian model serves for clause I an existing Phaselite treaty is retained (substantially) for clause II.

The decree was clear and had specific meaning for those whom it concerned; but for us all is allusive and vague. Even if our supplements are right, we can only guess what the 'existing treaty'

---

[1] Tod 118; 123 lines 24, 79: cf. the supplement [καθαπερ Χιοισ] in 121 line 7.

[2] Two things point this way. First, the particle μέν in line 6 requires some definite contrast between clauses I and II (p. 188, note 1 below). Second, the abolition of *ekkletoi* (?) *dikai* in clause III may be (but this is not certain) an advantage for Phaselis, and it would be unreasonable that Phaselis should have this advantage over Chios. Neither is quite conclusive. Hopper (see p. 186, note 3) has further objected (p. 42) to the use of the genitive Χιων, but perhaps Thuc. 5. 40. 2, τὰς Ἀθηναίων σπονδάς, is near enough. Tod 96, line 18, κατα τασ συμβολασ τασ οσασ, gives good support for οσασ.

had provided. I offer a hypothesis which I hope is consistent: the dogmatic tone aims at getting it clear.[1]

The decree's main purpose is contained in clause I. *Contracts made at Athens*: when litigation arises on these, *actio sequitur forum contractus*. This principle is new: in an earlier treaty with Phaselis (the 'existing treaty') some other principle had been used: perhaps the defendant was sued in his own city. The cases covered by clause I are no doubt a high proportion of the whole: and in all such cases a Phaselite defendant will now have to come to a foreign city. This hardship was mitigated by admitting him to the Polemarch's court.[2] This was a privilege usually given either to aliens domiciled in Athens or to individual foreign 'benefactors': it had apparently been given *en masse* to Chians (wherever domiciled) and is now given *en masse* to Phaselites.

Here then is the main business: the bringing of one large class of suits to Athens; and, for these, the Polemarch's court. This is clause I.

Clause II delimits it. 'In the remaining cases the existing arrangement is to stand':

'Except that' (clause III) in these remaining cases 'appeal is abolished.'

Clause IV reverts to the Polemarch's court. I have argued that this privilege is not given in clause II (nor of course III), so that clause IV is harking back to clause I. I believe this offers no difficulty. To those whom it concerned, clause I clearly held the substance of the decree and any later clause could hark back to it.[3]

There was, then, an older treaty, which did not prescribe *forum*

---

[1] I am assuming that whereas clause I announces changes over a named area, clause II affirms the *status quo* for the remainder. I infer that what has needed specifying in clause I is not part of the *status quo*.

[2] How did this privilege help? It is still bestowed on individuals late in the fifth century, when the Polemarch had long ceased to be judge in his own court, and the same kind of jury sat here as elsewhere (e.g. *A.T.L.* II. D23=*S.E.G.* X. 108, line 23: 416/5?). It may be that in this court an alien needed no *prostates*: somehow, at least, this court's rules of procedure gave him something like a citizen's status.—Lipsius, *A.R.* 65, note 46, infers from our document that in the fifth century all δίκαι ἀπὸ ξυμβολῶν came into the Polemarch's court. I infer the contrary, on the principle stated in note 1 above.

[3] *Ergo*, [παρα τοδε] in 18, rather than Wilhelm's [Αθηνησιν]. Not all cases at Athens, but all cases covered by the new provision. Note that clause IV gives its protection only to the Phaselite *defendant* ([κατα] in 18 is required by the genitive, τινοσ): the Phaselite *plaintiff* could look after himself.

contractus (at least, not systematically), did not admit to the Polemarch's court, and gave a status different from that of Chios. Our document revises this. Its main concern is to impose the *forum contractus* in all those cases (no doubt the majority of cases) where the *forum contractus* was Athens. Athens makes this demand on Phaselis, as she had on Chios and no doubt on all who accepted her hegemony. She mitigates it by granting Phaselis two particular favours: the Polemarch's court, and the abolition of appeal.

Understood in this way, can our document be as early as I have suggested? that is, earlier than the reform of 462?

Phaselis joined the League shortly before the Eurymedon battles, no doubt early in 469. It may be that the 'existing treaty' was made then, at once, and was modified by our decree within less than seven years. If it be thought that the treaty and modification thereof require more time, then quite possibly the 'existing treaty' is older than 469. Athens of course had these ξυμβολαί, these arrangements for litigation, with cities other than members of her League:[1] and Phaselis lay on a route where Athenian ships were often seen. In that case, the revision which our document contains could have been made as early as 469: as soon after the episode in Plutarch, *Cimon* 12. 3–4 as the persons concerned were back in Athens.[2]

Against quite so early a date as this there is, perhaps, the fact that the older treaty appears (from clause III) to have provided for *ekkletoi dikai*. We must next consider what these are and whether they allow the older treaty to be made before 469.

B. CLAUSE III

Clause III, as restored, abolishes *ekkletoi dikai*. The word ἔκ-κλητος is rare. The Attic dialect has its own range of words for the notion of 'appeal' (ἐφιέναι, ἔφεσις, ἐφέσιμος) and uses this foreign word only in connexion with various forms of 'foreign'

[1] Of course: and we have no doubt the evidence, close in date, in *S.E.G.* X. 6 (= Meiggs-Andrewes, *Sources* B8) A lines 40–3. The cities which are there assumed to have ξυμβολαί with Athens are surely the cities interested in the Eleusis festival.

[2] Plutarch l.c. (just before the Eurymedon battles): Kimon is besieging Phaselis: the Chians in his fleet are able, because of an old friendship, to bring her into the League and to mediate the terms between her and Kimon. Was Leon, the mover of our decree, one of Kimon's fellow strategoi (p. 183, note 1 above)?

appeal. I will first trace the word's usage, and then consider which form of 'foreign' appeal (that is, appeal from one city to another) is intended in our clause III.

The word is used in four different ways:

1. ἔκκλητος δίκη (or κρίσις): a judgment *that has been* (or *can be*) *appealed against*. Non-Attic: Tod 1 (sixth-century Chios), lines 20–3. δικασ [οqο]σαι αν εκκλητοι γενων[ται], cf. line 28, ηκκλητοσ δι[κη];[1] *Pap. Halenses* 1 (third century B.C., Egypt), line 68; *OGIS* 437 (first century B.C., Sardis and Ephesos), line 56; Plutarch *mor.* 493A.—Attic: our clause III; Tod 142, line 74.

2. ἔκκλητος πόλις: a city *which provides a court for a case originating in another city*:[2] Aischines, I. 89 *cum schol.*; Tod 142, line 49.

3. ἔκκλητος χρόνος: the time *within which notice of appeal must be given*: *Revenue Laws of Ptolemy Philadelphus*, 21. 15.

4. The ἔκκλητοι at Sparta, the persons *of whom the Ekklesia is composed*: Xen. *Hell.* 2. 4. 38, 5. 2. 33, 6. 3. 3; cf. Eur. *Or.* 612, 949.

The word is a verbal adjective and means, properly, what 'has been (*or* may be) "called out" '. Sense 4 is distinct from the others and is formed from the active ἐκκαλεῖν: persons who have been called out (of the town, or of their domiciles, into the open).[3]

---

[1] For this inscription, now republished in *B.S.A.* 51, see App. A.

[2] I give this cumbrous translation because, though it usually means 'city *to which appeal has been* (or *is to be*) *made*', 'appellate city', in Tod 142 line 49 it probably does not, the second hearing in the *ekkletos polis* being required by law. (The sense of ἔκκλητος is still the same if Feyel be right, *R.Phil.* 1945, 156–7, in restoring [εκκ]λητωι [βο]λει here and taking this 'appellate council' to be the body named in Tod 123, lines 57–8.) Certain persons are sentenced for treason in Keos, their names are to be listed by the Kean strategoi; anyone who claims that he is falsely listed may stand trial *at Keos and at Athens*, Athens being described as the *ekkletos polis*. Presumably he must clear both fences or his sentence stands. If he fails at the first, the second trial is purposeless and will not take place. But if he clears the first, the second trial is required by law and does not *depend on the volition* of either party, since the prosecution is (I presume) obliged to proceed.—The situation is different in Tod 162, line 21, where the prosecutor is allowed to *appeal against an acquittal* at Keos (the word used here is *ephesis*): here the second trial depends on the prosecutor's volition, as in Tod 142 I believe it does not.—A different situation again in ᾿Αθ. π. 55. 2 (cf. 45. 3), where the word *ephesis* is again used and again there is real 'appeal': see below, pp. 192ff.

[3] That is (no doubt: Plut. *Lyc.* 6) into the open space between Babyka and Knakion. The three places where Xenophon names these *ekkletoi* (Hell. 2. 4. 38, 5. 2. 33–5, 6. 3. 3–18) leave little doubt that they are the same as the Ekklesia; the word ἐκκλησία (= -τία) is simply the collective name for the ἔκκλητοι. Whether this implies that the word ἐκκλησία is of Spartan origin, is a question I cannot explore here (it is certainly the Spartan name for their Assembly: Thuc. 5. 77. 1), nor whether Euripides' use of ἔκκλητοι and ἔκκλητος ᾿Αργείων ὄχλος of the Argive Assembly in the *Orestes* is authentic local colour. The earliest occurrence of ἐκκλησία known to me is Herod. 3. 142. 2

In the first three it is formed from the middle ἐκκαλεῖσθαι, *provocare*. In this sense the verb is not Attic (the Attic is ἐφιέναι) and is very rarely found, but we may add to *L.S.J.*'s two instances in Plutarch the two inscriptions, Tod 1 (6th cent. B.C.: see App. A) and *Fouilles de Delphes* III. i, no. 486, II B, line 10 (3rd cent. B.C.): enough to assure its reality, and perhaps enough to show that the subject of this verb, as of ἐφιέναι, is the litigating party, not the organ of justice.[1] I know no other examples until Roman times, when it comes once or twice in Egypt (e.g. *Ox. Pap.* 1642. 21; 2104. 6) and also, incorrectly, in the passages cited in note 2 below. It means 'appeal *against*, challenge', *provocare*, not 'appeal *to*, invoke', *appellare*, so that ἔκκλητος δίκη, a judgment appealed against, is the original and proper use, and ἔκκλητος πόλις (city appealed to) a secondary and improper[2] extension of usage; and so of course is ἔκκλητος χρόνος.

In Tod 1, the words ἔκκλητος and ἐκκαλεῖσθαι are used for 'domestic' appeal, from one Chian organ of justice to another Chian organ. There was no room for them in this sense in Attic: but the adjective ἔκκλητος was appropriated in Attic for two, or perhaps three, kinds of foreign appeal. We may call these, roughly, 'hegemonic', 'third city' and 'reciprocal' appeal: 'hegemonic'[3] when Athens is the *ekkletos polis*; 'third city' appeal, as when Athens and the Boeotian League name Lamia to be the

---

(at Samos), unless the Theran decree in *S.E.G.* IX. 3, allegedly of the seventh century, be authentic in this particular.

[1] These two inscriptions are cardinal for the non-Attic vocabulary of appeal. For Tod 1 see App. A. Plutarch *mor.* 178 F, where Machaitas (father of the notorious Harpalos? *A.T.L.* III, p. 317, n. 70) appeals (ἐκκαλεῖται) from Philip asleep to Philip awake, may give us the fourth century Macedonian word: whence, perhaps, it passed to Greco-Roman Egypt.—Ἔκκλητον ποιεῖσθαι, used in Egypt as a periphrasis for ἐκκαλεῖσθαι (e.g. *Ox.Pap.* 1204. 5), has the party as its subject; but in Tod 142, line 74, the same phrase is restored in a quite other sense, the Kean swears that he will 'ensure that appeal is allowed', τασ δε δικασ - - - [ποιησομαι] πασασ εκκλητοσ. The restoration is justified, I think, by Dem. 7. 9, where Philip is said to be 'ensuring that appeal is allowed to himself', ἐφέσιμον τὴν - - - γνῶσιν ὡς ἑαυτὸν ποιούμενος. Cf. Aristotle, *Oecon.* 1348b14.

[2] Aischines, 1. 89, uses the phrase ἔκκλητος πόλις, and it is expounded by the scholiast, and by Hesychios and *Lex.Seguer.* s.v. (Bekker, *Anecd.* I. 247. 30). The grammarians take ἐκκαλεῖσθαι to mean *appellare*: but though they have support from the emperor Hadrian (who writes, *I.G.* II². 1100, lines 54–5, εαν δε εκκαλεσηται τισ η εμε η τον ανθυπατον) I think it is a solecism, the proper Greek translation of *appellare* being ἐπικαλεῖσθαι (*Acta Apost.* 25. 11). In Tod 1, line 10 εκκαλεσθω εσ is *provocato ad*, not *appellato*.

[3] The word 'hegemonic' is perhaps misleading since Athens may have claimed this from cities who did not accept her military hegemony.

ekkletos polis for both (*Syll.*[3] 464); 'reciprocal', as exemplified (outside the Attic sphere) by the judicial treaty between Delphi and Pellana (*Fouilles de Delphes* III. i, no. 486) where appeal may apparently go either way; the city which gives the first judgment is the *prodikos polis*, the other the *ekkletos polis*. Which kind of foreign appeal have we in the *ekkletoi dikai* of clause III? It is natural to think that Athens is waiving some hegemonic claim: that in the old treaty some cases judged in Phaselis could be appealed against and brought to Athens. This makes it hard to put the older treaty before 469, the year in which Phaselis accepted Athens' military hegemony. Yet possibly (p. 191, note 3 above) Athens might impose this judicial hegemony on cities which had not accepted her military hegemony: alternatively, the *ekkletoi dikai* hereby abolished were not hegemonic.[1]

5. 'Ephesis' at Athens

The foreign word ἔκκλητος had a certain latitude, but the native Attic terms are probably capable of stricter definition. Since their usage is important for my next section (The Lawcourts at Athens), I take this occasion for a short survey, particularly of the verb, ἐφίημι.

Ephesis (ἔφεσις) is always, I believe, the act of a 'litigating party' who, being dissatisfied with an authoritative pronouncement made about his case, *appeals against it* to some other authority. Most often he appeals to an Athenian lawcourt, εἰς τὸ δικαστήριον ἐφίησι: from the finding of his demesmen about his citizenship or of the Boulê about his fitness to hold office, or from the award of a public arbitrator;[2] similarly a Chalkidian may in certain cases

---

[1] *Sc.* they were 'third party' or 'reciprocal'. No example of either is known (I think) before 300 B.C.: though the ἔκκλητος πόλις which Aischines supposed in I. 89 is certainly not Athens. But for the period in question (say, the half century before 470) our sole evidence is the sentence which we are trying to understand.—The reader will also not forget the margins of doubt mentioned, pp. 183, note 1 and 187, note 2 and implied p. 188, note 1.

[2] *'Aθ. π.* 42. 1; Dem. 57. 6; Isaios fr. VI (from demesmen): *'Aθ. π.* 45. 3; 55. 2 (from the Boulê's scrutiny before office): 53. 2 (from arbitrators). Cf. Pollux 8. 62, who gives other cases, perhaps not all authentic. I do not go into the question (raised e.g. by Steinwenter, *Die Streitbeendigung* [Münchener Beiträge zur Papyrusforschung, Heft 8, 1925], pp. 68–78, and by Gomme, *Commentary* I, p. 342, n. 2) of whether the first hearing constitutes a 'trial' or 'erste Instanz'. What the notion of *ephesis* requires is, a verdict to be challenged: if not a δίκη, at least a κρίσις.

appeal from the court at Chalkis to the Athenian court.[1] But the second authority is not always the public lawcourt, as we see in the 'Demotionid' decrees (pp. 119 ff.). The person who introduces a candidate may appeal from the thiasos to the phratry (94–6, 100–2) or from the phratry[2] to the Demotionidai (30–1, 38–9).

The person who acts, when such appeal is made, is what I have called (rather loosely, perhaps) the 'litigating party': that is, a person whose case is submitted, to some official organ, to be pronounced on. The usage of the verb ἐφίημι is conclusive for this: the subject of this verb is always the party, never the organ of justice.[3] Consequently, the act of the magistrate in classical Athens, who first conducts an interrogation (ἀνακρίνει) and then without offering judgment takes the case into court (εἰσάγει τὴν δίκην εἰς τὸ δικαστήριον), is not *ephesis* and no ancient writer of any authority calls it *ephesis*.[4]

In the second decree of the Decelean phratry (note 2 below) the thiasos has to pronounce before the case goes to the phratry. There are two fences, first the thiasos, then the phratry: to get his candidate in, the introducer must *take* them both but he does not

---

[1] Tod 42 (=*I.G.* I². 39=*A.T.L.* II. D17), lines 73–6. This is perhaps the kind of thing which Pollux (see p. 192, note 2) means by ὅταν τις - - - ἐφῇ - - - ἐπὶ ξενικὸν δικαστήριον.

[2] That is, the Decelean phratry (Dekeleieis), see pp. 124 ff. I find nothing in the arguments of Latte (Pauly-Wissowa, XX, col. 750, lines 24–9, s.v. *Phratrie*) nor in the quite different ones of Nilsson (*Cults, Myths*, etc., 1951, p. 154) to make me change this opinion.

[3] '*Aθ. π.* 42. 1; 53. 2; Dem. 29. 59; 40. 17, 31 (bis.), 55; (for Dem. 34. 21 see note 4 below); *I.G.* II². 1237, lines 30, 38, 95–6, 101–2 (the Decelean phratry: note 2 above) ibid. 1183, lines 20–1: and in non-classical Greek Pollux 8. 62 (where τις means 'a party'); Lucian, *Abdicatus* 11; for *Lex. Cantabr.* λογισταί, see note 4 below.

[4] The grammarian in *Lex. Cantabr.* s.v. λογισταί (p. 672) says that the persons who render account to the Logistai ἀνακρίνονται πρῶτον εἶτα ἐφίενται εἰς τὸ δικαστήριον. This is intended to mean, presumably, that 'they are first interrogated, and then *referred* (or *taken?*) to the court': this use of ἐφίημι breaks all the rules and I am surprised that Lipsius, *A.R.* 104, note 201, should take the statement as it stands. The grammarian professes to be quoting Aristotle's '*Aθ. π.* (presumably 54. π. is fr. 447 in Rose's Teubner text of 1886, fr. 407 of the Berlin Aristotle), but there is nothing of this in our papyrus. The passage is slightly corrupted (the MS. has ανακρινοντεσ): whether we suppose that ἐφίενται is what the grammarian wrote or we change it to ἀφίενται (cf. Dem. 34. 21; and, for the procedure implied, '*Aθ. π.* 48. 4–5) I hope no one will want to use this passage as evidence of Attic usage.—In Dem. 34. 21, sometimes cited (e.g. by *L.S.J.*, ἐφίημι A IV) as ἐφῆκεν ἡμᾶς εἰς τὸ δικαστήριον and understood to mean 'the arbitrator *referred us* to the court'', the word ἐφῆκεν is now known to be false: the tenth-century *Parisinus* 2934 has ἀφῆκεν, see Lipsius *A.R.* 954, note 2. This false reading further misled *L.S.J.* in their next citation, Dem. 29. 59, where they propose to supply ἑαυτόν: but here as always the object to be supplied with ἐφίημι (in this sense) is no person but τὴν δίκην or the like, *provoco iudicium*: cf. Dem. 40. 31.

have to *clear* them both. If the thiasos accepts, the case goes to the phratry, automatically: this is not, and is not called, *ephesis*. If the thiasos rejects, the introducer may accept their verdict (and if so, that is the end: κυρια εστω η αποψηφισισ, 102–3), or he may appeal against it: and if he appeals (εαν εφηι εισ τοσ απαντασ) and wins his appeal, his candidate is inscribed in the register (94–8).

We have met something like these 'two fences' at Keos: Tod 142, lines 45–9: p. 190, note 2, above. But there both have to be *cleared*: unless both courts acquit the man listed as traitor, his sentence will stand. There is, there, no question of appeal: the first verdict is not *appealed against* by either party. If it goes against the defendant the case is finished; if it goes in his favour, the second hearing is not at the prosecutor's choice but is required by law. The fact that, in spite of this, Athens is called the *ekkletos polis* is an example of loose usage of the word ἔκκλητος.—But in the phratry, where the word ἐφίημι is used, there is a real appeal. If the first verdict goes against the introducer (and only then is the verb used), it lies with him whether the case shall come to the second organ; and the second organ can quash the verdict of the first.

All this is put out clearly by Nikodemos in his decree for the phratry. In the light of this clear case we may interpret the *scrutiny* (*dokimasia*) of the Nine Archons: 'Aθ. π. 45. 3; 55. 2. This case led Bonner and Smith to an opinion which I now believe wrong (*Admin. of Justice from Homer to Aristotle* II. 232, 244: see p. 174 above, note 1), namely that *ephesis* does not depend always on the volition of the losing party but is sometimes required by law. I believe that they, like Lipsius, *A.R.* 271, against whom they argue, have not distinguished between the *obligation on the organs of justice* to have a second hearing before an Archon is admitted, and the *right of the party* to have a second hearing if he is rejected at his first. The principle is the same as in the phratry. The Archon designate must (before he can take office) be scrutinized twice, by Boulê and lawcourt: two fences must be taken but only the second need be cleared. 'Appeal' occurs only when the first verdict goes against the applicant: and though Aristotle is less explicit than Nikodemos, we need not doubt that here too the applicant might if he chose accept that verdict, so that the second hearing is of his choosing.

This was an innovation: 'formerly the Boulê's rejection was final, but now the candidate may appeal' (45. 3; 55. 2). Formerly, the Archon, like the suspected traitor at Keos, had to *clear* both fences. We cannot date the change, but it was no doubt considerably after Ephialtes;[1] and so perhaps are some other types of appeal recorded by Aristotle as existing in his own day. The most numerous appeals were from the public arbitrators, and there was perhaps no public arbitration before 453.[2]

The verb ἐφίημι was no doubt used by Solon when he established *ephesis* in Attic law and allowed the litigating party, if dissatisfied with the magistrate's judgment, to *appeal against it* to a second authority, the Eliaia. When in 462 Ephialtes converted the Eliaia (greatly changed in this interval) into a court of first, and last, instance, he thereby put an end to the appeal allowed by Solon. It survived in, or was revived for, those few special cases which we have to cull from the Demosthenic corpus, from the *'Aθ. π.* and from inscriptions.

6. The Lawcourts at Athens

Three main stages in the evolution of the courts at Athens may now be distinguished:

1. Before Solon, the magistrates (that is, either one or other of the Nine Archons, or else the Areopagites) gave judgments without appeal.[3]

2. In 594, Solon allowed the parties to appeal to the Eliaia.[4]

3. In 462 Ephialtes abolished the magistrate's judgment and made the Eliaia the Court of first (and last) instance.

---

[1] Neither Lysias 26 (a scrutiny by the Boulê, 382 B.C.) nor the statement in Dem. 20. 90 that the Thesmothetai have faced two scrutinies (355/4 B.C.) gives us a *terminus ante*. Neither says anything of appeal, and in Lysias, 26. 14–15, it is perhaps rather implied that there is none.

[2] *'Aθ. π.* 26. 3, compared with 48. 5, 53. 1–3. It is, strictly, appeal from the Forty: the challenged verdict has been found by the arbitrator but given its authority by the Forty.

[3] *'Aθ. π.* 3. 5–6, cf. *Politics* 1298a30–1.

[4] *'Aθ. π.* 9. 1, cf. *Politics* 1273b41, 1274a3–5. The appellate tribunal is named Eliaia (or Heliaia?) in laws quoted by Lysias (10. 16) and Demosthenes (24. 105, cf. 114): the term *dikasterion* in *'Aθ. π.* is less technical, and the plural *dikasteria* in the relatively ill-informed passage of the *Politics* is no doubt a mistake, see p. 196, note 2, below. I prefer 'Eliaia' to 'Heliaia', see the instances quoted in p. 173 above, note 4, to which may be added the form *Ap-eliastes* in Aristophanes, *Birds* 110.

Between stages 2 and 3, the Eliaia no doubt changed its nature very considerably: what is constant is that this 'court of last instance' is, throughout, an 'unlearned' court. In Solon's law, the Eliaia is the assembled people, what he provides is *provocatio ad populum*. The use of the word in other dialects (with the non-Ionic vowel, αλιαια) to mean 'assembly' is well known (p. 173 above, n. 4): in the sixth-century Chian law which deals with appeal, the place of Solon's Eliaia is taken by the 'assembled people', δῆμος κεκλημένος.[1] But the Eliaia as Ephialtes left it is no longer the same as the Assembly: though the orators maintain a kind of fiction that the court which they address is the Athenian people, it was in fact an empanelled jury some few hundreds strong. Such panels must have been 'representing'[2] the Eliaia for some while before Ephialtes; they must have been used as soon as appeals became too many for the assembly to hear them all. In classical Athens, 'Eliaia' is a place (Dem. 47. 12) and was almost certainly a building; and it has been tentatively identified on the south side of the Agora, near the south-west corner.[3] The earliest building here is of the second quarter of the sixth century, perhaps not much before 550: it is thus about a generation later than Solon's law of appeal. We may perhaps infer that during this first generation no special building was needed, since all the appeals could be dealt with in the full assembly,—in what Solon had meant by the word 'Eliaia'. The building was needed when some of the work had to go to 'committees'.[4]

---

[1] Tod 1, line 7: see App. A.

[2] These representatives were no doubt always chosen by lot. The passage in the *Politics* which I have called ill-informed (p. 195, note 4) speaks as if the lot were already used for this purpose when Solon started (1274a4–5) and evidently conceives of several panels (*dikasteria*, 1273b41, 1274a3). The passage (1273b35–1274a21) quotes two views of Solon, friendly 1273b35–41 and hostile 1274a3–11; the remainder appears to be Aristotle's own. All three parts are (I think) equally ill-informed, Aristotle being himself responsible for 1273b41–1274a2 which is at variance with '*Aθ. π.* 8. 1–2. Cf. p. 197, note 2 below.

[3] *Hesperia* 23 (1954), 33–9: *The Athenian Agora* (Guide to the Excavations 1954), pp. 17, 81.

[4] Homer Thompson has informed me that one feasible place for the assembly to have met, before the Pnyx was taken into use (which was not much before 500), is outside the north face of this Eliaia building. There is here (largely covered later by the Hellenistic Middle Stoa) a fan-shaped area not unlike the Pnyx in shape: it is roughly a semicircle, the small platform on the north face of the building is its centre (the Bema?). If this be so, and the Eliaia building so closely adjoined the assembly, it might be regarded as a kind of Committee Room, where business could be done to which the whole body had no longer time to attend.

The building was excavated by Vanderpool who has, *qua est sua humanitate*, read

Such committees, or panels (*dikasteria*), would be well established before 462. If Perikles' law creating the salaries for jurors is rightly dated to before Ephialtes' main reform,[1] it was meant in the first place for such panels. Ephialtes required these panels no longer to hear appeals merely but also to be the courts of first instance, and for this they must be more rigorously organized. We may suppose that the Periklean salaries made possible the annual enrolment of 6,000 Eliastai, serving under oath and discipline; and that this enrolment was part of Ephialtes' main Reform.

Attic law was not unique in allowing appeal 'to the people'. In this, as in some other things, it is likely that Solon gave a settled procedure and the authority of law to a practice which was not unknown before, in Athens and elsewhere. But Solon's law created a bias towards 'unlearned' justice, and Ephialtes confirmed that bias: after 462, Athenian justice was irrevocably unlearned and had the virtues and vices of such. To Plato the vices were most apparent and this is one main cause of his deep quarrel with democracy. It is probably from some other Sokratic (Kritias?) that Aristotle quotes the 'hostile' view of Solon,[2] that his judicial arrangements paved the way for Ephialtes and Perikles and all the abominations of full-grown democracy. The defence of Solon which Aristotle sets against this criticism starts from the same premiss, that Solon could not have approved Ephialtes' work. That debate ran in a narrow circle and was largely personal: the experiment of committing justice to the unlearned deserves to be regarded with more detachment.

---

the above. He has confirmed and corrected my statement, but does not, of course, answer for the conclusions I suggest.—Our imperfect knowledge about the number, names and places of the lawcourt buildings in Athens is assembled and discussed by Jacoby on Androtion (*F. gr. H.* 324) F 59. For the possibility that the Eliaia building was also called 'Metiocheion' and was built (or re-built?) by Perikles' architect and friend Metiochos (*P.A.* 10131), see particularly *F. gr. H.* IIIb (Supplement), vol. II, pp. 147 n. 1, 148 n. 2, 150 n. 5, 152 nn. 12, 14, 15.

[1] Below, pp. 235–8.

[2] *Politics* 1274a3–11: see p. 195, note 4, p. 196, note 2, where I have called this passage, and the immediately preceding 'friendly' passage, ill-informed. This debate between Solon's friends and critics clearly preceded that scientific examination of Solon's work (whether by Theophrastos or another) whose fruits we find in Aristotle's *Constitution of Athens*.

Appendix A

Tod 1: the Chian Law about Appeal
(see pp. 190, note 1, 191, note 1, 196, note 1)

L. H. Jeffery republishes this valuable text, with some new readings, in *B.S.A.* 51, *The Courts of Justice in Archaic Chios*. The lines are re-numbered as follows: Tod, lines 1-9, 10-25, 26, 27, 28, 29-32 are now, respectively, A 1-9, C 1-16, B3, B2, B1, D 1-4. Miss Jeffery reads the faces in the order here indicated (viz. ABCD) and she reads the three lines in B upwards. I agree with all this, except that I am not certain which way the lines in B should be read. If downwards, we could restore, in B 2-1, ην δε αδικηται: παρα[χωρ]ηι δ ηκκλητοσ δι[κη]—'if he be suffering wrong, and the judgment appealed against be (consequently) put aside'.

In A8 Wilamowitz reads τιμαται: πρησ. Miss Jeffery and I, independently, read τιμηδιπλησ. Our serious divergence from Wilamowitz is that we read his *AT* as *H*. It was my impression (which Miss Jeffery does not confirm) that this *eta* had been superimposed on an earlier *alpha*.[1] I conceive that the cutter started to write αι τιμα(ι διπλησιαι) but, when he reached the sixth letter, saw that his copy had η τιμη διπλησιη: he corrected the word τιμα(ι), but left the word αι uncorrected. I suggest then that this sentence should have run: [ο εκκα-λεομενοσ ημ μ]εν δημο κεκλημενο αλοι (η) τιμη διπλησ[ιη]: 'if he appeal and lose his appeal before the assembled people, the fine is doubled'.

These suggestions, tentatively offered, may serve to get our notions concrete. It is fairly clear from A 7-8 that the Assembly meets in some connexion with 'doubled fines'; and from ηκκλητοσ in B1[2] that appeal has been already spoken of, probably in A.

Who heard these appeals at Chios? The appellant addresses his appeal to the Boulê (C 1-2): does this Boulê merely convey the appeal like other business, to the Assembly? or does it give its own final judgment? It is tempting to supply επι[κρινετω] in C 15-16, and this should probably mean that the Boulê is to give a final judgment. But what, then, is the 'assembled Demos' doing, in connexion with a 'doubled fine' in A 7-8? and are not these appeals included among the 'business of the Demos' in C 9-11? Perhaps we want some other word than επικρινετω in C 15-16? or perhaps the Boulê (or its presiding officers) acted *in the presence of* the Assembly?

---

[1] Wilamowitz believed that τιμααι had been corrected to τιμαται by the later imposition of the τ. Miss Jeffery's photograph gives some control for all this, but it is to be hoped that the stone itself will be checked by others.

[2] Wilamowitz wished to understand this word here as 'the Assembly' (like the *ekkletoi* at Sparta), but I cannot believe that the word should be used twice in one document (B1, C 12-13) in two senses of totally different derivation (pp. 190-1 above).

The Chian procedure interests us, because it may illustrate the Athenian. The Chian Boulê is surely probouleutic and is good evidence for the reality of Solon's 400. Should we conclude that Solon's 400 played a similar part in conveying appeals to the Eliaia? Without the Chian evidence we might have supposed that the magistrate, whose judgment was challenged, himself took the case to the Eliaia, since he does so in classical Athens (though in classical Athens he has offered no judgment). The question must (I think) remain open.

Appendix B

Lakritos
(see p. 185, note 3, and clause V)

In Dem. 35 the Athenian Androkles has tried to sue the Phaselite Lakritos, in the Thesmothetai's court, for certain debts claimed to be due on a contract made at Athens between Androkles and Lakritos' brother Artemon. Artemon is dead, Lakritos is alleged to be his heir.

Lakritos has entered a *paragraphê*, a plea in bar of action, and in our speech Androkles counters the plea. One part of Lakritos' case is to deny that he is heir, but there seems to be more: a question of some peculiar law (§ 4) and perhaps some contention about the appropriate court (§§ 47–9). Photiadis, in his paper mentioned p. 180 note 1 above, p. 63, has suggested that Lakritos invoked our decree, by whose terms a Phaselite in his circumstances must be sued in the Polemarch's court, not the Thesmothetai's.

It is hard to believe that our decree was still valid law in c. 350 B.C., that it had survived the general repeal of all laws of the year 403/2: and since our speaker says that over half the aliens who litigate at Athens are Phaselites (§ 2) one would suppose that if it was still valid the fact would be beyond argument. If Lakritos really invoked it, we must suppose that being an ingenious man[1] he had unearthed a decree which no one else knew of: or perhaps (as Prof. Andrewes has suggested to me) he did not claim that it was still valid, but cited it to show what favour the jury's ancestors had shown to Phaselis.

If he has invoked our treaty, two points will concern us. First, at §§ 47–9, where Androkles enumerates the courts which Lakritos may be supposed to fancy (concluding, § 49, ποῖ οὖν δεῖ ταύτην εἰσελθεῖν τὴν δίκην; δίδαξον ὦ Λάκριτε), the rare usage of παρά with the dative occurs

---

[1] Androkles describes him (§ 15) as οὑτοσὶ Λάκριτος Φασηλίτης, μέγα πρᾶγμα, Ἰσοκράτους μαθητής. This is satirical; and so perhaps is the description in [Plut.] *mor.* 837D (list of Isokrates' pupils) 'the man who legislated for Athens', ὁ νομοθέτης Ἀθηναίοις.

not less than four times.[1] This may be an unconscious, or a mocking, echo of lines 9–10 of our decree.

Second: Androkles is threatened with some kind of a fine which may land him in gaol (§ 46). This may refer to the *epobelia* which he must pay if Lakritos wins, cf. Dem. 45. 6, 56. 4; or it might be the 10,000 drachmas threatened in clause V of the decree (the *epobelia* would not come to more than 500 drachmas). Clause V (if we restore τισ in line 20) refers presumably to the party (not the magistrate), sc. to an Athenian plaintiff who cites a Phaselite in a manner contravening clause I. This is exactly Androkles' position.

[1] See p. 185, note 3 above.

THE PEACE OF KALLIAS[1]

THE Peace of Kallias, between Athens and Persia, is recorded by Diodoros under the year 449/8 as an immediate consequence of Kimon's last campaign in Cyprus, XII. 4. 4: Ἀρταξέρξης δὲ ὁ βασιλεὺς πυθόμενος τὰ περὶ τὴν Κύπρον ἐλαττώματα, καὶ βουλευσάμενος μετὰ τῶν φίλων περὶ τοῦ πολέμου, ἔκρινε συμφέρειν εἰρήνην συνθέσθαι πρὸς τοὺς Ἕλληνας. ἔγραψε τοίνυν τοῖς περὶ Κύπρον ἡγεμόσι καὶ σατράπαις, ἐφ᾽ οἷς ἂν δύνωνται συλλύσασθαι πρὸς τοὺς Ἕλληνας. (5) διόπερ οἱ περὶ τὸν Ἀρτάβαζον καὶ Μεγάβυζον ἔπεμψαν εἰς τὰς Ἀθήνας πρεσβευτὰς τοὺς διαλεξομένους περὶ συλλύσεως. ὑπακουσάντων δὲ τῶν Ἀθηναίων καὶ πεμψάντων πρέσβεις αὐτοκράτορας ὧν ἡγεῖτο Καλλίας ὁ Ἱππονίκου, ἐγένοντο συνθῆκαι περὶ τῆς εἰρήνης τοῖς Ἀθηναίοις καὶ τοῖς συμμάχοις πρὸς τοὺς Πέρσας, ὧν ἐστὶ τὰ κεφάλαια ταῦτα·

(i) αὐτονόμους εἶναι τὰς κατὰ τὴν Ἀσίαν Ἑλληνίδας πόλεις ἁπάσας

(ii) τοὺς δὲ τῶν Περσῶν σατράπας μὴ καταβαίνειν ἐπὶ θάλατταν κατωτέρω τριῶν ἡμερῶν ὁδόν

(iii) μηδὲ ναῦν μακρὰν πλεῖν ἐντὸς Φασήλιδος καὶ Κυανέων· ταῦτα δὲ τοῦ βασιλέως καὶ τῶν στρατηγῶν ἐπιτελούντων

(iv) μὴ στρατεύειν Ἀθηναίους εἰς τὴν χώραν ἧς βασιλεὺς Ἀρταξέρξης[2] ἄρχει.

(6) συντελεσθεισῶν δὲ τῶν σπονδῶν Ἀθηναῖοι τὰς δυνάμεις ἀπήγαγον ἐκ τῆς Κύπρου.

---

[1] I have used the following special abbreviations frequently:

A.T.L. Meritt, Wade-Gery, and McGregor, *The Athenian Tribute Lists*, Vol. I, Harvard University Press, 1939.

J. Jacoby, *Die Fragmente der griechischen Historiker*, I–II, Berlin, 1923–30. The historians are numbered serially: '115 F 153' means 'Theopompos (historian no. 115) fragment 153'.

This essay, based on papers I have read before the Oxford Philological Society, the Classical Club at Harvard, and elsewhere, owes much to the discussions on these occasions, and in its final form to the help of my wife and Mr. A. Andrewes.

[2] So the *Patmius*: Vogel brackets Ἀρταξέρξης: the inferior MSS. give Ἀρταξέρξης βασιλεύς. If the name is genuine (and the variation of order is of course no proof of its intrusion), it indicates that the treaty was 'with Artaxerxes' and would need renewal with Dareios.

Thucydides in his sketch of the years 476–439 (I. 98–117) does not mention the treaty: when, after the rather shameful Peace of Antalkidas in 386, it became by contrast a favourite theme of the Attic orators, Theopompos (J. 115 F 153) undertook to prove it was a myth. Kallisthenes (J. 124 F 16) appears to have accepted this proof: but Krateros, who later published extensive extracts from the Athenian archives, included a copy of it, of which a fragment perhaps survives.[1]

The contention of this paper is that Diodoros' account, like much of what he took from Ephoros, is true so far as it goes,[2] but a bit bowdlerized and unrealistic: and I seek to determine the actual terms more precisely and put the event in its historic context.

I

THE LITERARY PROBLEM

'Der Vertrag mit Persien oder der sogenannte Kalliasfrieden ist kein Problem der politischen, sondern der litterarischen Geschichte.' By these impatient words (*Hermes* XXXV. 111) Eduard Schwartz meant that the historical event is plain enough, what needs explaining is the way Kallisthenes and others wrote about it: in an acute footnote he adds that the (then) position of European settlements in the dominions of the Sultan, or in China, gives a good analogy. And though neither he nor anyone else has made the historical event plain enough for my taste, nor, I fancy, for the shrewd and uncompromising eyes of the great scholar* whom we are honouring, yet Schwartz did well to distinguish the two problems, and it is convenient to take the literary problem first.

The crux of the literary problem is not that Thucydides does not mention the treaty with Persia (he has other no less strange omissions) nor that Theopompos declared the inscribed treaty to be a forgery (though this is a matter of some interest): the crux lies, as both Schwartz and Ed. Meyer saw, in the words of Kallisthenes as quoted by Plutarch, *Kimon* 13. 4. Schwartz and Meyer give different solutions of this crux and neither solution is quite satisfactory. Plutarch, having given a description of the victory of the Eurymedon (evidently Kallisthenes' description: see Jacoby's note

---

[1] See pp. 231–2, *Appendix*.
[2] The date, as usual in narrative derived from Ephoros, is not more than approximate. I believe the treaty was sworn early in 449: see pp. 226–9.
*[W. S. Ferguson.]

on 124 F 15–16) concludes: 'This achievement so humbled the King's pride that he subscribed to the terms of the famous Peace, that he should keep a horse's ride distant from the Greek sea nor let his ships of war sail to the Greek side of Kyaneai and Chelidoniai. Kallisthenes says indeed that the King did not actually subscribe to these terms (οὔ φησι ταῦτα συνθέσθαι τὸν βάρβαρον), but observed them in fact through fear of that defeat, keeping indeed so far from Greece that Perikles sailed with 50 ships beyond the Chelidoniai, and Ephialtes with only 30, and no Persian fleet encountered them.'[1] It is perhaps arguable that Plutarch need not be understood as recording a definite denial of the treaty's existence: the words οὔ φησι, etc., might mean only that Kallisthenes did not mention it. This is, in effect, Meyer's contention: that Kallisthenes did not mention it in this context.[2] The difficulty here (apart from the fact that οὔ φησι commonly means *negat*) is that the context, as Meyer so persuasively shows, was a digression from the Peace of Antalkidas: if Kallisthenes contrasted that shameful treaty, not with the earlier treaty but merely with the situation produced by the Eurymedon, this suggests very strongly that he did not believe in the earlier treaty's existence. Schwartz, accepting Plutarch's statement that Kallisthenes denied its existence, infers that Kallisthenes must have known Theopompos' arguments against it, and further, that the passage must come from the only work of Kallisthenes which Schwartz believed later than the publication of Theopompos' arguments, viz. the *History*

---

[1] Plutarch's statement, *Kim.* 19. 4, that οὐδὲ γραμματοφόρος κατέβαινεν οὐδ' ἵππος πρὸς θαλάσσῃ τετρακοσίων σταδίων ἐντὸς ὤφθη στρατηγοῦντος Κίμωνος, is no doubt from this passage of Kallisthenes, since the famous clause (see p. 212, n. 2) is here put as a *de facto* result of Kimon's victories.

[2] Meyer, *Forschungen* II. 4–5, who however thinks Plutarch is just wrong. Kallisthenes illustrated his point by two instances (Plut. *Kim.* 13. 4): Perikles sailed beyond the Chelidoniai with 50 ships, and Ephialtes with only 30, and neither met an enemy fleet. Ephialtes was killed in 461, so that his voyage must certainly belong to the years immediately following the Eurymedon, before the Egyptian revolt. Perikles is mentioned first, which may suggest that he went first and therefore his voyage also belongs to those years. But Perikles was then very young: I suspect the order is rhetorical ('P. with 50 ships, E. with only 30') and that Kallisthenes refers to the voyage which Thucydides records (I. 116. 3) in 440 B.C.—Perikles sailed from Samos with 60 (not 50) ships, towards Kaunos and Karia (not beyond the Chelidoniai): such inexactnesses in a fourth-century historian should not surprise us. The central fact, that no enemy fleet ventured to show itself, is what matters. If this is right, then Kallisthenes' two instances are taken from very wide apart, and indicate that he conceives the situation created by the Eurymedon to extend right down to 440 (and no doubt beyond); and this will explode Meyer's hypothesis that Kallisthenes not only did not deny the treaty, but actually recorded it a few pages on.

of Alexander.[1] No one, I think, has followed Schwartz in this: it is indeed hardly conceivable that the account of the Eurymedon and its effects which lies behind Plutarch's *Kimon* 12–13, formed a digression on Alexander's march. Unless Plutarch has managed to change the whole tone, Kimon is there glorified by contrast to his successors, and his achievement is still unparalleled.

It looks, then, as if Kallisthenes denied the treaty in his *Hellenika* I, before the publication of Theopompos' *Philippika* XXV. He evidently admired the Athenian achievement; had he perhaps some reason for denial more cogent than Theopompos' imputation of forgery? *Omne ignotum pro magnifico*: the unknown arguments which may have moved Kallisthenes remain among the most potent weapons in the armoury of doubt. We move here amongst unknowns. Yet I would urge the possibility that Kallisthenes, writing his *Hellenika* in Philip's reign, could know of Theopompos' argument, although Book XXV of the latter's *Philippika* (where the argument finally stood) cannot have been published before Philip's death. It appears to me almost certain[2] that the two anti-Athenian 'pamphlets' which Theopompos inserted into *Philippika* X and XXV had done service as propaganda (i.e. had been in some form 'published') long before the publication of the complete history. Speusippos' complaint to Philip about Theopompos' malicious utterances (*Epist. Socrat.* 30. 14, see J. 69 F 1) was written in the late 'forties (τοσαύτην ἡμῖν σπάνιν βυβλίων βασιλεὺς Αἴγυπτον λαβὼν πεποίηκεν, ibid.): and unless Theopompos was known as a vitriolic pamphleteer, Anaximenes could not have fathered upon him his *Trikaranos*, no doubt in Philip's lifetime (Paus. VI. 18. 5: for the date see Jacoby's note on 72 F 20–1, sc. the fragments of the *Trikaranos*). I conceive then that Kallisthenes, aware that the treaty's authenticity had been questioned, preferred to contrast the Spartan treaty not with the earlier treaty but with the *de facto* situation after the Eurymedon. On that occasion he would be right in saying the king swore to no covenant, but observed its terms (or some of them) in fact.

---

[1] *Hermes* XXXV. 109: 'Kallisthenes knüpfte die Leugnung des Vertrages an eine Schilderung der Schlacht am Eurymedon: für eine solche Schilderung ist kein leichterer Anlass denkbar, als Alexanders Marsch durch Pamphylien im Jahr 333. Damals, vermutlich schon vor 334, müssen von Theompomps philippischen Geschichten mindestens die ersten 25 Bücher veröffentlicht gewesen sein.'

[2] Cp. p. 236, note 1, below.

My working hypothesis, then, is that Ephoros published his earlier fifth-century books (VIII–XII), with an account of the Treaty,[1] between 350 and 345: that in the middle 'forties Theopompos declared the Treaty a forgery: that in the later 'forties Kallisthenes retorted that that did not affect the magnitude of Athens' achievement, since Athens in fact broke Persia's power at the Eurymedon, and Persia only recovered when Athens had fallen and Sparta betrayed the Greek cause. This statement of the case misled Plutarch into dating the Treaty immediately after the Eurymedon (*Kim.* 13. 4), since by his time the authenticity was no longer questioned: it has been alleged that already the orator Lycurgus, writing in 331, drew the same false inference, *in Leocr.* 72–3 (τὸ κεφάλαιον τῆς νίκης [but this νίκη is not the Eurymedon?] - - - - συνθήκας ἐποιήσαντο). But this concerns fourth-century history more than fifth: such propaganda commonplaces tell us very little of the actualities of 450 B.C. I come back to Theopompos.

Theopompos in *Philippika* XXV undertook to expose the vanities of Athenian historic claims, including αἱ πρὸς βασιλέα Δαρεῖον Ἀθηναίων †πρὸς Ἕλληνας† (?περὶ Ἑλλήνων) συνθῆκαι (J. 115 F 153). His argument is preserved in two further fragments (J. 115 F 154, 155): the stele on which it was inscribed bore Ionic letters, not Attic, and the Ionic alphabet was not introduced till 403/2 B.C. Theopompos' conclusion (ibid. 154) that the Treaty was therefore a forgery (ἐσκευωρῆσθαι) goes far beyond this evidence and is in itself incredible: fourth-century Athens was anything but totalitarian and a public forgery of that kind (I submit) quite impossible. It is indeed very possible that the stele was inscribed in the fourth century. The publication of a document from the archives was frequently ordered; especially in the early years of the fourth century, when previous publications had perished in the troubles at the end of the fifth century (e.g. *I.G.* II². 6). If, as seems most likely, this publication was ordered about 380 B.C., it will not be, like those just mentioned, a publication of something still valid, but a piece of sentimental diplomacy, comparable to Isokrates' *Panegyrikos* of that date. Isokrates had there said (4. 120): μάλιστα δ᾽ ἄν τις συνίδοι τὸ μέγεθος τῆς μεταβολῆς εἰ παραναγνοίη

---

[1] And also the Ἑλληνικὸς ὅρκος: Diodoros, XI. 29. 3, gives it practically *verbatim* the same as Lycurgus *in Leocr.* 81, and no doubt both have it from Ephoros, since it is in ripe fourth-century style (e.g. no hiatus: contrast Hdt. VII. 132. 2). This too Theopompos undertook to explode (J. 115 F 153).

τὰς συνθήκας τάς τ᾽ ἐφ᾽ ἡμῶν γενομένας καὶ τὰς νῦν ἀναγεγραμμένας:
if the world was to compare the two treaties, the earlier one had
to be published. I am assuming that Theopompos was right in
contending that the inscription he knew was of the fourth century:
but the fact though probable is not certain. Could it not have
been inscribed as soon as the Treaty was concluded? The only
Attic decree in Ionic letters which is anywhere near the date of
the Peace of Kallias is *I.G.* I². 16: that was inscribed at the expense
of the Phaselites, who might use a foreign workman, whereas the
publication of the treaty with Persia was a matter for the Poletai,
who would surely use an Athenian. But it is too little observed
that Theopompos is reported as speaking of 'the treaty of the
Athenians with King Dareios': such a treaty was certainly concluded (Andok. 3. 29: see the following section) and would belong
to the year 423. At that date Ionic writing was getting commoner
in Attic decrees; *I.G.* I². 25 is of the same year and in some ways
an analogous document: it was no doubt commissioned by the
Poletai: it was begun in Attic, but continued in Ionic, script.[1]

Our evidence is, then, that the stele which Theopompos knew
contained the treaty with Dareios. It would be foolish to press
this too far, since the citation may be in error: but it looks as if the
headline of the stele read συνθῆκαι ᾿Αθηναίων πρὸς βασιλέα Δαρεῖον,
much like the slightly more elaborate heading of the treaty of
412/1 transcribed by Thucydides, VIII. 37. 1: ξυνθῆκαι Λακεδαιμονίων καὶ τῶν ξυμμάχων πρὸς βασιλέα Δαρεῖον καὶ τοὺς παῖδας τοὺς
βασιλέως καὶ Τισσαφέρνην. If so, the possibilities are many: I
suggest a few, not to be exhaustive but to indicate the uncertainty
of any one hypothesis:

> (*a*) The stele contained the original Treaty with Artaxerxes,
> inscribed in 449, with a new headline inscribed *in rasura* in
> 423 (cf. *I.G.* I². 51, 52), the headline only being in Ionic script.
> (*b*) The stele contained the Treaty with Artaxerxes on one
> face, that with Dareios on the other (cf. *I.G.* I². 24, 25), the
> latter face being in Ionic script. In cases both (*a*) and (*b*), the
> Ionic letters may be from the same hand as *I.G.* I². 25: in
> case (*a*) Theopompos must be presumed to have satisfied him-
> self with reading the headline only.

[1] See p. 209, (*d*).

(c) The stele contained only the Treaty with Dareios, inscribed in 423, in a hand similar to *I.G.* I². 25.

(d) The stele contained only the Treaty with Dareios, inscribed (as being the more recent) in 380 for comparison with the Peace of Antalkidas.

(e) The stele contained both treaties (cf. *I.G.* I². 57, II². 1), inscribed in 380 for comparison with the Peace of Antalkidas.

It is evident that a good deal turns on whether the Treaty with Dareios was a mere ratification of that with Artaxerxes [as implied in case (a)], or was something quite new. We probably cannot answer this question for certain, but at least we can get it formulated. That is our next concern.

II

THE TREATY WITH DAREIOS

The Treaty with Dareios (the Bastard, not the Great) is recorded by Andokides, 3. 29. Speaking in favour of the peace negotiations of 391 (see below, p. 225) he says, 'I fear we shall make our usual mistake, and give up our strong friends and choose weak ones. Remember how we made a treaty and covenanted friendship forever[1] with the King of Persia (and Epilykos my uncle was your ambassador to him), and later, persuaded by Amorges, a slave of the King and a runaway slave, we threw away the King's strength, as if it was no use to us, and chose Amorges' friendship: wherefore the King was indignant and made alliance with Sparta and gave them 5,000 talents for the war and finally brought our power to ruin.' Andokides does not expressly say that the King in question was Dareios: but he tells us elsewhere that when his uncle Epilykos was killed in Sicily in 414 he left as issue two young daughters, and this suggests that his mission to Sousa is not likely to have been very many years before that.[2]

---

[1] Σπονδὰς ποιησάμενοι καὶ συνθέμενοι φιλίαν εἰς τὸν ἅπαντα χρόνον.

[2] Epilykos and his three sisters (who married, one the strategos Glaukon, one Andokides' father Leogoras, one Perikles' son Xanthippos) appear all to have been born *c.* 460–450: he, as we shall see, was secretary of the first prytany in 424/3. Son of Teisandros, grandson of Epilykos, no doubt he was a member of the *genos* of Philaidai (like the elder Miltiades), since both Epilykos and Teisandros are among the descendants of Philaios in Marcell. *vit. Thuc.* 3. For the evidence for these relationships (not always quite conclusive) see *PA* under these names, and especially the *stemma* s.v. Ἀνδοκίδης, no. 828.

The date can be fixed precisely to 424/3, sc. Dareios' first year, by a comparison of the following documents.

(a) *I.G.* II². 8 (*Syll.*³ 118) : decrees in honour of Herakleides of Klazomenai. Of the main decree, which perhaps conferred Attic citizenship on him, only the last line survives; the bulk of the extant inscription is taken up by a presumably earlier decree which had made him a proxenos.

$[ε]δοξεν τηι βοληι [και τωι δημωι Πανδιο]$
$[ν]ισ επρυτανευεν Σ[ιμων? εγραμματευεν]$
5 $[N]εοκλειδησ επεστ[ατε \dots \dots ^{13} \dots \dots]$
$[ει]πεν· Ηρακλειδην [τογ Κλαζομενιον αν]$
$[αγρ]αψαι τογ γραμμ[ατεα τησ βολησ προξ]$
$[ενο]ν και ευεργετη[ν καθοτι αν τωι δημω]$
$[ι δο]κηι και θεναι ε[ν πολει επειδη ευ επ]$
10 $[οησ]εν τασ Αθηναιω[ν πρεσβειασ και εν π]$
$[ασι α]νηρ εστι αγαθ[οσ περι τον δημον τον]$
$[Αθην]αιων. Θοκυδιδ[ησ ειπε· τα μεν αλλα κ]$
$[αθα]περ τηι βοληι ε[πειδη δε οι πρεσβεσ]$
$[οι πα]ρα βασιλεωσ ηκ[οντεσ αγγελλοσι Η]$
15 $[ρακλ]ειδην συμπρατ[τεν εαυτοισ προθυ]$
$[μωσ ε]σ τε τασπονδασ [τασ προσ βασιλεα ε]$
$[σ τε α]λλο οτι επαγγε[λειαν,$ etc.]

Lines 13–16 make it certain that *spondai* have been made with the King. The supplements in 3–4 are suggested and explained by West, *A.J.P.* LVI. 73–6.[1] Neokleides, who is here epistates for his own tribe Pandionis, was (presumably earlier the same year, as member of the same Boule) secretary for the tribe Aigeis : as such he appears in perhaps three extant decrees, viz.

(b) *I.G.* I². 145

$Σωτιμο Ηερα[κ]λειοτο κ$
$αι εκγονον προχσενο κ$
$αι ευεργετο Αθεναιον$
$[εδοχσεν τει] βολει κα[ι] τοι [δεμ]$
5 $[οι Αιγεισ επρυτανε]υε Νε[οκλε]$
$[ιδεσ εγραμματευε,$ etc.]

Neokleides' name was first supplied here by Ferguson, *Ath. Sec.* 15, 17 : cf. West, *A.J.P.* LVI. 72 for the length of the line.

[1] I write περι in line 11, since εις conflicts with the spellings in line 16.

(c) *I.G.* I². 87, Treaty between Athens and Haliai: cf. Meritt, *A.J.P.* LVI. 65–71.

[Νε]οκλειδ[εσ — 6 or 7 — εγρα]μματευε
εδοχσεν τει [βολει και τοι δεμοι Αιγει]σ επρυτανευε
Νεοκλειδησ [εγραμματευε — 7 — επεσ]τατε Λαχεσ ε
ιπε· χσυνθεκα[σ, etc.]

That this year is 424/3 is demonstrated by Meritt l.c.

(d) *I.G.* I². 25: provision for the Priestess of Nike.

εδοχσεν τει βολει και τοι δε
μοι Αιγεισ επρυτανευε Νεοκ
λειδησ εγραμματευε Αγνοδε
μοσ επεστατε Καλλιασ ειπε· τ
5 ει ḥιερεαι, etc.

This is the inscription which was begun in Attic script but continued (lines 7 ff.) in Ionic. It is doubtless consequent on the news of the Treaty, being a renewal of 24 which itself was doubtless consequent on the news of the Treaty with Artaxerxes.

(e) *I.G.* I². 324, lines 25–6: text from Meritt, *A.F.D.* 138:

25 [ταδε παρεδ]οσαν ḥοι ταμιαι Θ[οκυ]διδεσ[1] Αχερδοσιοσ και χσυναρχοντεσ
επι Ισ[αρχο αρχοντοσ κα]
[ι επι τεσ βολεσ] ḥ[ει Επι]λ[υ]κοσ [προ]τοσ εγραμματευε, etc.

This is the year 424/3.

May we assume that Epilykos of (e), the secretary of the first prytany of 424/3, is the same as Epilykos who went on the embassy? That Neokleides, secretary of the prytany of Aigeis in 424/3 (b c d), is the same as Neokleides, epistates on the day when Herakleides was honoured for his services to the embassy (a)? That Laches who moved (c) is the same as the Laches who moved the decree for the armistice in 424/3 (Thuc. IV. 118. 11)? That Thucydides of (e), the tamias of 424/3, is the same as Thucydides who moved the amendment in (a), in which the Treaty with the King is mentioned? The case for these identifications (at least the first three) has been put by West, *A.J.P.* LVI. 72–6, to whom I refer: they provide a notable confirmation of the *a priori* arguments of

---

[1] This restoration is made certain by lines 34–5. Cf. Marcell. *vit. Thuc*. 28.

Koehler,[1] that (*a*) belongs to the year 423. If we accept them, Epilykos went to Sousa in his capacity as bouleutes, since his fellow bouleutes Neokleides is still in office when the embassy has returned, cf. (*a*) line 14. It is of course possible (see West l.c. 74, n. 7) that the bouleutes Neokleides in (*b c d*) is not the same man, or does not belong to the same year, as the bouleutes of the same name in (*a*): but the name is rare, the evidence is coherent: the economical hypothesis is that Epilykos went to Sousa, and came back, before midsummer 423. The statement of Andokides, that he had made a treaty with the King, is unequivocally confirmed by (*a*) line 16, τασπονδασ [τασ προσ βασιλεα]. In 424/3, Dareios the Bastard began his reign.

It is very remarkable that Thucydides does not mention this treaty. In IV. 50 he tells how in the winter of 425/4 the Persian Artaphernes had been captured in Thrace, on his way from King Artaxerxes to Sparta: and how an Attic embassy was sent with him as far as Ephesos, but no further, since on the news of Artaxerxes' death they returned home. To have recorded this abortive embassy, and then said nothing of the embassy which a year later made a treaty with the new King, is something of quite a different order from his silence on the Treaty with Artaxerxes. In 424/3 he is in the main stream of his proper subject, and the attitude of Persia is part of the story (as IV. 50, and again VIII. 5. 5, 6. 1, 16. 3, etc., show). No doubt this extraordinary silence is partly due to the unfinished state of the history. In this winter of 424/3, the historian was commanding in Thrace, failed to save Amphipolis, and was exiled: and the narrative from then onwards was perhaps due for more revision than the earlier years of the ten-year war. But this silence is evidence of the reality of the treaty with Artaxerxes. If Athens had not before been in treaty with Persia, the treaty of 423 becomes so cardinal an event that no lack of revision really explains its absence from a narrative which devotes twenty-eight chapters to the winter of 424/3, and seventeen chapters to the summer of 423 (IV. 89–116 and 117–133). But if the treaty of 423 was no more than a reaffirmation, with the new king, of the treaty which had existed with his predecessor,[2] it becomes less momentous.

---

[1] *Hermes* XXVII. 68–78, accepted (before the further evidence of the names was known) in *Syll.*[3] 118.

[2] See p. 201, n. 2.

I conceive, then, that the Treaty of 424/3 was in essentials a renewal of that of 450/49: possibly a verbatim renewal [as suggested on p. 206, under (a)]. But this is not proved; and in our attempts to recover the terms of the treaty of 450/49, that of 424/3 will perpetually obtrude itself. The *status quo* which was upset in the last ten years of the Peloponnesian War was of course that of 424/3: the treaty which Theopompos saw inscribed on a stele was very probably that of 424/3. Are the terms which Isokrates and the orators report (see p. 213) those of 450/49 or of 424/3? Was the document which Krateros transcribed (pp. 202, 231) that of 450/49 or of 424/3? It is never easy to say: and though I conceive the two treaties to have been in essentials identical, let us remember that this is not proved.

III

THE TERMS OF THE TREATIES WITH ARTAXERXES AND DAREIOS

I have called Diodoros' account of the Treaty 'bowdlerized and unrealistic': this applies especially to his summary of the terms. Of his four heads (see p. 201), the first two may be classed as 'autonomy clauses', the last two as 'non-aggression clauses'. It is true, I believe, that the Treaty prescribed autonomy for the Greek cities, and non-aggression between Athens and Persia: it will be convenient, then, to examine the further evidence under these two heads.

A. Autonomy clauses (and tribute*)

In the *Panegyrikos*, published in 380, Isokrates invited the world to compare τὰς συνθήκας τάς τ' ἐφ' ἡμῶν γενομένας καὶ τὰς νῦν ἀναγεγραμμένας (4. 120). Whether 'the treaty made in our time', which he wishes to compare with the Peace of Antalkidas, is the treaty with Artaxerxes or with Dareios, is not clear: but I am assuming there was little essential difference between the two Athenian treaties.[1] From the Athenian treaty, he then cites three clauses: τότε μὲν γὰρ ἡμεῖς φανησόμεθα

*[But cf. *A.T.L.* III. 275.]
[1] The most striking of the clauses which Isokrates here cites is (ii), the fixing of the tribute payable to the King. Herodotos implies such a clause for the Artaxerxes treaty (VI. 42. 2), Thucydides for the Dareios treaty (VIII. 5. 5).

(i) τὴν ἀρχὴν τὴν βασιλέως ὁρίζοντες
(ii) καὶ τῶν φόρων ἐνίους τάττοντες
(iii) καὶ κωλύοντες αὐτὸν τῇ θαλάττῃ χρῆσθαι.

Of these (i) and (iii) are 'non-aggression clauses', see below p. 213. The clause which concerns the conditions of autonomy is (ii).
Athens fixed the scale of certain tributes payable to the King. What tributes could these be except those from the Greek cities of Asia Minor? A famous sentence of Herodotos (VI. 42. 2) tells us how the scale was fixed: the tribute payable was that laid down by Artaphernes after the reduction of the Ionian revolt. A mild assessment, based on area,[1] and containing no punitive advances: κατὰ δὴ τούτους μετρήσας φόρους ἔταξε ἑκάστοισι, οἳ κατὰ χώρην διατελέουσι ἔχοντες ἐκ τούτου τοῦ χρόνου ἔτι καὶ ἐς ἐμὲ ὡς ἐτάχθησαν ἐξ Ἀρταφρένεος. The King then was entitled to certain limited revenues from the Greek cities, but had no further authority over them. Diodoros' 'autonomy clauses' say that the Greek cities were left autonomous, and that the satrap covenanted not to move to the west of Sardis:[2] the latter is one of the most constantly reported terms.
Walker in C.A.H. V. 470 says: 'as Persia never resigned her claim to the tribute of the Greek cities in Asia, she cannot possibly have recognized their autonomy'. Ancient diplomacy thought otherwise. Substitute Artaphernes for Aristeides, and the terms could be expressed in the words of the Peace of Nikias (Thuc. V. 18. 5): τὰς δὲ πόλεις φερούσας τὸν φόρον τὸν ἐπ' Ἀρταφέρνους αὐτονόμους εἶναι. The Peace of Nikias was between two Greek powers: that the concept is equally possible between a Greek power and Persia, may be seen in Xen. Hell. III. 4. 25. Tithraustes there conveys to

---

[1] Not, therefore, tapping the industrial or mercantile wealth of Ionia.
[2] I take this to be the sense of Diodoros' μὴ καταβαίνειν ἐπὶ θάλατταν κατωτέρω τριῶν ἡμερῶν ὁδόν: cf. Hdt. V. 54. 2; Xen. Hell. III. 2. 11. Sardis to Ephesos was 540 stades (Hdt. l.c.), the distance forbidden to Persian officials is given by Plut. Kimon 19. 4 (presumably from Kallisthenes, see p. 203, n. 1) as 400 stades. These 400 stades may be the distance to Smyrna (for fifth-century Smyrna see A.T.L. 560, n. 2: for the possibility of a road, Xen. Hell. I. 1. 10): more likely perhaps they indicate a covenanted point on the Ephesos road some miles S.W. of Sardis. The same distance is called a day's journey on horseback by Dem. 19. 273, Plut. Kim. 13. 4, Suidas Κίμων. In Aristodemos, J. 104 F1, 13. 2, we should perhaps read ἐντὸς τριῶν ἡμερῶν ὁδόν, ⟨ἣ⟩ ἦν ἂν ἵππος ἀνύσῃ διωκόμενος, μὴ κατιῶσιν. The Halys boundary (Isok. 7. 80, 12. 59) is part of the non-aggression clause, quite another matter: see below.

Agesilaos the terms which Artaxerxes II proposes:[1] βασιλεὺς ἀξιοῖ
. . . τὰς ἐν τῇ 'Ασίᾳ πόλεις αὐτονόμους οὔσας τὸν ἀρχαῖον δασμὸν
αὐτῷ ἀποφέρειν.

I would summarize the autonomy clauses thus:

> The Greek cities shall pay a fixed yearly sum to the satraps, but the
> Satrap and his officers shall not come beyond a certain point westward and,
> provided they receive their money, shall have no authority beyond that point.

This rather precarious balance was materially steadied by the
'bilateral demilitarization' which accompanied the non-aggression
clauses.

B. Non-aggression clauses (and de-militarization)

Diodoros says (p. 201 supra) that the King covenanted that no
Persian ship of war should come west of 'Phaselis and Kyaneai',
and Athens on her side covenanted, if the King observed his obligations, not to attack 'the land over which King Artaxerxes rules'.
The former of these clauses is very frequently mentioned, in
slightly varying form:

(1) Isokr. 12. 59, οὔτε (sc. ἐξῆν) μακροῖς πλοίοις ἐπὶ τάδε πλεῖν
    Φασήλιδος (cf. idem 7. 80, 4. 118, and more vaguely, 120).

(2) Dem. 19. 273, ἐντὸς δὲ Χελιδονίων καὶ Κυανέων πλοίῳ μακρῷ
    μὴ πλεῖν.

(3) Lycurg. in Leocr. 73, μακρῷ μὲν πλοίῳ μὴ πλεῖν ἐντὸς Κυα-
    νέων καὶ Φασ‹ήλ›ιδος.

(4) Diod. XII. 4. 5, μηδὲ ναῦν μακρὰν πλεῖν ἐντὸς Φασήλιδος καὶ
    Κυανέων.

(5) Plut. Kim. 13. 4, ἔνδον δὲ Κυανέων καὶ Χελιδονίων μακρᾷ
    νηὶ καὶ χαλκεμβόλῳ μὴ πλέειν.

(6) Aristodemos J. 104 F1, 13. 2, ἐντὸς Κυανέων καὶ Νέσσου
    ποταμοῦ καὶ Φασήλιδος (ἥτις ἐστὶν πόλις Παμφυλίας) καὶ
    Χελιδονέων μὴ μακροῖς πλοίοις καταπλέωσι.

(7) Suidas s.v. Κίμων, ἐκτὸς Κυανέων καὶ Χελιδονέων καὶ Φασή-
    λιδος (πόλις δὲ αὕτη τῆς Παμφυλίας) ναῦν Μηδικὴν μὴ πλεῖν
    νόμῳ πολέμου.

These points are in south or east Lykia (pace Aristodemos and
Suidas): Kyaneai is the southernmost point;[2] the Chelidonian

---

[1] This is a proposal to restore the Kallias terms: see p. 225, and note 1 ibid.
[2] See Pauly-Wissowa, s.v. Kyaneai (2), and cf. Robert Études anatoliennes ch. XIX
But see p. 214 n. 2.

islands are off the south-east point; Phaselis is on the east coast; the River Nessos is unknown.[1] Of the latest writers, Aristodemos gives all four names, Suidas three: the intermediate writers give two apiece: Isokrates, the earliest, gives Phaselis only. What is the meaning of this variety? 'If the inscription contained the limits by sea and land,' asks Walker in *C.A.H.* V. 471, 'how can we account for such discrepancies in our authorities? They had only to use their eyes, and to see what stood written on the stone.' I do not know what answer he intends to the rhetorical question. He does not, presumably, suggest that Theopompos was wrong in saying that the Peace was engraved on stone: forgery or no, the alleged terms were on public view.

I am inclined to think that all these places were named in the Treaty, and the writers chose such as took their fancy, or as they remembered. No doubt the accumulation of names in the latest writers is due to their love of erudition. Isokrates was content with the furthest limit, Phaselis, which gave the essential fact: if the King's warships might not approach Phaselis, *a fortiori* they might not Kyaneai. Why then were so many places named? If the limit were inclusive, it might well be laid down that the King's warships could sail 'as far as Phaselis and Chelidoniai and Kyaneai'. But I find this incredible: can Phaselis have been left exposed to such visits? The limit was surely exclusive. It could no doubt even so be laid down that the King's ships must not approach either Phaselis or the Chelidoniai; i.e. they could move south of Phaselis if they kept east of the Chelidoniai. But Kyaneai cannot be thus explained.[2] Possibly Phaselis-Chelidoniai was the limit in 449, Kyaneai in 423,[3] and Demosthenes contaminated the two treaties. Far more likely the clause was reciprocal, and Kyaneai-Chelidoniai-Phaselis defined the zone into (and beyond) which neither party should send ships of war. A demilitarized zone: this would help to explain the growth of piracy in these waters: Thuc.

---

[1] See Müller's note in *F.H.G.* V, pp. 15–16. In the list of rivers in Hesiod *Theog.* 337 ff., Νέσσον in 341 is usually understood as the Nestos in Thrace, which is called Νέσος in a few passages (e.g. Theophr. *hist. plant.* III. 1. 5: cf. schol. Thuc. II. 96). But in 450 B.C. the Nestos as a boundary would concern the rising Odrysian power, not Persia.

[2] Could Kyaneai be Kyaneai (3) in Pauly-Wissowa, sc. the mouth of the Bosporos? So Walker assumes, *C.A.H.* V. 470, and finds it ridiculous: but such a limit might be meant to deny the Black Sea to Athenian (rather than allow it to Persian) ships: and if so, Perikles' expedition in the middle 'thirties was a breach of treaty. But the explanation in the text is a lot simpler. *[But see *A.T.L.* III, pp. 114–17.]

[3] But Phaselis paid tribute to Athens in 418/7 or later: *A.T.L.*, p. 153, no. 37, I. 17.

II. 69 says that in 430, Peloponnesian pirates based on Lykia were interfering with cargoes from Phaselis and the east. Was there a similar demilitarized zone on land? Isokrates 7. 80 says οὔτε μακροῖς πλοίοις ἐπὶ τάδε Φασήλιδος ἔπλεον οὔτε στρατοπέδοις ἐντὸς Ἅλυος ποταμοῦ κατέβαινον: cf. 12. 59, οὐκ ἐξῆν αὐτοῖς οὔτ᾽ ἐντὸς Ἅλυος πεζῷ στρατοπέδῳ καταβαίνειν οὔτε μακροῖς πλοίοις ἐπὶ τάδε πλεῖν Φασήλιδος. Walker (C.A.H. V. 470) appears to regard this Halys line as a variant of the three days' limit of the autonomy clause. It is no such thing: the three days' limit, or the 'Sardis line', is the eastern limit of Greek autonomy; the 'Halys line' is the eastern limit of demilitarization. As such, Isokrates properly brackets it in both passages with Phaselis.

The King covenanted not to move west of the Halys with a land army. — We have probably to distinguish three elements in the army of the Persian empire:[1] (1) what I will call the 'Palatine Army'; that is, the King's own army, consisting primarily of the 10,000 Immortals: (2) the native levies of the provinces, under command of the satraps: (3) the royal garrisons in the provinces, under phrourarchs immediately responsible to the King.

The 'Palatine Army' is what Isokrates in the Panegyrikos (4. 145) calls τὴν στρατιὰν τὴν μετὰ τοῦ βασιλέως περιπολοῦσαν: what Xenophon, in a difficult passage of the Oikonomikos (4. 6) calls τοὺς μὲν ἀμφὶ τὴν ἑαυτοῦ οἴκησιν, which at the annual inspection the King himself inspects, in contrast to τοὺς πρόσω ἀποικοῦντας to which he sends inspectors. Its ideal institution by Kyros the Great is described in Xen. Cyrop. VII. 5. 66–70. It is this Palatine Army of whose maintenance Herodotos speaks, when he says, I. 192. 1, βασιλέι τῷ μεγάλῳ ἐς τροφὴν αὐτοῦ τε καὶ τῆς στρατιῆς διαραίρηται γῆ πᾶσα ὅσης ἄρχει:[2] this was a charge additional to the tribute (πάρεξ

[1] I am conscious how superficial this account is. E. Herzfeld, Altpersische Inschriften, Berlin, 1938, pp. 51–4, makes suggestions about the feudal organization, which he believes the pseudo-Smerdis sought to abolish (Hdt. III. 67. 3) and Dareios restored (Behistun § 14). The system he infers seems to me intrinsically probable, but I cannot estimate its evidence: see R. Zaehner's criticisms in 'Aparmānd', in the J.R.A.S., 1940, p. 35—I have not followed Ed. Meyer's view that the satrap commanded all the troops of his satrapy, but I recognize that, of the evidence I use, Xenophon's Cyropaedia is romance and his Oikonomikos largely unintelligible.
[2] But in the next sentence it is Babylonia and ἡ λοιπὴ πᾶσα Ἀσίη, Babylonia paying for four months, 'the rest of Asia' for eight: so Egypt is not included (cf. III. 96). The passage of Theopompos quoted below (J. 115 F 113) suggests that the four months represent four months' actual sojourn of the King and his army (ὅταν βασιλεὺς εἴς τινας ἀφίκηται τῶν ἀρχομένων). Herodotos writes of the Kallias period; Theopompos, though he writes presumably of the Antalkidas period, says ἐκ παλαιοῦ.

τοῦ φόρου), and one-third of it was borne by the Satrapy of Babylonia. When Ktesias and Deinon are quoted for the astounding figures (Athen. IV. 146c) that the King would dine with 15,000 men and his dinner would cost 400 talents, these are of course exceptional and outside figures, and the second is taken from Herodotos VII. 118, where it is part of a petulant anecdote and anyway includes the whole of the apparatus of gold and silver plate which was a capital and not a routine expense. But for both figures the army's dinner is included in the King's: and in the 400 talents, the dinner of the whole Army of Invasion. The first figure, 15,000 diners, no doubt includes the 10,000 Immortals and is the Palatine Army; it is to this peace-time 'dinner' that Theopompos refers in J. 115 F 113: 'when the King comes to any of his subjects, twenty and sometimes thirty talents is spent on the dinner, sometimes indeed much more. For each city has had apportioned to it from of old the tribute it must pay and the dinner it must provide'.

Such was the Palatine Army. Herodotos says it was maintained by the peoples of Asia; and, comparing this with his careful phrasing in III. 96, we may conclude it did not normally move into Egypt. I suggest that neither did it move into Asia Minor, but stayed at the heart of the Empire east of the Euphrates. This was *de facto* true; and Herodotos and Theopompos speak of the routine provision for something which looks like a fixed annual royal progress (see p. 215, n. 2). The simplest meaning of the famous Halys clause in the treaty with Athens is, that the King covenanted not to move this Palatine Army into the western satrapies, ἐντὸς "Αλυος πεζῷ στρατοπέδῳ μὴ καταβαίνειν. By covenanting this, the Persian Empire was converted from an offensive power, treating the world as its prey, into a defensive power, living on terms with its neighbours.

It is possible that the western satrapies were even further demilitarized, having neither native levies at the satrap's command, nor royal garrisons.

Xenophon (*Cyrop.* VIII. 6. 1) ascribes to Kyros the Great the institution of a system whereby satraps did not command the 'garrisons' in their satrapies: he decides to send out satraps, τοὺς μέντοι ἐν ταῖς ἄκραις φρουράρχους καὶ τοὺς χιλιάρχους τῶν κατὰ τὴν χώραν φυλακῶν οὐκ ἄλλῳ ἢ ἑαυτοῦ ἐβούλετο ἀκούειν. He makes a speech to the satraps designate, and explains he does not wish to supersede the phrourarchs (6. 3), ἄλλους δὲ σατράπας πέμψαι μοι δοκεῖ οἵτινες ἄρξουσι τῶν ἐνοικούντων καὶ τὸν δασμὸν λαμβάνοντες τοῖς τε φρουροῖς δώσουσι μισθὸν καὶ ἄλλο τελοῦσιν ὅ τι ἂν δέῃ. Such 'garrisons' possibly include the feudal establishments which Kyros had charged those Persians to maintain who owned property in the conquered provinces (*Cyrop.* VII. 5. 72 ff., esp. 85–6: cf. VIII. 1. 1 ff.). The *Cyropaedia* is not history, but Xenophon knew the Persian military system well, and these two categories appear in Herodotos: the feudal landowners in V. 102. 1, οἱ Πέρσαι οἱ ἐντὸς Ἅλυος ποταμοῦ νομοὺς ἔχοντες, and the fortress garrisons in his account of Egypt; they had stations at Elephantine and Daphnai (II. 30. 3) and at Memphis (III. 91. 3), they are composed of Persians and ἐπίκουροι (presumably not natives), and elaborate measures are taken for their commissariat. They do not appear to have accompanied Xerxes to Greece: Egypt only provided sailors, who served under the satrap Achaimenes. When Aeschylus in the *Persae* talks of the governors of Memphis and Thebes (lines 36 to 38) no doubt he has in mind the phrourarchs: that they were not in fact with Xerxes would be no matter. We shall meet another 'royal garrison' in Syria (Xen. *Anab.* I. 4. 4, see below). These royal troops in the provinces are no doubt οἱ πρόσω ἀποικοῦντες whose annual inspection Xenophon distinguishes from that of the Palatine army, *Oikon.* 4. 6. — The satrap Achaimenes, on the other hand, commands his Egyptian sailors; and where we can control it, the army list of Xerxes shows satraps regularly in command of the native levy of their provinces.

We have no specific information about royal fortresses or garrisons in the western satrapies. Certainly none were allowed in the autonomous zone, and I take Isokrates' 'Halys clause' to indicate that none was allowed west of the Halys. There had been plenty in the earlier reigns: Xerxes had built a royal fort (βασίλεια ἐρυμνά) near Kelainai, on the road to the Halys Gates (Xen. *Anab.* I. 2. 8–9: cf. Hdt. VII. 26. 3); and the army which pursued the Greeks to the coast after the burning of Sardis in 498 was composed, according to Herodotos, V. 102. 1, of οἱ Πέρσαι οἱ ἐντὸς Ἅλυος ποταμοῦ νομοὺς ἔχοντες. Did they remain under the Treaty? Herodotos, V. 52. 1–2, describes the road to the Halys Gates[1] and mentions no fortresses

---

[1] Calder, *C.R.* XXXIX. 7 ff., argues that this is not the Royal Road, though none the less real for that (ibid. 8–9). Kelainai lay south of the straightest route from Sardis to the Halys Gates.

till he comes to the Gates: ἐκδέκεται δὲ ἐκ τῆς Φρυγίης ὁ Ἅλυς ποταμός, ἐπ' ᾧ πύλαι τε ἔπεισι, τὰς διεξελάσαι πᾶσα ἀνάγκη καὶ οὕτω διεκπερᾶν τὸν ποταμόν, καὶ φυλακτήριον μέγα ἐπ' αὐτῷ. This may perhaps be compared with the position at the Amanos Gates, at the entrance to Kilikia from Syria. Kilikia was not indeed demilitarized, but was in alliance with (rather than subject to) the King[1] and consequently did not admit royal garrisons. When the Ten Thousand reach the Amanos Gates, they find two fortresses, τὸ μὲν ἔσωθεν τὸ πρὸ τῆς Κιλικίας Συέννεσις εἶχε καὶ Κιλίκων φυλακή, τὸ δὲ ἔξω τὸ πρὸ τῆς Συρίας βασιλέως ἐλέγετο φυλακὴ φυλάττειν (Xen. Anab. I. 4. 4). In both cases the King maintains a fortress on his military frontier.

What of the native levy? The commission of the younger Kyros in 407 was (Xen. Hell. I. 4. 3) καταπέμπω Κῦρον κάρανον τῶν εἰς Καστωλὸν ἀθροιζομένων (cf. Anab. I. 1. 2, 9. 7):[2] in the Cyropaedia Xenophon sets the last battle between Kyros the Great and Kroisos in Thymbrara (VII. 1. 45), ἔνθα καὶ νῦν [4th century] ὁ σύλλογος τῶν ὑπὸ βασιλέα βαρβάρων τῶν κάτω (ibid. VI. 2. 11). The Kastolos plain lay some fifty miles east of Sardis, and Thymbrara is presumably the same place:[3] Kyros' commission in 407 appears to be the remilitarization of the Sardis area, the final shaking off of the treaty restrictions. Herodotos, writing whilst the treaty was in force, says (I. 155-7) that Kyros the Great made the Lydians put away their armour and wear chitons, and unlearn their warlike ways: consistently, he makes the troops which pursued the Ionians from Sardis in 498 be all Persians (V. 102. 1, quoted just above), though certain Lydians fought in Sardis itself (ibid. 101. 2). But in VII. 74, the Lydians serve in Xerxes' army, in their native equipment, and do not appear to have been disarmed. Is it possible that their disarming was not the work of Kyros the Great, but a consequence of the treaty with Athens? Whenever it began, the disarming of the Lydians seems to have been real. The Satrap's

---

[1] The native Syennesis dynasty was ended after the younger Kyros had compelled the last of the name to rebel. For Kilikia's comparative independence, cf. Xen. Anab. I. 2. 26; Hdt. III. 90. 3. Cf. the status which Euagoras of Cyprus demands (and gets): to speak not ὡς δοῦλος δεσπότῃ but ὡς βασιλεὺς βασιλεῖ, Diod. XV. 8. 3, 9. 2.

[2] In Anab. I. 9. 7, his style is σατράπης Λυδίας τε καὶ Φρυγίας τῆς μεγάλης καὶ Καππαδοκίας, στρατηγὸς δὲ καὶ πάντων οἷς καθήκει εἰς Καστωλοῦ πεδίον ἀθροίζεσθαι.

[3] The village of Kastolos is fixed some 60 miles east of Sardis by Ditt. O.G.I. 488, cf. Robert Études anatoliennes 159 f.: the 'plain' (n. 2 above) perhaps lay west of the village. Thymbrara is unknown: Adala, 30 miles east-north-east of Sardis, where Radet wished to site it (Lydie 249, 313), is the ancient Satala, according to Robert, Villes d'Asie Mineur 101-2.

troops, during the period of the treaty, are mainly Greek mercenaries: when Pissouthnes revolts from Dareios II, the issue is settled
by the defection of his army of Greeks (Ktesias, *Pers.* 52). In his
action against Kolophon (Thuc. III. 34) the main troops appear to
have been Arkadians: the few βάρβαροι there mentioned are no
doubt Persians. Until the alliance with Sparta in 412, the Persians
in the western satrapies were militarily powerless (cf. Thuc.
VIII. 5. 5).

If the Persians might not bring a land army west of the Halys,
there was presumably some reciprocal engagement by Athens: this
was, probably, the dismantling of the fortifications of Ionia.[1] This
is noted in general terms by Thucydides III. 33. 2, ἀτειχίστου οὔσης
τῆς Ἰωνίας: specifically of Klazomenai (VIII. 31. 3), Knidos (ibid.
35. 3), Lampsakos (62. 2), Kyzikos (107. 1). Ionia became a war
area in 412 (perhaps sooner, see infra) and the treaty was broken
on all sides: in Xen. *Hell.* I, we hear of the fortification by Athens
of Lampsakos, Chrysopolis, perhaps Phokaia (2. 15, 1. 22, 5. 11).
It was perhaps by a breach of treaty, on one side or the other,
that Pygela had been fortified (2. 2):[2] many years earlier the
treaty had certainly been strained by Pissouthnes' intervention
at Kolophon, and the fort at Notion (Thuc. III. 34) was evidently
a consequence. The most instructive passage is perhaps Thuc.
VIII. 16. 3: a sea force and a land force of Peloponnesians both
arrive before Teos in 412, and the Athenian fleet has to retire. The
Teians, he says, did not at first admit the land force, until the
Athenian fleet left: once admitted, this force proceeds to demolish
the landward wall: τὸ τεῖχος ὃ ἀνῳκοδόμησαν οἱ Ἀθηναῖοι τῆς Τηίων
πόλεως τὸ πρὸς ἤπειρον. This is a wall on the landward side, giving
protection from the interior: the Athenians had *re*built it. When
had it been pulled down, and when had they 'rebuilt' it? It seems
to me the most likely hypothesis that it was pulled down by the

---

[1] The importance of this phenomenon for the treaty was first pointed out, so far as
I know, by A. J. Toynbee in a work on modern Turkey, *The Western Question* (1922),
p. 221. It is confirmed in some measure by excavation, see especially Schefold *Jahrbuch*
XLVIII (1933) Beiblatt 147–8; ibid. XLIX (1934), Beiblatt 388; von Gerkan *Milet*
I. 8 (1925), 120–3; II. 3 (1935), 120–24. Cf. *A.T.L.* in the Gazetteer, under Δηρισαῖοι
(pp. 511–12), Ἰασῆς (492), Μιλήσιοι (520). We hear of similar dismantling of *island*
fortifications, and the measure was no doubt partly intended to make control easy for
Athens.
[2] Cf. Thucydides' remark on the fortification of Polichne near Klazomenai (for the
site, see *A.T.L.* 487 s.v. Ἐρυθραῖοι): ἐν τειχισμῷ τε πάντες ἦσαν καὶ παρασκευῇ πολέμου
(VIII. 14. 3).

terms of a treaty with Persia, and had recently been 'rebuilt' by Athens in contravention of that treaty: and there may be some confirmation of this in the words which follow in Thucydides: 'and a few barbaroi came later and joined in the demolition of the wall, commanded by Stages, one of Tissaphernes' governors'. *Τῶν βαρβάρων οὐ πολλοί* — this help was hardly needed: was it a gesture of protest because their treaty rights had been infringed?

The land zone thus demilitarized (roughly from the Halys to the Aegean Sea) will have been exactly delimited: Isokrates' *ἐντὸς "Αλυος* is no more documentary than his *ἐπὶ τάδε Φασήλιδος*. Since the Persian empire was essentially a road system, the line was perhaps defined by naming a point on each of the great roads: the Halys Gates were one such point. In the *Panegyrikos* 4. 120, Isokrates said *ἡμεῖς φανησόμεθα τὴν ἀρχὴν τὴν βασιλέως ὁρίζοντες*: this, I conceive, refers especially to the Athenian undertaking, if the King performs his part, *μὴ στρατεύειν εἰς τὴν χώραν ἧς βασιλεὺς 'Αρταξέρξης ἄρχει*. For this definition of the King's *ἀρχή*, which Athens covenanted not to attack, I am inclined to think neither the Halys line nor the Sardis line was used, but rather the Aegean coast. Two passages of Thucydides (both phrased, apparently, with reference to the treaty) speak of the King's (or the satrap's) *ἀρχή* as including the autonomous zone: VIII. 5. 5, *ἐκ τῆς ἑαυτοῦ ἀρχῆς* (=*ἀπὸ τῶν Ἑλληνίδων πόλεων*) and VIII. 56. 4, *παραπλεῖν τὴν ἑαυτοῦ γῆν* (=the Aegean coast). This would imply no more (and no less) than that Athens covenanted not to land troops on the Asiatic coast:[1] when in fact she does, it is perhaps as much a breach of treaty as Pissouthnes' intervention in Kolophon (e.g. Thuc. II. 69, III. 19, 34, and of course frequently in VIII). This concept, that the Greek cities of Asia 'belonged to' the King, but were not subject to his writ, is (as Schwartz suggested, see p. 202 above) not unlike the 'capitulations' once enjoyed by Europeans in the dominions of the Sultan.

For an actual fragment of the text of this delimitation of the King's dominion, see infra, *Appendix* (p. 231). Athens there recognizes the King's ownership of (sc. covenants not to invade) the provinces of Egypt and Libya.

---

[1] Accordingly, when Tithraustes proposes to Agesilaos to renew the Kallias terms (Xen. *Hell.* III. 4. 25; see p. 213, n. 1 and p. 225, n. 1), he requires first that Agesilaos shall withdraw his force from Asia: *σὲ μὲν ἀποπλεῖν οἴκαδε*.

I would summarize the non-aggression clauses thus

A zone shall be marked out on sea, between Phaselis and Kyaneai, into (or beyond) which neither party shall send ships of war; and a zone on land, between the Halys and the Aegean Sea, into (or beyond) which neither party shall lead troops, nor shall they maintain fortresses in it. The King's dominions are defined, and guaranteed against Athenian attack: they include the provinces of Egypt and Libya, and the whole seaboard of Asia Minor.

The autonomy clauses then follow:—

But in the area west of Sardis, inhabited by Greeks, the King shall send no functionaries nor exercise any authority: his sole right shall be a yearly tribute, of a fixed amount based on the survey of Artaphernes in 493.

I submit that these terms are reasonable: that they cover the evidence (without assumption of forgery or lying), and do not go beyond the indications of the evidence. How do they stand in the historical context?

IV

THE HISTORICAL SEQUEL

The first serious strain to which the Treaty was put was the Samian War of 441–439. It was a bad moment for Athens, and a temptation to the two powers with whom she was in treaty, to seize their opportunities. Both Sparta and the satrap Pissouthnes considered taking action, but neither actually did: Perikles reconnoitred towards the neutral sea-zone, but sighted no Persian fleet (Thuc. I. 116. 3: cf. 115. 4–5, 41. 2, Plut. *Kim.* 13. 4). Incidents then became frequent: shortly before the Peloponnesian War* Athens occupies Sinope (Plut. *Per.* 20. 1–2, *I.G.* I². 944), Astakos (Diod. XII. 34. 5: see *A.T.L.* in the Gazetteer, 472), perhaps a little later Pythopolis (ibid. 544). In 430 Pissouthnes intervenes at Kolophon (Thuc. III. 34). Sparta seeks many times to induce Persia to denounce the treaty (Thuc. II. 7. 1, 67, IV. 50), and just before Artaxerxes' death, a Persian emissary to Sparta is intercepted. Athenian embassies had no doubt been visiting Sousa during these years, cf. Arist. *Ach.* 61–125; Strabo I. 3. 1; Plato *Charm.* 158a. Incidents on the Athenian side are constant (Thuc. II. 69,

*[But see *A.T.L.* III, pp. 114–7.]

III. 19, 34), culminating in the grave provocation of the Tribute assessment of 425, which not only trebled Athens' claims on the Ionian coast, but included places far beyond the neutral zone (e.g. Aspendos, Kelenderis in Kilikia, possibly Doros in Palestine), and in the interior of Karia (see *A.T.L.* A9. II. 143, 146–7, 156, and note on 155, p. 206, and Gazetteer, s.vv. Ἄσπενδος, Δῶρος, Ἐδριῆς, Ἰτύρα, Κελένδερις). It was no doubt to explain these matters that the embassy recorded by Thucydides, IV. 50. 3, set out for Sousa in the winter of 425/4, but turned back on the news of Artaxerxes' death. A year later, in 424/3, when Dareios II had disposed of his rivals, the treaty was renewed with him (section II supra).

This was in 423. We do not know how long it lasted, but almost certainly less than ten years, perhaps much less. Perhaps trouble was already afoot in 422 when Pharnakes, the northern satrap, 'gave' Atramyttion to the Delians whom Athens had expelled from Delos.[1] It began when Pissouthnes, at a date unknown but probably early in the reign, revolted from Dareios. Faced with this delicate situation, Athens did not officially side with or against him: but the mercenary force on which he depended was commanded by an Athenian, Lykon, who decided his fate by accepting the money of Tissaphernes, sent by Dareios to supersede him: the mercenaries deserted, and Pissouthnes was captured (Ktesias *Pers.* 52). The revolt was continued by his son Amorges (Thuc. VIII. 5. 5): and, for whatever reason, Athens decided to support him, officially, against Tissaphernes (Andok. 3. 29, quoted p. 207 supra); that is, against Dareios.

When was this? I suggest not later, and perhaps not much earlier, than 414. In the expense accounts for the year 415/4, on the second day of the eighth prytany (i.e. 21 March 414), a payment is made to a strategos εν Εφ[εσοι?] (*I.G.* I². 302 line 69: but I quote from Meritt's text in *A.F.D.* 163 where it is line 79).[2] A strategos in

---

[1] Thuc. V. 1. 1. Atramyttion is on the coast, but was a Lydian town, and at the head of a deep gulf: I am not sure that the settling of Delians there was a breach of treaty. In Thuc. VIII. 108. 4, it appears to be in the southern satrapy: its disposal now by the northern satrap is possibly a sign that Pissouthnes' revolt has begun.— Krateros is cited by Stephanos Byz. s.v. Ἀδραμύττειον for the form Ἀδραμύττιον, and it has been suggested that the name stood on one of the two assessments which Krateros transcribed (see *A.T.L.* 203). It seems to me much more likely that the name occurred in some *decree*, e.g. the decree which recalled the Delians from Atramyttion to Delos, Thuc. V. 32. 1.

[2] Cf. *Hesperia* V. 381–2 (no. 5), for an honorary decree of the same prytany, in Ionic script: for services to this force?

Ephesos (if this supplement be right) was, as I understand it, a breach of the treaty: and Ephesos is the natural base for a force operating against the satrap of Sardis (Xen. *Hell.* III. 1. 8, 2. 11, and especially 4. 4–26). Two years later, Tissaphernes·is eagerly seeking the alliance of Sparta: ὑπὸ βασιλέως γὰρ νεωστὶ ἐτύγχανε πεπραγμένος τοὺς ἐκ τῆς ἑαυτοῦ ἀρχῆς φόρους, οὓς δι᾿ Ἀθηναίους ἀπὸ τῶν Ἑλληνίδων πόλεων οὐ δυνάμενος πράσσεσθαι ἐπωφείλησεν· τούς τε οὖν φόρους μᾶλλον ἐνόμιζε κομιεῖσθαι κακώσας τοὺς Ἀθηναίους, καὶ ἅμα βασιλεῖ ξυμμάχους Λακεδαιμονίους ποιήσειν. καὶ Ἀμόργην τὸν Πισσούθνου υἱὸν νόθον, ἀφεστῶτα περὶ Καρίαν, ὥσπερ αὐτῷ προσέταξε βασιλεύς, ἢ ζῶντα ἄξειν ἢ ἀποκτενεῖν (Thuc. VIII. 5. 5).

Dareios had made Tissaphernes pay the arrears.[1] These arrears cannot have run (since he could not have paid them) since 449 or even 423; they must be arrears for the last year or two, i.e. since the Athenians had begun, in breach of the treaty, to prevent his collecting the revenues. This I conceive they had done since their alliance with Amorges: we do not know its date, but I suggest the strategos in Ephesos in March 414 is already there to prevent Tissaphernes collecting tribute; and further (since the arrears were something which Tissaphernes' exchequer could still, even in 412, bear), that he had not been there in 415. The rebuilding of the landward fortifications of Teos (Thuc. VIII. 16. 3: cf. p. 219 supra) was no doubt part of these operations.

In 414, when Athens was badly wanting money, and perhaps already contemplating the abolition of phoros (Thuc. VII. 28. 4), —at such a date to denounce the treaty with Dareios and support a rebel satrap, was gambling very high: the gamble failed, and Athens paid exceedingly heavily.

We now reach firmer ground: treaties whose actual text we have, and negotiations reported by trustworthy contemporaries. Tissaphernes got his treaty with Sparta, and three successive forms were sworn to, within twelve months between summer 412 and spring 411. Thucydides gives all three verbatim. Many of the clauses

---

[1] On this passage see Dundas, *C.R.* XLVIII. 167, who points out the impossibility of long arrears. But I do not see why the new claim should have started in 412 (p. 168 'from this year onward'). Dundas' question 'What was Dareios demanding?' suggests that πεπραγμένος means 'he was asked for the money'. But does it? I take it to mean 'he was made to pay', as πράσσεσθαι just below means 'to make them pay him': Athens could hardly prevent his 'asking'.

refer to the conditions of alliance and the actual circumstances of the war: I quote from the third and final form the two clauses which are essential for our enquiry: χώραν τὴν βασιλέως, ὅση τῆς Ἀσίας ἐστί, βασιλέως εἶναι· καὶ περὶ τῆς χώρας τῆς ἑαυτοῦ βουλευέτω βασιλεὺς ὅπως βούλεται (Thuc. VIII. 58. 2):

(i) The King's territory, so far as it is in Asia, shall belong to the King:

(ii) and concerning his own territory the King may do as he pleases.

Against the background of the treaty with Athens, the rather surprising second clause becomes clear. Dareios may militarize the demilitarized zone, he may put garrisons in the autonomous zone (cf. Thuc. VIII. 84. 4–5, 109). In the language of the peace of Nikias, Ionia has sunk from the status of Argilos, Stageiros, etc. (φερούσας τὸν φόρον αὐτονόμους εἶναι) to that of Skione, Torone, etc. (the contracting claimant may βουλεύεσθαι περὶ αὐτῶν ὅτι ἂν δοκῇ αὐτοῖς: Thuc. V. 18. 5, 8). The King may even bring ships into the Aegean (VIII. 59, etc.); just before, in spite of her desperate need, Athens had refused to waive that fundamental clause of her old treaty.[1]

Once again,[2] before the end of the war, it seemed as if Persia might patch up her quarrel with Athens. After his successes in the Bosporos, Alkibiades persuades Pharnabazos, probably in 408, to give five ambassadors escort up to Sousa (Xen. Hell. I. 3. 13). At that moment, Athens came nearer to salvation than at any moment after 413: but early the next year, before they reached Sousa, they were met by Kyros, who bore a message from the King: καταπέμπω Κῦρον κάρανον τῶν εἰς Καστωλὸν ἀθροιζομένων (ibid. I. 4. 3):

I send down Kyros to take military command of the forces of the west:

and the ambassadors were allowed to go no further. This was the final repudiation of all the obligations of the Kallias treaty. Dareios is using the liberty granted him in the Spartan treaty, denied to him in the Athenian: he is converting the west once more into a military area.

---

[1] Thuc. VIII. 56. 4. Sparta does not give Dareios any islands (such as Athens had been prepared to, ibid.), and Tissaphernes is still very shy of bringing ships beyond Aspendos (VIII. 59, 78, 81. 3, 87–8, 99, 108. 1).

[2] At least once: how little our information is exhaustive is shown by I.G. I². 113, an undated decree (Attic script) in honour of Euagoras of Cyprus, in which there is mention of the King and Tissaphernes (lines 38–9).

Soon after, Dareios died, and Kyros rebelled against the new King, Artaxerxes II. Sparta had backed Kyros rather heavily and her relations with Persia went bad: she took the remains of Kyros' forces into her service and declared war on the King. Tissaphernes is no match for Agesilaos, and treats for peace: he asks Agesilaos what his terms are: Agesilaos states them (Xen. *Hell.* III. 4. 5):

αὐτονόμους καὶ τὰς ἐν τῇ 'Ασίᾳ πόλεις εἶναι, ὥσπερ καὶ τὰς ἐν τῇ παρ' ἡμῖν 'Ελλάδι:

> The cities in Asia shall be autonomous, like the cities in European Greece.

These are victor's terms, and Tissaphernes says he will lay them before the King. So bad are they, that the King orders Tissaphernes' execution: they are far worse, for Persia, than the Peace of Kallias had been. Tissaphernes' successor, Tithraustes, states the King's counter proposal: it is a compromise between the utter complaisance of Sparta in 412, and her utter defiance now: it is, in fact, the Kallias treaty[1] (ibid. III. 4. 25):—βασιλεὺς δὲ ἀξιοῖ σὲ μὲν ἀποπλεῖν οἴκαδε, τὰς δ' ἐν τῇ 'Ασίᾳ πόλεις αὐτονόμους οὔσας τὸν ἀρχαῖον δασμὸν αὐτῷ ἀποφέρειν:

> The King thinks right[2] that Agesilaos evacuate Asia, and the cities of Asia be autonomous but pay to Persia the ancient tribute (sc. the tribute assessed by Artaphernes in 493).

The offer was not, however, sincere. Artaxerxes had had ample warning of his danger and had prepared his counter offensive: he appointed the Athenian Konon his admiral in chief, and gave him a free hand if he would drive Sparta off the seas. It worked completely: the Spartan offensive in Asia collapsed at once, and no more is heard of any revival of the Kallias terms. That was in 395. The next we hear of negotiations is in 391. The terms offered are preserved in Didymos' commentary on Demosthenes: it is these which Andokides was recommending when he referred to the Peace of Epilykos (3. 29): Didymos says Athens would not look at them, and Andokides was exiled for his pains. The terms were sent down by the same Antalkidas who brought down the final peace five years later: and the clause quoted is τοὺ[ς τὴν 'Ασ]ίαν οἰκοῦντας

---

[1] See p. 213, n. 1; and for the demand that Agesilaos shall evacuate Asia (the Kallias 'non-aggression clause'), p. 220, n. 1.
[2] Compare the formula of the Antalkidas treaty (*Hell.* V. 1. 31), βασιλεὺς νομίζει δίκαιον.

"Ελληνας ἐν βασιλέως οἴκ[ῳ π]άντας εἶναι συννενεμημένους (Didymos in Dem. Phil. X. col. 7, 19–23 [=Philochoros, F. gr. H. 328 F 149.]):

> The Greeks who dwell in Asia shall all be attached to the King's household.

Athens fought for another five years, and went some way towards recreating her empire, but Persia was now on Sparta's side, and in 386 Antalkidas brought down from Sousa the famous peace whose text is given, no doubt abridged, in Xen. Hell. V. 1. 31.

> The King thinks right that the cities in Asia be his, and of the islands, Kypros and Klazomenai: and that the Greek cities, great and small, shall be autonomous.

It was a wonderful achievement for Persian diplomacy and the King's chancellery must have enjoyed drafting it. No more talk from the Greeks of Europe about how the King shall behave in Asia: no: now he prescribes how they shall behave in Europe. And that is how it struck Isokrates, 4. 120:

> 'A man can see the greatness of the change, if he will read and compare the treaty which we made, and this which has just now been concluded. He will find that we named frontiers to the King's dominions, prescribed in some cases the amount of tribute he should receive, forbade him to sail the sea: and now it is the king who directs and prescribes the business of the Greeks, telling us what each should do, and only stops short of putting his quartermasters in our cities.'

Fortunately Persia was now so decrepit that no first-class danger was to be apprehended from her. Had she been more genuinely dangerous, Greek disunion would have been healed, and Artaxerxes would not have been able to employ this tone.

Compared with this, the Peace of Kallias was glorious. In the freshness of his indignation Isokrates lets out the old treaty's most disreputable clause (4. 120): ἡμεῖς φανησόμεθα ---- τῶν φόρων ἐνίους τάττοντες. It is never mentioned again.

V

The Date of the Treaty with Artaxerxes

Diodoros makes the Treaty with Artaxerxes the immediate consequence of Kimon's last expedition to Kypros: he dates it to 449/8.

The exact year is perhaps (as so often in Diodoros) wrong, but the occasion is evidently right. A treaty which in fact prescribed the relations of the two powers for the rest of Artaxerxes' reign cannot have been made before the intensive hostilities of the 'fifties; the misapprehension which led certain ancient writers to put the Treaty immediately after the Eurymedon has been noted above (p. 205).

For the exact year: I take the firm core of Pentekontaetia chronology to be that Kimon was ostracized between spring 461 and spring 451, and that the Five Years' Truce, which he made, ran from summer 451 to summer 446. Kimon's last expedition to Kypros (closely consequent on this truce, Thuc. I. 112. 2) will therefore be in 450. It is not impossible *per se* that the campaign should have lasted into 449; but for the reasons following it seems likely that the negotiations for peace occupied the winter of 450/49, and the treaty was sworn fairly early in 449.

The Treaty ended the war, and ended therefore the obligations of the allies under that assessment of 478/7, whereby the Athenians ἔταξαν ἅς τε ἔδει παρέχειν τῶν πόλεων χρήματα πρὸς τὸν βάρβαρον καὶ ἃς ναῦς (Thuc. I. 96. 1). It did not of course end their alliance with Athens, which was in perpetuity, 'Αθ. π. 23. 5:[1] but it ended their obligations to serve or pay tribute on a scale assessed πρὸς τὸν βάρβαρον. It was however evident, to Athens at least, that the League's fleet (under Athenian control) whose maintenance was the chief charge on League revenues, could not be simply discharged: on Perikles' motion, Athens invited all Greek states to send representatives to consider peace-time expenditure.[2] The agenda of this congress is given by Plutarch, *Per.* 17. 1, who evidently keeps close to the wording of the decree: the three expenditures to be discussed are (i) rebuilding the temples, (ii) maintaining the festivals started in 479, (iii) policing the seas. No one came (since Sparta, who was asked first, declined) and Athens decided to help herself. Perikles moved a second decree, that the money accumulated κατὰ τὴν 'Αριστείδου τάξιν (i.e. the assessment πρὸς τὸν βάρβαρον) should be used for rebuilding the Athenian temples. So at least I understand the difficult lines 3–8 of the *Anonymus*

---

[1] Cf. Larsen, *C.P.* XXVIII. 267; Highby *Erythrae Decree* 64.

[2] This decree is evidently the immediate consequence of the Treaty: see p. 254 below, n. 2. The words καὶ τὴν εἰρήνην ἄγωσιν (Plut. *Per.* 17. 1) are presumably from the text of the decree and, if so, are a contemporary mention of the Peace.

Argentinensis: see the text proposed in *A.T.L.*, p. 572, T9. This second decree was voted before the end of the year 450/49:[1] the Treaty cannot therefore be later than the early summer of 449, since Perikles' two motions, that inviting the Congress and that appropriating the reserve of Phoros, must come (in that order) between the Treaty and the end of the Attic year.

Money had thus been found for the temples. But the fleet could hardly continue to be maintained out of a capital sum, however large: the revenues had to be renewed. It is now well known that no quota-list was inscribed on the 'First Stele' for one of the years between 449/8 and 447/6; it is assumed in *A.T.L.* that the missing year is 449/8.[2] It would seem that tribute was still paid for 450/49, that the war was formally ended in the latter part of that (Attic) year, and that consequently no tribute was due for 449/8. What is certain is that after one year's interval it was reimposed.

There is one other indication of date. Herodotos, VII. 151, reports that 'many years after 480' τυχεῖν ἐν Σούσοισι τοῖσι Μεμνονίοισι ἐόντας ἑτέρου πρήγματος εἴνεκα ἀγγέλους ᾿Αθηναίων, Καλλίην τε τὸν ῾Ιππονίκου καὶ τοὺς μετὰ τούτου ἀναβάντας, ᾿Αργείους δὲ τὸν αὐτὸν τοῦτον χρόνον πέμψαντας καὶ τούτους ἐς Σοῦσα ἀγγέλους εἰρωτᾶν ᾿Αρτοξέρξην τὸν Ξέρξεω εἴ σφι ἔτι ἐμμένει τὴν πρὸς Ξέρξην φιλίην συνεκεράσαντο, ἢ νομιζοίατο πρὸς αὐτοῦ εἶναι πολέμιοι· βασιλέα δὲ ᾿Αρτοξέρξην μάλιστα ἐμμένειν φάναι καὶ οὐδεμίαν νομίζειν πόλιν ῎Αργεος φιλιωτέρην. It is likely that the ἕτερον πρῆγμα for which Kallias was at Sousa, is the peace which bears his name. Now Argos had embarked on an adventurous foreign policy in 462, and involved herself on Athens' side in the war which followed between Athens and Sparta (Thuc. I. 102. 4, 107. 5). Those were the years when Athens was fighting both Sparta and Persia with success. But when under the strain of the disaster in Egypt, Athens made a truce with Sparta in 451,

---

[1] The papyrus says [ἐπ' Εὐ]θυδήμο[υ] Περικλέους γνώμη[ν] εἰσ[ηγησαμένου]. The archon of 450/49 was Euthynos, but he is called Euthydemos by Diodoros (XII. 3. 1). Meritt's observation (*A.T.L.* l.c.) that the comments in this papyrus all depend on lemmata beginning with ὅτι, leaves no choice but to take this decree as part of the comment on the building of the Parthenon.

[2] *A.T.L.* 133, 175, with references to *B.S.A.* XXXIII. 112 and Meritt *D.A.T.* 65, 69. It should be specially noted (*a*) that the lists there numbered 7 and 8 are so alike that it is reasonably certain that they belong to successive years, and (*b*) that list '7' is unique (after list 1) in having no serial number, and a plausible explanation of this is that it was awkward to give the serial number 7 to the list which stood immediately below 5.

Argos evidently felt nervous lest she might find herself isolated among stronger powers:[1] the clearest sign is her thirty-year peace with Sparta, concluded perhaps in the autumn of 451, perhaps a year later (Thuc. V. 14. 4, 28. 2, 40–1: cf. Busolt *G.G.* III. 339, n. 3). There is evidence of the same anxiety in a clause of the thirty-year peace between Athens and Sparta (446/5), to the effect that while Argos was not included in this peace, it did not preclude Argive-Athenian friendship (Paus. V. 23. 4): it is clear that Argos had been anxious to know how this peace would leave her relations with Athens. That at the same juncture she should have enquired about her standing with Persia is likely enough.

This will not of course give us a close date. We cannot, e.g. argue that Argos is likely to have made this enquiry as soon as Athens' truce with Sparta had isolated her: for is it not caused rather by the knowledge that Athens is negotiating with Persia?[2]

VI

ESTIMATE[3]

The Persian empire revealed high qualities in its ruling nobility: courage, energy, ·intelligence, humanity. It was a searching test of these qualities when it encountered, in the Greeks, a higher civilization, and a creativeness almost unique in history. In practically all the arts of peace and war, Greece was, in virtue of this creativeness, Persia's superior—in architecture, in medicine, in

---

[1] It is much the same position as in 420: ἔδεισαν μὴ μονωθῶσι, Thuc. V. 40 1.

[2] Just so, in 446 the knowledge that Sparta was negotiating with Athens caused Argos to make the *démarche* at Athens which resulted in the clause Pausanias quotes. I note that the question 'or are we considered to be enemies?' presupposes that Argos is or has been in alliance with Athens, so that the embassy cannot have been sent (as has been suggested) on Artaxerxes' accession. It has also been suggested that it went immediately after the alliance with Athens, *c.* 461 (and therefore that Kallias, like Antalkidas, paid two visits to Sousa, the first one unsuccessful). This seems to me incredible: both Athens and Argos felt, in 461, at the top of the world, and Persia was not formidable. But we should remember that Herodotos does not guarantee his story (152. 1).

[3] Is the fifth-century silence (but see p. 227, n. 2, p. 231, n. 1) due to shame? I think Hdt. VII. 151 is euphemistic (cf. 152. 2). Demosthenes, 19. 273, says that Kallias was fined 50 talents for making the treaty: but Plutarch, *Kim.* 13. 5, reports that he was exceptionally honoured for it, and Pausanias, I. 8. 2, that he was some time honoured with a statue. Diodoros, XII. 7, names Kallias as one of the two chief envoys to Sparta for the thirty-year peace: if this is true, and the same Kallias, his disgrace was at least not permanent. It was no doubt his grandson who moved *I.G.* I². 25, for whose connection with the Treaty see p. 209; no. 24, however, was not moved (as suggested in *I.G.* I²) by Hipponikos (sc. Kallias' son), see *J.H.S.* LI. 78, n. 80.

naval construction, in military technique. In the clash of the two civilizations, the Persians had two advantages: their resources in material (whether accumulated or exploitable) and in men, appeared inexhaustible: and war was their essential function. Without war the Persian nobility and monarchy had comparatively little *raison d'être*: there is evident truth in the observation that Herodotos puts in Atossa's mouth (III. 134. 1–2), that a Persian King must justify himself by conquests.

The Greeks were a fighting race: but since their civilization did not lack other functions also, we find in their literature, besides militarist sentiments which may sometimes surprise us,[1] much praise of peace and much sensibility to the havoc which war makes of rational felicity. This contrast is not yet poignant in Archilochos' famous couplet, *I am a servant of the Lord God of War, and I understand the lovely art of the Muses:*[2] but begins to be in the second choros of the *Septem* (288 ff.).

The fighting energy of Athens in the invasion of Xerxes and the decades following needs no argument:[3] the disparity between her energy, and that of her Ionian allies, was the profound cause of the failure of that union, conceived with such exultant hopes in 478 (cf. Thuc. I. 99). Her war aims no doubt, like all war aims, varied with circumstance, but two can be picked out as fairly constant:

   (i) to win an indemnity for the damage done in 480/79, by an offensive against Persia.[4]

   (ii) to exterminate Phoenician sea power.

(The strategic point, for both aims, was Kypros.) But apart from the booty of the Eurymedon, which paid for the artificial platform on which the Parthenon later stood,[5] very little was got in the way of indemnity: and the breaking of Phoenician sea power was reserved for Alexander. But after some thirty years of encounter with Athens, Persia was wounded mortally, and her inexorable de-

---

[1] Sappho 16, Alkaios 357 (Lobel and Page); Pindar fr. 66 (Bowra); Thuc. II. 31, VI. 41. 3; Xen. *Hell.* V. 1. 17.

[2] Fr. 1 (Diehl). The translation is Yeats', *The Cutting of an Agate* 125.

[3] The casualty list of the tribe Erechtheis, of the early 'fifties, may be cited: *I.G.* I². 929. Athens' temper in the Kimonian period seems to me expressed very faithfully in *Hymn. Hom.* XI: Παλλάδ' 'Αθηναίην ἐρυσίπτολιν ἄρχομ' ἀείδειν, | δεινήν, ἧ σὺν "Αρηι μέλει πολεμήϊα ἔργα | περθόμεναί τε πόληες αὐτή τε πτολεμοί τε, | καί τ' ἐρρύσατο λαὸν ἰόντα τε νισόμενόν τε. | χαῖρε θεά, δὸς δ' ἄμμι τύχην εὐδαιμονίην τε. Is the poem in fact of this date?

[4] Thuc. I. 96. 1, πρόσχημα γὰρ ἦν ἀμύνεσθαι ὧν ἔπαθον δῃοῦντας τὴν βασιλέως χώραν.

[5] Plut. *Kim.* 13. 5, τὸ νότιον τεῖχος.

cline begins: the picture in Xenophon, *Cyrop.* VIII. 8, is of the reformed marauder who has settled down to live on his *rentes* and gone soft. It was Artaxerxes' treaty with Athens which started this: by it Persia formally abjured conquest and accepted a *modus vivendi*.

The world was thus made, if not quite safe, yet safe enough, for the development of Greek civilization: not only for the arts and sciences, but for experiments in government and social order and rational felicity. It was left to Alexander to break the Persian empire. Kimon's friends believed that Athens might have secured better co-operation from her allies and from Sparta, and by more concentration of energy against Persia have done more of what Alexander was to do.[1] It may be: but to some of us, the conquest of Persia appears as the end of the especial quality of Greek civilization, and we may think that Perikles did better to bring Persia to terms than to break her.

APPENDIX

A FRAGMENT OF THE TEXT OF THE TREATY?

'Εν δὲ τοῖς ψηφίσμασιν ἃ συνήγαγε Κρατερὸς ἀντίγραφα συνθηκῶν ὡς γενομένων κατατέτακται (Plut. *Kim.* 13. 5). Krateros included the text of the Treaty among his collection of documents,[2] and so presumed it genuine. The Treaty with Artaxerxes or Dareios? It is commonly said that Krateros copied from the *stele* which Theopompos had condemned as a forgery, and there is some reason to think that this *stele* held the treaty with Dareios (see p. 206). It seems to me that, for Krateros, the treaty with Artaxerxes was more interesting, and I conceive he would know which one he was copying (even though Theopompos may not have known which one he was criticizing): and my impression is that Krateros was not a στηλοκόπας but worked from the archives. So that the chances that his text was of the Treaty of 450/49 are, I think, strong.

I believe we have a fragment of it. The Townleyan scholiast on *Iliad* XIV. 230, Λῆμνον δ' εἰσαφίκανε πόλιν θείοιο Θόαντος, may perhaps be restored as follows:—

---

[1] Plut. *Per.* 12. 1–2, where the words ταύτην (sc. τὴν πρόφασιν) ἀνῄρηκε Περικλῆς are a reference to the Treaty; ibid. 28. 6.

[2] The best account of Krateros' work is in Krech, *de Crateri ψηφισμάτων συναγωγῇ*, Berlin, 1888; cf. *A.T.L.* 203. The psephismata included various sorts of "documents" from the archives, not necessarily all decrees: though the Treaty was, quite possibly, a decree: cf. *I.G.* I² 26, 39, 51, 52, etc.; Thuc. IV. 118. 11. *[See now *F. gr. H.* 342.]

πόλιν θείοιο ‹Θόαντος: ὡς Εὐριπίδης, " Εὔβοι' 'Αθήναις› ἐστί τις γείτων πόλις," ἀντὶ τοῦ " νῆσος "· οἱ δὲ ἀντὶ τοῦ " χώρα," ‹ὡς› ἐν ψηφίσματι ‹ὃ παρα›τίθεται Κρατερός, " ἔστε ἐπὶ Αἴγυπτον καὶ Λιβύην τὼ πόλεε." Lacunas explevit Meineke, modo ὡς Εὐριπίδης addidi, coll. Strab. VIII. 3. 31 : καρτερός ms., Κρατερός Meineke : in fragmento psephismatis, ἐστὶν ms., delevit Meineke, ἔστε ἐπὶ (sc. εστ‹ε επ›ι) ego. Krech fr. 12; apud *F.H.G.* non exstat. *[Now *F. gr. H.* 342 F 18.]

This restoration is essentially Meineke's, given in his edition of Stephanos, p. 718. The scholium is evidently corrupt, but none of the restorations are vital; it is certain that we have a quotation from one of Krateros' 'documents', containing the words Αἴγυπτον καὶ Λιβύην τὼ πόλεε. These words are cited to illustrate the use of πόλις in the sense of 'island' or 'country'. This usage occurs in poetry, though rarely;[1] its presence in documentary prose needs accounting for. I have long thought that the phrase might be from the Treaty: τότε μὲν γὰρ ἡμεῖς φανησόμεθα τὴν ἀρχὴν τὴν βασιλέως ὁρίζοντες (Isokr. 4. 120). Since Persian documents were drafted in Aramaic, I asked G. R. Driver if any Aramaic word was likely to be responsible for this curious usage in the Greek translation, and he tells me that the Aramaic *medinah*, 'juridical area', is used sometimes of a city, sometimes of a province. '[*As far as?*] the two administrative areas of Egypt and Libya.' The King's dominions are being defined; they are to stretch, in this direction, to the areas which had rebelled under Inaros (Thuc. I. 104. 1). Athens renounces her support of such rebellion.

Was the translator an Ionian? If my suggestion ἔστε ἐπὶ is right, he probably was, since ἔστε is not Attic. Perhaps the form πλέειν, for which Lindskog quotes no variant in Plut. *Kim.* 13. 4, is another Ionicism: if so, ἔνδον δὲ Κυανέων καὶ Χελιδονίων μακρᾷ νηὶ καὶ χαλκεμβόλῳ[2] μὴ πλέειν (μηδετέρους?) may be almost textual (Krateros being by then available). I do not think, even so, that a *stele* commissioned by the Poletai in 449 B.C. is likely to have been inscribed in Ionic script (see p. 206); but it becomes a little less impossible.

[1]See the passages cited by Strabo, VIII. 3. 31. The loose apposition of Σικελίαν etc. to πόλεις πολλάς in [Lysias] 6. 6 should not be cited for this usage.

[2] Χαλκέμβολοι in Diod. XIV. 59. 7 (Phoenician); Plut. *Ant.* 35. 7. In the former, are they armed merchantmen?

TWO NOTES ON THEOPOMPOS, *PHILIPPIKA*, X

I. KLEON AND THE ASSESSMENT

IN volume LVII of this *Journal** (pp. 377–94) Meritt and I sought to establish that Kleon came back from Pylos about the end of the second prytany of 425/4 and that Thoudippos (who sponsored the motion for the remarkable tribute-assessment of that year) had expected him back in time to get the business finished within the prytany, but that in fact the bill was not passed until the third prytany had begun.[1] The crux was that whereas Thucydides leaves in everyone's mind the impression that Kleon had been notoriously punctual, there was nevertheless this unexpected delay. We argued, therefore, that the actual capture of the Spartans was achieved in an absolute minimum of time; so that, if Kleon took things easier on his way home, he might have fulfilled his twenty-day promise and yet have been later than Thoudippos calculated. We could, however, give no direct evidence that Kleon had relaxed his pace.

Yet there is, I believe, evidence that Kleon did cause delay which Thoudippos could hardly have foreseen. It was not quite as we imagined, sc. on the way back (*A.J.P.* LVII, pp. 392–3), but after his return to Athens.

Theopompos is cited (fr. 92 Jacoby=sch. Lucian, *Timon*, 30) for the palmary instance of Kleon's effrontery: 'Once when the Athenians had assembled, he came to the Ekklesia with a wreath on his head; and telling them to postpone the meeting (since he was sacrificing and had to entertain guests) he dismissed the Ekklesia.' The story finds its perfect context if this is the meeting summoned so urgently by Thoudippos, if Kleon's sacrifice is the thanksgiving for Pylos, if his behaviour is the licensed effrontery of the hero of the hour.[2] I have given the flat version of the

*[*American Journal of Philology.*]
[1] *I.G.* I². 63; see Meritt and West, *The Athenian Assessment*, pp. 44–5, lines 3, 34.
[2] Compare the tone of his notorious dispatch beginning 'Dear Boule and Demos' (cf. *A.J.P.* LVII, p. 391, note 35).

Lucian scholiast. Plutarch tells the story with more gusto (*Nicias* VII. 7; *Moralia* 799 D): Kleon kept them all waiting;[1] when he came, he said, 'I am busy today. I am going to entertain guests and have sacrificed to the gods'; and the assembly broke up in laughter and applause. The laughter was no doubt due to high spirits, but was there a joke as well? Were Kleon's guests (ξένους) his Spartans?

Thoudippos fixed the time for debate on the assessment επει[δαν ηεκει ηε] στρα[τια] ες τριτεν εμεραν (Meritt and West, *The Athenian Assessment*, p. 45, line 34). This is not unlike a clause in the 'resolution of the allies' touching the debate on the peace with Philip in 346 B.C. (Aeschines, II. 60: ἐπειδὰν ἐπιδημήσωσιν οἱ πρέσβεις καὶ τὰς πρεσβείας ἀπαγγείλωσιν - - προγράψαι τοὺς πρυτάνεις ἐκκλησίας δύο). Here, too, a debate is to be postponed till certain individuals can attend it, not in their official capacity (it is to be 'after they have reported') but because their presence might make some difference.[2] The clause was in fact disregarded (ibid. 61) since the allies' resolution bound no one; nor in any case need we suppose that if they had been late the Ekklesia would wait for them. But imagine such a clause, when joined to Kleon's exceptional standing after Pylos: in the story, he comes from his private affairs (not from the council-house) and has evidently no official position, yet the Ekklesia waits for him. Thoudippos' clause, *plus* Kleon's personal standing at the moment, explains this. It surely cannot have been usual.

Plutarch does not cite Theopompos by name; the scholiast commenting on the two names Ὑπερβόλῳ and Κλέωνι in Lucian's text quotes Theopompos three times: fr. 95, Θεόπομπος ἐν τῷ περὶ δημαγωγῶν; fr. 96, Θεόπομπος πάλιν ἐν δεκάτῳ Φιλιππικῶν; fr. 92, Θεόπομπος. All three have always been ascribed to the 'Demagogue' section of *Philippika* X (see below), no doubt rightly. This might be taken as further proof that the Ekklesia in question was due to consider the assessment, since 'reckless treatment of

---

[1] τὸν μὲν δῆμον καθήμενον ἄνω περιμένειν πολὺν χρόνον ὀψὲ δ' εἰσελθεῖν ἐκεῖνον. In this, and the laughter, Plutarch need hardly be suspected of embroidering Theopompos. The laughter at any rate is what makes the story à *propos* in *Nicias* VII. The incident is no doubt glanced at Arist. *Eq.* 929 ff., and Kleon must have suggested leniency for Miletos. The Sausage-seller hopes that next time he will burst.

[2] Similarly, Thoudippos does not enact that an Ekklesia be called 'for the strategos' (cf. Andocides, I. 11) in which case Kleon would be on duty (which he clearly is not); but simply, that the Ekklesia be at a time when the strategos can attend.

public finance by demagogues' was the subject of that section. But this is not cogent: a pejorative anecdote did not, for Theopompos, have to be strictly relevant.

2. DATE OF JURYMEN'S PAY

The introduction of pay for Jurymen was dated 462 + by Busolt (*Gr. Gesch.* III, p. 263; cf. p. 255) but there has been a tendency to lower the date a little[1] or a lot. Unquestionably this has been due to a sense that Ephialtes should be off the scene before Perikles appears in full career, and Walker in *Cambridge Ancient History* (V, p. 101) puts this explicitly (the italics are mine):

> The only indication of date is afforded by the statement of Aristotle ('Aθ. Πολ. XXVII 3) that the measure was brought forward by Pericles as a bid for popular favour, and in order to counterbalance the wealth of Cimon. This would point to a period when Pericles *had succeeded to the leadership* of the popular party, and Cimon was still the leader on the other side. The date, therefore, *cannot be before the ostracism* of Cimon, for Ephialtes, not Pericles, was then the leader of the popular party; and it cannot be during the exile of Cimon, for Aristotle's statement implies his presence at Athens. It must, therefore, fall between his return from exile, which happened probably in 451 B.C., and his sailing for Cyprus in 450 B.C.

Like too many arguments from residue, this will not bear scrutiny. Put the plain question, cannot this story of rivalry belong to the time before Kimon's ostracism? I seek to show that it not only can but does. The story occurs first, for us, in Theopompos, and he (I seek to show) put it before both Kimon's ostracism and Ephialtes' legislation.[2]

---

[1] Meyer, *Gesch. d. Alterthums* III. pp. 571–3, Beloch, *Gr. Gesch.* II², p. 155, Glotz, *Histoire Grecque* II, p. 138, Berve, *Gr. Gesch.* I, p. 273, all imply, without argument, that it is *after* Ephialtes' anti-Areopagite laws, but not much after.

[2] This means that fr. 89 should stand before fr. 88. The traditional (but arbitrary) inverse order, already in Müller's *F.H.G.* (I, p. 293), has I imagine helped the tendency to lower the date of fr. 89. This will not prove that Theopompos is right. Walker indeed puts the legislation after the ostracism, εἴη δ' ἂν πᾶν. I insist only that the 'rivalry' story cannot be used to support the 451 date. Bonner and Smith, *Administration of Justice*, pp. 226–30, discuss the two dates 462 and 451, and advance (but finally reject) two considerations for the latter: (1) If (what they rightly think very doubtful) Aristotle, 'Aθ. Πολ. XXVII. 1, records a second anti-Areopagite law dated 451, Plutarch might mean this as the law which succeeded the invention of pay. But Plutarch 'specifies' the law which caused Kimon's ostracism. (2) The Jurymen, if

The closing chapters of *Philippika* X (all our fragments are from these 'closing chapters') existed separately as a pamphlet called 'The Demagogues at Athens'.[1] As an excursus to Bk. X,[2] it is evidently motivated by the comptrollership of Euboulos in Athens. This is described in fr. 99, 100, not flatteringly: he has completed the ruin of Athens' morale by his administration of the Theorikon. So far Theopompos' judgment does not differ materially from Demosthenes', nor indeed from the truth: men like Euboulos make a 'power-policy' impracticable for the state they serve. But what Demosthenes thought was treason to Athens' past, Theopompos thought the due culmination of a century or more of Athenian demagogy.

The thesis, then, is that this vicious system, the use of the state revenues for the pleasures of the poor, was rooted in Athens' past. There are named Kimon, Kleon, Hyperbolos, Kallistratos, Euboulos: these all with reference to Bk. X or to the pamphlet. Fragments 85–7, on Themistokles, are from Plutarch, who never gives book numbers: not strictly relevant to the thesis, they speak of bribery and peculation, cognate themes which Theopompos did not disdain.[3] There is little of Perikles in our fragments: he and his rival Thucydides[4] are named in 91 (cf. 261: neither gives the book number): but clearly Perikles must have been one of the main villains of the piece, and Kimon and Thucydides were there as foils. This can, I think, be proved.

---

already paid, might have resented the circuit justices of 453/2. But the new courts were not really a form of poor-relief, and anyway (see the acute remarks of Calhoun, *Growth of Criminal Law*, pp. 102 sq.) it was not the dikastai but the thesmothetai who were relieved of work thereby. I once thought Aristophanes, *Eccles.* 303–8, rather favoured 451, the 'fifties being Myronides' great time: but Aristophanes is thinking of Ekklesia pay. For the date in the early 'fifties I can find no reason except compromise: its constant repetition (p. 235, note 1) seems to be a matter of habit.

[1] Fr. 100 Jacoby=Athen., 166 D. Fr. 95 is quoted as from the pamphlet. The *Philippika* cannot have been published before Philip's death (fr. 27, which stood ἐν ἀρχῇ τῆς Φιλίππου συντάξεως, seems to me to prove this as clearly as the more scandalous passages: see further Jacoby's judicial comments on fr. 330, 340, *ad loc.* and also p. 358), and I imagine this pamphlet, and the similar one in Bk. XXV, had earlier separate circulation: this one in the late 'fifties, the other in the early 'forties.

[2] Theopompos' narrative had reached the later 'fifties: fr. 52, 63, 78, 101.

[3] E.g. fr. 94 (no book number, but not to be separated from 93 which cites Bk. X) on Kleon's peculation. In fr. 90 'Kimon' is needed for Cyril's context, but Theopompos must have said 'Kleon' and Cyril has confused the names. These peculation passages are probably (fr. 86 certainly?) from Kritias: I hope later to develop the case for Kritias as a major source for *Philippika* X.

[4] Theopompos calls him son of Pantainos: but that he means the son of Melesias is made virtually certain by fr. 261.

Fragment 89 tells the well-known story of Kimon's great personal generosity, and concludes '*it was to this that he owed his position of first citizen in Athens*'. Its bearing on the thesis is clear: what Kimon achieved by personal liberality, his successors had to achieve by *misthos*. This is made explicit by Aristotle ('*Aθ. Πολ.* XXVII), who tells the same tale as motivation for Perikles' invention of Jurymen's Pay. The '*Aθηναίων Πολιτεία* is probably later than Theopompos' pamphlet (see p. 236, note 1) but does not of course derive from it. Theopompos has told the story in more detail, but Aristotle in one respect more carefully (Kimon, he says, kept open house *for all his demesmen* of Lakiadai, where Theopompos says *for all Athenians*). We have to posit a common source, which each has used in his fashion: I suggest it is Kritias (see p. 236, note 3).

Plutarch twice tells the story, in *Pericles* IX. 2–3, and in *Cimon* X. 1–3. He follows Theopompos, not Aristotle, having the greater detail and also the error. But he (or his original) has checked Theopompos by Aristotle: he notes, in the *Cimon*, that Aristotle says 'demesmen only', and in the *Pericles* he quotes Aristotle for Damonides' name. This is his regular way with a secondary source, and it is generally recognized that his primary source, here, is ultimately Theopompos.[1] Now a little later (*Pericles* X. 1; for the *Cimon* see below) he has a second bit which is recognizably Theopompos (fr. 88), and the narrative between is consecutive and coherent; it may, I think, rank as certain that this narrative is all, in its main lines, Theopompos.[2] It is as follows, *Pericles* IX. 2–X. 1 (I condense it to the essentials): 'Perikles competing with Kimon could not compete with his wealth and generosity [here comes Theop. fr. 89], so he bribed the masses with theorika and Jurymen's and other Pay,[3] and used them against the Areopagites. By his power with them he destroyed that Boule's[4] standing, and in consequence Ephialtes reduced their jurisdiction and Kimon was ostracized. Such was Perikles' power. Yet

---

[1] E.g. Wilamowitz, *Aristoteles und Athen* I, p. 300; Busolt, *Gr. Gesch.* III, p. 36; Jacoby, *Frag. Gr. Hist.*, comm. on 115 F 89. The reckless exaggeration of VII. 8 (Ephialtes was Perikles' *homme de paille*) is not of course Theopompan: nor XVI. 3.

[2] Note that Theopompos is nowhere named: if he had been used for two isolated bits in a consecutive narrative, this would be most surprising.

[3] Is this accumulation due to Plutarch or Theopompos? We can hardly say, but it does not matter. Here, as in the matter of the demesmen, the careful Aristotle corrects the recklessness of our other witnesses: it is clear that the common source spoke of Jurymen's Pay, not of the other *misthoi*.

[4] Sc. the Areopagites. The verb κατεστασίασε is Theopompan, cf. fr. 240.

Kimon did not stay away his full ten years, but was recalled under stress of war [Theop. fr. 88].'

In the *Cimon* the same material is split up. Kimon's generosity (X. 1–3), the Areopagites' loss of jurisdiction *owing to Perikles' power with the masses* (XV. 2), the ostracism (XV. 3–XVII. 3 [a digression on Ithome, as contributing to his fall, makes this so long, but XVII. 3=*Pericles* X. 1 *init.*]), Tanagra and the recall (XVII. 4–8). The order is identical, but the story has lost its coherence. Perikles the villain, not Kimon the hero, was the central figure in Theopompos; so that in a life of Perikles the story stays coherent, in a life of Kimon it is a framework to be filled out with other matter.

THUCYDIDES THE SON OF MELESIAS

A STUDY OF PERIKLEAN POLICY

AT the crisis of Perikles' career, in the middle 'forties, Thucydides of the deme Alopekê, the son of Melesias, withstood the great man for a little while, until he was swept aside. He was ostracized (the last important ostracism of which we hear) and with that Perikles begins his fifteen years' principate.

Impar congressus Achilli, Thucydides is damned by another Latin tag also: he is *magni nominis umbra*. Thucydides, for us and for most ancient writers, means the son of Oloros, the historian; and it has long been recognized that the second *Vita* prefixed to our texts of Thucydides' *History* contains information about the son of Melesias.[1] The difficulty of disentangling him from his namesakes,[2] more perhaps than the overtoweringness of his rival, has deterred historians from constating about the son of Melesias things which I think can yet be constated and should be. For indeed Kimon's political heir, who resisted Perikles on behalf of the Attic aristocracy, in the days when this aristocracy (to Athens' own irreparable damage) was being ruined,[3] is a sufficiently important figure.

His importance in the aristocratic tradition of Plato and Aristotle is unmistakable, if rather surprising. Ἀθ. πολ. 28, Aristotle names the leaders of the upper classes, after Kimon, as Thucydides, Nikias, Theramenes: and adds, 'the best statesmen in Athens, μετὰ τοὺς ἀρχαίους, seem to have been Nikias and Thucydides and Theramenes. As to Nikias and Thucydides, practically

---

[1] See Appendix A. Busolt, *G.G.* III. 1, pp. 442 and 497 sq., is rather doubtful how far the reference to Melesias' son may be safely assumed. The identification of Melesias (v. infra) enables me to claim for his son with more confidence certain hitherto doubtful passages.

[2] I regret extremely that Kirchner's *Beiträge zur Geschichte attischer Familien* in the *Festschrift für d. Berl. Friedrich-Wilhelms-Gymnasium* (Berlin, 1897), in which he disentangles these namesakes, is inaccessible to me. Its conclusions are incorporated in the *Prosopogr. Attica*.

[3] Meautis, *L'Aristocratie athénienne*, Paris, 1927, pp. 17 sqq.

everyone is agreed that they were not only fine gentlemen (ἄνδρας καλοὺς κἀγαθούς) but statesmen also, who treated the whole city πατρικῶς, as a nobleman treats his inheritance.' A tendencious judgment, but striking. In the opening speech of the *Laches*, Plato pairs him with Aristeides: and in the *Meno*, he is instanced along with Themistokles, Aristeides and Perikles, to show that virtue is a thing unteachable, since none of these managed to have it taught their sons.

So he was undoubtedly important. For what he did, however, we must turn to late writers, especially Plutarch. From him we learn that after Kimon's death he organized the opposition to Perikles and brought matters to the issue of ostracism.

I. *The Ostracism and its Causes.*

He was ostracized in spring 443, and eleven of the *ostraka* cast against him are extant (*I.G.* I². 911). The date is not absolutely certain, but the probability is strong. Plutarch says (*Perikles* 16. 3) that after Thucydides' ostracism Perikles held a single and continuous position of power and authority of not less than fifteen years in his yearly *strategiai*. The phrase is rhetorical, the figures possibly round (cf. in the preceding clause τεσσαράκοντα μὲν ἔτη πρωτεύων, etc.): but the probable interpretation is, that Perikles was elected Strategos fifteen times running, beginning with the election of 443 for the year 443–2. This is true at the lower end: Perikles was elected Strategos in 430 for 430–29, and again in 429 for 429–8. In neither year did he serve the full twelve months: he was deposed in the course of 430–29, and died in the course of 429–8. But if we are not to count these uncompleted years, then the first of the fifteen elections is put back to 445, and this is out of the question. The ostracism was preceded by a period in which Thucydides had almost equal authority[1] with Perikles: this is impossible in 446. We may be more exact: since the fifteen years of continuous strategia begin from the ostracism, it is a fair inference that Perikles was *not* Strategos in the year immediately preceding: yet he was certainly elected in 446 for 446–5. I take it, therefore, as the most probable hypothesis, that Perikles failed of election in 444 for 444–3; that an ostracism was demanded that

---

[1] Plut. *Perikles* 11. 1, εἰς ἀντίπαλον. Cf. 6. 2. δυεῖν οὐσῶν ἐν τῇ πόλει δυναστειῶν: and *Vita Anon. Thuc.* §§ 6–7 (see Appendix A).

winter, and in spring 443 Thucydides was ostracized and Perikles was elected for 443–2, the first of his fifteen continous elections. I hope what I say later may serve to confirm this hypothesis.[1] On the actual issue between the two men, Plutarch says (*Perikles* 14): '§ 1. When the speakers on Thucydides' side abused Perikles for squandering the money and destroying the revenues, he asked the Ekklesia if they thought the expense had been heavy: and when they replied "Very heavy," "Then charge it", he said, "not to yourselves but to me: and I will dedicate the offerings in my name." § 2. So, whether struck by his generosity or moved to overbid him in noble zeal, they cried out and bade him spend from the revenues and spare nothing. § 3. And at last he faced the struggle and ordeal of ostracism against Thucydides, and removed him from Athens and ended the opposition.'

One issue, then, was the opposition to the building programme: for it is clear that by 'the offerings' (τὰ ἀναθήματα) Plutarch means (as he does in 12. 1, ἡ τῶν ἀναθημάτων κατασκευή) the great buildings of the Akropolis. The Peace with Persia in 449 ended the hopes of a specific indemnity for the burnt temples: the failure of the Panhellenic Congress immediately after (see p. 254, note 2 infra) decided Perikles to use the resources he had, of which a very large proportion was surplus Tribute: it is possible that he put through in 449 a special statute authorising this (see Appendix B). As to the date of the opposition offered, it may be that his opponents fought him inch by inch and kept the question open till the ostracism of 443: but such accounts as we have refer (I think) to the first broaching of the question, in the early 'forties. In the *Perikles*, ch. 12, where Plutarch describes the controversy at most length, the last sentence of § 1 indicates the morrow of the Peace with Persia.[2] The story I quoted above (*Perikles* 14) is perhaps legendary and not to be dated: but it suits the early (better than the later) 'forties,[3] when the principle of large expense was still in

---

[1] There is no other indication of exact date. A fragment of the Θρᾷτται of Kratinos (quoted Plut. *Perikles* 13. 10) mentions τοὔστρακον but should probably not be referred to this time; since another fragment mentions Euathlos, who is still a young man in 425. Geissler, *Chronologie der altattischen Komödie*, pp. 21–2.

[2] "Ἡ δ' ἔνεστιν αὐτῷ πρὸς τοὺς ἐγκαλοῦντας εὐπρεπεστάτη τῶν προφασέων, δείσαντα τοὺς βαρβάρους ἐκεῖθεν ἀνελέσθαι καὶ φυλάττειν ἐν ὀχυρῷ τὰ κοινά, ταύτην ἀνῄρηκε Περικλῆς.

[3] The ostracism is the *ultimate* result (14. 3, τέλος δὲ) of the rivalry of which this is an (early) instance. The rivalry was a matter of years (8. 5, πλεῖστον ἀντεπολιτεύσατο χρόνον).

16

doubt and before the total outlay was yet enormous. For Perikles was only moderately rich (᾽Αθ. πολ. XXVII. 4) and cannot have offered to pay for the Parthenon!

The building programme involved a good deal. Athens had been, like Sparta, a war executive: it made of her a peace-time capital also, with absolute disposal of her imperial revenues. Further, it involved the question of taste, it could be called pretentious and hubristic. And the question of the disposal of Tribute touched the Kimonians more nearly if Prof. West's thesis in a recent important paper[1] is right, that Kimon was responsible for making Euboea tributary just before his death, so that the Peace, instead of ending her service, merely confirmed her new (and now inferior) status. (There is little doubt, I think, that when Sparta, having encouraged Euboea to revolt,[2] left her, as usual, to face the consequences, the solid gain for Athens was the formal admission of her right to Tribute in peace-time.) Euboea, then, may have been especially on the conscience of Kimon's political heir, and the question of the use of her Tribute a vital question.

The case against and for the building programme is excellently put by Plutarch in his *Perikles* 12. The opposition chose to see it as a question of political morality and of taste. Perikles defended it on economic grounds. He desired, in peace as in war, an ἔμμισθος πόλις, a population in government service. For a community can accustom itself to a high or low standard of living, to this or that economic basis: only the standard or basis must (for economic health) be constant. It was not merely that Athens was now facing demobilization for the first time since before Salamis. Suppose she could make that effort, reabsorb her sailors, once more become a private city like another: what was to happen at the next emergency? Neither the economic miracle (the discovery of the Maroneia vein at Laureion) nor the moral miracle (the abandonment of the city) was to be looked for regularly. Those two miracles had made of Athens the Imperial City that Sparta could not be:

[1] *Amer. Hist. Rev.* 35, pp. 267 sqq.

[2] I imagine the crisis of 446 was staged when the Spartans went to Delphi, probably in 448: we find the confederates in West Boeotia next year (Thuc. I. 113. 2). For Tolmides is aware of it, and first takes a cleruchy to Euboea (Diod. XI. 88. 3: Andok. *Peace* 9) and then seeks to nip the bud of revolt in West Boeotia. He succeeds in precipitating events in that one area: the rest synchronises, according to plan, with the expiry of the Five Years' Truce. *[But see *A.T.L.* III. 178.]

to this destiny Perikles meant to hold. The Opposition, with narrower (perhaps intenser) vision, saw only what was being lost: the modest, proud, spontaneous aristocracy which trusted in God and valour to preserve the sweetness of their life. Let Persians or Semites organize and govern: the Greeks knew how to live.[1]

Perikles and his rival, then, were making for different worlds. If the building programme first crystallized their end, it is not likely to have been the only issue: I suggest later that the proximate cause of the ostracism was the question of Thouria. The rivalry had one profound and disastrous result: it created the Class War. The son of Melesias first clearly constated that the successes of the Demos were against his party's interest, that Perikles' difficulty was his opportunity. The tone of the Pamphlet on the *Constitution of Athens*, preserved among Xenophon's works, is the natural development of this: so too is that disease of *Stasis* (the Class War) so bitterly diagnosed by the historian Thucydides. The method which the son of Melesias invented is comparable to the modern Caucus, or the Whip system: the Opposition was instructed to vote, not on the merits of the case, but as it bore on the question of breaking Perikles; not by their private judgment, but as the party decreed. The party, a state within the state, sat as one body on the Pnyx: after the Revolution of 411 the Demos made these tactics, in the Boule at least, illegal.[2]

So much is familiar enough. I wish, however, to explore further the *milieu* of this statesman; especially his family connexions, which I believe to be both discoverable and important.

II. *Melesias.*

Melesias, to modern scholars, is nothing but the father of Thucydides. Thucydides in his turn had a son called Melesias after his grandfather, and he in his turn a son called Thucydides. The younger Melesias, and his son the younger Thucydides, are characters in Plato's *Laches*: we do not indeed learn much of them, except that Young Thucydides is completing his education, and

---

[1] Pindar's view: in its extremest form in Pythian VIII, to which I come soon.

[2] The system is described in Plut. *Perikles* 11. The Bouleutai, in 410 and thenceforth, have to swear to take their seats by lot; Philochoros *F. gr. H.* 328 F 140; the Class War, Thuc. III. 82–4. The judgment of Aristotle, 'Aθ. πολ. XXVIII. 5, is emphatic that Thucydides himself was not a mere class leader. He stands indeed half-way between Kimon and Kritias.

Melesias is regretting that he himself had not been educated with more care and less indulgence.

The date is somewhere about 420, after the battle of Delion (181*b*) and before Laches' death in 418: Thucydides II is of young undergraduate age.[1] Melesias II will have been the same about 450, Thucydides I about 480, Melesias I about 510. They can hardly have been much younger than this. Marriage under thirty (for a man) was not common.[2] Moreover, though some scholars regard Plato's dramatic dates with more scepticism than Prof. Taylor does, yet I cannot doubt that Lysimachos II and Melesias II, Aristeides II and Thucydides II, respectively, were in fact (as Plato represents them, *Laches* 179) more or less contemporaries: and I am already making Thucydides I considerably younger than Aristeides I, who was archon in 489 B.C.[3]

Thucydides then was older than Perikles: he was born about 500 B.C. or perhaps earlier. The adventurous thesis of M. Cavaignac (to which I come later), that he is maternal grandfather of his namesake the historian,[4] is suited by this date: and the bent old man in Aristophanes, *Acharnians* 703, may well, so far as the dates go, be our Thucydides.

The *Acharnians* was played in the spring of 425, when he would be seventy-five years old or more. The Choros say (I paraphrase briefly lines 703–710), 'Shall a bent old man like Thucydides wrestle with Kephisodemos and be ruined! It made me cry to see the old man so muddled; when he was the Thucydides we knew, he'd have thrown ten Euathloi.'[5] Euathlos was a notorious young accuser; Kephisodemos, it seems, another: from line 716 it appears that Alkibiades was of their gang. Many scholars[6] have noted that the wrestling metaphors (συμπλακέντα 704, κατεπάλαισε 710) were especially applied to our Thucydides; and since the point is cardinal, I assemble the instances.

Plutarch, *Perikles* 11. 1, says of him that 'wrestling with Perikles' (περὶ τὸ βῆμα τῷ Περικλεῖ συμπλεκόμενος) he soon brought things level. Ibid. 8. 5 (= *Moral.* 802*c*), King Archidamos of Sparta asked

---

[1] Μειράκιον, νεανίσκος, Plato, *Laches* 179 *b, c.*
[2] Solon, fr. 19 (Diehl, *Anth. Lyr.*), line 9.
[3] And therefore born about 520: not later certainly, nor, I think, much earlier.
[4] *RevPhil.* 1929, pp. 28 sqq.
[5] I have omitted the difficult line 709, which deserves further attention.
[6] Kirchner, *Prosop. Att.* 7268: van Leeuwen, *Acharnenses* (Leiden, 1901), p. 121: Rennie, *Acharnians* (London, 1909), pp. 197 sqq.

him whether he or Perikles were the better wrestler (παλαίει
βέλτιον), and he replied, 'Who can tell? When I throw him, he
argues that he never fell, and wins his point and persuades the
crowd.' Thucydides' wrestling is metaphorical: but his sons
wrestled literally. In Plato's *Meno* Sokrates maintains that statesmen cannot teach their sons statesmanship, though they teach
them (or have them taught) much else: thus Thucydides brought
up his two sons to be the finest wrestlers in Athens. 'Επαίδευσεν
τά τε ἄλλα εὖ καὶ ἐπάλαισαν κάλλιστα 'Αθηναίων · τὸν μὲν γὰρ Ξανθία
ἔδωκε τὸν δὲ Εὐδώρῳ (*Meno* 94c). They were the best wrestlers in
Athens and had the best masters.

Seeing we know so little of Thucydides altogether, this is a
striking accumulation, and I think justifies us in identifying the old
wrestler and broken great man of the *Acharnians* with Perikles'
rival. That is to say, the accumulation is not accidental but has a
reason.[1] What reason? No one, to my knowledge, has found or
even sought it; yet I believe it lies close enough to hand. *Thucydides'*
father, Melesias, was in his day the greatest wrestling master in Greece.
We know him from three Odes of Pindar, of which one, Olympian
VIII, belongs to 460 B.C.: the other two, Nemeans IV and VI,
cannot be so certainly dated, but they are both, I think, considerably earlier.[2] By 460 Melesias has a long career behind him and
thirty victories to his credit (Olympian VIII. 66). In Nemean V,
which is probably nearer 490 than 480, another Athenian[3] wrestling master, Menandros, is mentioned in terms which suggest
that Melesias has already started practice.[4]

Melesias is a rarish name: but I am convinced of the identification not so much by this rarity, as because the wrestling *motif*
is hereby perfectly explained. It is the family's heraldic symbol:
the Master's son wrestles in metaphor: his grandsons revert to
literal wrestling. I think no one who knows much of Pindar or
indeed of the structure of early fifth-century Greek society will

[1] 'Apparet cum patrem tum filios *luctae* fuisse peritissimos': van Leeuwen on Ar. *Ach.* 703 sqq.
[2] See Appendix C. I hope to deal elsewhere in detail with the chronology of all Pindar's Aeginetan Odes (Melesias' pupils are all Aeginetans).
[3] Melesias was an Athenian, sch. Nem. IV. 155a. [The suggestion in the *inscriptio* to O. VIII. (Drachm. pp. 236, line 2, 237, line 12), that he was Aeginetan, is evidently guesswork.]
[4] Line 49: χρὴ δ' ἀπ' 'Αθανᾶν τέκτον' ἀθληταῖσιν ἔμμεν, 'the masters all come from Athens.' This suggests to me that Pindar was especially interested in the other Athenian. i.e. that Melesias was already his personal friend.

doubt that poet, trainer, and athlete alike belong to the same class, the international aristocracy of Greece: so that Plato aptly says of Thucydides (*Meno* 94*d*), οἰκίας μεγάλης ἦν καὶ ἐδύνατο μέγα ἐν τῇ πόλει καὶ ἐν τοῖς ἄλλοις Ἕλλησιν.

Melesias was probably growing up, we saw, about 510 B.C.: so he was born not much after 530, and was not much under seventy when he trained his thirtieth victor in 460. He is an older contemporary of Pindar, five to ten years older. The three passages in which Pindar mentions him are all rather obscure, nor will I here try to expound them (see p. 248 infra). It is clear at least that the two men were friends; I should think indeed that Melesias was Pindar's closest Athenian friend. Trainer and praiser of athletes, especially Aeginetan athletes, they had certain fundamental tastes (and distastes) in common.

My thesis, therefore, brings Melesias' son, Thucydides, into the intimate circle of Pindar: and this is, to me, its most valuable and pregnant result.

M. Cavaignac has recently sought to establish the following *stemma* (*RevPhil.* 1929, 28): [I add the sons and grandson of Thucydides I]—

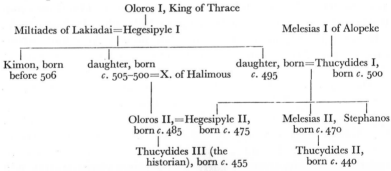

Oloros I, King of Thrace

Miltiades of Lakiadai=Hegesipyle I   Melesias I of Alopeke

Kimon, born   daughter, born   daughter, born=Thucydides I,
before 506   *c.* 505–500=X. of Halimous   *c.* 495   born *c.* 500

Oloros II,=Hegesipyle II,   Melesias II, Stephanos
born *c.* 485   born *c.* 475   born *c.* 470

Thucydides III (the   Thucydides II,
historian), born *c.* 455   born *c.* 440

It is a most ingenious piece of reasoning. For the historian's paternal ancestry, it agrees with Kirchner in the *Prosopographia Attica*, no. 7264, and, I think, is convincing. His maternal ancestry is more adventurous. It depends on the truth of Marcellinus' statement (*Vita*, § 2) that his mother was Hegesipyle. [The statement is commonly rejected, since (*a*) the name Hegesipyle may be 'simply taken' from the elder Oloros' daughter, (*b*) it is not easy to see what document or tradition would have preserved the name of the historian's mother. Neither objection is very cogent.] If true, it makes it probable that he descended on both sides from Miltiades' family: and since the statesman Thucydides is known to have married into Miltiades' family, it becomes exceedingly likely that the historian's mother was the issue of that marriage, and the historian's name thence derived.[1]

Aristotle says and Plutarch repeats that the statesman was κηδεστὴς Κίμωνος.[2] His wife, who bore him a son not much after 470 (Melesias II, p. 244 supra), can hardly be Kimon's daughter, so that κηδεστής must here mean *brother-in-law*. So too, I imagine, does γαμβρός in the well-informed scholiast on Aelius Aristeides (III. 446 Dind.).[3]

By 460, then, Thucydides had been for some years married to Kimon's sister.

III. *Pindar and the First Peloponnesian War.*

By 460 Kimon was ostracized, Ephialtes murdered, and Perikles (little over thirty years old) the first man in Athens. Athens had quarrelled with Sparta and the Spartan group, and was on the verge of that war whose early outcome was the conquest of Aegina, and the Thirty Years' Peace its shabby end. In this year, 460, Pindar wrote his last words of praise for any Athenian; their difficult and apologetic phrase may excuse the harshness of my version (O. VIII. 54–66).

> *If for Melesias I should lead back my song*
> *To the fame he has from young athletes,*
> 55 *Let no sharp stone of envy strike me.*
> *I will tell, too, of this joy he won*
> *Himself at Nemea,*
> *And that later he fought with men*
> *In the Fighting Match.*[4] (*Who knows for himself*

---

[1] The historian inherits, on his mother's side, *both* Miltiades' blood (if her name be Hegesipyle) *and* the statesman's name (if it be the statesman who brought the name Thucydides into Miltiades' family). The historian inherits the latter *on his mother's side*, since the statesman cannot be father of Oloros (their demes are different).

[2] *Ἀθ. πολ.* XXVIII. 2: Plut. *Perikles* 11, § 1.

[3] Γαμβρός most often means *son-in-law*, but by no means always: e.g. Herod. I. 73. Astyages is γαμβρός of Croesus, having married his sister Aryenis. It means someone who has married into the family: Croesus could not be called γαμβρός of Astyages.

[4] I.e. Melesias in his youth won the boys' wrestling and the men's pankration.

60 *Will more easily teach: not to learn first, is folly,*
   Since untried men have less weight to their minds.)
   But here is the Master, to say beyond others
   The right way for the man to go
   Who'ld get from the holy Games
   His heart's desire of glory.
65 *Now Alkimedon is his pride, and wins him*
   A thirtieth victory.

Here (especially 59–61) is Pindar's stickiest style: he is embarrassed. 'Il le loue dignement,' says Puech:[1] yet how different are these careful platitudes, from the high-spirited *argot* of the earlier mentions.[2]

The poem was sung at Aegina,[3] where it was difficult to praise any Athenian: the death-struggle between the two sea-powers was in sight.[4] Melesias was indeed an international figure: he had had many years' connexion with Aegina especially: his son was closely allied, by marriage and policy, with Kimon the leader of the pro-Peloponnesian party. The fall of Kimon, the breach with Sparta, the victory of democracy, were still provoking the angriest resentment in Athens,[5] and Melesias was moved by every tie to deplore what was now inevitable. Nevertheless, he was Athenian, and when the pull came, no proud Athenian, not Kimon himself, was going to favour the enemy: the few traitors were shamed into silence by the crisis of Tanagra.[6] And the exaltation of the following months, when Boeotia and Aegina were conquered, healed all divisions in Athens.

The First Peloponnesian War, which began so splendidly, ended in failure. Athens' star was crossed this time by Egypt: next time by Syracuse. I hold this double thwarting for sheer disaster: it means the failure of Athens, the failure of the fifth century, the failure of Greece as a world power. And the first

---

[1] Puech, *Olympiques*, p. 104.

[2] Nemean IV. 93: VI. 64. For the *argot*, see the editors *ad loca*; also Bury's *Nemean Odes*, Appendix A, notes 5 and 7, for some ingenious suggestions; δελφινίζω is interesting.

[3] Puech, *Olympiques*, pp. 101–2.

[4] Olympian VIII. 28–9, ὁ δ' ἐπαντέλλων χρόνος τοῦτο πράσσων μὴ κάμοι.

[5] The most vivid contemporary document is the *Eumenides* of Aeschylus, played in the spring of 458. See Livingstone, *The Problem of the Eumenides*, *J.H.S.* XLV. 1925, pp. 120 sqq.

[6] Thuc. I. 107. 4: Plut. *Kimon* 17. 4–9: *Perikles* 10. 1–5. The appearance of Kimon on the battlefield, and his recall after the battle, are flourishes of fourth-century rhetoric.

thwarting is so much the more tragic as Athens held more promise, material and spiritual, in 456 than forty years later. Yet it was hardly for Pindar to agree. He lived in that dying world which Athens meant to break and build again: which, instead, was broken and remained so.

In 455 (or 454) the armada in Egypt was destroyed. The *mirage orientale* lingered a few years more, but on Kimon's death in 450 Perikles resolved to abandon that shadowy quest and secure something substantial. With pealings of bells and dedications to Victory, peace with Persia was concluded at last.[1] Cyprus and Egypt and the sovranty of those waters were lost, and the *mirage* with them; the hope of the endless gold of Persia, or the endless corn of Egypt. After all, the Athenian League was extremely rich, and could with a little care control the corn-supply from the Black Sea. Perikles set about making sure of these things.

The next ten years, the 'forties, are the crisis of Perikles and Athens. The process on which Perikles now embarked is thus described by the Mytileneans: 'When we saw Athens drop the war with Persia and prepare slavery for her allies, we felt no longer safe' (Thuc. III. 10. 4). That is a hostile statement: but the words put in Perikles' own mouth in his last speech to the Athenians (Thuc. II. 63. 2) say in effect the same: 'Your Empire is now a Tyranny; and if you were wrong to take it, yet you dare not let it go.' It was this 'crisis of the 'forties' (it, and the means used to meet it) which turned the League into a Tyranny: the widespread cleruchies, the absolute disposal of the Tribute surplus, above all the suppression of the two major revolts, of Euboea and of Samos and Byzantion. Athens was left with a large treasure at her disposal and the North-East corn route absolutely secure (these, to console her for the Oriental *mirage*), and by the Thirty Years' Peace Sparta formally acknowledged her rights over the Empire, including the taking of Tribute.

Yet neither Perikles nor Athens was unharmed. Once the iron hand had been used, the velvet glove was never again convincing; and Athens was to enter the Second Peloponnesian War weaker, in the moral elements of power, than she did the First.[2] More-

[1] *I.G.* I². 24: Welther, *A.M.* XLVIII. 1923, pp. 190 sqq.; *Vom Nikepyrgos.* For the Ionic lettering of the Peace (Theopomp. fr. 154, Jacoby) cf. *I.G.* I². 16. *[For full discussion see pp. 205 ff.]

[2] Ionian hoplites fight at Tanagra: Perikles dares not use them in 431.

over, Athens had lost her land Empire. This is sometimes called a slight loss; and no doubt the 'sailor crowd', henceforward always more powerful, cared little. Their vision was hardly wider or acuter than the average Spartan's: for such, the dualism was good enough. But others (we may perhaps take Tolmides as their type) cared greatly: and for myself, I cannot see where else the salvation of Greece lay: I think we take too readily as inevitable the failure of fifth-century Greece: the steady decline from 450 onwards, the ultimate futile chaos. Sparta was always just too tough for Athens: incapable of leading Greece herself, she can prevent Athens doing so, and plays always for stalemate and no decision. Yet before Tolmides' death in 447, things were nearer decision than ever before or after, except perhaps on the morning of the battle of Delion. The disasters of 447 and 446 (cf. Thuc. IV. 21. 3) compelled Athens to accept a provisional solution, which Perikles (I think) never meant to be more than provisional,[1] the Sparta-Athens dualism. Unhappily this provisional solution became canonized: with every restatement of it (the most grotesque was in 369 B.C., Xen. *Hell.* VII. 1. 14) Greece sinks a little lower: it was especially dear to Persia.

Rome made a world-power of Italy: Athens (in spite of Salamis, the Eurymedon, Oinophyta) made none of Greece.

The First Peloponnesian War was Athens' first bid for the control of Greece, and it had failed. Perikles handled the crisis well, and Athens emerged with three useful gains, namely Naupaktos, Aegina, and Sparta's acknowledgment of her Empire. Enough to make the nucleus of a second attempt: but little to show for fifteen years of intermittent fighting, for the exaltation and sacrifices of the early 'fifties.

---

[1] Wilamowitz says of Perikles: Er hat sein Volk, das über Rhodos und Miletos gebot, allerdings zum Herrn auch über Sparta und Korinth machen wollen: die Herrschaft in Hellas war sein Programm 462: er hat es trotz den Zwischenstreichen der kimonischen Politik und trotz dem schweren Frieden von 445 nicht geändert (*Arist. und Athen* II. 98). It was harder after 445. The loss of the Land Empire meant beginning again: it meant also, that henceforth hoplites and farmers count little, sailors and cockneys much. This caused, if not all the harm the conservatives imagined, at least the discontent of valuable citizens. The fears of 457 (Thuc. I. 107. 4) are realised by the evacuation in 431 (Thuc. II. 14–16). For the good old days of the Land Empire, Μυρωνίδης ὅτ᾽ ἦρχεν ὁ γεννάδας, see Aristoph. *Ekkles.* 303 sqq.: lament over the hoplite, Plato, *Laws* 706c–707b: cf. Xen. *Hipparch.* 7 (the ἄλλη πόλις cares little about beating the Boeotians).

When the crisis was past, a certain psychological reaction set in, such as often follows when men have reached out after greatness and not attained it completely. It was the ἐπίβδα, the day after the feast, the morning headache:[1] in the wreck of hope, the once desired greatness seemed tawdry. Thucydides the son of Melesias caught at this moment of disillusion and nearly broke his rival: in the spring of 444, Perikles (for the last time in his life) failed to be elected Strategos.[2]

Here let me turn once more to Pindar, the friend of Melesias, the most articulate voice of that aristocratic order for which Thucydides stood. In 446, Pindar wrote the Eighth Pythian. He was an old man; and once more, after fourteen years, he is praising a boy wrestler from Aegina, Aristomenes son of Xenarkes. It seems to me one of his very greatest poems, passionate, rapt, serene. I have no space to quote the whole; and short of that, comment is to little purpose. It begins with the invocation of Peace, daughter of Right, and ends with the prayer for righteous Aegina's freedom. The heart of the poem is the αἴγλα διόσδοτος, the sunlight of God: it alone makes man more than a shadow in a dream: no man can command it, so that confident ambition is folly.

I believe Pindar's moral (not explicit nor very systematic) is this: *Leave Athens to the Gods: you violent young man, delight is a brittle thing, be careful.* But his mind is filled not so much with this moral as with the facts (as he saw them) of light and darkness. In righteous Aegina, in this Procession with Right standing beside it, with the Aiakidai close round and Apollo raining melody, here is Quietness, and shining light, and life sweet as honey. The light is crossed by death in war, by the peace-breakers (the Giants— and Athens), by the element of violence in Aristomenes himself, by the crooked twists of thought.[3]

In the circumstances of 446 there was no mistaking the reference to Athens. Pindar was not a statesman, he is seldom concerned to diagnose forces or prescribe action: poet and prophet, he discerns and proclaims the intimate or the eternal values. The Athenian Empire sought to build a confident structure by troubling other

---

[1] There was also something of a famine: sch. Ar. *Wasps*, 718, *I.G.* I². 31.

[2] Vide supra, p. 240.

[3] Μείλιχος αἰών, 97, and ἀμείλιχος κότος, 8–9. The detail of the passages referred to is: [Light] 21–2, 70–1, 22–3, 68, 1 sqq., 96–7, 97: [Darkness] 51–3, 6–17, 73–82, 94.

men's peace: a pretentious, contemptible thing, outside real joy, an offence to God.[1]

The effect of the poem was, I expect, tremendous: especially on those Athenians who were sensitive to that sort of opinion and disillusioned with greatness.[2] Those who knew pre-Persian Athens might remember the giant-slaying Athena, in that Gigantomachy pediment which the Persians threw down and our generation has recovered.[3] I think Pindar remembered it.

> *Kind-hearted Quiet, daughter of Right,*
> *You who make mightiest cities*
> *And hold the last keys of counsel and war:*
> *—Porphyrion did not know you*
> *When he aroused you too far!*

The new Parthenon was now going up, and made the city like a vain, extravagant woman who took men's money.—Or so the opposition said.

IV. *Perikles and the Athens-Sparta Dualism.*

With all this, Perikles waged war to the knife. Anticipating, let me quote words put in his mouth some fifteen years later, whose concentrated contempt I cannot translate (Thuc. II. 63).

ἧς [sc. the Empire] οὐδ' ἐκστῆναι ἔτι ὑμῖν ἔστιν, εἴ τις καὶ τόδε ἐν τῷ παρόντι δεδιὼς ἀπραγμοσύνη ἀνδραγαθίζεται· ὡς τυραννίδα γὰρ ἤδη ἔχετε αὐτήν, ἣν λαβεῖν μὲν ἄδικον δοκεῖ εἶναι ἀφεῖναι δὲ ἐπικίνδυνον. τάχιστ' ἄν τε πόλιν οἱ τοιοῦτοι ἑτέρους τε πείσαντες ἀπολέσειαν καὶ εἴ που

---

[1] See Appendix D.

[2] I do not know how Pindar's poems were published. It is quite possible that Thucydides was one of the house party at Aegina, or at least met members of it. The host (Aristomenes' father) was Xenarkes: a comparison of P. VIII. 70–1 with N. IV. 12 makes me suspect some play on the name, and that Xenarkes was perhaps there when Nemean IV was sung. If so, he and Melesias were fellow-guests. And Thucydides did not drop his Aeginetan friends: at least, I infer from the malicious tale in *Vita Anon. Thuc.* 7 (cf. Marcell. *Vita* 24) that he spent part of his ten years of ostracism with them. (The story cannot apply to the historian, since Aegina became a cleruchy in 431, Thuc. II. 27. There is difficulty indeed about the son of Melesias, if we accept the inevitable correction ἐκτὸς for εντος in the law of 480, 'Αθ. πολ. 22. 8: yet laws may be broken.)—For other possible connexions of Xenarkes and the πάτρα Μειδυλιδᾶν, see Xenarkes the great Akarnanian pankratiast (?) in Paus. VI. 2. § 1–2 (on which passage cf. Robert in *Hermes* 35. 176), and the name Meidylides current in Athens in the fifth and fourth centuries (*Prosop. Att.* 9731–9734).

[3] *Acropolis Museum Catalogue*, No. 631. Pindar was in youth passionately devoted to Athens and had lived there. The Panathenaia commemorated Athena's defeat of the Giant Asterios (Aristotle fr. 637): she is armed, with raised spear, on the Panathenaic amphoras (which Pindar liked, *Nem.* X. 35–6).

ἐπὶ σφῶν αὐτῶν αὐτόνομοι οἰκήσειαν· τὸ γὰρ ἄπραγμον οὐ σώζεται μὴ
μετὰ τοῦ δραστηρίου τεταγμένον, οὐδὲ ἐν ἀρχούσῃ πόλει ξυμφέρει, ἀλλ'
ἐν ὑπηκόῳ, ἀσφαλῶς δουλεύειν.[1]

I anticipate these words here, because they point sharply the
contrast to Pythian VIII. I think also they aim at the son of
Melesias. He had come back in 433, to form once again the
nucleus for any movement against Perikles: whom indeed he
survived, and found his successors, Alkibiades[2] and company,
more merciless (Aristoph. *Acharn.* 703 sqq., *immo* 679 sqq.).

Perikles meant the Sparta-Athens dualism to be provisional.
The years 445–431 were not, nor were meant to be, a millennium:
Athens had recoiled, to jump better. The Korkyra treaty of 433
was a stage in a process of whose earlier stages we are not wholly
ignorant: possibly Phormion's Akarnanian alliance (Thuc. II.
68. 8, cf. 9. 4), more certainly the treaties with Rhegion and
Leontinoi.[3] This relentless pressure westwards was aimed directly
at Korinth, indirectly at Sparta: Korinth was to be forced out of
the Spartan league (Thuc. I. 71. 4) or, if necessary, ruined.[4]

A recent study of Atheno-Korinthian relations (O'Neill, *Ancient
Corinth*, Baltimore, 1930) arrives at a contrary conclusion by
omitting these earlier stages. The treaties with Leontinoi and
Rhegion are assumed [impossibly: see note 3] to have been first
made in 433 (op. cit. p. 237): the alliance with Akarnania is
ignored altogether. [I believe indeed that the Akarnanian Treaty
is subsequent to the battle of Sybota: though prevailing opinion
at present puts it in the early 'thirties,[5] and it certainly made an

---

[1] 'You cannot drop the Empire now, not though loss of nerve in the crisis drive some
to make a virtue of inaction. For what you have now is like a tyranny, which (so it
seems) it is wrong to take but unsafe to let go. Men of the sort I mean quickly ruin
a city, if anyone listens to them, or if anywhere they are their own masters: since the
inactive cannot survive except by the support of the active: and the safety of submission
may do for a subject city, but not for a leading Power.'

[2] The way to ruin the Empire is 'quietism and aristocratic niceness': εἴ γε ἡσυχάζοιεν
πάντες ἢ φυλοκρινοῖεν οἷς χρεὼν βοηθεῖν, according to Alkibiades in 416 (Thuc. VI. 18.
2). That whole speech is the last and desperate plea against acquiescence in the dualism, which has now become almost canonised.

[3] *I.G.* I². 51 and 52. The treaties were renewed in 433–2, after the battle of Sybota:
that is the date of the existing prescripts. The texts of the treaties are about ten years
older (*I.G. ad loca*). [This can be verified on the stone easily: 51 is in the British
Museum.]

[4] Each successive Athenian attempt at domination involved more destruction:
though of course never anything comparable to Rome's record in Italy.

[5] See, e.g. Busolt, *G.G.* III. 2, p. 763, note 6, Beloch, *Att. Polit.* 299. Yet personally
I am convinced that Phormion made it in the spring of 432, and that the previous

implacable enemy of Ambrakia and was a direct check to Korinthian expansion.] Keulen, *De Pericle Pacificatore* (*Mnemosyne*, 1920,
pp. 239 sqq.), nourishes his thesis yet more scantily: he just affirms
that the Decree inviting first-fruits for Eleusis (*I.G.* I². 76) and
the Decree inviting delegates to a Congress at Athens (Plut.
Perikles 17) both belong to the years immediately following the
Peace of 445: so in these years Perikles was Peacemaker. But
in fact neither Decree belongs to those years, nor illustrates his
policy at that time. The Eleusis Decree is a very great deal later
(probably Peace of Nikias):[1] the Congress Decree belongs to 449,
448, or early 447.[2]

The Eleusis Decree is not Periklean: moreover, it is issued under
Delphic Sanction, and does not compare with the Congress Decree
in which Athens aims at a position like (or better than) Delphi's.
I therefore leave it out of account.

The Congress Decree aimed at making Athens the capital of
Greece. She would be the seat of an Amphiktyony greater than
Delphi's, and the naval executive for the whole Greek world.
When Sparta refused to bless this reorganization and extension of

---

seizure of Argos (Thuc. II. 68. 6) is parallel to the seizure of Anaktorion (I. 55. 1),
two attempts by Korinth, on the morrow of Sybota, to secure at least the Ambrakiot
Gulf. Thucydides' narrative of near-western events is *not* continuous after the battle
of Sybota; and Phormion had time for such action before he was sent to Poteidaia.
[I think the appearance of Poteidaia and Strepsa in the Quota List of 433-2 is decisive
against putting the events of Thuc. I. 59–62 before the spring of 432. See Jacoby,
Thukyd. und d. Vorgesch. d. Pelop. Krieges, in *Gött. Nachr.* 1928: Kolbe, *Ein Beitrag zur
Ekrlärung d. I. Buches in Thukyd. im Lichte d. Urkunden* (Stuttgart, 1930): Pohlenz in
Gött. gel. Anz. 1932, pp. 21–8: Keil in *PhW.* 1932, 513–18.]

[1] See Koerte in Noack's *Eleusis* (1927), p. 313; Dinsmoor, *Archons of Athens* (1932),
p. 340; Merritt, *Ath. Financ. Documents* (1932), p. 172.

[2] I.e. after peace with Persia, and before the Parthenon was begun. Keulen in
doubting the latter gravely misconceives the programme of the Congress: e.g. p. 240,
'ut communi sumptu et certa ratione tota Graecia artis operibus exornetur.' Perikles
said περὶ τῶν Ἑλληνικῶν ἱερῶν ἃ κατέπρησαν οἱ βάρβαροι: the Persians did not burn
temples all over Greece. The land they most ravaged was Attica: the temples to be
rebuilt are *imprimis* the Akropolis temples: and then perhaps Hera in Xypete (*A.J.A.*
1929, p. 400) and a few in the still intact Land Empire (Abai, Haliartos; Paus. X.
35. 2); which in the event were left ruined (Paus. l.c.): some too in Ionia (Isokr.
IV. 156): but none in Peloponnese or in any Korinthian sphere. Again, after the
Peace of 445 there was no question who should police the seas: Athens, out of the
tribute of her now acknowledged Empire! In fact, the two questions before the
Congress were: (1) Who should pay for the Parthenon? (2) Who should pay for the
Athenian fleet? Questions actual enough on the morrow of the Peace with Persia,
when the indemnity had been foregone and the tribute had become questionable
(cf. West, *Am. Hist. Rev.* 35, pp. 267 sqq.; and even if West's general thesis be denied,
there is the Quota List of 448–7 *of about one-third the normal length*; it is decisive as to the
questionableness of tribute payment). In 445 these questions were settled. *[See note
to p. 270.]

Athens' League, and staged instead the crisis of 446, Athens lost her chance of peaceful hegemony. The dualism had now to be accepted until it could be smashed. I have argued that the means she chose to smash it was Western expansion. I now come to my *crux*, the colony of Thouria in 444–3.

V. *Thouria*.

The events which culminated in the founding of Thouria[1] in 444–3,[2] in what had been Sybarite land, appear to have offered a heaven-sent opportunity to Athens to establish herself in Western Greece. It all came in the end to very little. After ten years, the colony disowned its Athenian parentage: after the Syracusan disaster, the Thourian ships joined the Peloponnesian fleet. The story is so parallel to that of Amphipolis, that some of this failure must be ascribed to a general wane of Athenian prestige. Yet Thouria's defection is more gradual (she takes half-hearted part in the siege of Syracuse, Thuc. VII. 57. 11), it was not precipitated by the genius of Brasidas, and it begins as early as 434–3, when Perikles was still powerful and Athens' prestige was on the whole sound.[3] The failure therefore must lie partly in the special circumstances.

Thouria, though founded by Athens, was a 'Panhellenic colony'. They sent heralds, Diodoros says, round the cities of

---

[1] *Thouria* is the Thucydidean form: his usage is probably constant, *Thouria* for the town (VI. 61. 7, 88. 9, VII. 33. 5, 6), *Thourias* for the land (VII. 35. 1), *Thourioi* for the people (VI. 61. 6, 104. 3). [Pappritz (see next note) curiously denies this in VII. 33: he says *Thouria* there means the land, and translates VII. 33. 5: 'they met (in the district) the anti-Athenians expelled (from the town)'. I think no one will doubt that the words really mean 'they found (on arrival at the town) that the anti-Athenians had just been expelled'.] On the coins, Thourioi (like Athenaioi, etc.) means the people. *Thourioi* for the town, ps.-Andok. IV. 12. The Roman form varies, but *Thurii* has good authority.

[2] The mid-century coins of Sybaris-Thouria reveal three stages: (1) Sybaris proper, (2) an Atticized Sybaris, (3) Thouria. This enables us to disentangle the confused narratives, and constate that Athens reinforced the Sybarites probably in 446–5; quarrelled with them; and sent out a fresh colony in 444–3 (ἐπὶ Πραξιτέλους, ps.-Plutarch 835d) led by the oracle-expert Lampon, who determined the new site of Thouria. Diodoros confuses the Sybaris and Thouria missions. It is not more than a slight anachronism of language, when Aristotle (*Pol.* 1303a) puts the quarrel with the Sybarites (Strab. VI. 1. 13, Diod. XII. 11. 1–2) ἐν Θουρίοις, *among the Thourians*. The detail is in Busolt, *G.G.* III. 1, pp. 518 sqq., who follows Pappritz, *Thurii* (Berlin, 1890: this dissertation, though unmethodical and full of misprints, is still most useful).

[3] The stream of discontented allies to Thouria (ps.-Andok. IV. 12) will hardly have begun by then. For the influence of Kleandridas, see Appendix E.

Peloponnese, offering a share in the colony to any who chose to take it (XII. 10. 4). It is usual to see in this a gesture of conciliation, a disavowal of specifically Athenian ambition in the West, a sop to Korinth. So O'Neill (*Ancient Corinth*, p. 196, etc.) conceives it, and takes the Korinthian action in not supporting the revolt of Samos in 440 as proof that Korinth had picked up the sop. I do not think this is wholly false, though Korinth does not appear to have accepted the invitation to a share in Thouria,[1] and though the treaties with Leontinoi and Rhegion are probably before 440 and cannot have seemed friendly. I think in 440 Korinth was trying to leave ill alone:[2] yet the gesture of Thouria may have helped in some degree. The problem to my mind is, Why did Athens make that gesture?

If the 'Panhellenism' of Thouria meant that Athens 'did not meditate any further aggrandisement' (O'Neill, p. 236), then it has little in common with the Congress Decree of *c.* 449: it is a new notion and needs to be accounted for. If on the other hand it (like the Congress Decree) aimed to make Athens the capital of Greece, the aim was very bad. Now Perikles might indeed aim badly: but it is pertinent to observe that 444–3 is the year when Perikles was out of office. *I submit that we see, in the execution of the Thouria project, the hand of his rival.*

Thucydides the son of Melesias was, like his father, a Panhellenic figure.[3] He was the true Panhellenist: and I think Perikles, in the Congress Decree, stole his thunder. To Perikles, Panhellenism was a thing which could be made to serve Athens: to Thucydides, it meant equality of all Greek states, the renouncement of Athenian domination. I think the Panhellenism of Thouria is of this second sort. That enterprise had begun as an imperial venture. Athens had accepted the Sybarites' invitation to help to refound their

---

[1] I judge from the Thourian tribe-names (Diod. XII. 11. 3): the Peloponnesians who took part come from Achaia, Arkadia, Elis. A possible share in the tribe *Doris* was hardly proportionate to Korinth's pretensions.

[2] Mr. O'Neill will excuse me if I quote a sentence of his (p. 193) and deliberately misdate it. 'Modern historians do not sufficiently bring out the helplessness of Corinth at this stage of her history.' He writes this of the later 'fifties: it is true, I believe, of 440 also. War with Athens could hardly fail to be disastrous to Korinth and she knew it. After Sybota, in 433, she was just desperate: the war ruined her more surely than Athens.

[3] Οὐκ ἦσαν αὐτῷ πλεῖστοι φίλοι Ἀθηναίων καὶ τῶν συμμάχων; . . . ἐδύνατο μέγα ἐν τῇ πόλει, καὶ ἐν τοῖς ἄλλοις Ἕλλησιν. Plato, *Meno*, 94d. This agrees well with the Panhellenism of Thouria: the tribes there were named Arkas, Achais, Eleia, Boiotia, Amphiktyonis, Doris, Ias, Athenais, Eubois, Nesiotis (Diod. XII. 11. 3).

town, and had soon ejected the Sybarites.[1] Lampon thereupon produced oracles that Athens should colonize the land, with a new city on a new site. But then the co-operation of Peloponnese was invited, and this ruined Thouria as an imperial venture. Athens seems to be speaking with two voices, and we know there were just now, in fact, fluctuations of power. Fortunately we are not left to mere conjecture, and it is worth while to assemble the facts.

Both the two founders[2] were Perikleans: Lampon the prophet prophesied Thucydides' defeat (Plut. *Per.* 6. 2), Xenokritos hastened it by a prosecution (*Vit. Anon. Thuc.* § 7). The latter passage, torn as it is from its original context,[3] yet preserves valuable information. We hear that Thucydides resisted Perikles in the law-courts, became προστάτης τοῦ δήμου, and was elected Strategos [this if true (see Appendix A) refers to the year 444–3]: but he soon lost his standing, since *after a visit to Sybaris he was prosecuted by Xenokritos and then ostracized for ten years.* For a detailed treatment of these alleged facts, I refer to Appendix A: but that Thucydides took more than a casual interest in the Thouria project seems beyond all doubt, and it appears that his action was resented by the Periklean founders.[4] I imagine he sent the heralds round Peloponnese.

For the dates, probably Lampon produced his oracles (see especially sch. Ar. *Clouds* 331) in the course of 444, and Thucydides sent the heralds to Peloponnese, etc., in the winter following. He was ostracized next spring, and I imagine the colonists set sail soon after.

The ostracism had decided the personal issue between the two statesmen: but as regards Thouria, it left Athens committed to a mongrel policy. We have here a first instance of what we meet too often later: a project conceived by imperialists, but its execution marred by men who dislike it. Later, this ruined the campaigns of Mantineia and Syracuse. The orthodox solution was

---

[1] Strabo, VI. 1. 13, speaks (at this stage already) of 'Athenians and other Hellenes' —i.e. Athenian allies.

[2] Lampon and Xenokritos: Diod. XII. 10. 3: Photius, s.v. Θουριομάντεις (see Appendix E).

[3] The *Anonymus* intends it for the historian: but I think it certain that his ultimate source meant it for the son of Melesias. See Appendix A.

[4] There was, naturally, little mutual confidence between the 'Periklean' founders and the 'Thucydidean' colonists whom they had to lead. See Diod. XII. 35. 1.

ostracism, and in 443 it was applied: too late for Thouria, but in time to prevent further inconsistency.[1] [Had it been applied as honestly in 417, after Mantineia, it might have saved the ruin in Sicily: for the failure to choose between Nikias and Alkibiades, one way or the other, was a main cause of that disaster.] The need for both Policy and Executive to be continuous is now recognized, and Perikles enjoys henceforth a virtual principate, expressed constitutionally by his special position amongst the Strategoi. His nine colleagues are chosen 'one from each tribe',[2] Perikles 'from all Athenians'.

We find this system first in 441–0,[3] when we have the full list of Strategoi for the year: again in 439 (whether 440–39 or 439–8) in a document I have recently published (*Cl.Ph.* XXVI, 309–313) regarding the conclusion of the Samian War. It evidently held for the rest of Perikles' life.[4]

VI. *The Return of Thucydides.*

'Εξοστρακίζεται ἔτη δέκα (*Vita Anon.* 7):[5] we may assume he returned in the spring of 433,[6] and I think he made himself felt.

It was in the course of that year that Perikles took the decisive step of accepting Korkyra's alliance and sending out a fleet with

---

[1] The treaties with Leontinoi and Rhegion may belong to that year, and mark the resumption of imperial ambition. The Quota-List for 443–2 [*A.T.L.* List 12] more certainly reflects Perikles' new security: the five *Provinces of the Empire* (Ionia, Hellespont, Thrace, Karia, Islands) appear for the first time; and in 443–2 and 442–1 the Hellenotamiai have an additional secretary, to cope with the new organization.
The Chairman of the Hellenotamiai in 443–2 (as we know from the same document) was the poet Sophokles: who is thus one of Perikles' right-hand men at the critical moment. In 441–0 he was elected Strategos—on the strength of his *Antigone*, we are told (Antigone ὑπόθεσις), which was thus produced in the spring of 441. The Athenian people saw statesmanship in the play, and deemed its author a proper man for the highest Executive. We should not forget this in reading it: for it is, as it were, the στάσιμον following the violent ἐπεισόδιον of the 'forties. [The picture of Sophokles as a munitions profiteer, in *A.J.Ph.* XLVII, 1926, pp. 358–60, seems to me malicious.]
[2] Nine, from ten tribes: which tribe is left out? I have given elsewhere (above, p. 115) my reasons for inferring from Plato, *Laws* 759 D, the following, viz.: the whole Demos elects one Strategos from *each* of the ten tribes; then he of the ten elected who has fewest votes is dropped.
[3] See the lists in Beloch, *G.G.*[2] II. 2, pp. 260 sqq. This full list is quoted in a scholium first published complete by Wilamowitz, *De Rhesi Scholiis*, p. 13. *[See now *F. gr. H.* 324 F 38.]
[4] He has a colleague from his own tribe in 433–2 and 432–1. We have no details between 439 and 433.
[5] Cf. sch. Ar. *Wasps* 947.
[6] Carcopino, in support of his untenable thesis that the *ostracisés* never stayed away their full ten years, proposes to identify him with the Thucydides in Thuc. I. 117. 2 (*Hist. de l'Ostrac. athén.* pp. 210 sqq.). This is quite groundless.

orders to fight, if necessary, against the Korinthians. The intransigence which Perikles showed from this moment to the declaration of war was ascribed by some to his personal embarrassments. Plutarch and Diodoros record a series of criminal trials directed against his dependents and intimates, Pheidias, Anaxagoras, Aspasia:[1] and Satyros[2] says that the prosecution of Anaxagoras was conducted by the son of Melesias. Perikles (I need not say) did not make war solely to put a stop to this nuisance, yet these tales, if true, are not irrelevant: though it is more likely that the prosecutions were meant to stop the war than *vice versa*.

But first, do the prosecutions belong in this context at all? Satyros[3] (Prof. Taylor observes) appears to imagine that Thucydides prosecuted Anaxagoras soon after 450, for he makes the charge not only impiety but Medism: a charge obsolete in 433, but not perhaps soon after 450 amongst those who disliked the Peace with Persia. I am not sure that this really indicates more than that Thucydides' politics in 433 were old-fashioned—that he had forgotten nothing and learnt nothing: and I cannot grant that Prof. Taylor has 'decided the point absolutely' that Anaxagoras was tried soon after 450:[4] still less (what Prof. Taylor does

---

[1] Plut. *Perikles* 32: Diod. XII. 39. 2.   [2] Quoted by Diog. Laert. II. 12.

[3] A considerable fragment of Satyros, dealing with Anaxagoras' influence on Euripides, has been found at Oxyrhynchos: *Ox. Pap.* IX. 1176. The statement quoted by Diogenes Laertius was probably parenthetic to the Life of Euripides.

[4] *On the Date of the Trial of Anaxagoras, Cl.Qu.* 1917, 81 sqq. It is agreed he lived from about 500 to soon after 430: the question at issue is where, in that space, his Athenian period comes. On this the ancient statements are contradictory (the materials in Diels, *Vorsokratiker*). Since therefore there has been definite error somewhere, it is unsafe to argue (as Prof. Taylor does constantly) from the *necessary implications* of our sources. It is not safe to say what Demetrios *meant* by the entry in his *Archontes* (*Cl.Qu.* p. 81). That Isokrates, XV. 235, 'states in so many words that Anaxagoras' connexion with Perikles went back to the early years of the latter' is untrue: what he does say applies to Damon equally, and it is notorious that Perikles was Damon's 'pupil' late in life, Plato, *Alkib.* I. 118c. No one suggests that Anaxagoras 'died almost as soon as he reached Lampsakos' (*Cl.Qu.* p. 85), for even if he was condemned in 433, he lived there five years: and the 'doxographers' tradition' that Archelaos 'succeeded Anaxagoras and was succeeded by Sokrates' (so in effect *Cl.Qu.* p. 86 top) is (*a*) not a safe inference from the statements (D. Laert. II. 16, Suidas Ἀρχέλαος) that he was pupil of Anaxagoras and teacher of Sokrates, and (Clement, *Strom.* I. 63) that Anaxagoras was succeeded by Archelaos, Sokrates' master: (*b*) sufficiently accounted for if Eusebios is right (*Prep. Ev.* X. 14, § 13) in saying that Archelaos took over the Lampsakos school, presumably in 427.

Prof. Taylor has been more decidedly answered by M. Derenne in *Les Procès d'Impiété* (Liége-Paris 1930). I did not know his book when I wrote this note: which I leave, since it puts the *negative* case as strongly as I am prepared to. The *positive* arguments for 433 are well marshalled by M. Derenne, pp. 34 sqq.: especially the anecdote in Plut. *Per.* 6, §§ 2–3, which presupposes that Anaxagoras was in Athens in the middle 'forties; Plato, *Cratylus* 409A, ὃ ἐκεῖνος νεωστὶ ἔλεγεν; and the likelihood of a

not, I think, contend) that there was no attack on the 'impiety' of Perikles' friends about the year 433. The Decree of Diopeithes, which launched that attack, is not to be moved from the date at which Plutarch puts it:[1] not, certainly, back to 450, for Diopeithes the χρησμολόγος is familiar in the War Comedians, and we find him still practising his trade in Sparta at the beginning of the next century (Xen. *Hell.* III. iii. 3). Indeed if Plutarch is wrong in dating Anaxagoras' trial about 433, his error is that he wrongly connects it with Diopeithes' Decree.[2] We have therefore to constate that the return of Thucydides coincides with an outbreak of malicious litigation.

Thucydides the historian, his namesake and possibly his grandson, says no word of this, nor anywhere anything of the son of Melesias' career. I think this is due, like many Thucydidean silences, to contempt: contempt for mere obstruction, for the ἀπράγμων who stands in the way of the δρᾶν τι βουλόμενος.[3] For the younger Thucydides was caught wholly by the glamour of Perikles: he thinks his Principate (gained over the elder Thucydides' body) most admirable:[4] to him, the pity was that Perikles' ideas were inherited by Alkibiades, a man bound to ruin them by the fatal resentments which he created.[5] He makes the Korinthians say of Athens[6] the same things in effect which Pindar had said in Pythian VIII: yet what Pindar saw with disdain, Thucydides' Korinthians see with admiring envy. Perikles made him drunk with the idea of power, nor to the end of his life did Thucydides forget it.

> *Fall'n Cherubs! to be weak is miserable,*
> *Doing or suffering.*

reference to Anaxagoras' trial and exile in Eurip. *Medea* 292–301 and 214–24 (spring of 431 B.C.).

[1] Plut. *Perikles* 32, περὶ τοῦτον τὸν χρόνον: sc. just before the beginning of the war.

[2] It is pretty certain that the trial of 'Ασπασία καὶ κύριος (i.e. Perikles: sch. Ar. *Knights* 969) cannot be so early in her career as *c.* 450. Her crime was ἀσεβεία, Athen. XIII. 589E: she apparently gave her girls the names of the Muses (sch. Hermog. in Walz, *Rhet. Gr.* VII. 165). Some at least of this information must come from the documents of the trial.

[3] II. 64. 3–4. Moreover, Thucydides, the scientist aiming at control and power, is in strong reaction against Pindar's acquiescent obscurantism which culminates in P. VIII. 73–7. Contrast, e.g. Th. I. 144. 4, V. 111. 3, VIII. 27: and see, for his intellectual affinities, Cochrane, *Thucydides and the Science of History* (Oxf. Univ. Press, 1929).

[4] II. 65. 9–10.   [5] VI. 15. 4: cf. 28. 2 and II. 65. 11.

[6] I. 70, 71: especially 70. 9, πεφυκέναι ἐπὶ τῷ μήτε αὐτοὺς ἔχειν ἡσυχίαν μήτε τοὺς ἄλλους ἀνθρώπους ἐᾶν.

APPENDIX A

Vita Anon. Thuc. §§ 6–7. (*See pp.* 239, *note* 1 *and* 257, *note* 3.)

The *Vita Anon. Thuc.* § 6 says that the historian πρὸ τῆς συγγραφῆς προέστη τῶν πραγμάτων 'before writing his history was a leading statesman'. This is manifestly untrue of the son of Oloros, who was little over thirty when he was exiled. (This follows from Marcellin. *Vita* 34, and much else: see *Prosop. Att.* 7267, and Schwartz, *Das Geschichtswerk des Th.*, p. 217.) The 'leading statesman' is, I have no doubt, the son of Melesias; and I imagine the information which follows in §§ 6–7 is from a 'Life' of him[1]: not a very good one, though we must not attribute all the stupidity of the *Anonymus* to his source. The alleged facts are:—

1. He defended Pyrilampes who had killed a boy in a love affair, and though Perikles prosecuted, won his case.
2. He was consequently elected Strategos and became προστάτης τοῦ δήμου (i.e. the dominant statesman in Athens: cf. ᾿Αθ. πολ. XXIII. 3, XXV. 1, etc.).
3. Owing to his pride and avarice, he soon lost this position: since
4. he went to Sybaris, and when he returned he was accused by Xenokritos [one of the founders of Thouria, Diod. XII. 10] and condemned; and later was ostracised.
5. He spent part of his ostracism at Aegina.

1. Pyrilampes, Plato's stepfather, was wounded at Delion in 424 (Plut. *Gen. Socr.* 581D): but since his son was by then a famous beauty (Plato, *Gorgias* 481e, 513b) and was a grown man before Eupolis died (Eup. in sch. Ar. *Wasps* 98), Pyrilampes' wild oats were probably sown well back in the 'forties. We may perhaps date the trial to c. 445, if its result was really the next stage, viz.:—

2. The brief political eclipse of Perikles. I question Thucydides' actual *strategia*, since the word Strategos is used inexactly by the late grammarians. The sentence clearly refers to the year 444–3.

3. [The taunt of avarice[2] betrays the democratic source: unless it be the general malice of Stesimbrotos of Thasos, ἐν τῷ ἐπιγραφομένῳ περὶ Θεμιστοκλέους καὶ Θουκυδίδου καὶ Περικλέους (Athen. XIII. 589D).]

4. His fall is connected with a visit to Sybaris[3] and a successful prosecution[4] by Xenokritos: this precedes the ostracism. [Sch. Ar.,

---

[1] Ultimately, perhaps, from Stesimbrotos (see Athen. 589D).

[2] Its recurrence in both the Sybaris and Aegina stories suggests that this whole narrative (§§ 6–7) hangs together and refers *en bloc* to the son of Melesias.

[3] He is perhaps a *Kataskopos* (cf. Thuc. IV. 27. 3): ἀποδημήσας does not necessarily imply a private visit, even in good Greek: e.g. Derkylidas is φιλαπόδημος because he likes foreign commands, Xen. *Hell.* IV. iii. 2.

[4] Συγχύσεως δικαστηρίου: otherwise unknown. Lipsius in his revision of Meier-Schoemann, *Att. Process*, withholds any opinion of its content: and in his *Att. Recht.*

Wasps 947, says the same: κατεδικάσθη εἶτα ἐξωστρακίσθη.] Since the execution of the Thouria project was (I have argued) a main preoccupation of his year of power, this seems entirely credible. Xenokritos then (like Lampon, see p. 257 supra) is a Periklean, and attacks him on the Thouria question. 'Sybaris' is correct: there is no 'Thouria' till Lampon has arrived there, identified the spot and chosen the name. Yet ostracism only touched the highest, and is not a usual sequel to a judicial condemnation: οὐ γὰρ τοιούτων εἵνεκ' ὄστραχ' ηὑρέθη.

5. For the likelihood, and the difficulty, of this story, see p. 252, note 2 supra. It recurs in Marcellinus § 24.

I would trust the details (the causation, sequence) of this narrative extremely little: but I think it refers beyond question to the son of Melesias. I add a short note on two other passages, where it is questionable which Thucydides is meant.

Timaios says the son of Oloros spent [some part of] his exile in Italy, and died and was buried there (ap. Marcellin. 25 and 33). Timaios had the reputation of an indefatigable bookworm with little judgment: it is likely he has got the wrong Thucydides, but there is no great reason to suppose it is the son of Melesias.

Finally, Ar. *Wasps* 946-7. The scholiast (whom I have quoted above) refers this to the prosecution by Xenokritos *c.* 444: but if it refers to the son of Melesias at all, it will be to the prosecution by Kephisodemos *c.* 426 (*Acharn.* 703 sqq.). However, the *historian* Thucydides had been exiled (and perhaps stood his trial) the year before the *Wasps* was played, so that it may be he.

Appendix B

Who Paid for the Parthenon? (*See page* 241.)

The enemies of Perikles (Plut. *Perikles* 12. 2) said, *Hellas* paid for the adornment of Athens: τοῖς εἰσφερομένοις ὑπ' αὐτῆς (sc. τῆς 'Ελλάδος) ἀναγκαίως πρὸς τὸν πόλεμον ἡμᾶς (sc. τοὺς 'Αθηναίους) τὴν πόλιν καταχρυσοῦντας καὶ καλλωπίζοντας 'The money contributed by Hellas perforce for the war' means, Tribute money.

The actual accounts[1] of the Parthenon, and the Chryselephantine Athena, give the λέμματα, the moneys received by the officers in charge of the works; and, as a rule, the first item is from last year's officers, the second (and sometimes third) from the Tamiai of the Goddess, the third or fourth from the Hellenotamiai. We never have sufficient

---

he leaves it unnoticed. It can hardly be bribery ('Αθ. πολ. XXVII. 5). Possibly a form of ἀπάτη, 'failure to substantiate,' cf. Dem. XX. 100, ἐάν τις ὑποσχόμενός τι τὸν δῆμον ἢ τὴν βουλὴν ἢ δικαστήριον ἐξαπατήσῃ.

[1] Parthenon, *I.G.* I². 339–353: Chryselephantine Statue, ibid. 354–362. The latter contains no moneys received from Hellenotamiai.

of the actual figures to determine the amounts of these receipts, but it is probable that the more substantial amounts stand first, and are from the Tamiai. And in the accounts of the Propylaia we get at last a description of the money paid by the Hellenotamiai (*I.G.* I². 364, lines 63–5, and 365, lines 17–19): το χσυμμαχικο φορο μνα απο ταλαντο: i.e. it is Athena's Quota of the Tribute, that sixtieth part which she received as her own.

If this were all the Tribute money spent on these works, Perikles' enemies were unfair in their accusations: nor could Athena's Quota be called 'money contributed for the war' (Plut. *Perikles* 12. 2). I think they spoke with better reason than that, and that the Tribute money spent on these works is to be sought in the moneys received from the Tamiai of the Goddess. There is (I think) little doubt that Mr. Stevenson[1] is right in supposing that the mass of surplus Tribute money was in the hands of these Tamiai throughout the 'forties, as we know it was in the 'thirties and later. However we estimate the amount of this surplus, it certainly formed a considerable proportion of the total treasure of these Tamiai: and justified those who said that the Parthenon, built out of that treasure, was built out of Tribute money.

Did they hold, then, that once Athena had taken charge of this Tribute surplus, she was bound to use none of her Treasure for her own temple and cult? I think not: the complaint is that she spends *so much*: like an extravagant woman's, the money runs through her fingers. The magnificence of the Parthenon was due to the fact that the Tamiai held that surplus.

It is just possible that we have the law whereby Perikles established this principle, that the surplus of Tribute be spent on the Akropolis buildings. The *Anonymus Argentinensis*,* lines 5 to 8, contains a law of Perikles': it is too fragmentary for certain restoration and I know none which is free from objection. It stands after a note on the beginnings of the Parthenon and before one on the Boule's shipbuilding duties. It is probably part of one or the other: which? Wilcken, *Hermes* XLII, 1907, pp. 390 sqq. thinks the latter, and refers the law to the legislation of 431 (Thuc. II. 24). His thesis will not stand, unless την πολιν be corrected to τον πολεμον.[2] Beloch's thesis (*G.G.*² II. 2. p. 328) that the law belongs to 450–49, and is preliminary to the building of the Parthenon, has never been presented in detail: I have suggested (*J.H.S.* LI, 1931, p. 85) that the new note on shipbuilding perhaps begins in line 8, οτι νο|[μοσ ην Αθηνησιν, etc. This leaves μετεχειν

---

[1] *J.H.S.* XLIV. 1924, pp. 5 sqq.

*[Most recently, Wade-Gery and Meritt, *Hesperia* xxvi (1957) 163 ff.]

[2] I do not think [αναλισκ]ειν εις την πολιν could mean 'spend on state purposes, i.e. the war'. See my note in *J.H.S.* LI, 1931, pp. 84 sq.

(before *ὅτι*) unexplained: could it perhaps introduce the new excerpt (='item')[1]? Or, since the Parthenon and shipbuilding notes are in fact out of sequence (being glosses on Dem. XXII. § 13 and § 8, respectively),[2] was it once a marginal adjustment (='this note should come after the next')?

If the law belonged to 450–49, it would tighten the chronology of these years. Winter 450–49, negotiations with Persia: early spring 449, the Congress Decree (Plut. *Perikles* 17): the present Decree is consequent on the failure of the Congress (see p. 254 supra) and gives the alternative answer to the question, How shall the temples be rebuilt? It must come before midsummer 449.

The Archon, Euthydemos, will do for either year: for though the Archon of 450–49 was Euthynos in fact, we know from Diodoros XII. 3 that his name in the Archon lists was at some stage corrupted to Euthydemos.

APPENDIX C

The Dates of Nemeans IV and VI. (See p. 245, note 2.)

The only sure indication of the date of Nemean VI is that Praxidamas, the victor's grandfather, was himself a victor in 544 B.C.[3] Put sixty-six years for the two generations, and deduct six, since Praxidamas' was a man's victory and his grandson's a boy's, and this brings us to (544−60) about 484 B.C. This cannot be held, of course, to within ten years either way: but (in spite of the sombreness of the first *strophe*) I get an impression of youthfulness (esp. 24–6, cf. P. X. 4, N. V. 14) and would put it before the Sicilian journey:[4] and Melesias is still as quick as a dolphin (64).

Nemean IV I would date, with more precision, to the Nemead of 477. The Aiakidai come in all Aeginetan odes: but here, the rapid succession, in lines 46–9, of Aegina, Cyprus, Salamis, the Euxine, and the long Thessalian development in the next lines, are due, I am confident, to the exploits of the Aeginetan fleet: which fought at Salamis in 480, at Cyprus and the Euxine[5] in 478, and had now sailed to Thessaly and would spend the winter of 477 at Pagasai.[6] I add a few

---

[1] This is against the custom of the excerptor.

[2] See Wilcken, l.c. p. 403.   [3] Line 15, Paus. VI. 18. 7.

[4] Lines 24–6 have echoes in Pyth. I. 43–5, Ol. II. 89: compare also line 57 with Ol. II. 32–3, and line 30 with Pyth. I. 94.

[5] See Pausanias' dedication, quoted Athenaeus XII. 50 (p. 536B).

[6] Plut. *Themistokles* 20. 1: for the date, Beloch, *G.G.*[2]. II. 1, p. 62, II. 2, p. 190: Busolt, *G.G.* III. 1, p. 83: Lehmann-Haupt, *Klio*, XVII, pp. 67–73: Heichelheim, *Zeitschr.f. Num.* XL (1930), pp. 17–22: Johnston, *Hermathena* XLVI (1931), pp. 106–111. Leotychidas was deposed in consequence of this campaign (Hdt. VI. 72): this must be after the poem of Timokreon quoted Plut. *Them.* 21. 4 was written (I think this invalidates the date given in *C.A.H.* V. 466). I believe the seven years between this deposition (476) and the 'accession of Archidamos' (469, see Plut. *Kimon*. 16. 4)

words on the difficult lines 33–43. They correspond, in general, to such lines as Isth. V. 51–3, VIII. 6 sqq.; the Theban poet feels his shame. The victor has won at Nemea (17) and Athens (19) and Thebes (19)—a town of friends, since Herakles and Telamon were partners (20–32). Then come the lines in question (33–43): then the Aiakidai (44 sqq.). The ἴνγξ which pulls at his heart (35), and the ἐπιβουλία which he bids his heart pull against (37), are the same or nearly the same: his own distress, his enemies' malice.

APPENDIX D

Ἡσυχία and ἀπραγμοσύνη. (See pp. 252, note 1, 253, note 1, etc.)

I have taken Pindar's Ἀσυχία in Pythian VIII to be that Peace which Athens, like Porphyrion, tries to destroy. Prof. Robertson, reviewing *The Pythian Odes of Pindar* (translated by Mr. Bowra and myself, Nonesuch Press, 1928), has questioned this, on the ground that ἀσυχία means rather 'internal concord', the opposite not of πόλεμος but of στάσις (*Cl. Rev.* XLII. 1928, p. 178). I think the distinction is unreal: ἀσυχία is a brightness of the spirit (μεγαλάνορος Ἡσυχίας τὸ φαιδρὸν φάος, frag. 109 Schr.) which is darkened equally by πόλεμος and στάσις. But how constantly it is opposed to 'restless external ambition' will be clear from the following instances:[1]

Hdt. I. 66: καὶ δή σφι οὐκέτι ἀπέχρα ἡσυχίην ἄγειν, ἀλλὰ καταφρο-νήσαντες Ἀρκάδων κρέσσονες εἶναι ἐχρηστηριάζοντο ἐν Δελφοῖσι ἐπὶ πάσῃ τῇ Ἀρκάδων χώρῃ.

Hell. Oxyr. *cap.* II, § 2: οἱ δ' ἐν ταῖς Ἀθήναις ἐπιθυμοῦντες ἀπαλλάξαι τοὺς Ἀθηναίους τῆς ἡσυχίας καὶ τῆς εἰρήνης καὶ προαγαγεῖν ἐπὶ τὸ πολεμεῖν καὶ πολυπραγμονεῖν.

Hdt. VII. 150. 3 [The Argives, wishing to keep out of the Persian War, demand a share in the High Command]: ἵνα ἐπὶ προφάσιος ἡσυχίην ἄγωσι.

Xen. *Hell.* VI. 1. 14 [Polydamas is urging the Spartans to fight Jason if they can fight in full force]: εἰ δὲ νεοδαμώδεις καὶ ἄνδρα ἰδιώτην οἴεσθε ἀρκέσειν, συμβουλεύω ἡσυχίαν ἄγειν.

Thuc. I. 124. 2: ἐκ πολέμου μὲν γὰρ εἰρήνη μᾶλλον βεβαιοῦται, ἀφ' ἡσυχίας δὲ μὴ πολεμῆσαι οὐκ ὁμοίως ἀκίνδυνον.

About twenty further instances could be quoted from Thucydides: see especially the sentence quoted above p. 260, note 6: the Athenians neither want ἡσυχία themselves nor allow it to others (I. 70. 9).

---

are probably due to Archidamos' minority, and are the real cause of the famous seven years' error in Diodoros' dates for the Eurypontid Kings (Meyer, *Forsch.* II. 504 sqq.).

[1] My instances are from the historians. We find the word in more *private* senses in, e.g. Lysias VII. 1, IX. 4, 'keeping oneself to oneself'.

66   ESSAYS IN GREEK HISTORY

Pindar says, *Hesychia* is daughter of *Dikê*, and so makes the quality connote 'keeping to your own'. 'Not keeping to your own' is ἀδικία, and this is how Periklean Athens doubtless appeared to him. But short of actual ἀδικία, the quality could be less contentiously named πολυπραγμοσύνη: a word commonly of blame which Athens accepted with pride. Πράσσειν σὺ πόλλ' εἴωθας ἥ τε σὴ πόλις: and Theseus answers τοιγὰρ πονοῦσα πολλὰ πόλλ' εὐδαιμονεῖ.[1] In an exhaustive study of the word ἀπραγμοσύνη and its cognates,[2] Nestle shows that this *fainéance* is, on the whole, unsympathetic to Thucydides the historian, and sympathetic to Plato: and he suggests that the attack on the ἀπράγμων in Thuc. II. 63 (which I believe is aimed at the son of Melesias, p. 253 supra) is aimed at Sokrates. I cannot believe that Sokrates in 430 was a figure of any political consequence: and I hope Nestle would accept my alternative. The pretensions of Athens were of course repugnant to the aristocratic tradition, and both Pindar and Plato are inevitably hostile: Pindar, because that tradition was still so good a thing: Plato, because those pretensions had, in fact, done such harm.

I may add that the leadership of the ἀπράγμονες, after the son of Melesias' death, devolved to some extent on Nikias:[3] cf. Thuc. V. 16. 1, and VI. 18. 6, ἡ Νικίου τῶν λόγων ἀπραγμοσύνη. Also the ἀπράγμων in Eupolis' *Marikas*, quoted Plut. *Nikias* 4. 6, is a devout Nikian: ὑμεῖς γάρ, ὦ φρενοβλαβεῖς, λάβοιτ' ἂν ἄνδρ' ἄριστον ἐν κακῷ τινι;

Appendix E

Kleandridas at Thouria. (*See pp.* 255, *note* 3 *and* 257, *note* 2.)

Photius Θουριομάντεις should, I think, be read as follows:—

Τοὺς περὶ Λάμπωνα· τὴν γὰρ εἰς Σύβαριν ἀποικίαν οἱ μὲν Λάμπωνι ἀνατιθέασιν οἱ δὲ Ξενοκρίτῳ οἱ δὲ τῷ Χαλκῷ (codd. Χαλκιδεῖ) Διονυσίῳ οἱ δὲ Κλεαρίδᾳ (codd. Καθάριοι) τῷ Λάκωνι οἱ δὲ Λυσίᾳ τῷ (codd. Πλησίππῳ) Ἀθηναίῳ.

Χαλκῷ: cf. Plut. *Nikias* 5. 3: *Prosop. Att.* 4084. Κλεαρίδᾳ: this form must, I think, lie behind Καθάριοι (ΛΕ in many hands was written as like ΛΘ as possible), as behind Κλέαρχον in Diodoros XIII. 106. 10. Λυσίᾳ: *Vit. X Orat.* 835*d*.—Neither Klea[nd]ridas nor Lysias was a 'Founder': the former was an exile, ἄπολις, and therefore unqualified. Kleandridas had been Ephor in 446 and exiled from Sparta after

---

[1] Eurip. *Suppl.* 576–7. Contrast the ironical opening of the *Herakleidai*. The case is formally argued both ways in the scene between Zethos and Amphion in the *Antiope*: see von Arnim's *Supplementum Euripideum*, pp. 11–15.

[2] *Philologus*, LXXXI, 1925, pp. 129 sqq.

[3] Aristotle regards Nikias as successor to the son of Melesias: Ἀθ. πολ. XXVIII. § 2–3: ibid. § 5.

the fiasco of that year, when the Spartan army retreated and left Perikles leisure to reduce Euboea.[1] We know nothing of how he came to Thouria (perhaps he went straight to Sybaris in 446), but once there he proved himself the most capable man in their frequent emergencies. He was Commander-in-Chief against the Lucanians and against Taras.[2] His service against Taras, a Spartan colony, makes it unlikely that he ever recovered his status at Sparta. [His son Gylippos was given the Syracuse venture, to 'make good', but was later disgraced himself.[3] The ex-Spartan Kleandridas,[4] who in the fourth century fought with Thebes against Sparta, is possibly a grandson.]

He is dead by 414, for when his son Gylippos arrived that year at Thouria (Thuc. VI. 104. 2), he 'revived in his own person[5] his father's title of citizen'. From this we may perhaps infer that Kleandridas had been no more than a πολίτης. However, he must have been an outstanding figure. The leading Athenians (e.g. Dionysios and Lampon) did not stay at Thouria, but went home: men of the first mark did not usually, unless they had been 'unfortunate', stay in a colony. This must have contributed to the decline of Attic prestige there.

APPENDIX F

*The Chronology of Plutarch's 'Perikles'; and Χεϱϱονεσῖται in the Quota Lists.**

I have read Weizsäcker's *Untersuchungen über Plutarchs biographische Technik*[6] (which throughout uses the *Perikles* as the basis of discussion) with so much pleasure and profit that I regret to find how frequently I have to reject his historical conclusions.

With his main thesis I agree. Plutarch is a moralist, who liked history because it is morality in action. He therefore approaches the material of history (which is, by its nature, in the time-dimension) with the moralist's classifying mind: whence comes what Weizsäcker calls his chronographisch-eidologische Polarität. Plutarch (that is to say) categorises incidents by their kind (*eidologisch*); and though his task of biography compels him to relate events in the time-dimension (*chrono-*

---

[1] Plut. *Perikles* 22. 3: Diod. XIII. 106. 10.
[2] Polyainos II. 10: Strabo VI. 1. 14.
[3] Plut. *Lysandros* 16–17: Diod. XIII. 106. 8–10: Suidas Ἔφοροι.
[4] Diod. XV. 54: codd. Λεανδριας.
[5] This is the force of the middle, ἀνανεωσάμενος, cf. ἀνανεώσασθαι, V. 43. 2: Gylippos 'revived' his dead father's citizenship exactly as Alkibiades meant to revive his dead grandfather's proxeny. The middle voice is decisive against translating 'he revived (in Thouria) the *Constitution* of Kleandridas': nor indeed was Gylippos in a position to make constitutional changes. The Thourians had had to admit him because they had under-estimated his fleet (Thuc. VI. 104. 3), but they refuse to help him (104. 2) and continue to help Nikias (VII. 57. 11, cf. 33. 6).
*[See note on p. 270.]   [6] *Problemata* Heft 2, Berlin 1931.

graphisch), the compulsion remains external and the homage to chronography is perfunctory. [And how misleading this perfunctory homage can be, Weizsäcker (p. 62) well illustrates from the *Kimon*, ch. 8: Kimon and his colleagues are appointed judges of tragedy in the spring of 468: Plutarch groups this (*eidologisch*) with other 'Ehrungen überhaupt', and attaches them all (perfunctory *chronographisch*) to the Skyros exploit. Weizsäcker well insists that this chronography is wrong: the incident of spring 468 has no connexion with Skyros, but is the result of the Eurymedon, which we may therefore date (at last!) to 469.]

But he proceeds to discriminate between 'universal eidologies' where the time-dimension is irrelevant, and 'period-eidologies' where it is not: and placing *Perikles* 19–20, § 2 in the latter category, to present to us the dilemma '*is the period* (to which the expeditions to the Gulf of Korinth, the Chersonese, the Pontos, *all* belong) *the early 'forties* (which Plutarch seems to imply) *or the late 'fifties* (which he might with difficulty be held to mean)?' In this dichotomy Weizsäcker, with a nice show of reluctance, decides for the latter: since Thucydides puts the expedition to the Gulf beyond question in the late 'fifties. He concludes, the cleruchy in the Chersonese was created in the late 'fifties.

In insisting, as against this, on Plutarch's pragmatische Uninteressiertheit, I should have thought I had Weizsäcker with me (see, e.g., his p. 38). I certainly deny cogency to all stages of this special argument (pp. 33–44 and Exkurs A).[1] The date (447 B.C.) which I have assumed in the narrative, and given in the Time-Table, for the cleruchy in the Chersonese, is based chiefly on the Quota Lists. The Χερρονεσῖται pay eighteen talents' Tribute in spring 447 (as in 453 and 451), and Tolmides is killed in the course of that year: *ergo* the cleruchy in the Chersonese was created not earlier than 447, that in Naxos (since Tolmides led it) not later: and Diodoros XI. 88 makes it probable they were created in the same year.[2] It is as near certain as may be that the Χερρονεσῖται could not have paid so high a Tribute after the cleruchy: when we next have their Tribute (in 441) it is one talent only (and so steadily in 440, 439, 434, 432), and a cleruchy (whose *terminus post quem* is spring 447) is the obvious explanation of so sensational a reduction.

Weizsäcker does not seriously attack the evidence of the Quota Lists,

---

[1] There is no chronological implication in the passage: and if there were, it would have little weight in a passage primarily 'eidological', by a man with little concern for [and therefore little grasp of] the time-dimension. The ingenious dilemma on pp. 88–9, as to Diodoros XI. 88 and 85, rests on the fallacy that Diodoros required some cogent reason before assigning an event to a given year. Since he had to assign every single event he mentions to some specific year, he could not afford to be so fastidious.

[2] Ἅμα δὲ τούτοις πραττομένοις Τολμίδης ὁ ἕτερος στρατηγός: the text then becomes obscure, but it appears that Diodoros' source (and not his own arbitrary framework) synchronized the two cleruchies.

but only Kirchhoff's and Busolt's presentation of it. Those scholars believed the reduction of Tribute was accompanied by an Apotaxis: Weizsäcker denies this. I need not broach this controversy, since it is irrelevant (indeed if Weizsäcker be right, he only strengthens the case against himself and makes the reduction more sensational). Instead, I recapitulate the relevant evidence. Χερρονεσιται pay eighteen talents in 454–3, 452–1, 448–7,[1] and one talent in 442–1, 441–0, 440–39, 435–4, 433–2. In the latter cases, Χερρονεσιται means inhabitants of *Agora*,[2] a town on the neck of the Peninsula between Kardia and Paktye. It was on this neck that the Athenian cleruchs were settled:[3] probably in Kardia and Paktye, since neither of these ever appears as paying Tribute later, even in the years for which we have the Hellespontine list complete. I imagine, then, that the eighteen talents had been paid by Kardia (ranking since Miltiades as the capital of the peninsula) on behalf of itself and Agora and Paktye, and probably on behalf of the rest of the Peninsula except Alopekonnesos.[4] After the cleruchy, the southern cities pay separately:[5] the natives remaining on the neck are represented by the one talent from Agora.

Our disagreements on the chronology of *Perikles* 12 (Weizsäcker, pp. 13–14) are on detail rather than principle. Two details. In § 1 ἀδοξεῖ and κακῶς ἀκούει do *not* reden von etwas bereits-sichtbarem: they refer to the transfer of the money. In § 5 he overlooks γάρ, which (I believe) makes the στρατεῖαι and Perikles' motion (φέρων εἰς τὸν δῆμον) the causes of, *ergo* antecedent to, the events of §§ 1–4.

TIME-TABLE

451. Kimon returns: five years' Truce.
450. Kimon in Cyprus: dies.
      Winter: ambassadors go to Sousa.
449. Early spring: Peace with Persia: [Euboea retained as tributary].
      Spring: invitations to Congress: Sparta refuses.

[1] In 450–49 they pay just under fourteen talents.
[2] Χερρονεσιται απ Αγορας in 441–0, 435–4, 433–2.
[3] See Plut. *Per.* 19, § 1. When Lysander sent them home after Aigospotamoi, the gap was felt: Xen. *Hell.* III. ii. 8–10.
[4] Alopekonnesos pays separately in 451–0 and 450–49. Is Πακτυ - - in 451–0, the town of Paktye, or rather Pakty[es] the ruler of the Ἰδυμες in Ionia? West and Merritt seem to imply the latter in their index to *S.E.G.* V.
[5] It is probable they all appeared from 447–6 onwards. The following names are extant: Limnai Elaious 447–6, Limnai Elaious Sestos 446–5, Elaious Sestos 445–4, Limnai Elaious Sestos Madytos 444–3 and 443–2. There is in each case ample room on the stone for the missing names. The aggregate for all the separate towns (including Alopekonnesos and Agora) is about two and a half talents: e.g. in 435–4.

[Early summer: Decree to spend Tribute on the Building Programme?]

448. Sacred War: [Crisis of 446 planned by Sparta].

448–7. Abnormally short Quota List (about one-third normal length).*

447. Cleruchies in Chersonnese and Naxos [?Euboea: Diod. XI. 88].

Parthenon begun: [first protests of Thucydides?].

Koroneia: loss of Boeotia.

446. Five years' Truce expires: Megara, Euboea, in revolt: Spartan invasion. Pindar's Pythian VIII.

445. Early spring: Thirty Years' Peace. [Acquittal of Pyrilampes.]

444. Thucydides' year of power: Perikles is not elected Strategos.

Project to colonize Thouria, modified in execution by Thucydides.

Thucydides visits Sybaris: prosecuted by Xenokritos.

443. Spring: Thucydides ostracized: Perikles elected Strategos paramount.

Early summer: the colonists sail to Thouria.

[Alliance with Leontinoi and Rhegion.]

Sophokles Hellenotamias: the five Provinces of the Empire.

433. Spring: Thucydides returns.

Decree of Diopeithes: prosecution of Aspasia [and Anaxagoras].

Korkyra alliance: Sybota in early September.

432. Alliance with Akarnania: later, Phormion goes to Poteidaia.

429. Perikles dies during his fifteenth consecutive Strategia.

426. Thucydides prosecuted by Kephisodemos.

*[Wade-Gery later discovered that *S.E.G.* V. 7, assigned to 448/7, was part of the list for 453/2 (see p. 228, with note 2, and *A.T.L.* III 278 ff., 289 ff.). There is thus no evidence for the tribute of the Chersonese between 450/49 and 447/6, but other arguments support the dating of the Cleruchy to 447.]

ADDITIONAL NOTE

I have not sought to compile a doxography of modern opinion on Athenian policy, but De Sanctis' essay *La pace di Nicia* (*RivFil.* 1927, pp. 31 sqq. republished in his *Problemi di Storia Antica*, Bari, 1932) should have been cited pp. 250 note 1 and 253 note 2. I am glad of the support of a writer of such force and authority, in regarding the Sparta-Athens dualism as politically futile.

KRITIAS AND HERODES

THE purpose of this paper is to put forward the hypothesis that the author of 'Herodes περὶ πολιτείας'[1] is Kritias. The speech bears Herodes' name: did Herodes' well-known interest in Kritias amount to the transcription of a whole speech? The speech concerns Thessalian affairs at approximately the time when Kritias was in Thessaly: is it exactly the time? and is the tone what we would expect Kritias' tone to be? We have much description of Kritias' prose style, and a few verbatim fragments: does the style of this speech correspond?

On these (or indeed other) lines, I hope the hypothesis may be further tested and either refuted or confirmed. The identification would add materially to our knowledge both of the speech and of Kritias: I hope the enquiry may at least help our understanding of them.

A. THE SUPERSCRIPTION

The speech is preserved for us in a manuscript of the thirteenth century now in the British Museum (Burneianus 95). The bulk of the manuscript (150 pages out of 170) is taken up with the speeches of Andokides, Isaios, Deinarchos, Antiphon, Lykourgos: as a sort of appendix it has a miscellany of pieces under the names Gorgias, Alkidamas, Lesbonax, and finally our speech, which is headed *ΗΡΩΔΟΥ ΠΕΡΙ ΠΟΛΙΤΕΙΑΣ*. Three fifteenth-century manuscripts (which appear to be simply copied from this, and henceforth I will disregard them) repeat this superscription.[2]

---

[1] The speech is published in Reiske's *Oratores Graeci*, vol. viii; Bekker's *Oratores Attici*, vol. iv (Oxford), vol. v (Berlin); Dobson's *Oratores Attici*, vol. iv (with Dobree's *Adversaria*, pp. xx–xxi); K. Müller's *Oratores Attici*, vol. ii: also separately by Hass, *De Herodis Attici oratione περὶ πολιτείας* (Leipzig, 1880); Drerup ['Ηρώδου] περὶ πολιτείας in *Studien z. Gesch. und Kult. d. Alt.* ii. 1 (Paderborn, 1908: the most serviceable text); Meyer, *Theopomps Hellenika*, pp. 201 ff. (Halle, 1909: his text is substantially a reprint of Drerup's with less apparatus). I refer to the works of Reiske, Dobree, Hass, Drerup, Meyer, by the author's name only: for the discussions by Beloch, Adcock, Knox, Morrison, see p. 275, n. 3.

[2] I take this account of the MSS., and all my knowledge of them, from Drerup, pp. 1–2 and his *apparatus*.

Herodes, to whom the speech is thus ascribed, is no doubt Herodes Atticus, the sophist of the second century A.D. We have no other works of his.

It was not till near the end of last century that this superscription was questioned. Beloch in 1897, in the first edition of his *Griechische Geschichte* ii, p. 132, note 2, stated his belief that the author was no sophist of Roman date but a contemporary of the events discussed, that is, of about 400 B.C.: Ed. Meyer in 1902 agreed (*GdA* v, pp. 56–8). Suspicion so far was confined to the author's name, *ΗΡΩΔΟΥ*: it was left to a defender of Herodes' authorship (see p. 279, n. 1) to doubt whether the speech's title, *ΠΕΡΙ ΠΟΛΙΤΕΙΑΣ*, was authentic. The speech is not about a form of government but about an issue of foreign policy: as announced in §§ 2–4, it is an issue of peace or war: in concrete terms it is whether Larisa should join Sparta in a war against Archelaos of Macedon. Forms of government are incidentally discussed in a short passage in §§ 30–1.[1] These 10 lines (out of over 200) are indeed both difficult and interesting, and no reader forgets them. When the speech's main issue, Sparta versus Archelaos, was dead (as it soon was), no doubt these 10 lines which boost a certain type of oligarchy retained their interest. Unless the superscription is irrelevant altogether, the words περὶ πολιτείας are no doubt somehow connected with the peculiar interest of this short passage.

The passage has of course no interest at all if it is the work of a Hadrianic sophist. If, as I believe, it is the work of Kritias, it is intensely interesting. Herodes Atticus was a devotee of Kritias and 'brought his works to the notice of the reading public':[2] sc. he either edited them, or perhaps wrote essays on them which may have involved extensive quotations—we may imagine something not quite so serious as Dionysios, not so childish as Athenaeus. I suggest, as one way of accounting for our superscription,

---

[1] Ἴσως ἄν τις εἴπῃ . . . πολιτεύεσθαι. This is a sub-section of the wider question discussed in §§ 28–31: 'what have we to apprehend from Sparta's known behaviour? She does not bully her neighbours: *someone may say that she demands oligarchy, but that is nothing to fear*: so her known behaviour gives no cause for apprehension.' This section is enclosed between its opening and closing sentences: ἐκ ποίων χρὴ παραδειγμάτων ὀρρωδεῖν; . . . παραδείγματα τοιαῦτα παρεχομένους ὀρρωδεῖν οὐκ εἰκός. Incidentally this puts the meaning of παραδείγματα in § 31 beyond question and makes it unlikely that παράδειγμα ibid. is used in another sense.

[2] Philostratos in his *Life of Herodes* (*vitae sophistarum*, ii. 1), § 14: τῷ δὲ Κριτίᾳ καὶ προσετετήκει καὶ παρήγαγεν αὐτὸν ἐς ἤδη Ἑλλήνων τέως ἀμελούμενον.

that Herodes included this speech in his work on Kritias in a sub-section of it to which he gave the title περὶ πολιτείας. The passage in question would justify his placing it under that head. There are of course other possibilities: Herodes may have written a treatise of his own *On Government* in which he quoted this speech (again in virtue of §§ 30–1). Some such hypothesis (we do not have to determine exactly which) would spare us the double absurdity of supposing that our speech was composed by Herodes[1] and that its own title was περὶ πολιτείας.

B. The Author

(a) Not Thrasymachos

In previous discussions the name most mentioned has been Thrasymachos. He has been suggested as the author or else (by those who hold to Herodes' authorship) as the source of information.[2]

We have two fragments of Thrasymachos' speeches.[3] First, a long passage from the opening of a speech which shows remarkable resemblances to the opening of ours. I will call it the 'longer fragment'. The title περὶ πολιτείας which has been attached to it in Diels and elsewhere has no authority and is unfortunate: while not so glaringly inapposite as the same title is to our speech, it is in no way apposite, and it is confusing (to say the least) that it should bear the title which our speech already bears. The second fragment, a hostile reference to Archelaos, is from a speech entitled ὑπὲρ Λαρισαίων. Both fragments are thus rather closely related to our speech: the longer fragment, while on a different subject, opens in a very similar manner; the other is on a very similar subject. Neither, however, is part of our speech: our writer (a) closely imitates the opening of a speech by Thrasymachos on a different topic, and (b) writes a speech on a topic on

---

[1] This seems 'absurd' to me. On the general problem of how to distinguish a real from a bogus speech I may refer to Meyer's excellent pages, 209–18. As a 'work of art' our speech is incredible. A sophistic speech puts all its cards on the table and is nothing if not explicit: our speech is maddeningly allusive: contrast e.g. the naïve ὑφ' ὑμῶν δ' ἐπὶ σοφίᾳ in Gorgias' *Palamedes* 16 with the gloss-provoking ᾧ γὰρ ἡμεῖς ἰσχύομεν of 'Herodes', § 32. Among examples of the transitional idiom of *c.* 400 B.C. I note the use of ξενικῷ πολέμῳ for 'foreign war in § 11, whereas ξένους in § 15 is 'mercenaries'.

[2] Nestle, *N. Jahrb.*, 1903, pp. 191 ff.; Köhler, *SB Berlin* xxvi, 1893, 504–7: id. ib. 1895, 457. Cf. Meyer, p. 213, n. 1, Diels-Kranz, *Vorsokratiker*[5], n. on 85 B 2.

[3] Diels-Kranz, *Vorsokratiker*[5], 85 B 1–2.

which Thrasymachos was also to write.[1] This is interesting, but not surprising if the two writers are contemporary: we see the same thing, e.g. in Pindar and Bakchylides, or Sophokles and Euripides. And though we have less to judge from, I believe that here too imitator and model are very different personalities.

The ὑπὲρ Λαρισαίων ought (to judge by its title) to plead for the Larisans before some other party. A priori one might expect the speaker, like the audience, to be non-Larisan: so e.g. Demosthenes speaks in Athens ὑπὲρ Μεγαλοπολιτῶν: but the use of the first person plural in our only fragment shows that the speaker is a Larisan, like the Plataean speaker of Isokrates' Πλαταικός. A Larisan, then, pleads his city's case: probably at Sparta. There are many such speeches in Thucydides and other historians. In our single fragment ('shall we submit to Archelaos?') an undesirable alternative policy is mooted; it is as if the Korkyran were to say at Athens (Thuc. 1. 36. 3) 'shall we hand our fleet to Korinth?', or the Athenian at Sparta (Herodotos, 9. 11. 1) 'shall we accept Mardonios' offer?' or the Korinthian at Sparta (Thuc. 1. 71. 4) 'shall we seek another hegemon?' or the Pharsalian Polydamas at Sparta (Xen. Hell. 6. 1. 13–14) 'shall I take Jason's terms?': the question is addressed to the foreign audience, and is either an appeal ad misericordiam or a threat. It seems to me most likely that the audience is Spartan[2] and that the situation is that caused by the Eclipse Battle:[3] Larisa is asking Sparta to protect her against Lykophron, otherwise she will have to come to terms with Archelaos.

Of what party in Larisa is the speaker of the ὑπὲρ Λαρισαίων? I imagine the Aleuad party, the party which had opposed the speaker of the 'Herodes' speech. They had declined in the earlier part of 404 to join a Spartan alliance against Archelaos; but the Eclipse Battle has turned them from choosers into beggars. Before that defeat no doubt they could have had support from Archelaos on good terms;[4] now Archelaos was grooming his own pretender, Hellanokrates (cf. Morrison, p. 70).

---

[1] I assume that Thrasymachos' longer fragment is earlier than our speech, whereas the ὑπὲρ Λαρισαίων is later. I discuss the date of the ὑπὲρ Λαρισαίων in my text: the occasion of the longer fragment is clearly before the fall of Athens (Athens is still at war, and is ridden by faction: sometime between 413 and 405).

[2] The fragment shows that the audience cannot be Kyros.

[3] See below, p. 276. (For a summary of the speech, and for the general situation, see Morrison, pp. 69 ff.)

[4] Such is clearly the thesis of the opponents of the 'Herodes' speaker.

Is the ὑπὲρ Λαρισαίων written for a real occasion? is it, like Lysias 34 (and, as I believe, the 'Herodes' speech), written by a professional writer for a speaker in a real debate? or is it, like Isokrates' *Plataikos* or *Archidamos* (and, I believe, Thrasymachos' own longer fragment), a piece of high-class journalism, topical and intended to influence opinion, but fictional in form? The latter, I imagine:[1] but whether or no, it appears that Sparta did not help Larisa, which turned accordingly not to Archelaos but to Kyros (Xen. *Anab.* i. 2. 1; cf. Morrison, p. 66, n. 3).

The 'Herodes' speech, then, cannot be the same as Thrasymachos' ὑπὲρ Λαρισαίων. It is complete, and does not contain the sentence which is quoted from Thrasymachos: it is *ad Larisaeos*, not *pro Larisaeis*. Those who contend that here is another speech by Thrasymachos on Larisan affairs have the burden of proof on them. There is no reason to think it is written on behalf of the same party: rather the contrary. Thrasymachos was certainly not the only sophist or speech-writer to whom Larisans could apply. There remains the longer fragment, and the remarkable echoes of it in the 'Herodes' speech: I submit that we see here one contemporary echoing another, not one writer repeating himself. Certain ideas are taken over, but the hard-bitten positivist tone of the 'Herodes' speech is as unlike the academic melancholy of Thrasymachos as can well be.[2]

(b) Perhaps Kritias?

Many dates have been proposed for the 'Herodes' speech:[3] this has been used as an argument by the supporters of Herodes'

---

[1] From a title and one sentence it is rash to conclude very much: but Thrasymachos, like Gorgias and Isokrates, was an educationist, a purveyor of ideas, a 'philosopher', whereas Lysias and Kritias were men of affairs.

[2] Meyer, p. 280, n. 2, remarks that Thrasymachos' longer fragment 'operates throughout exactly as our speech does with the notion of ἀνάγκη'. I speak below in Section E of our author's use of ἀνάγκη: he welcomes it (§ 2 ἀναγκαῖον καὶ προσῆκον, § 4 πρῶτον μὲν ὡς ἀγαθόν ἐστι . . . δεύτερον δ' ὡς ἀναγκαῖον), but Thrasymachos regards it as an evil (e.g. our sedition is the *necessary* result of folly). The difference appears to me fundamental. Even in the opening argument, so nearly identical (note ἐβουλόμην μέν in § 3 and in Thrasymachos), the tone has this essential difference: 'I think some God has had us in his especial care' our author says: Thrasymachos says 'since God has brought us to this pass'.

[3] Beloch *G.G.*[2] iii. 2. 16–18 (400/399), Costanzi, *Studi ital. d. filol. class.* vii. 137–59 (410/409), Drerup (404), Meyer (400/399), Morrison, *C.Q.* xxxvi. 68 ff. (404): Adcock and Knox in *Klio*, xiii. 249 ff., Münscher in Pauly-Wissowa, viii. 952–3 (art. 'Herodes'), Wilamowitz in *SB Berlin*, 1925, p. 335, n. 5, and others, regard it as a

authorship, who apparently forget how frequently this has happened to documents which are beyond all question contemporary and authentic.[1] Our science is not exact enough to prevent many wrong answers being offered; yet we may hope by repeated enquiry to eliminate them. It may perhaps now be taken as certain that the situation of the 'Herodes' speech is after the battle of Aigospotamoi. Athens is mentioned, but as a factor in the past, and in such a way as to show that she is wholly absent from the 'parallelogram of forces' of the present (§§ 19–20). On the other hand, it is before Archelaos' death in 399. Within these fairly narrow limits, the decisive question is, is it before or after the Eclipse Battle?—that is, the defeat of Larisa by Lykophron in September 404 (Xen. *Hell.* 2. 3. 4). *After*, according to Beloch and Meyer, who put it in 400/399; *before*, according to Drerup and Morrison, who therefore put it in 404. We owe this sharp formulation of the issue to Morrison (pp. 73–4), and I have little doubt he gives the right answer. The battle of the Eclipse involved great slaughter (Xen. l.c.), and Lykophron and Larisa were still at war in 395 (Diod. 14. 82. 5): after September 404 Lykophron was a factor which the speaker could not (as he does) simply ignore.[2]

Meyer's most positive argument against Drerup is the mention of Elis in § 28: 'this presupposes the war of 402–400, for not till then did Elis rejoin the Peloponnesian League' (p. 272). This mention of Elis is a famous stumbling-block: it is in fact Adcock's chief weapon[3] in his proof that the speech can have no real date.

product of Roman times (Herodes Atticus) whose dramatic date is incapable of being fixed. I refer to the works of Beloch, Morrison, Adcock, Knox, by the author's name only: for Drerup and Meyer, see p. 271, n. 1.

[1] See Morrison, p. 68, n. 3: 'This principle would prove that e.g. the Decrees of Callias and the Pirate Law on the Aemilius Paulus monument at Delphi were spurious'. I might add the ps.-Xenophon's Ἀθ. πολ., or will someone say that this too is by a Roman sophist? Adcock's *jeu d'esprit*, in which he undertakes to prove that no date *could* be right, is more reasonable: but he has nothing against 404 except the Eleans in § 28, for whom see pp. 276–8.

[2] Meyer, p. 268, n. 1, seeks to meet this by saying that there is no proof that Lykophron was yet supported by Sparta (as he certainly was in 395, Diod. l.c.). The hypothesis of Drerup and Morrison, that he was already on the Spartan side in 404, and that his attack was a consequence of our speaker's policy being rejected, seems to me good and economical; but it is not essential to their decisive argument viz. that his action (whatever its nature) could not simply be disregarded, as it is in e.g. § 13. [After the battle, if Lykophron were Sparta's ally, Larisa might still look to Sparta for protection, much as Finland has done to America: this was, I conceive, the plea of the ὑπὲρ Λαρισαίων (see above)—an unsuccessful plea.]

[3] Adcock puts the Elis War in 399–397, so that Archelaos is dead before Elis 'rejoins

I cannot quite accept Morrison's solution (p. 72, n. 4) that Elis
rejoined the Spartan alliance before 414: why in that case did
Elis provide no ships in 413 (Thuc. 8. 3. 2)? Nor do I much
believe in my own solution of twenty years back (*J.H.S.* xliv,
p. 61, n. 25) that 'Ηλείους is a corruption due to πλείους immediately above. But is perhaps the whole thing a mare's nest?
The speaker neither says nor (that I see) implies that Elis is in the
Spartan League. He is meeting the contention that Archelaos
is preferable to Sparta, and he says that propinquity to Sparta
(ἀστυγείτονας ὄντας) has not had as unpleasant results for Elis
as propinquity to Archelaos (τοιοῦτος ὢν πρόσοικος § 26) has had
in Larisa.[1] I do not mean to be unreasonably literal. Argos too
was on the borders of Laconia, as Elis and Arkadia were, and
Argos is not named; so that (unless we have the historical blunder
which Adcock supposes) it was in some way more reasonable
to name Elis than Argos. As I understand it, the speaker does
regard Sparta as having more pretensions in Elis than in Argos:
but he claims that these pretensions have not led her to behave
like Archelaos. Well: *after* the Sparta-Elis war, Elis was not much
evidence for Sparta's niceness as a neighbour: the main grievance
against Archelaos was that he had robbed Larisa of her *perioikis*
(§ 6); and that is just what Sparta did to Elis in 400. But *before*
that war, the speaker's language is not unnatural: although we
do not know Elis' exact status,[2] the Spartan demand that she

the League'. Cary in *C.A.H.* vi, p. 33, puts it in 401–399. Though it is indifferent to
my view of the 'Herodes' speech, I think Meyer's date for the war is right (sc. 402–400).

[1] In § 29 I suggest (p. 290) ὥσπερ οὖν ἐνθάδε Μακεδόνα, which reinforces this point:
but my argument does not depend upon this correction. The speaker is in either case
contrasting Sparta and Archelaos as neighbours, and the ὥσπερ clause either points
(ὥσπερ οὖν) or modifies (ὥσπερ οὐδ') the contrast.

[2] Diodoros, 14. 17. 5, says τὰς δαπάνας τοῦ πρὸς Ἀθηναίους πολέμου κατὰ τὸ ἐπιβάλλον
αὐτοῖς μέρος ἀπῄτουν: Elis is treated like an Athenian tributary who is in arrears [for
ἀπαιτεῖν see Meritt, Wade-Gery, and McGregor, *A.T.L.* I, pp. 212–13]. The contrast
with Thuc. 8. 3. 2 is interesting: Elis was clearly seeking to establish her claim to a
religious neutrality (Diod. l.c., perhaps preferable to Xen. *Hell.* 3. 2. 22), and it looks
as if Sparta did not insist on ships or service but did insist on payment: or is it (more
simply) that after Aigospotamoi Sparta felt stronger? Since our speech is certainly
after Aigospotamoi, our argument does not require us to choose between these alternatives: but the problem is interesting. It might be maintained that Sparta's demand in
402 was a bolt from the blue, and that up till then no one could have dreamt that
Elis was less independent than Argos: but this seems to me unlike Spartan diplomacy.
The spokesman of Elis in most of the negotiations was no doubt Hippias, who appears
to have dwelt on the early history of the two states (Plato, *Hippias mai.* 281 B, 285 D, E):
I have little doubt that the very remarkable theories about Elis' 'sacred neutrality'
which Ephoros recorded (*F. gr. Hist.* 70 F 115) are the theories advanced by Hippias

should pay her share of the cost of the war against Athens (Diod. 14. 17. 5) shows that Sparta did not recognize Elis to be as independent as Argos, and our speaker of course shares that view.

If the speech was written in 404 (a few months at least must have passed since Aigospotamoi), and before the September eclipse, then there is no reason of *date* why Kritias should not be the author. There are many considerations which suggest him: he was an oligarch of just that temper, he was in Thessaly at just that time, and the fact that he was Herodes' favourite author might have some bearing on the manuscript title ʽΗρώδου περὶ πολιτείας. The reasons he has never been suggested are perhaps two: first, a certain misapprehension of Kritias' political colour, before his last phase (see below); secondly, the style of our speech. Drerup gives a short characterization of Kritias' style, based on the extant fragments, and concludes that our speech is in most respects 'the exact opposite' (p. 66): it is, more positively, in 'a style like Gorgias' ' (p. 67).[1] I confess these determinations surprise me: in the next section I put my case for thinking it the sort of speech Kritias might have written for a Thessalian speaker.

Drerup believes (p. 113) that the speech was primarily intended for an Athenian public: it was a contribution to the discussions περὶ πολιτείας which preceded the establishment of the Thirty. Not primarily, I think: primarily it was for use by a real Larisan on a real occasion, as much as Lysias 34 was for use by a real Athenian on a similar occasion. The Thessalian context is not

---

in this context. The thesis is that Sparta had guaranteed the neutrality in old days. Whether (as I believe) these theories were embodied in Hippias' *Olympionikai* need not be discussed here: I have elsewhere urged that it was in the *Olympionikai* that the famous diskos was first published (p. 60 above, n. 4); it proved that Lykourgos of Sparta had joined in guaranteeing the Sacred Truce. Elis' claim to neutrality is perhaps further illustrated by *IvO* 30 (=*IGA* 105 *cum addendis*) εδοξεν Αλειοισι· | Διφιλον τον Αθαν[α|ι]ον Μελανοπο ηυιυν | προξενον και ευεργε|ταν τον Αλειον γραφο|αι· εν Ολυνπιαι εδοξεν. The Αλειοι take their decision in Olympia (the punctuation in ll. 1 and 6 is mine, but it seems necessary): they must surely be the Eleans. Diphilos, of a famous family of kaloi and strategoi, is no doubt Laches' brother, and no doubt the same man as the strategos who was stationed at Naupaktos in 413, Thuc. 7. 34. 3. I suspect his Elean proxeny is connected with that strategia. The arrival of Alkibiades' πλοῖον φορτηγικόν at Kyllene (Thuc. 6. 88. 9) is quite consistent with neutrality: the presence of Korinthian hoplites in Pheia (ibid. 7. 31. 1) is perhaps more of a borderline case, but cf. Ephoros l.c. τοὺς δι' αὐτῆς τῆς χώρας ἰόντας στρατοπέδῳ τὰ ὅπλα παραδόντας ἀπολαμβάνειν μετὰ τὴν ἐκ τῶν ὅρων ἔκβασιν.

[1] Philostratos says that Kritias could adapt Gorgias' manner to his own style by adding εὐγλωττία: *Epist.* 73 (see p. 285, n. 4). If I have rightly understood this phrase, it seems to me a very exact account of what we have here: the antithetical and sometimes purple style, but kept closer to natural speech.

'halbdunkel' (not, at least, in the sense that the hearer's attention is not closely invited to it): it is hard for us to grasp and define just because it is taken for granted as real and we are plunged *in medias res*. But secondarily, yes: no Athenian oligarch could read § 30 in the circumstances of 404 without taking to himself the words τοιαύτην γε, οἵαν ἡμεῖς εὐχόμενοι πολὺν χρόνον καὶ ποθοῦντες, ὀλίγον χρόνον ἰδόντες, ἀφῃρέθημεν: cf. Thuc. 8. 97. 2, Ar. 'Αθ. π. 34. 1. [The very next words, εἰ δὴ προσήκει ὀλιγαρχίας λέγειν ἐκείνας πρὸς τὰς ἐνθάδε, show that Athens is secondary, Larisa primary.] And the 'hoplite' basis of citizenship in § 31 recalls the Athenian oligarchic doctrine (e.g. Thuc. 8. 97. 1), and the juxtaposition of χρήμασι—σώμασι in § 4, though in a non-political context, recalls the same doctrine (Thuc. 8. 65. 3, etc.). It is these interesting marks of the writer's political prepossessions which account (I believe) for the curious superscription περὶ πολιτείας:[1] the question now is, were they Kritias' prepossessions?

Kritias' known activities in 411/410 are two: he was responsible for two motions, one recalling Alkibiades from exile, one pronouncing the dead Phrynichos guilty of treason: Plut. *Alc.* 33. 1, Lycurg. *in Leocr.* 113. He was thus not only an active member of the 5,000, but one of those who eagerly dissociated themselves from the specific policies of the 400.[2] In view of his later record (especially his endorsement, early in 403, of the Eetioneia policy: 'Αθ. π. 37. 1) it was easy to lose sight of this, and the ps.-Dem. in 58. 67 makes

---

[1] The acute Dobree wished to correct the title to περὶ πολέμου: *an e compendio* πο i.e. πολέμου? Münscher, in Pauly-Wissowa, viii, p. 952, speaks of 'den Titel περὶ πολιτείας der wohl nicht vom Verfasser stammt': he maintains Herodes' authorship, but does not explain how the superscription came to be right in one particular but wrong in the other.

[2] Alkibiades was recalled, presumably on Kritias' motion, immediately the 5,000 took power (Thuc. 8. 97. 3): the 400 had refused to recall him (8. 70. 1) and Alkibiades (now at Samos) had declared against the 400 and for the 5,000 (8. 86. 6). The fortress at Eetioneia was the answer of the 400 to the threats of Alkibiades from Samos (90. 1–3), and it was suspected that they meant not only to keep Alkibiades out but to let the Spartans in (90. 3). Phrynichos was one of the chief authors of this plan (90. 1) and went on the embassy to Sparta which was believed to be treasonable and for which Antiphon was later condemned to death by the 5,000: on his return Phrynichos was assassinated (92. 2), and the rioters demolished the Eetioneia fortress (92. 4–11): to take part in demolishing Eetioneia ranged you with the 5,000 and Alkibiades, against the 400 and Phrynichos (92. 11). It is thus certain that ps.-Demosthenes is wrong in calling Kritias a pro-Eetioneia man in 411: Eetoneia was, as Kritias recognized, the acid test, and in 411 he took one side, in 403 the other.—In view of Thuc. 8. 97. 3, there can be no doubt that Xenophon is wrong in saying that Alkibiades was still an exile in 407 (or 408?) just before his return to Athens (*Hell.* 1. 4. 10). Kritias' motion for Alkibiades, like his motion against Phrynichos, clearly belongs to 411.

him the author of the Eetioneia policy in 411. Inevitably: to a fourth-century orator, Kritias was a conventional villain (Dem. 24. 90, Aeschin. 1. 173), and few cared to remember the 'respectable' Kritias of 411.[1] But his contemporary Xenophon is concerned to account for the change: it was his sojourn in Thessaly which spoiled the good of his earlier association with Sokrates (*Mem.* 1. 2. 24). Xenophon's explanation is moralistic and naïve and *ex parte*. It was the opportunity which was new: Kritias was ruined by the temptation to make party capital out of his country's defeat. The process may have begun while he was in Thessaly. Our speech shows whole-hearted Lakonism and a thirst for revenge—disquieting symptoms:[2] but its constitutional doctrine is consonant with Kritias' past and his immediate future, sc. his period of collaboration with Theramenes (Xen. *Hell.* 2. 3. 15).

What was Kritias doing in Thessaly? In exile certainly: he had quarrelled with Kleophon (Ar. *Rhet.* 1. 15. 13), and probably shared Alkibiades' fall (see p. 292, n. 1). Xenophon says he associated with lawbreakers (ἀνομίᾳ χρωμένοις, *Mem.* l.c.) and lets his enemy Theramenes say (*Hell.* 2. 3. 36) that he 'worked for democracy with Prometheus[3] and armed the Penestai against their masters'. Seeing what confidence Sparta reposed in him in 404, we must suspect that this 'democracy' was not extreme: he evidently helped an agrarian revolt against the Aleuads and their like,[4] and we may reasonably associate this with the attempted Larisan 'constitution' at which Gorgias (the Aleuads' friend) mocks,[5] and to which our speaker looks back fondly: a hoplite

---

[1] 'If you want to praise Kritias,' says Aristotle (*Rhet.* 3. 16, 1416ᵇ28), 'you have to tell the whole story, for not many people know it.' Was his memory kept green in the Academy?

[2] It seems to me that our speaker has to make out the case (sc. cannot take it for granted) that the sort of constitution which Sparta imposes is the same as the sort he has himself worked for. If Kritias is the author, and the speaker is one of his confederates [is he Prometheus? see next note], this may suggest that Kritias had at least not been a recognized Spartan agent in the years when Athens was still fighting Sparta. But this indication is far from certain: Kritias may have worked openly for Sparta and against Athens: and if he did, it would certainly have been demoralizing for a man of his temper (cf. his judgment on Kimon, *Vorsokr.*⁵ 88 B 52=Plut. *Cim.* 16. 9).

[3] Is Prometheus our speaker? is this in fact a reference to the known circumstances of the περὶ πολιτείας?

[4] Morrison, p. 65 f.

[5] Aristotle reports the jest, *Pol.* 3. 2, 1275ᵇ27, and adds τὰ μὲν ἴσως ἀπορῶν τὰ δ' εἰρωνευόμενος 'perhaps in some degree he really didn't know the answer, in some degree was pretending not to'. See Morrison, p. 71. I agree with Morrison that he is mocking the arbitrary choosiness of the demiourgoi, whose function seems to be more or less exactly that of the katalogeis of 411 at Athens: are the politophylakes of Ar.

franchise.[1] From our speaker's words (ἀφῃρέθημεν, § 30) as well as from Theramenes' (ὧν μὲν οὖν οὗτος ἐκεῖ ἔπραττε μηδὲν ἐνθάδε γένοιτο) it seems not to have gone smoothly[2] Compared with the feudal serfdom of the Aleuads and the Menons (e.g. Dem. 23. 199) such a hoplite franchise could well be called 'democracy': our speaker himself asks 'if oligarchy be the name for it, compared with what we have here' (§ 30). Kritias in his *Constitution of Thessaly* blamed Thessaly's Medism on the extravagance of the Aleuads (*Vorsokrat.*[5] 88 B 31 = Athen. 663 a): our speaker in the same vein asks 'shall my opponents a second time involve Thessaly in disgrace?' (§ 22, 36).

Kritias, then, in Athens in 411 and in Thessaly later (from before Arginousai till after the surrender of Athens)[3] was an upholder of 'hoplite' oligarchy, of the sort which our speaker says that Sparta approves. This was the man who could start, in 404, by collaborat-

---

Pol. 1305^b28 perhaps the successors of the demiourgoi? if so, the passage is illustrated by ps.-Lysias, 20. 13, cf. 2. [In Larisa, as in oligarchic Boeotia and in the Attic experiments, there was thus created (by exclusion) a new category, neither *politai* nor *xenoi*, whom I have proposed to call *hypomeiones*: cf. § 31 of our speech.] Gorgias (I am assuming) not only taught the Aleuads and their friends, but shared their political outlook, sc. their attitude both to the Larisan *bourgeoisie* and to Archelaos. The remarkable and serious attack on Archelaos in Plato's *Gorgias* is surely no casual irrelevance: is it not due to Gorgias having identified himself with Archelaos' friends? ὡς καλῶς οἶδε Πλάτων ἰαμβίζειν. I feel confirmed in this by the fact that Antisthenes' *Archelaos* contains an attack on Gorgias (Athen. 220 d). Antisthenes, a cruder moralist than Plato, will surely have harped on Archelaos' enormities. Gorgias no doubt maintained they were irrelevant, and Polos' unskilful argument will be a travesty of this. [I suspect this is the plagiarism of Antisthenes of which Plato was accused by Theopompos (*F. gr. Hist.* 115 F 259 = Athen. 508 d): of minimal importance in the dialogue to us, it is just what Theopompos would notice.]

[1] Philostratos' words (in his *Life of Kritias* [*vitae sophistarum*, i. 16], § 2 = *Vorsokr.*[5] 88 A 1), βαρυτέρας ἐποίει τὰς ὀλιγαρχίας, can hardly be taken as a serious corrective of Xenophon's Theramenes. Philostratos is indeed combating Xenophon's thesis in *Mem.* 1. 2. 24 that Kritias was corrupted by the Thessalians, and he professes to base himself on what Kritias *said* in Thessaly: διαλεγόμενος τοῖς ἐκεῖ δυνατοῖς καὶ καθαπτόμενος μὲν δημοκρατίας ἁπάσης διαβάλλων δ' Ἀθηναίους ὡς πλεῖστα ἀνθρώπων ἁμαρτάνοντας. Has Philostratos been reading Kritias' Thessalian speeches (e.g. the 'Herodes' speech)? I doubt it. Just above he has said that Kritias βουλεύματος . . . ξυνελάμβανεν ὡς μηλόβοτος ἡ Ἀττικὴ ἀποφανθείη [cf. Isokr. 14. 31]: this seems to me an obvious lie based on school declamations [cf. the subject for debate in Hermogenes, pp. 33–4 Rabe: 'Kritias has taken sanctuary with the Tyrannicides: shall he be dragged away?'] and I suspect a similar origin for these conversations with Thessalian magnates. I think little was known of Kritias' Thessalian visit beyond Xenophon's two passages (*Hell.* 2. 3. 36; *Mem.* 1. 2. 24): he was there at the time of Arginousai (*Hell.* l.c.) though he had been in Athens shortly before (see p. 292, note 1, below), the bulk of his exile was spent in Thessaly (*Mem.* l.c.), he probably came back when Athens surrendered (Lysias 12. 43 f.; Andokides 1. 80).

[2] Aristotle, *Pol.* 1305^b28, may refer to the duration of this hoplite constitution: see p. 280, n. 5, above.

[3] Cf. n. 1 above.

ing with Theramenes: what later drove him to his 'tyranny' and his death (revenge? fear?) is another story. This speech, which is before the eclipse of September 404, is well before his quarrel with Theramenes: I imagine it is written between the surrender of Athens in April (perhaps indeed a little before the surrender) and the establishment of the Thirty in September 404, and that Kritias, at the time of composition, either was in Thessaly or had left it very recently.[1]

It survived, not because everything Kritias wrote survived, still less because a political speech by a Larisan would survive; but because of the great interest of §§ 30–1 in the mouth of a man like Kritias. To contemporaries these lines touched on the vital issues at Athens; to Herodes perhaps they threw light on Kritias' constitutional theory. The first may have ensured its survival at the start: the second is perhaps responsible for its survival till today.

C. STYLE AND LANGUAGE

Drerup after careful examination (pp. 36–65) concludes (p. 66) that the language and style of our speech are not Kritias'.[2] For comparison we have, first, the prose fragments of Kritias, and secondly, what the ancient critics say of his style. Neither is very helpful. Descriptions of a writer's style may be recognized as just if we have his works: when we have not, they may easily be misunderstood. The actual prose fragments are few, and those which can reasonably be thought to be quoted verbatim are far fewer still:[3] none of all of them is from a speech. Such as they are, they suggest two discrepancies: our speech uses -σσ- (not -ττ-), and avoids hiatus, the fragments do neither.

---

[1] Cf. p. 281, n. 1. He would presumably not cut his Thessalian connexions at once. —I follow the chronology set out by G. Colin, *Xénophon historien d'après le livre II des Helléniques*, 1933 (*Annales de l'Est*), pp. 112–16. Surrender of Athens, April; the Thirty take office, September; Thrasyboulos in Phyle, December 404: death of Theramenes, February; of Kritias, May 403.

[2] He is rebutting the thesis [not that it is by Kritias himself, but] that it is by Herodes; who (he says) would imitate Kritias, whereas this speech does not. More positively he says (p. 67) it is in Gorgias' style (though not of course by Gorgias). I note that Philostratos says that Kritias, like Thucydides, shows Gorgias' influence: they both adapted his grand manner to their own style, Kritias by adding εὐγλωττία. See p. 285, n. 4; p. 289, n. 4; p. 278, n. 1.

[3] Kritias' fragments are in Diels-Kranz, *Vorsokr.*⁵ 88: the prose fragments are 88 B 31–73. Of these, 53–73 are single words: only 31–6, 39–40, 42, 44 contain sentences *verbatim*.

The avoidance of hiatus (Drerup, pp. 55-7) is much stricter than in any extant passage of Gorgias: stricter even than Thrasymachos: comparable with the earliest Isokrates.[1] Few as Kritias' verbatim fragments are, they suffice to show he did not mind hiatus in his philosophic or historical writings (e.g. *Vorsokr.*[5] 88 B 33, 42). It may of course be that Kritias avoided hiatus in his speeches, though not in his other prose works: I am more inclined to think it is special to this speech (we have to remember that if it is by Kritias it must be one of the very latest of his works). Avoidance of hiatus, a feature of non-dactylic verse, came into prose with Gorgias and (still more) with the *prosa numerosa* of Thrasymachos: of the Attic orators of the first half of the fourth century Isokrates and Isaios practise it. Our speech (which is thus a very early example) is for export, and I suggest this early avoidance is a symptom of the taste of the export market.[2] The use of -σσ- may conceivably be the same: but the evidence here is far less satisfactory. The assertion that Kritias' prose fragments show -ττ- regularly (Drerup, p. 66) rests in fact on one single example, sc. Θετταλικός in *Vorsokr.*[5] 88 B 33=Athen. 463 E: 88 B 31 and 37, which are commonly cited in support, are not strictly verbatim (*nedum* 41 *a*): and anyway all are from the single work, the *Politeiai*. Our speech has -σσ- usually, -ττ- once (§ 3). Since late writers (or at least their MSS.) are very indifferent to this matter of spelling,[3] it is uncertain whether this apparent discrepancy is a

---

[1] Gorgias' fragments are in *Vorsokr.*[5] 82 B: Thrasymachos' ibid. 85 B. Of Isokrates, 18 gives perhaps the best comparison; it is still fifth century: 21 is notoriously exceptional, admitting hiatus freely.

[2] Plato had been close to Kritias at the time our speech was written (*Ep.* 7. 324 D), so that perhaps his words in *Meno* 70 A–B, 76 C–E, are specially in point, on Thessalian literary taste and how you had to cater for it. [I agree with Burnet that Kritias in the *Timaeus* and *Critias* is our K.'s grandfather.] See too Philostratos Epist. 73: παρ᾽ οἷς τὸ ῥητορεύειν γοργιάζειν ἐπωνυμίαν ἔσχεν: on Kritias' adaptation of Gorgias' style see p. 285, n. 4. We do not indeed know that Gorgias ever avoided hiatus as strictly as our speech does. He tolerates it in the *Epitaphios*, an early work: the *Palamedes*, where he tends to avoid it, is presumably a little later than Euripides' *Palamedes* of 415 (Ael. *VH* 2. 8): so that avoidance may well have been the modern practice in Thessaly by 404; the influence of Thrasymachos may have helped (cf. *Vorsokr.*[5] 85 B 2).

[3] Some papyri of Thucydides have -ττ-: on -σσ- in Alkidamas see Luria, *Riv. d. Fil.* liv, 1926, p. 220, n. 1. Athenaeus 151 *d* quotes θαρσαλέως from Xenophon *Anab.* 7. 3. 29. Dionysios appears (for his own part) to write γλῶσσα (*Ant. R.* 1. 66. 1, 67. 3) γλῶττα (ibid. 1. 68. 1; 2. 7. 3–4) θάλασσα (1. 2. 3–4, 3. 3, 9. 1, 10. 1) θάλαττα (1. 3. 5, etc.) quite indifferently: and in spite of Marcellinus *vit. Th.* 52, he quotes Thucydides as writing (1. 22. 4) κτῆμα ἐς ἀεί ... σύγκειται (*de comp.* 22). Whether himself or his copyists, the result is the same for us: but his habit of translating Herodotos into Attic suggests that he himself thought spelling unimportant to style, and that the 'scent of

matter of *Textgeschichte*, or of the writer's (or writers') practice.
The same is true of, e.g. Antiphon v and vi, where our manuscripts
give -σσ- in v and -ττ- in vi: is this a real variation in Antiphon's
practice, or is it an accident of transmission?[1] If we may trust the
prima facies of our tradition, it looks as if -ττ- was vernacular
'*Attic*', and -σσ- a '*Hellenic*' compromise, at a time when Attic
was just beginning to be the language of all Greece.[2] In the fourth
century, after Thucydides and Gorgias (who use -σσ-), the pure
vernacular (-ττ-) became the norm: but -σσ- reappears in Hellenistic Greek (e.g. Chares of Mytilene, *F. gr. Hist.* 125). The use of
-σσ- in a speech to be spoken by a Thessalian in Thessaly is in
line with this.

Apart from these two concessions to the 'Hellenic' speaker and
audience, is our speech in what we may suppose to be Kritias'
style? The fragments, few and indistinctive as they are, plain
description mostly and not argument, show a style more abrupt
and less insinuating than Xenophon or Lysias or Isokrates: e.g.
B 32, 34 (the famous *asyndeton*, see below), cf. 46, 47: but there is

---

antiquity, to be essential, should breathe of something rarer than an odd arrangement
of type' (Quiller-Couch, Preface to *Oxford Book of English Verse*, p. viii).
　[1] Antiphon's spelling has been discussed e.g. by Luria, op. cit. (previous note),
p. 220, n. 1, Rosenkranz, op. cit., infra (next note), p. 144. The statistics for the orator
always include the Tetralogies, but surely should not: whoever wrote them, they are
no evidence for the language or style of Antiphon's actual pleadings. [See e.g. *Hermes*,
lviii, p. 104.] Nor do I think much gained by including the single example from I
(ἔλασσον in 1. 19); the curiously 'tragic' context (Klytaimnestra in 17, ἐκπίνουσιν
ὑστάτην πόσιν in 20, the general tone of 19 itself) makes it rather unsafe to build on.
The important statistics are from V and VI, and roughly we may say -σσ- is regular in
V, -ττ- in VI. This materially alters the look of things: moreover, the common view
that VI is later than V (and thus -ττ- a modernism) is not certain nor even very
probable: Meritt wishes to date VI to 419 (*A.F.D.*, p. 174) and V is probably later
than that. The divergence of V and VI, then, may be due to their having a different
Textgeschichte: if it is due to Antiphon himself, it may be that -σσ- in V is 'hellenism'
(see the next note), suited to Antiphon's foreign client. No doubt he often had foreign
clients and therefore often 'hellenized'. [It is perhaps worth noting that in Vogel's
statistics of *Kürzenmeidung*, *Hermes*, lviii, pp. 87 ff., 'Herodes' ' 33·5 per cent. disregard
is high, but is pretty exactly the same as Antiphon v, Lysias xxiv and xxx.]
　[2] The problem of -ττ- and -σσ- is discussed by Rosenkranz 'Der lokale Grundton und
die persönliche Eigenart in der Sprache des Thukydides und der älteren attischen
Redner' (sc. down to Andokides; excluding Lysias, etc.), in *Indogermanische Forschungen*,
xlviii, 1930, pp. 144–5, with statistics from early Attic writers. He concludes (p. 145):
'wer speziell für Athen schrieb, wählte *TT*: das gilt für die Inschriften, Reden,
politischen Schriften und dergl. Dagegen scheinen die Autoren, die für ihre Werke
auf das gesamte griechische Publikum rechneten, die Schreibweise *ΣΣ* vorgezogen zu
haben, da *TT* als Provinzialismus erschien'. Our speech (which he does not take into
account) fits well into this. I use the terms 'hellenize', 'Hellenic' on the strength of
Posidippus Comicus fr. 28 Kock, to which Jacoby drew my notice: a Thessalian,
blamed for his bad Attic, claims the right of Greeks at large to 'hellenize'.

little room in them[1] for the speed and energy of thought which mark our speech (a speed and energy not quite comparable with Thucydides', though enough [e.g. §§ 9–10] to endanger the lucidity at which the careful antitheses aim). Falling back on the ancient critics, we find, I believe, that our speech accords closely with Philostratos' account of Kritias' style.[2] Our author βραχυλογεῖ ἱκανῶς, and δεινῶς καθάπτεται ἐν ἀπολογίας ἤθει:[3] when he seeks τὸ σεμνόν (as e.g. in the purple patch, §§ 16–18) he is capable σεμνολογῆσαι οὐ τὴν διθυραμβώδη σεμνολογίαν, building his effect out of κυριώτατα ὀνόματα.[4] The exact degree of his 'Atticism' is no doubt hard to gauge: the πνεῦμα (ἐλλιπέστερον μέν, ἡδὺ δὲ καὶ λεῖον), especially when balanced against the σκληρότερος λόγος of another critic,[5] may perhaps be recognized in a certain rather gauche restraint, an avoidance of climax. Philostratos' two most interesting points, the Κριτίου ὥρα and Κριτίου ἀγών being allusive and perhaps slightly corrupt, are worth quoting in full:

(a) καὶ τὸ ἀσυνδέτως δὲ ⟨χωρίον⟩ χωρίῳ προσβαλεῖν Κριτίου ὥρα.

(b) καὶ τὸ παραδόξως μὲν ἐνθυμηθῆναι ⟨μὴ⟩ παραδόξως δὲ ἀπαγγεῖλαι Κριτίου ἀγών.[6]

'Kritias' beauty[7] lies in his asyndeton: his power,[8] in his com-

---

[1] Occasional turns of phrase (e.g. B 44 καὶ τὸ ἔτι τούτων αἴσχιστον, § 22 καὶ τὸ μέγιστον) are not very distinctive. [In view of the irony in § 22 fin. should we put a question mark after φήμην in this fragment?]

[2] In his Life of Kritias (vitae sophistarum, i. 16), § 4=Vorsokr.⁵ 88 A 1.

[3] 'His attack is formidable when his tone is defensive': cf. §§ 1–4, 25–33. This is one facet of the Κριτίου ἀγών (below with n. 8), if my insertion of ⟨μὴ⟩ in that passage be correct.

[4] In Epist. 73 (=Vorsokr.⁵ 82 A 35, 88 A 17) Philostratos makes a very similar point: Gorgias' grand manner was adapted (cf. p. 289, n. 4) by Thucydides and Kritias, Thucydides converting it into his own by ῥώμη, Kritias by εὐγλωττία. This is no doubt similar to the κωμικὴ εὐγλωττία so much admired in Herodes (Philostr. vit. soph. 2. 1. 14): the racy idiom of natural speech, as seen e.g. in good dialogue in a novel. The 'Herodes' speech has, I believe, exactly this: an archaist might find it more telling than Gorgias because closer to real speech [asyndeton, 'Kritias' own beauty' is, in its simplest form, a mark of comic style: in our speech, §§ 6, 7, 8, 10, 16, etc.]. To use κωμική for interpreting what Philostratos meant by Kritias' εὐγλωττία, is not of course to suggest that Kritias copied comedy: both copied life. The word no doubt suggested (to Philostratos) New Comedy rather than the fantastic vocabulary of Old: it is amusing to compare the closing words of § 31 (in a typical comic rhythm) with, e.g. Ar. Knights 878. [See below, on § 31.]

[5] Aristides, Ars rhet. 2. 15=Vorsokr.⁵ 88 B 46.

[6] Diels adds ⟨χωρίον⟩, I have added ⟨μὴ⟩.

[7] Dionysios uses ὥρα of Plato's style (ad Pomp. 2), Plutarch of Herodotos' (de Her. mal. 43).

[8] I translate ἀγών 'power' to give the contrast (which I take to be intended) with 'beauty': the means he uses to defeat his adversary, opposed to what charms his hearers with.

bination of a daring originality of thought with a reasonableness (normality) of expression.' Κριτίου ὥρα and Κριτίου ἀγών are evidently allusions to some well-known critique of Kritias' style: no doubt Herodes'. In further detail—

(a) Is this simple 'asyndeton' (e.g. §§ 6–7, the clauses ἔχει μέν γε χώραν . . . , μία μὲν αὕτη πρόφασις . . . , begin without a conjunction: cf. § 8 διὰ ταῦτα . . . , § 10 οὕτω μέν . . . , § 16 τούτων πάντων, and cf. below on § 3 δοκεῖ δή μοι . . . , § 17 τότε [Reiske] καὶ τοῖς γέρουσιν . . .)? or is it rather wider, what Drerup calls (p. 55) 'Unbeholfenheit der Satzfügung'?[1] Both are characteristic, both of the fragments and of our speech.

(b) As corrected (with insertion of ⟨μὴ⟩) this is appropriate to our speech: the speaker's values are very individual in fact, but his manner implies they are self-evident. The uncorrected text is perhaps defensible:[2] to me it seems weak in itself, not much of an ἀγών, and it also combines rather ill with the πνεῦμα ἡδὺ καὶ λεῖον which immediately follows. [See also p. 285, n. 3.]

Finally, Philostratos calls Kritias δογματίας καὶ πολυγνώμων, rich in *sententiae*. Our speech offers little occasion for this, but perhaps §§ 7, 11, 31, are examples of what is meant.

Does Philostratos base himself (or did Herodes, whom no doubt he follows) on speeches? or does he think primarily of the 'Sokratic'?[3] I have not much doubt that Herodes studied the speeches:[4] but in case of any doubt, there is perhaps value in Hermogenes' critique, which is explicitly based on speeches.[5] He

---

[1] Compare the taste of George Moore's dictum: 'No writer ought ever to use either "which" or "that"' (reported by Harold Nicolson, *Spectator*, 17 April 1942). What is valued is the immediacy of a paratactic style: not unlike what we admire in the narrative style of a ballad (e.g. *Clerk Saunders*), the stark unexplained juxtaposing of ideas or episodes.

[2] It would make the flattish point that Kritias is unlike Isokrates; or it might imply an *enfant terrible* manner, such as Xenophon perhaps adumbrates, e.g. *Hell.* 2. 3. 16 (I do not think this is what Philostratos means).

[3] As Dionysios does, *Thuc.* 51: 'orators like Andokides Antiphon Lysias, Sokratics like Kritias Antisthenes Xenophon' write a vernacular and prove that Thucydides does not. This list is abridged in *Lysias* 2 to οἵ τε 'Ανδοκίδου λόγοι καὶ οἱ Κριτίου καὶ ἄλλοι συχνοί (which likewise use the vernacular, opposed to the 'Old Attic' of Plato and Thucydides): λόγοι=literary compositions.

[4] See the next note.

[5] Hermogenes, *de ideis*, 2. 11 (pp. 401–2 Rabe).=*Vorsokr.*[5] 88 A 19. Hermogenes' words μάλιστα ἐν τοῖς δημηγορικοῖς προοιμίοις are the only explicit reference which

compares Kritias with Antiphon: equally σεμνός (with a blunt categorical manner):[1] more καθαρός: εὐκρινής, ἐπιμελής, and σαφής, but not so tediously as Antiphon and so more convincingly: moderately ἐπιεικής and ἀφελής. This does not go very far, but so far as it goes it all applies well enough.

D. TEXT AND INTERPRETATION

i. ὑμεῖς, ἡμεῖς

I cannot accept Morrison's distinction (p. 70) between the first and second persons (ἡμεῖς ὑμεῖς, etc.), and that for three reasons:

(1) This shift between the first and second persons is common in all political oratory: in Perikles' funeral speech, for example, ὑμῶν in 2. 35. 3 is the same as ἡμῶν in 36. 2: the people addressed in the second person in 35. 1, 46. 2, are the same Athenians as those spoken of in the first person throughout.

(2) If any distinction was intended, it was a matter which Greek (and the Greek of this speech) is well qualified, by particles, order of words, etc., to make explicit. There is for instance a real distinction between ἡμεῖς (=the Thirty) and ὑμεῖς (=the Boule) in Kritias' speech in Xen. *Hell.* 2. 3. 24–34, and it is never for a moment in doubt. In our speech it is *nowhere* made explicit, though the writer is not sparing of particles and is lucidly logical.

(3) Though there undoubtedly is use of both first and second persons, there is also undoubtedly itacistic confusion between ἡμεῖς, etc., and ὑμεῖς, etc. (as there is also e.g. in

we have to Kritias' speeches. But on p. 403 Hermogenes expressly classes Kritias with the 'Ten Orators', as being comparable with Demosthenes rather than with Plato and as practising τὸ δικανικόν and τὸ συμβουλευτικόν. Dionysios had classed him with the Sokratics (see note 3, above). Herodes has come between: it looks as if Herodes' 'publication' (p. 272, n. 2) had converted Kritias from a Sokratic into an orator.

[1] τὰ πολλὰ λέγων ἀποφαντικῶς (so Rabe: Diels prints ἀποφατικῶς, but Hermogenes is simply repeating what he has just said of Antiphon, on p. 401, where the meaning is not in doubt. In both places it is a form of ὄγκος). This 'apophantic' manner is illustrated in two 'fragments' of Kritias (*Vorsokr.*[5] 88 B 46–7) in which the sophist Aristides compares some words of Xenophon with how Kritias would say the same thing. Blunt, downright, authoritative: not urbane like Xenophon or Lysias. In ps.-Lysias xx there are several indications which prove that §§ 1–10 are by a different speaker from §§ 11–36, among them the 'apophantic' tone of §§ 1–10. In our speech the tone is tempered to the speaker's youth, yet e.g. §§ 1, 3, 31, 33, are as 'apophantic' as Antiphon.

Xen. *Hell.* 2. 3. 28 and 51): twice the reflexive possessive ὑμέτερα αὐτῶν is written, where the verb is in the first person (§§ 5, 23).

ii. *Individual Passages*

The following notes on individual passages take Drerup's text as their starting-point.

§ 2: D's punctuation is harsh and involves a difficult order of words: is there a lacuna? E.g. ἔχοι τις ἂν ἐγκαλεῖν τοῖς λέγουσι ματαιότητα ἢ πολυπραγμοσύνην, αἰτιασάμενος ‹αὐτοὺς λέγειν οὐ δυναμένους› ἐπίστασθαι, etc.

§ 3: the Aldine punctuation (εἰ δὲ τοῦτο διατρίβετε, καὶ δι᾽ ἄλλους εὖ πράττειν ἡδύ. δοκεῖ δή μοι, etc.) gives καί its point (cf. καὶ πράσσειν in § 10), gives a better sense to ἡδύ, and also better logic. The asyndeton is a mark of Kritias' style (p. 286): the abrupt δοκεῖ δή μοι is perhaps 'apophantic' (p. 287, n. 1).

§ 4: for ἑκόντας write ἄκοντας: cf. ἄκων in a similar connexion in § 6.

§§ 5–6: the writer is fond of the logical νῦν δέ (§§ 23, 33: cf. § 26 below), which is usually preceded by an alternative unfulfilled condition (cf. Xen. *Hell.* 2. 3. 28). Knox has restored this by writing ἡμεῖς μὲν γὰρ ε‹ἰ ἠ›πιστάμεθα . . . προγιγνώσκοντες [τ᾽] ἂν πρὶν παθεῖν ηὐλαβούμεθα, . . . νῦν δέ, etc.

§ 9: ᾧ γὰρ ἁλίσκεται μάλιστα καὶ πόλις καὶ χώρα τοῦτο τὸ χωρίον οὐκ ἔλαθεν αὐτόν: Knox says that χωρίον here gives the Latin *locus* in the sense of *occasio*. I know no Latin parallel for this vivid and pregnant phrase. The aggressive use of 'balance of power' (to support the weak against the strong) is given under the figure of a strategic *vantage-point*[1] which does not escape Archelaos' eye for country. The image is sustained all through the phrase (ἁλίσκεται, ἔλαθεν), it is not simply that χωρίον means *occasio*.

Ibid.: Beloch's στασιάζοντας ἡμᾶς ‹πρὸς ἡμᾶς› αὐτούς is surely right.

§ 10: so too Hass's τοῖς ὀλίγοις (MS. πολλοῖς).

§ 11: *stasis* is as much worse than war as war is than peace. Knox notes that this is repeated in Ael. Aristides, Ῥοδίοις περὶ ὁμονοίας, § 19 (i. 830, Dind.=ii. 60, Keil): this would be natural

---

[1] Cf. the χωρίον in Xen. *Hell.* 7. 5. 11.

enough, if our speech was 'published' by Herodes (see p. 286, n. 5), but in fact Aristides is quoting, almost verbally, Herodotos 8. 3. 1. The sentiment is specially appropriate to the preoccupations of the outgoing fifth century,[1] and Xenophon puts something not unlike it in Kritias' mouth, *Hell.* 2. 3. 29.

Ibid.: μήτε τοὺς ἀπο‹θανόντας μήτε τοὺς ἀπο›κτείναντας gives a substantial homoioteleuton and also picks up ἀποθνῄσκουσιν just above.

§ 13: τὸν διαλύσοντα γάρ (Hass: MS. τὸν διάλογον γάρ) gives a motive for the postponement of γάρ, viz. to avoid hiatus.

§ 14: keep ἐξαγομένων: ἐξάγεσθαι of the purchaser (or as we should say, the importer), Andoc. 2. 11. For the fact cf. Xen. *Hell.* 6. 1. 11.

§ 15: δια‹κω›λύομεν (Knox): cf. Xen. *Hell.* 2. 3. 16.

§ 17: there is no construction for the accusatives οἰκίας, χρήματα. Is there a lacuna? E.g. χρήματα ‹διαρπαζόμενα διὰ τί μάτην› διαλέξομεν;

Ibid.: ὁ ταῦτα δρῶν (generalizing participle, like ὁ βουλόμενος)[2] does not refer to Archelaos (as both Drerup, pp. 86 and 21, and Meyer, p. 261, n. 2, suppose), but to the individual Larisan, who-ever he happens to be (cf. ὁπότε τύχοι). Accordingly we should not correct προσῆκον[3] of the manuscript to προσῆκεν. ὁ ταῦτα δρῶν (whatever Larisan does Archelaos' dirty work) is distinguished from τούτων τὸν αἴτιον in §§ 16 and 18, who is of course Archelaos himself.

Ibid.: ἡ νεότης for ὡσαύτως (Hass) perfectly restores this eloquent sentence: at what date could *eta* be twice misread as *omega* (ὠνεότως)? Reiske's τότε for ὅτε is attractive, and gives a Kritian asyndeton.

§ 18: the triad ἀμυνομένους μέν . . . τιμωροῦντας δέ . . . οἰκτείρον-τας δέ . . . reminds me of Thuc. 3. 84. 2 ἀκρατὴς μέν . . . κρείσσων δέ . . . πολεμία δέ.[4]

---

[1] Enough to cite Thuc. 3. 82-4; Xen. *Hell.* 2. 4. 22.

[2] Cf. Kritias' proclamation εἴ τις τὸν 'Αθηναῖον φεύγοντα δέξοιτο (Philostr. *Vit. soph.* 1. 16. 1 = *Vorsokr.*[5] 88 A 1).

[3] Sc. προσῆκόν ἐστι, cf. e.g. Plato, *Theaet.* 196 E. The present tense suits the generaliz-ing participle.

[4] Both perhaps are adaptations (p. 282, n. 2) of the weighty 'tetrads' in Gorgias' *Epitaphios* (*Vorsokr.*[5] 82 B 6): θεράποντες μέν . . . κολασταὶ δέ . . . αὐθάδεις . . . εὐόργητοι: ὑβρισταί . . . κόσμιοι . . . ἄφοβοι . . . δεινοί: οὔτε ἐμφύτου ἄρεος οὔτε νομίμων ἐρώτων οὔτε ἐνοπλίου ἔριδος οὔτε φιλοκάλου εἰρήνης: σεμνοὶ μέν . . . ὅσιοι δέ . . . δίκαιοι . . . εὐσεβεῖς δέ.

19

290   ESSAYS IN GREEK HISTORY

Ibid.: for ἀποδιδάξομεν τοὺς ἄλλους, etc. . . . ἐπιβουλεύειν ἡμῖν cf. the last sentence of Xen. *Hell.* 2. 3. 34, οὗτος σωθεὶς μέν, etc., ἀπολόμενος δέ . . . ὑποτέμοι ἂν τὰς ἐλπίδας.

§ 20: ἐπειδὴ τοίνυν ⟨τού⟩τοις [Πελοποννησίοις]. τούτοις will mean Λακεδαιμονίοις, as it should: just below, in τοὺς μὴ ⟨συμ⟩πολεμήσαντας αὐτοῖς, αὐτοῖς must be the Spartans (and must also refer to ⟨τού⟩τοις), since just below again συμπολεμεῖν μετὰ Πελοποννησίων means 'to join the Spartans' wars *along with* the Peloponnesians'.

§ 22: πρότερον μὲν ὅτι τὸν [πρότερον] Μηδικὸν οὐ συνεπολεμήσαμεν ⟨πόλεμον⟩.

§ 23: καίτοι rams the argument home: 'and the case is even stronger than that, since . . .'. Cf. Xen. *Hell.* 2. 3. 29.

§ 25: I suggest keeping ὅ μοι (=τοῦτο δέ μοι), and putting a full stop at λέγω (Hass). Then (keeping the asyndeton) τοῖς ἐναντιωσομένοις εἴπερ, etc.

§ 26, last clause: εἰ μὲν ἀνάγκην ἑώρων . . . ἐβουλευσάμην ἄν . . . νῦν δέ, etc. (Reiske: MS. τὴν δέ). Cf. §§ 5–6 above.

§ 29: ὥσπερ οὖν (MS. οὐδ') ἐνθάδε Μακεδόνα. This changes the sense (as e.g. Beloch, p. 24, n. 4 on p. 25, wishes it changed): we do not of course know for certain whether there had or had not been a Macedonian governor in Larisa at any stage, but ὥσπερ οὖν seems to me to give a more convincing sentence (see p. 277, n. 1).[1] For ηὕρηκε (MS. εὕρηκε) just above, perhaps write ἑόρακε, cf. ὁρῶμεν in § 28.[2]

§ 30: αὐτόθι at the end is not (as Knox supposes) tautologous, but means *in those parts*, as it does in § 28: 'where, *in the Spartan sphere*, will you find a city so small',—etc. So in ps.-Xen.'Ἀθ. πολ. αὐτόθι always means 'in the place under discussion', sc. 'at Athens': 1. 2, 10, 11, 13; 3. 1, 6.

§ 31: locus desperatus. The sense of παραδείγματα is certain (cf. § 28), but παράδειγμα just above cannot bear this sense and is therefore probably corrupted (see p. 272, n. 1). I think there must be a lacuna and that Dobree has divined the sense: he suggests that παράδειγμα conceals παράλληλα, and he corrects θῆται παρὰ δὲ

---

[1] Ὥσπερ οὖν makes explicit something which so far is only *implied*, e.g. by the protasis of a conditional sentence. See Denniston, *Greek Particles*, pp. 421–2. The presence of a Macedonian governor has been implied by the contrasted absence of Spartan governors.

[2] The writer likes to associate εὑρίσκω and ὁρῶ: §§ 3, 26: the distinction, if any, is fine.

to παραθῆτε. The following proposal utilizes his suggestions: ἕως ἂν ‹κτήσηται· δῆλον δέ, ἐὰν › παρ' ἄλληλα παραθῆτε ταῦτα ‹καὶ › ἅ, etc. Dem. 19. 174 (or 18. 265) should be compared and might suggest a more convincing restoration.—It is hardly necessary to say that the subject of εὔξασθαι is not (as Knox supposes) the Spartans, but the same as of εὐχόμενοι in § 30.

Ibid.: ἃ μὴ γενέσθαι δεινόν ἐστι μᾶλλον ἢ γενέσθαι: a verse of a metre frequent in comedy.[1]

§ 32: Morrison objects (p. 71, n. 3) to Drerup's bracketing [πλησίοι εἶναι αὐτῷ] as a gloss: but in a speech which so carefully avoids hiatus I do not believe the words are genuine. There is consequently (I think) no such reference as Morrison sees to Herakleia or Pharsalos: I imagine ᾧ ἰσχύομεν is cavalry. Immediately after the gloss, πρῶτον μὲν γάρ is meaningless: Reiske's μὲν οὖν gives sense but does not explain the corruption: is there a lacuna? There is no δέ to answer Λακεδαιμονίοις μέν just above: this may have stood in the lacuna; or is the unanswered μέν part of that tacit contrast with Archelaos which is also implied in the (surely *logical*, and not as Morrison takes it *temporal*)[2] οὐκέτι?

Ibid.: ἐὰν δὲ ἐγχωροῦσιν MS., ἐγχειρῶσιν edd.: perhaps ἐγχωρῇ σφίσιν (cf. Xen. *Hell.* 2. 3. 16)?

§ 33: ἀφελόντες τῶν ἐκείνου κακῶν MS.: perhaps τῶν ἐκεῖ or τῶν παρ' ἐκείνῳ? 'rescuing them from their hardships in Macedonia'.

E. Ἀνάγκη (Xen. *Hell.* 2. 3)

In the foregoing section I have given a few references to those parts of Xen. *Hell.* 2. 3, in which Kritias is the speaker. These parallels do not indeed do much to support Kritias' authorship, since no doubt as many parallels could be found elsewhere: Xenophon's idiom is his own (cf. e.g. 6. 5. 39 ff. for many verbal echoes of 2. 3), though he is not insensitive to dramatic propriety. But perhaps a certain insistence on *necessity* in this chapter is a Kritian feature: 16 ἀντέλεγεν ὅτι οὐκ ἐγχωροίη: 51 οἶδε οἱ ἐφεστηκότες οὔ φασιν ἡμῖν ἐπιτρέψειν: 24 πλείστους δὲ ἀνάγκη ἐνθάδε πολεμίους εἶναι. In all these cases (even in the one quoted last)

---

[1] See p. 285, n. 4. The metre (iambic tetrameter catalectic) is no doubt fortuitous: the words hardly look like a *quotation* from Old Comedy (cf. e.g. Ar. *Knights*, 878). But the words might be a sort of proverb, since it is a popular and proverbial, as well as a comic, metre: e.g. οὐ φροντὶς Ἱπποκλείδῃ, ἄριστα χωλὸς οἰφεῖ, etc.

[2] The temporal sense is precluded by πέφυκεν and by the following γάρ.

the necessity, though remorseless, is to some degree welcomed. So in our speech, § 4 πρῶτον μὲν ὡς ἀγαθόν—τοῦτο ὑμᾶς διδάξω, δεύτερον δὲ ὡς ἀναγκαῖον: cf. §§ 19 ff., also §§ 1–3.

'Ανάγκας ἔδυ λέπαδνον. With all his tempered and sensitized intelligence, Kritias professed himself, finally, to be driven by remorseless logic. He deceived himself: the remorselessness was his own, he was feeding his hunger for revenge. The passion of revenge breathes in our speech, surprisingly, more than the topic seems to admit. Is not this Kritias, emotional (§ 16), remorseless, now approaching his last phase?

Necessity drove him far before it had done with him: his last phase is no doubt in Thucydides' mind in 3. 82–3, especially 82. 8. Kritias had ranged himself, between 411 and 407, under the great triumvirate of Theramenes, Alkibiades, and Thrasyboulos: of these, he executed Theramenes, got his foreign friends to execute Alkibiades,[1] and was himself killed by Thrasyboulos. The quisling's progress. Our speech only adumbrates this: the political doctrine of §§ 30–1 is still Theramenean.[2]

---

[1] So Plut. Alcib. 38. 5; Nepos, Alcib. 10. 1: no doubt all accounts of the murder were tendentious, more or less. Ferguson, C.A.H. v. 365 in his brilliant account of these events speaks as if Alkibiades had let Kritias down whilst he (Alkibiades) was still in power: 'his leader either could not or did not protect him—an omission which Critias remembered later.' But Kritias' poem to Alkibiades (Vorsokr.⁵ 88 в 4–5) was surely written when Alkibiades was actually in Athens, in 407; and it was not written from exile. Alkibiades' own fall is so soon after this that it is unlikely that Kritias' exile came first: Kritias in fact was involved in Alkibiades' fall. It may be just this which he could not forgive. I imagine Kritias was one of those who had urged Alkibiades to attempt a coup d'état before he left Athens on his last campaign (Plut. Alcib. 34. 7): without doubt Kleophon would take the first opportunity he could to ruin either of them. A. von Blumenthal in his essay Der Tyrann Kritias (Stuttgart, 1923), p. 7, quite misconceives the order of events: 'wird verbannt, kehrt wieder, wirkt für Alkibiades'.

[2] τῷ μὲν οὖν πρώτῳ χρόνῳ ὁ Κριτίας τῷ Θηραμένει ὁμογνώμων τε καὶ φίλος ἦν (Xen. Hell. 2. 3. 15).

INDEX I: GENERAL

INDEX II: PASSAGES DISCUSSED